"BLACK ST[illegible] is a fast-moving, twisting futuristic thriller ab[illegible]ntest of survival . . . The bo[illegible]n array of natural vistas a[illegible]tive, colorful ways, help[illegible]essive science fiction graphic novel."
—Foreword Reviews

"BLACK STAR is a sci-fi thriller about a competition for survival in a distant and dangerous planet, beautifully told with gripping, relentless comic book storytelling."
—Multiversity Comics

"[Readers] who view stories like an artifact they are slowly, carefully exhuming, however, will find much to love in BLACK STAR . . . Like all great science fiction stories, *Black Star* puts its characters first. For that reason alone, Glover and Jovellanos' excellent graphic novel deserves to find a readership."
—Nerd Daily

"A cat-and-mouse tale of two astronauts stranded on a desolate planet."
—*New York Times*

"Jovellanos injects energy with fluid action, expressive character design, and a radiant color palette with blazing red wildfires and icy blue shuttle scenes . . . this offers a nifty take on interpersonal conflicts in interspace, bolstered by snazzy art."
— *Publishers Weekly*

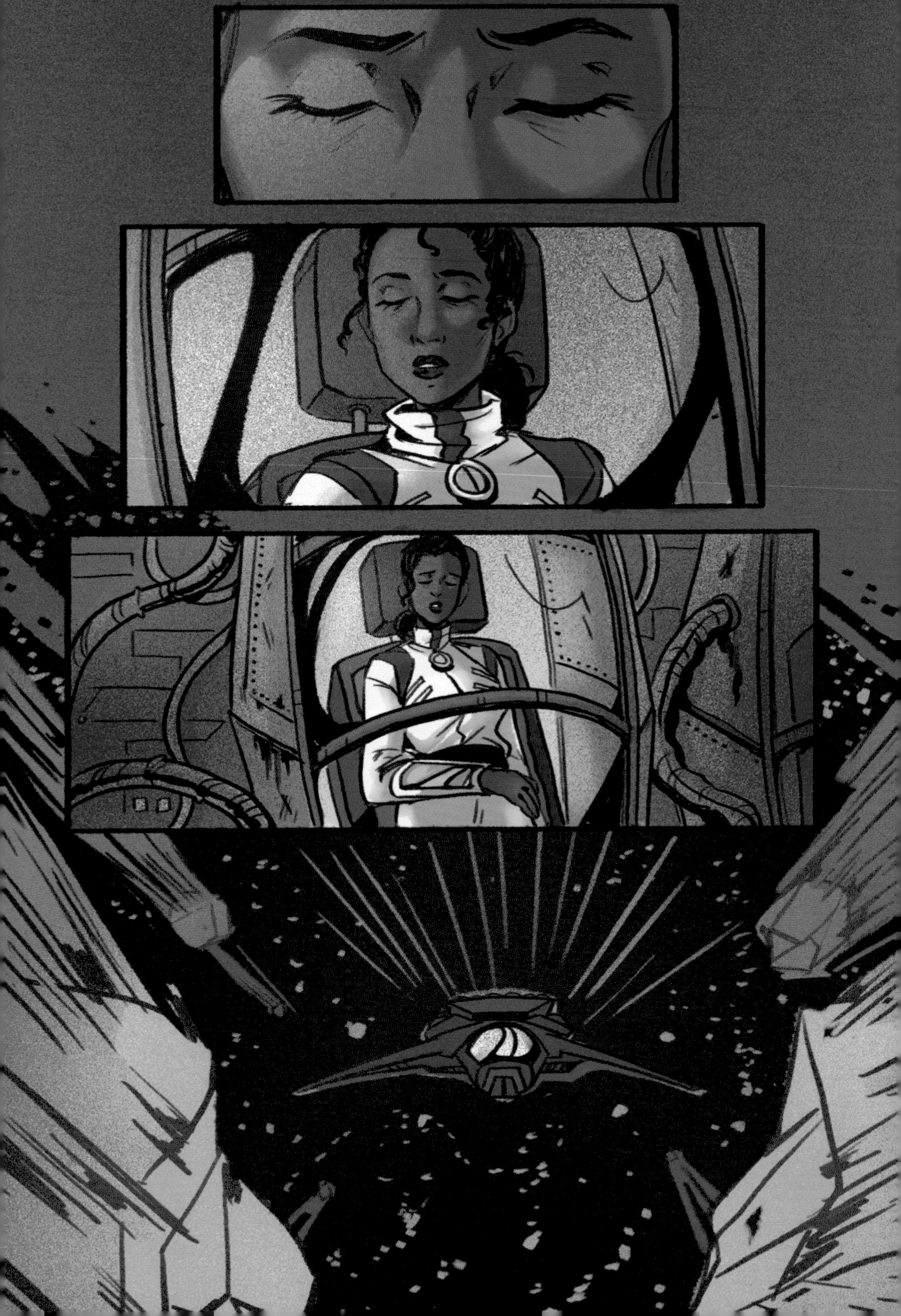

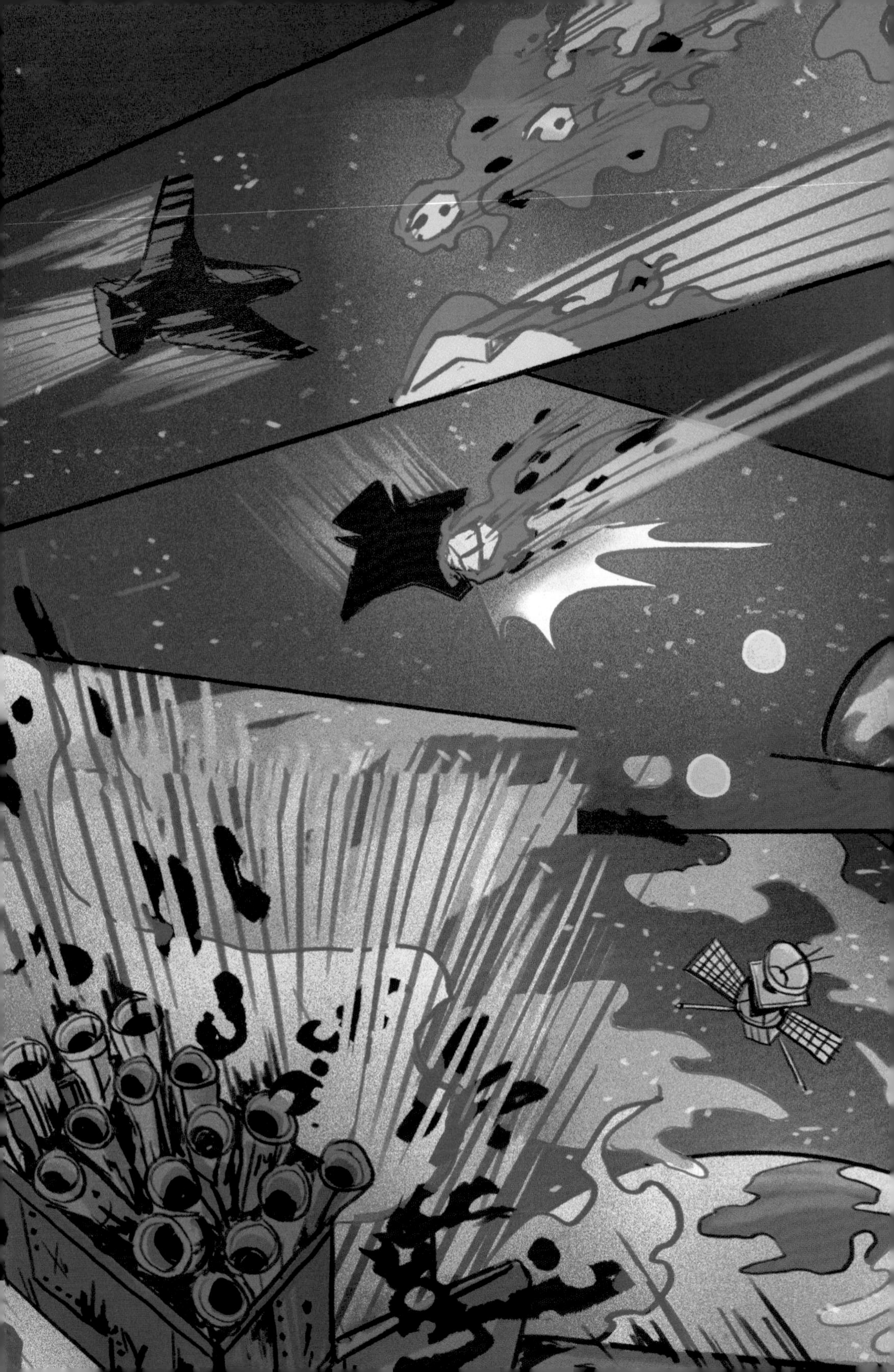

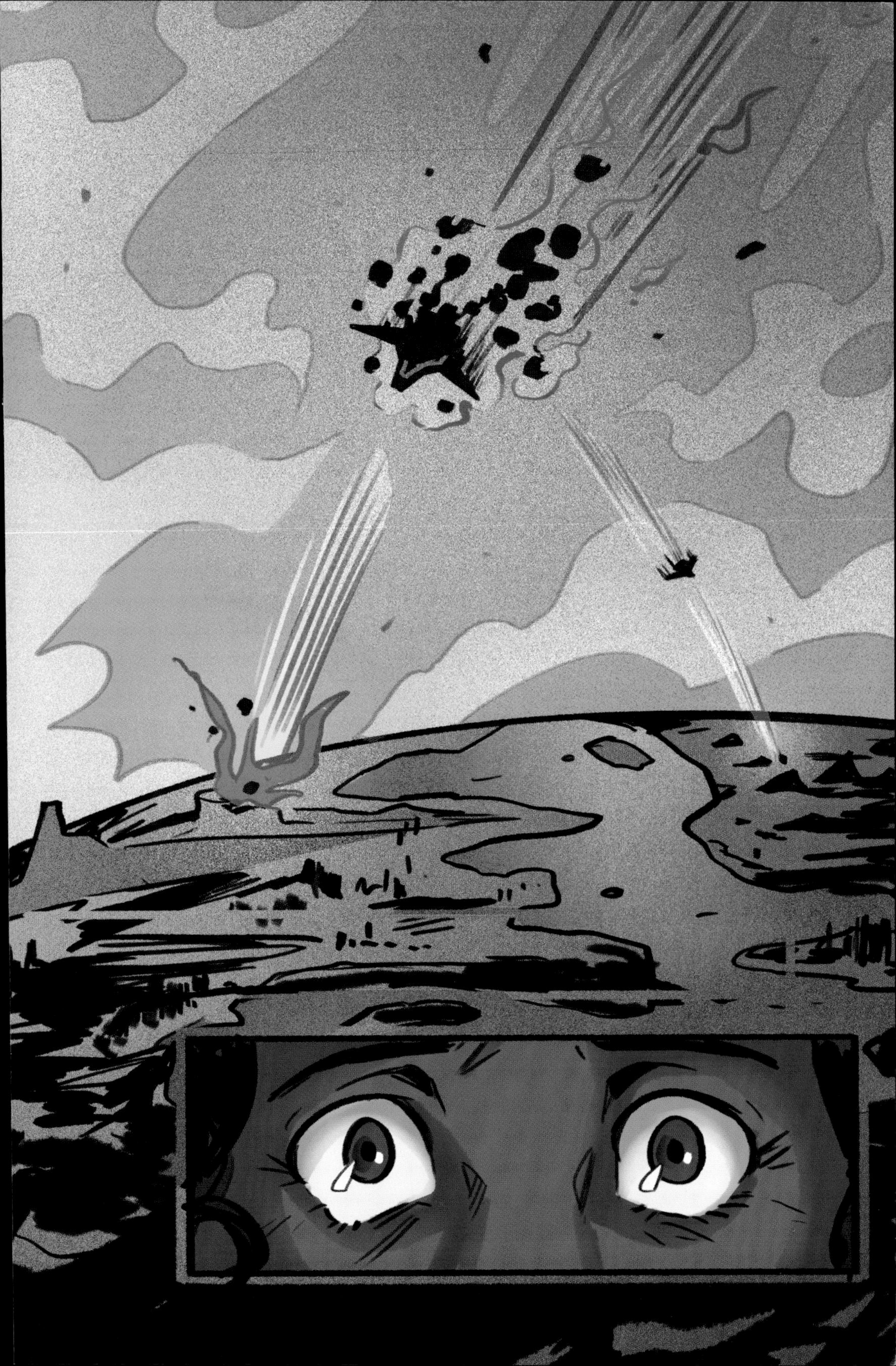

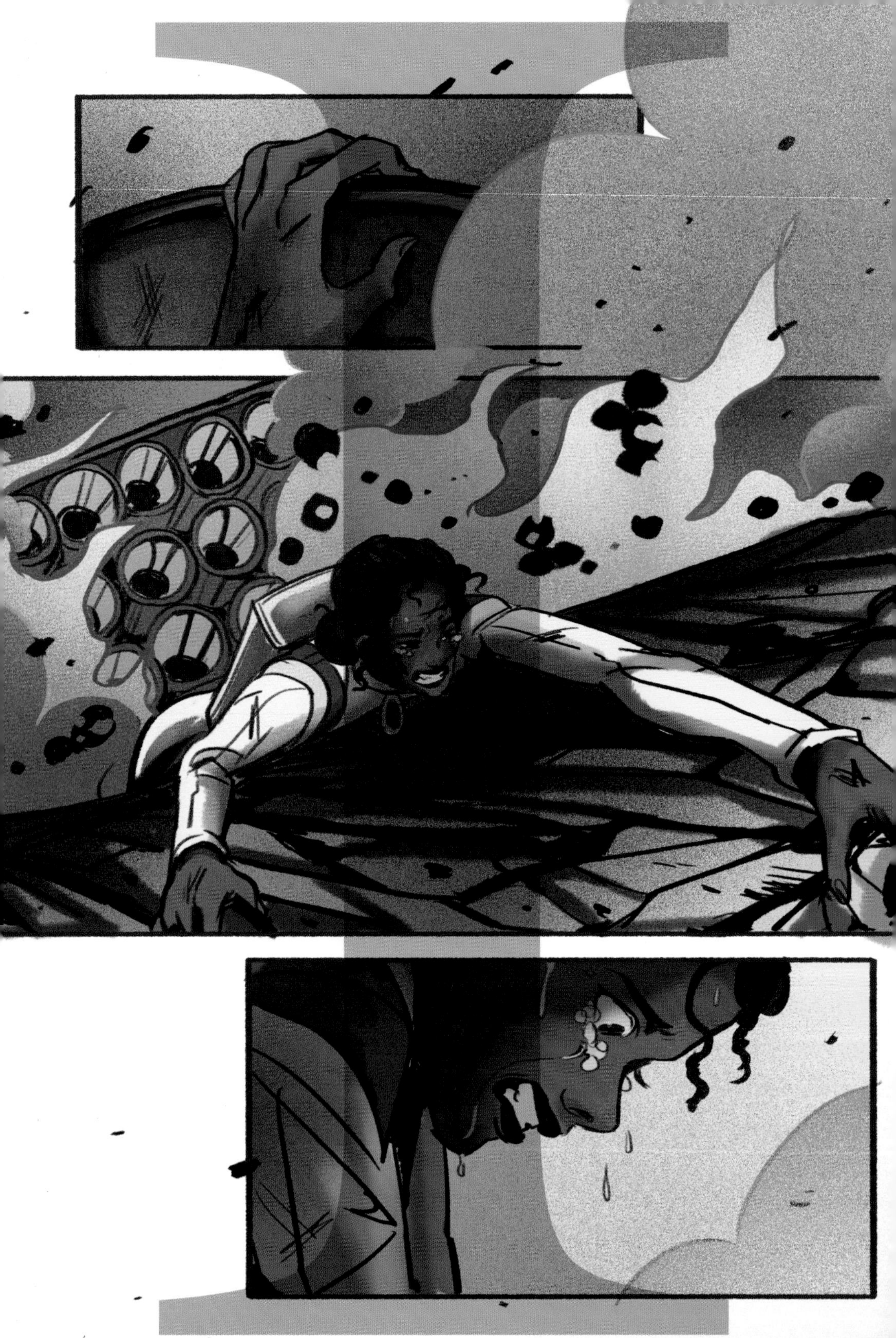

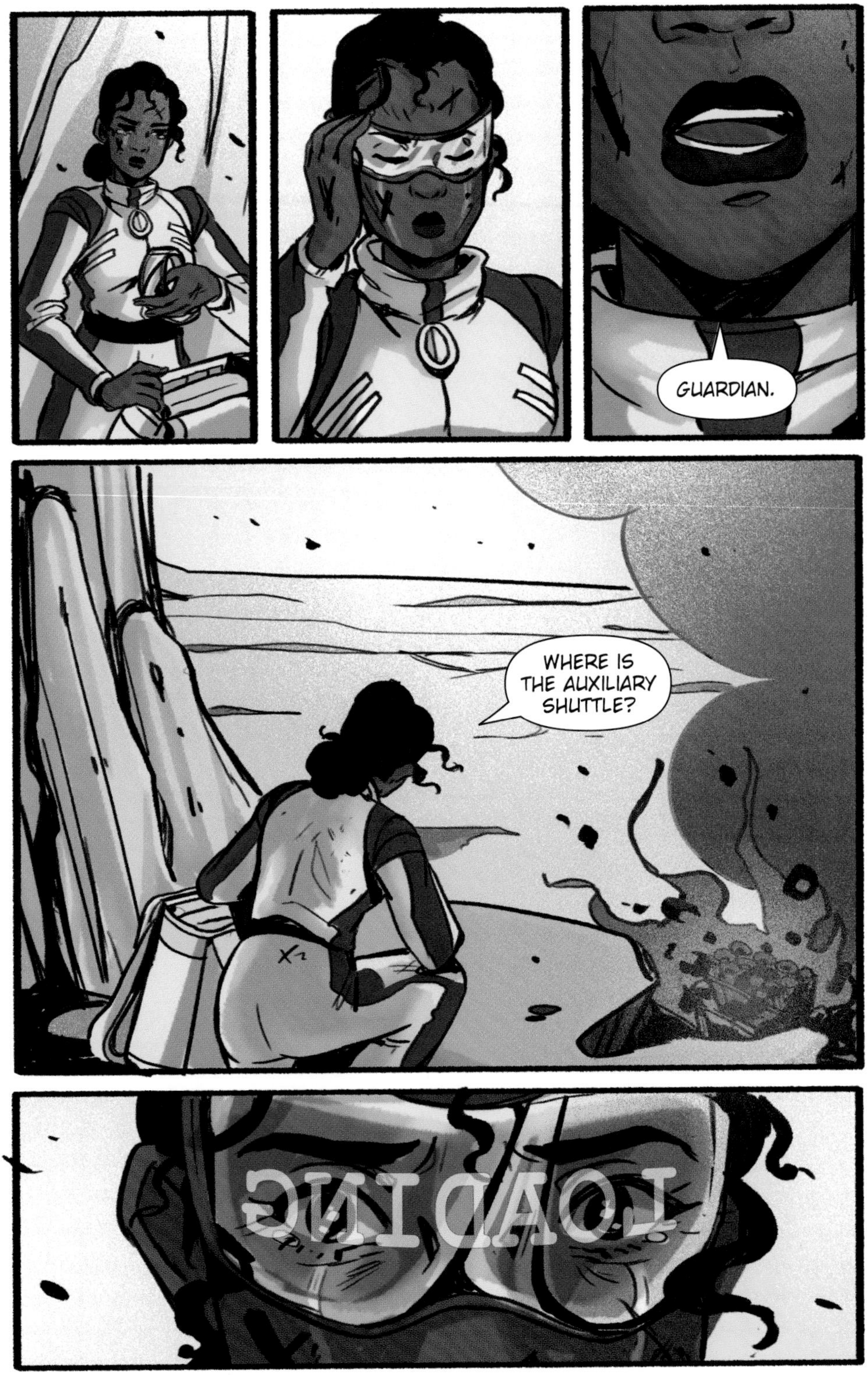
GUARDIAN.
WHERE IS THE AUXILIARY SHUTTLE?
LOADING

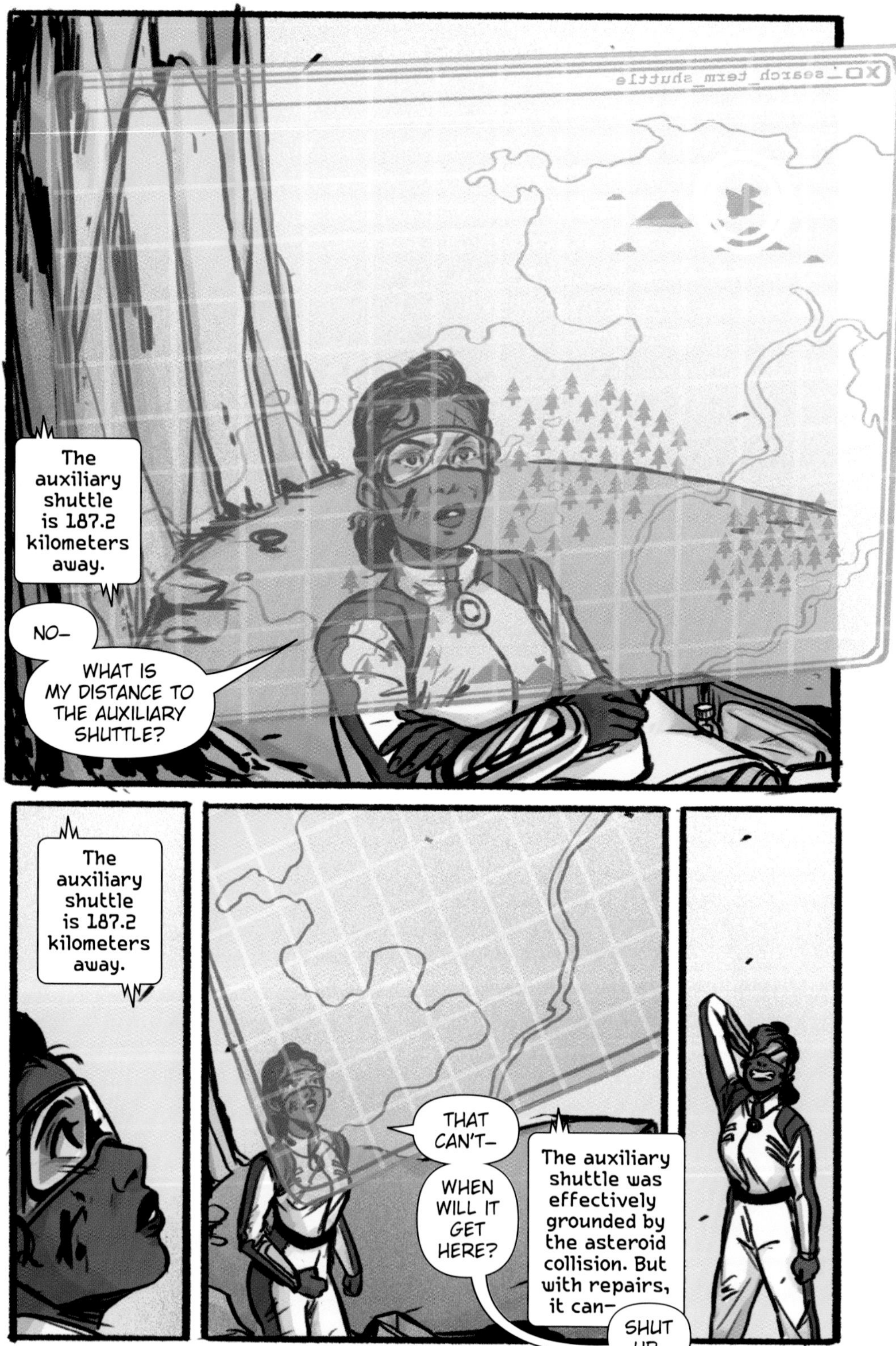
The auxiliary shuttle is 187.2 kilometers away.
NO–
WHAT IS MY DISTANCE TO THE AUXILIARY SHUTTLE?
The auxiliary shuttle is 187.2 kilometers away.
THAT CAN'T–
WHEN WILL IT GET HERE?
The auxiliary shuttle was effectively grounded by the asteroid collision. But with repairs, it can–
SHUT UP.

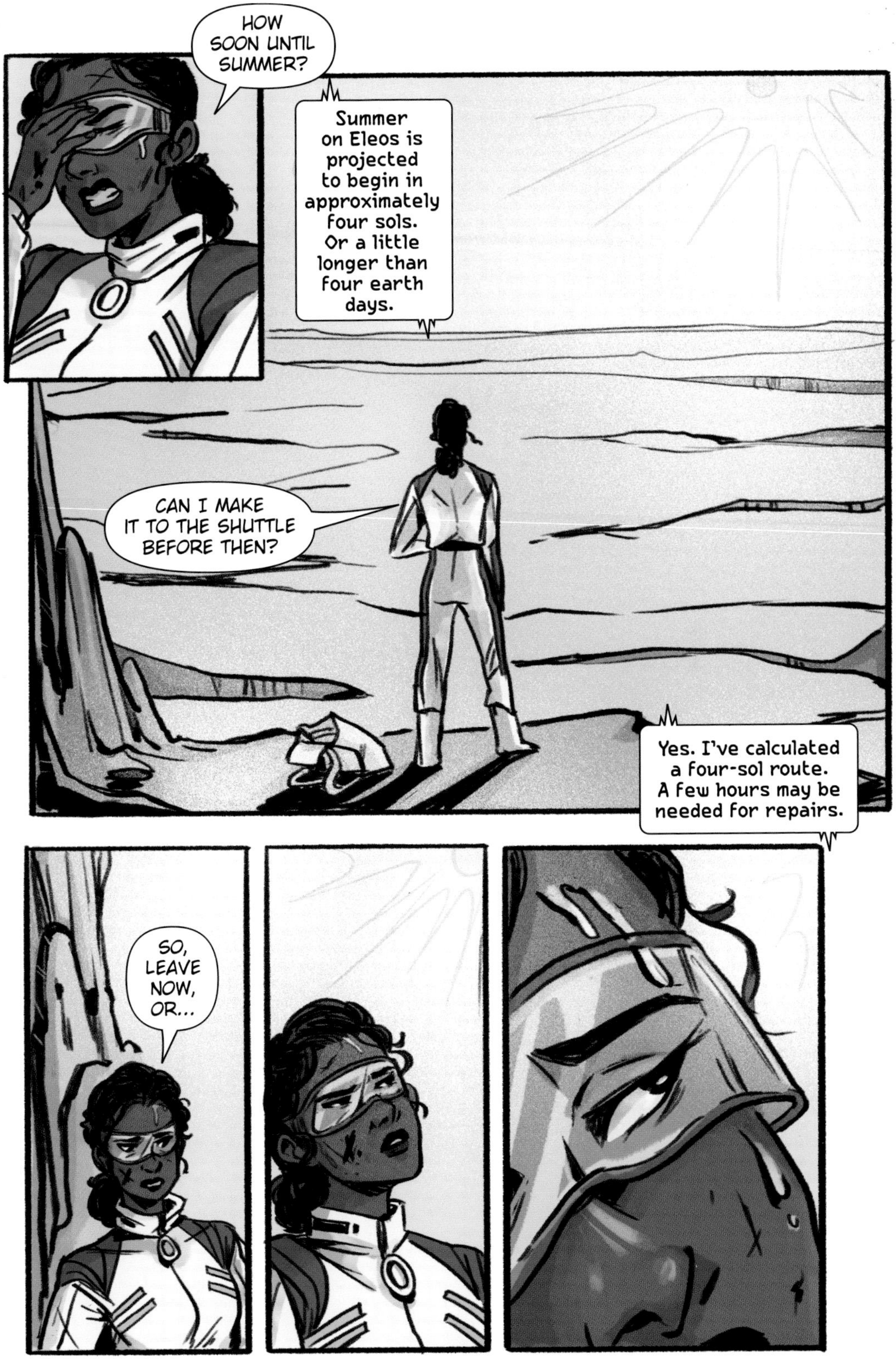
HOW SOON UNTIL SUMMER?
Summer on Eleos is projected to begin in approximately four sols. Or a little longer than four earth days.
CAN I MAKE IT TO THE SHUTTLE BEFORE THEN?
Yes. I've calculated a four-sol route. A few hours may be needed for repairs.
SO, LEAVE NOW, OR...

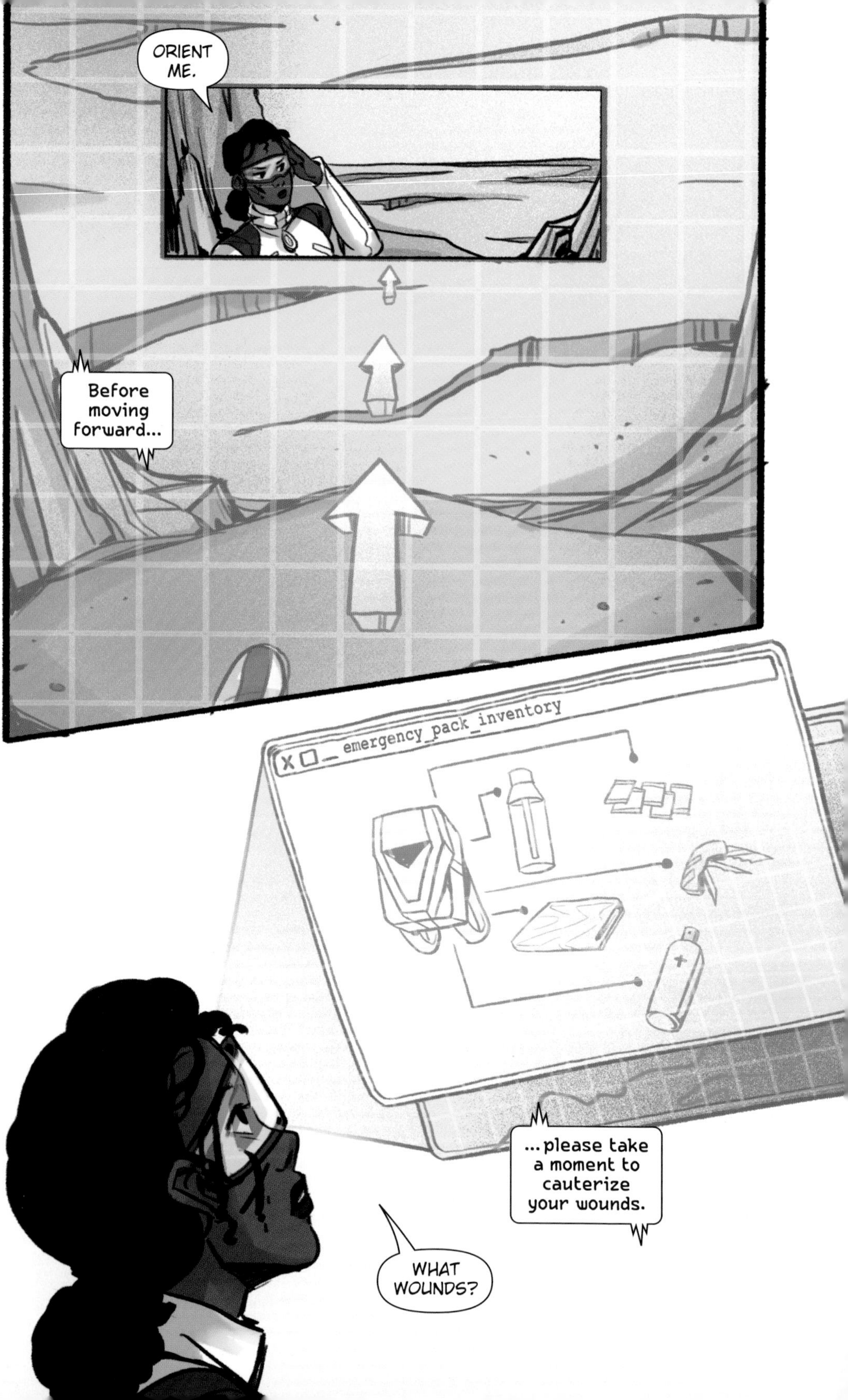
ORIENT ME.
Before moving forward...
emergency_pack_inventory
...please take a moment to cauterize your wounds.
WHAT WOUNDS?

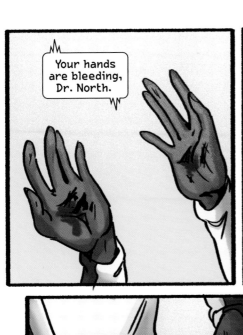

Your hands are bleeding, Dr. North.

Please use the cauterizing agent from your emergency pack.

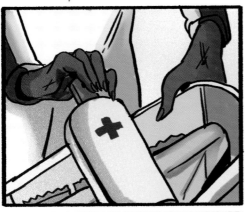

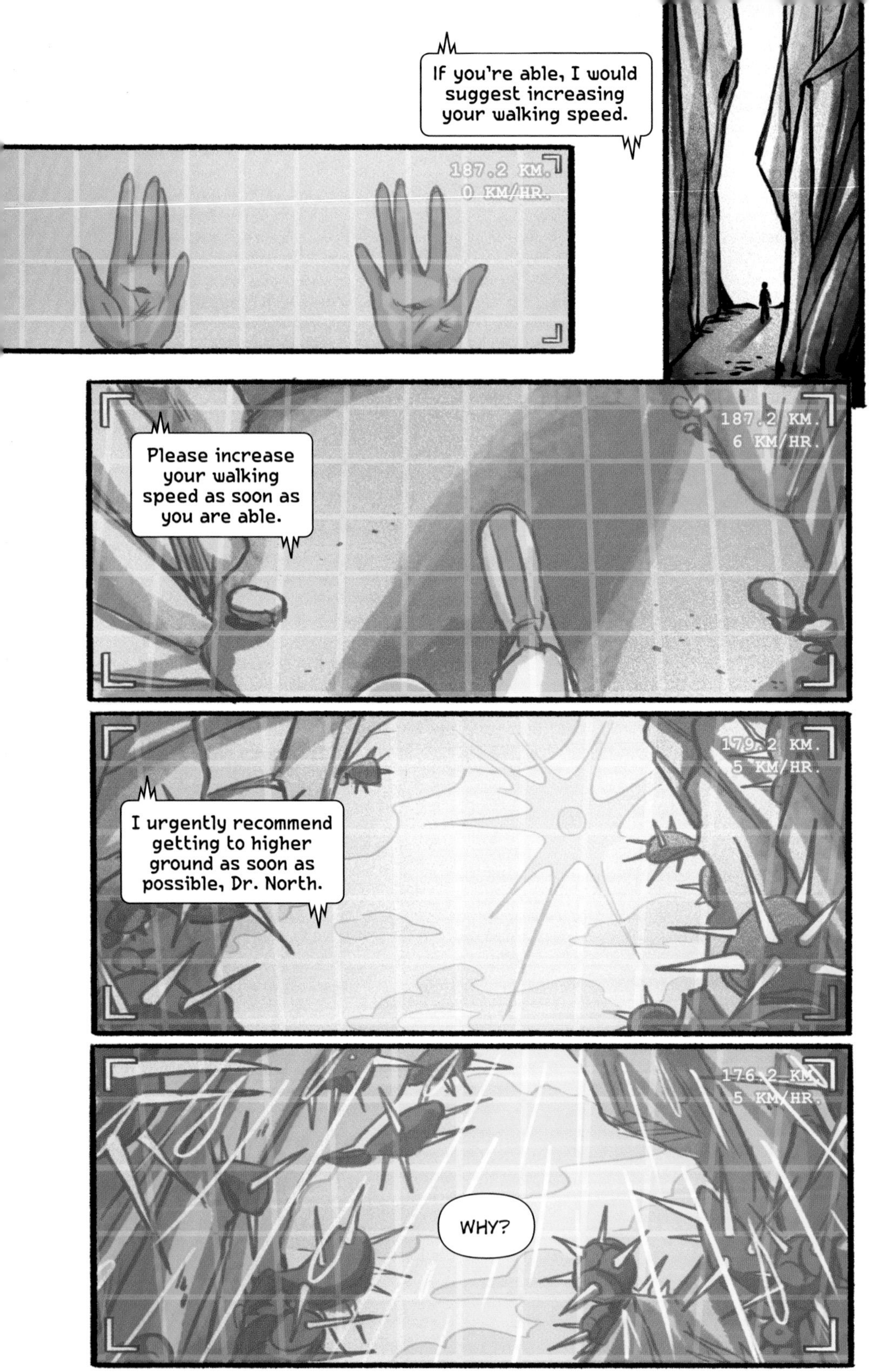
If you're able, I would suggest increasing your walking speed.
187.2 KM.
0 KM/HR.
187.2 KM.
6 KM/HR.
Please increase your walking speed as soon as you are able.
179.2 KM.
5 KM/HR.
I urgently recommend getting to higher ground as soon as possible, Dr. North.
176.2 KM.
5 KM/HR.
WHY?

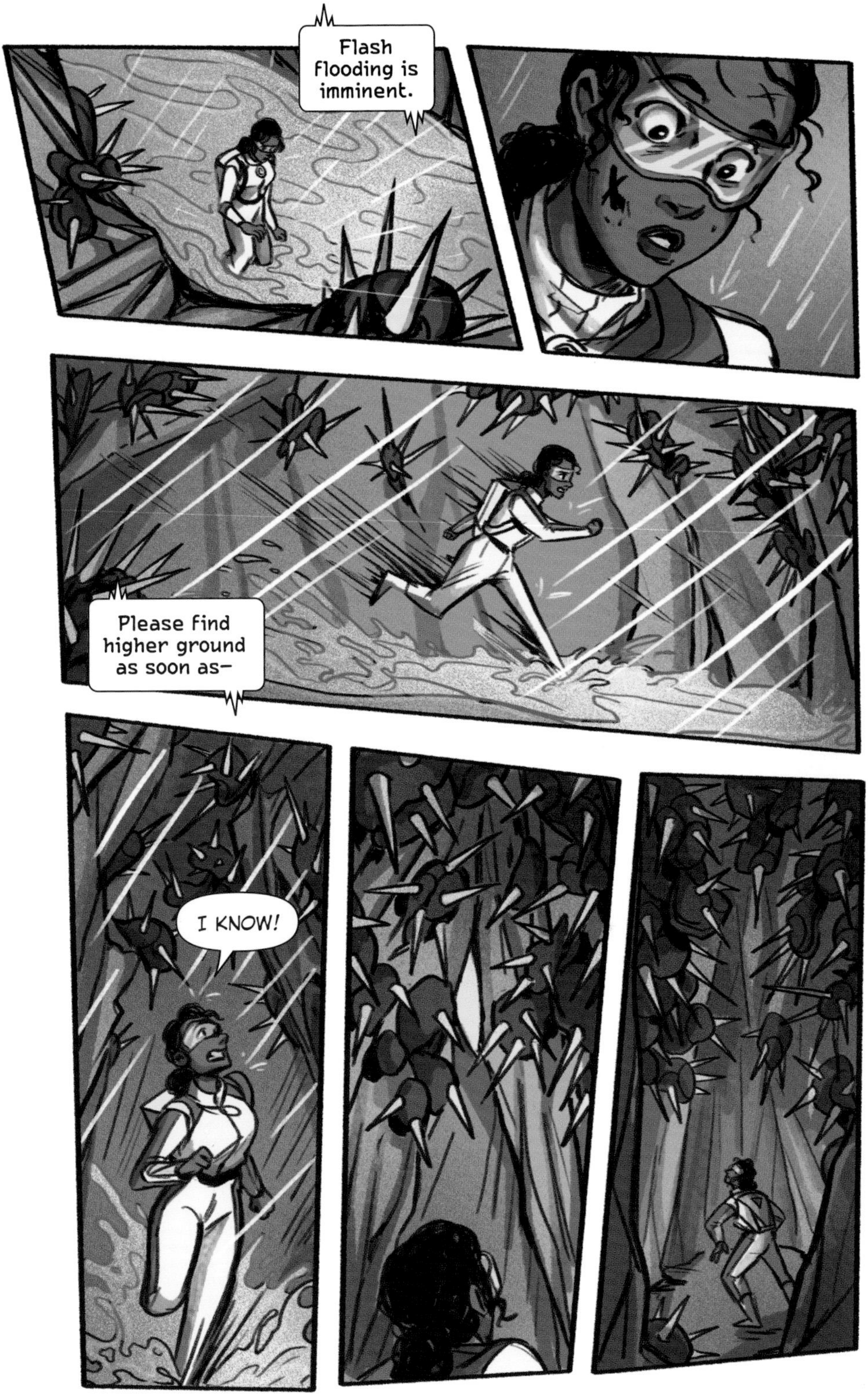
Flash flooding is imminent.
Please find higher ground as soon as—
I KNOW!

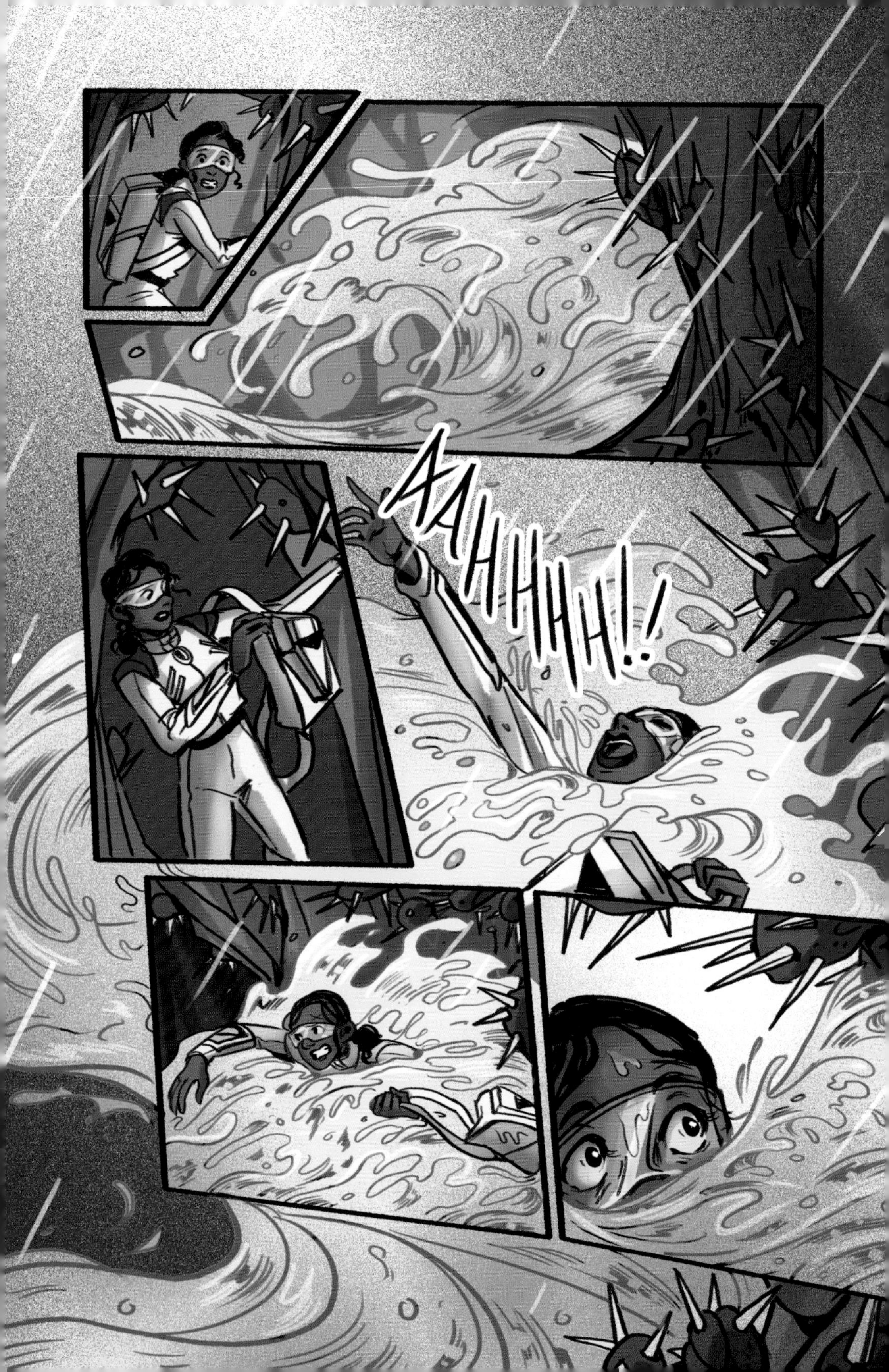
AAAHHHHH!!

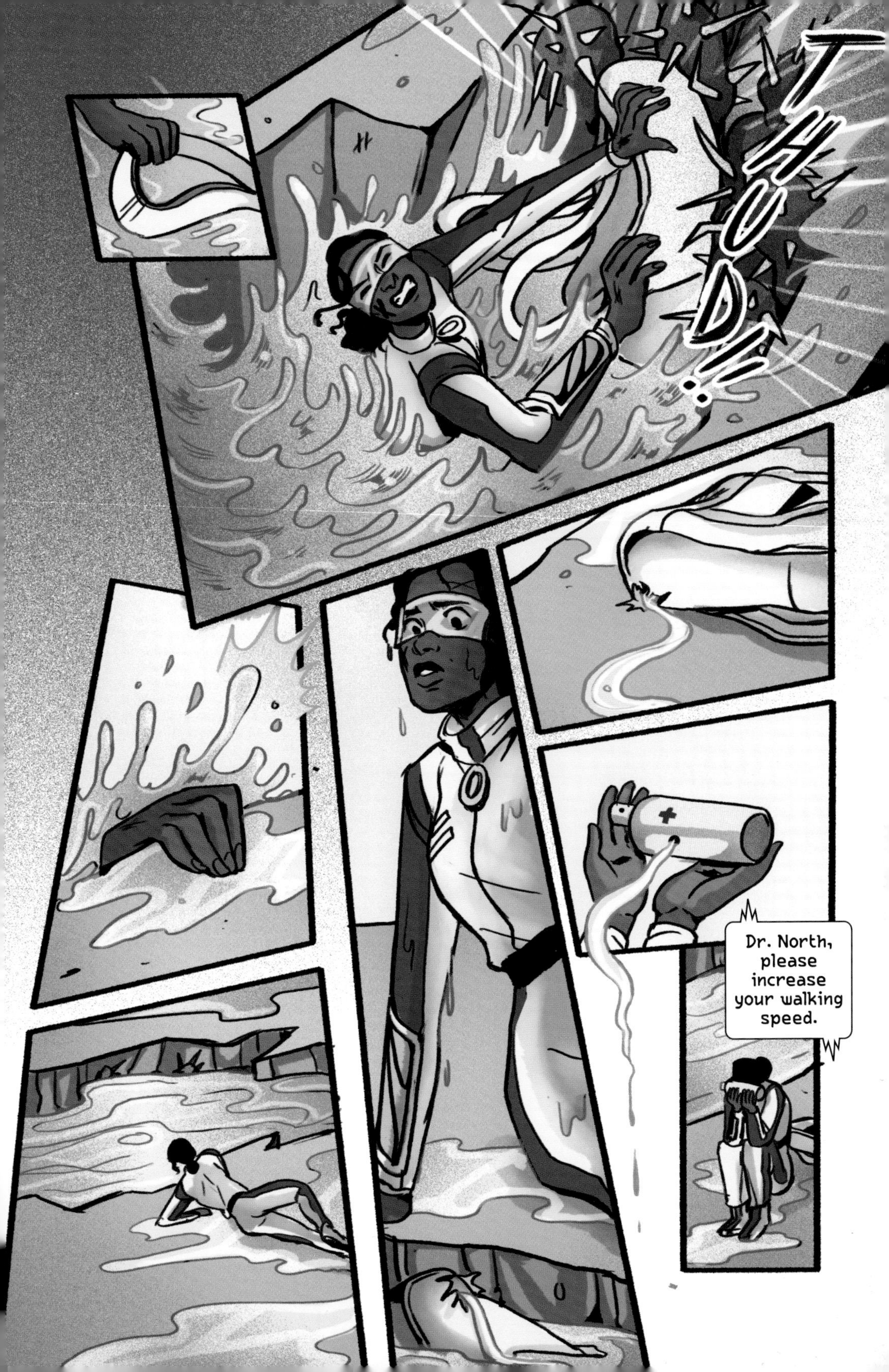
THUD!!
Dr. North, please increase your walking speed.

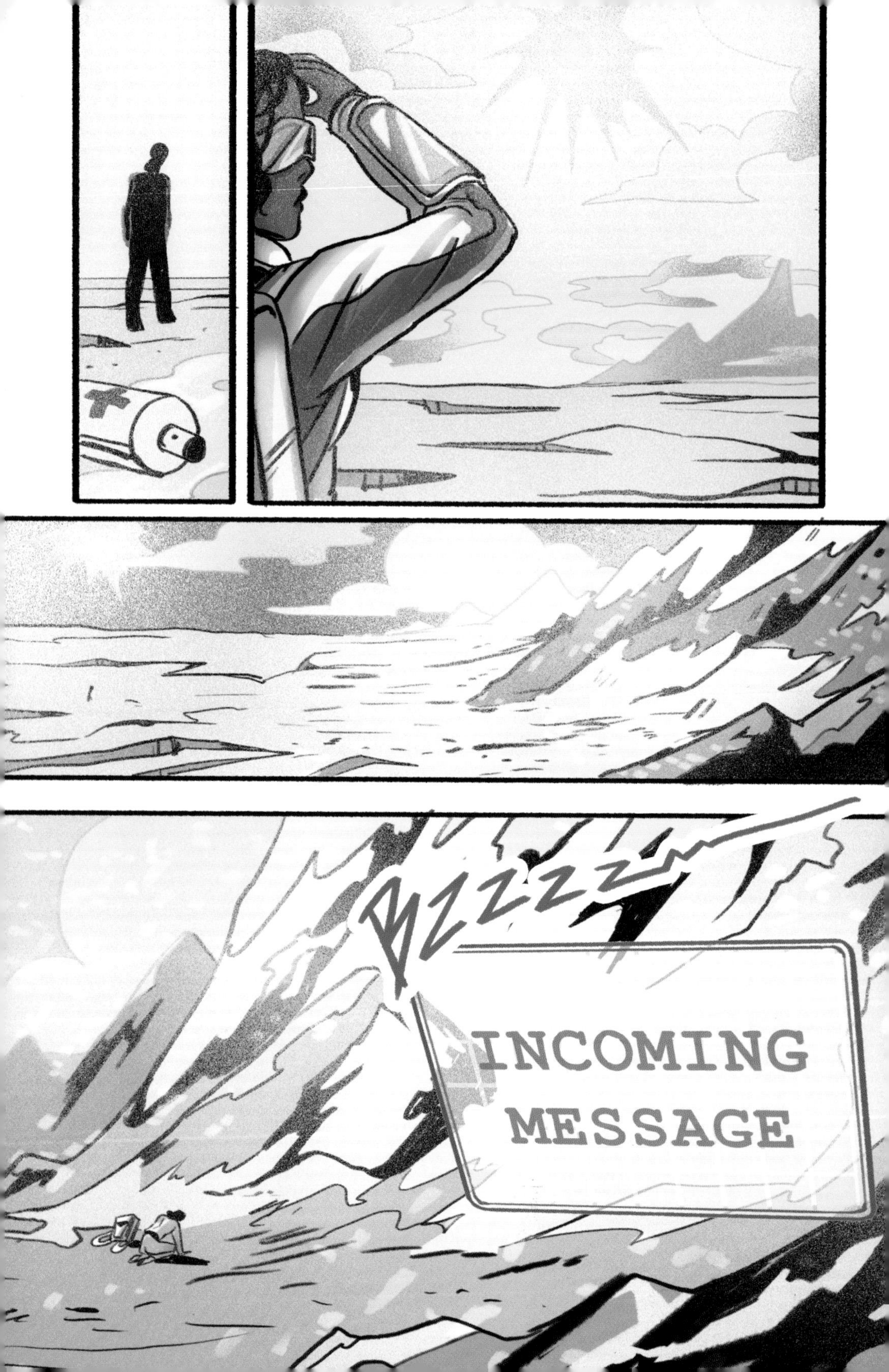
BZZZZ
INCOMING MESSAGE

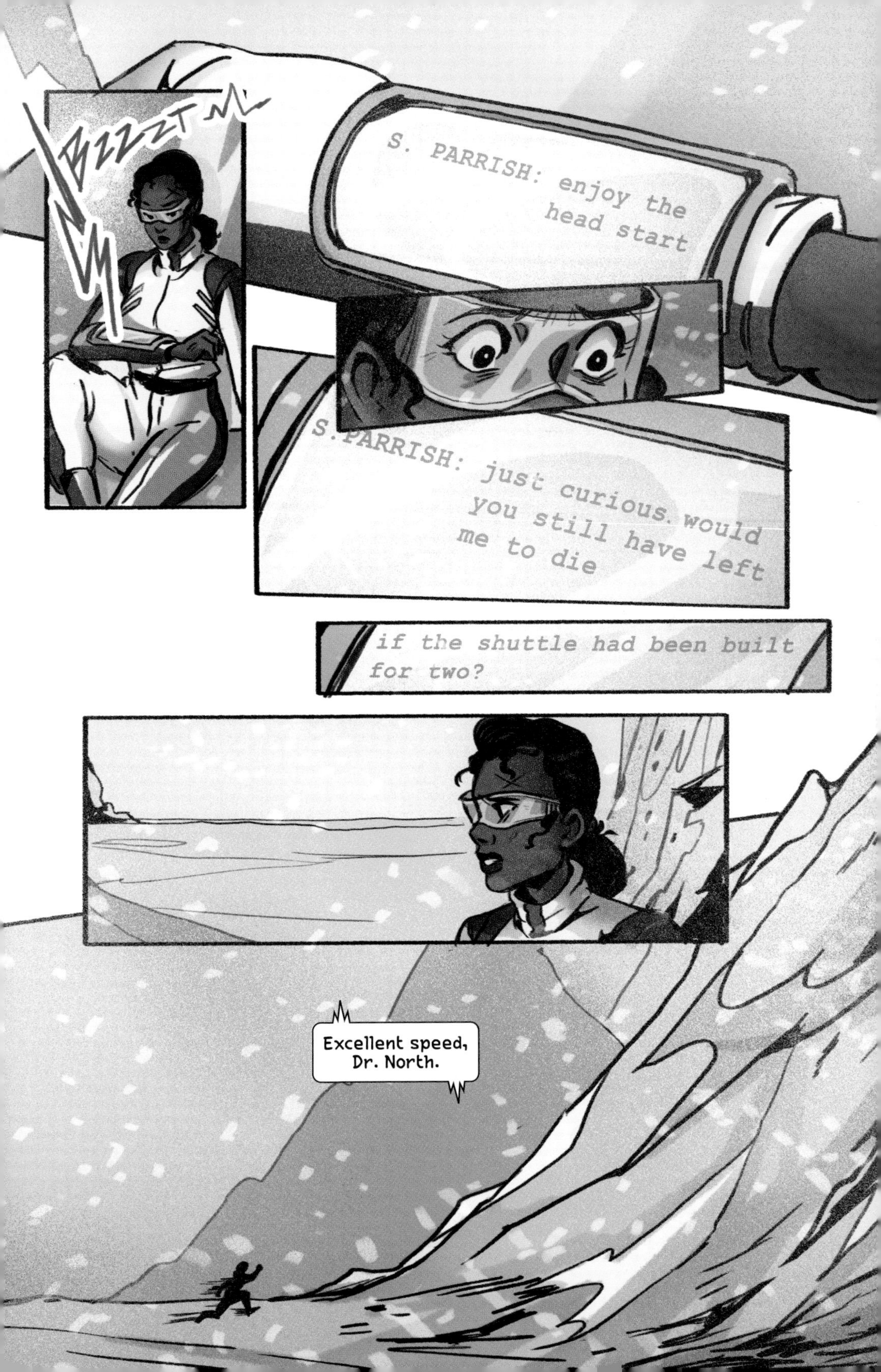
BZZZT
S. PARRISH: enjoy the head start
S. PARRISH: just curious. would you still have left me to die
if the shuttle had been built for two?
Excellent speed, Dr. North.

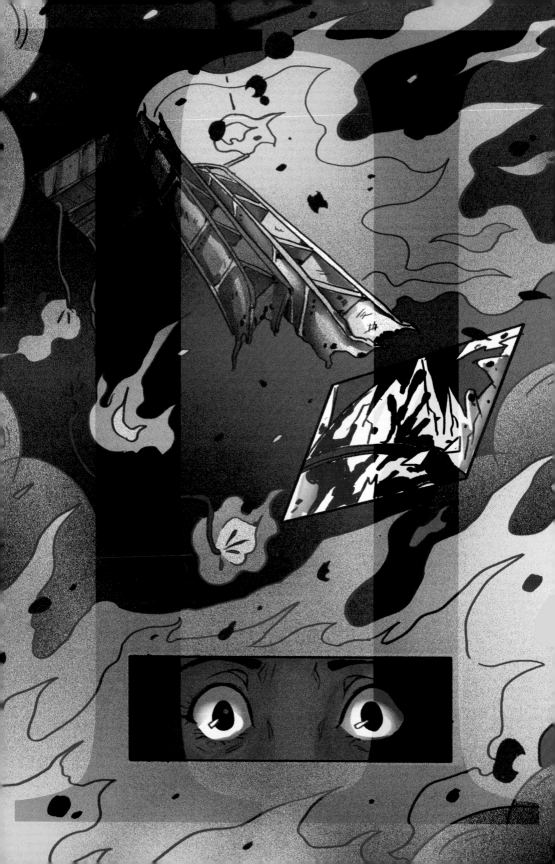

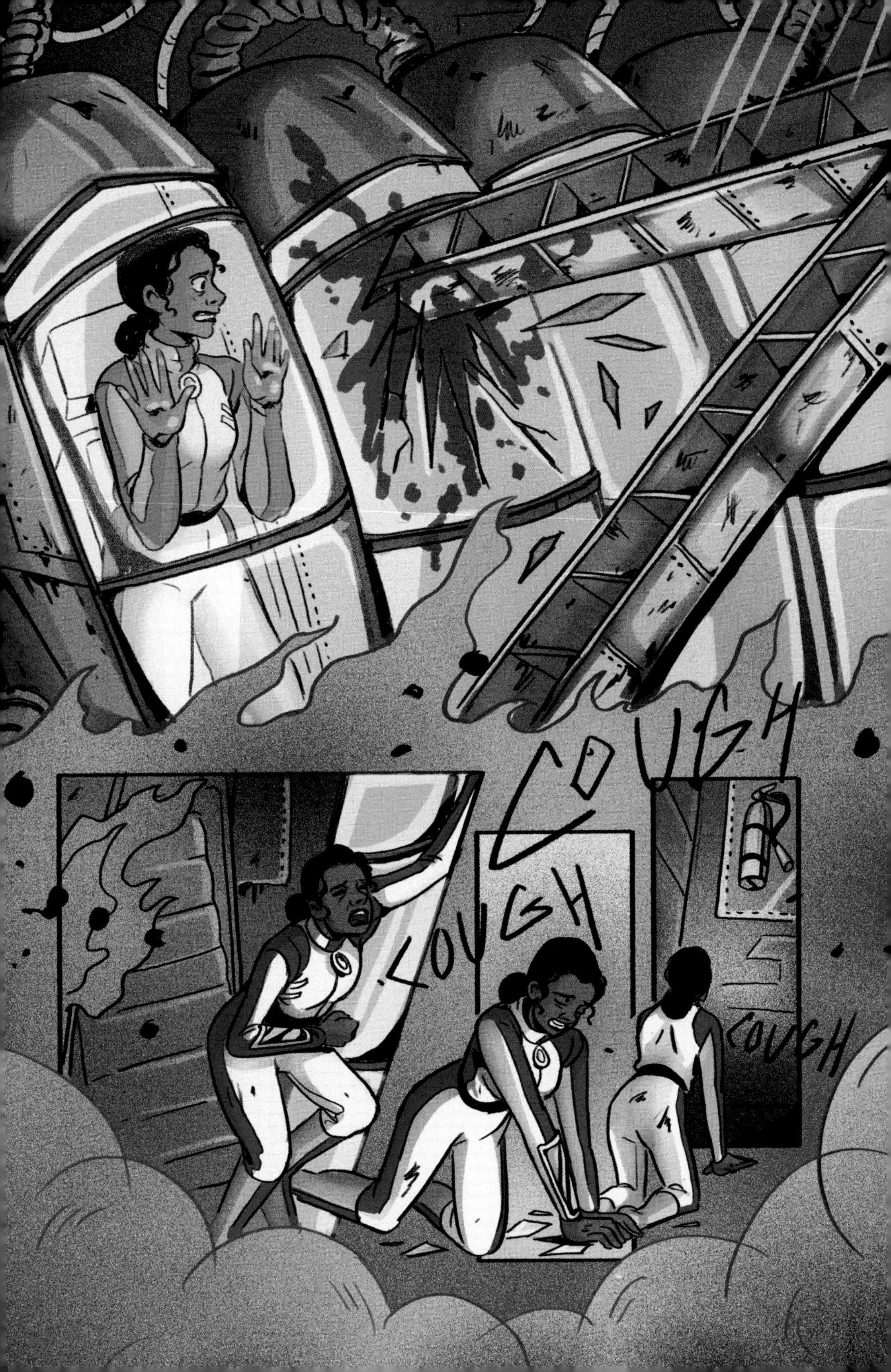

COUGH
COUGH
COUGH

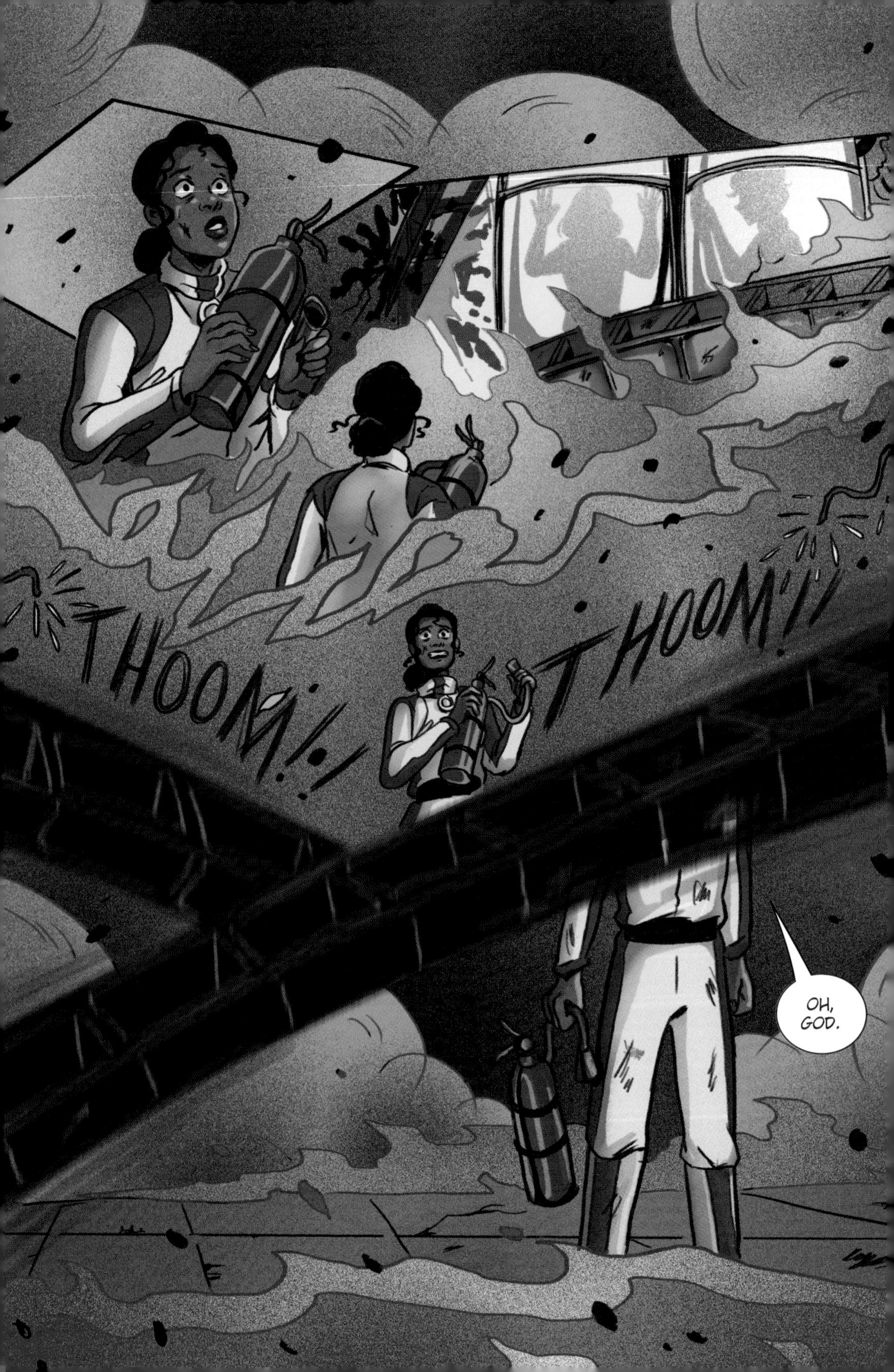
THOOM!!
THOOM!!
OH, GOD.

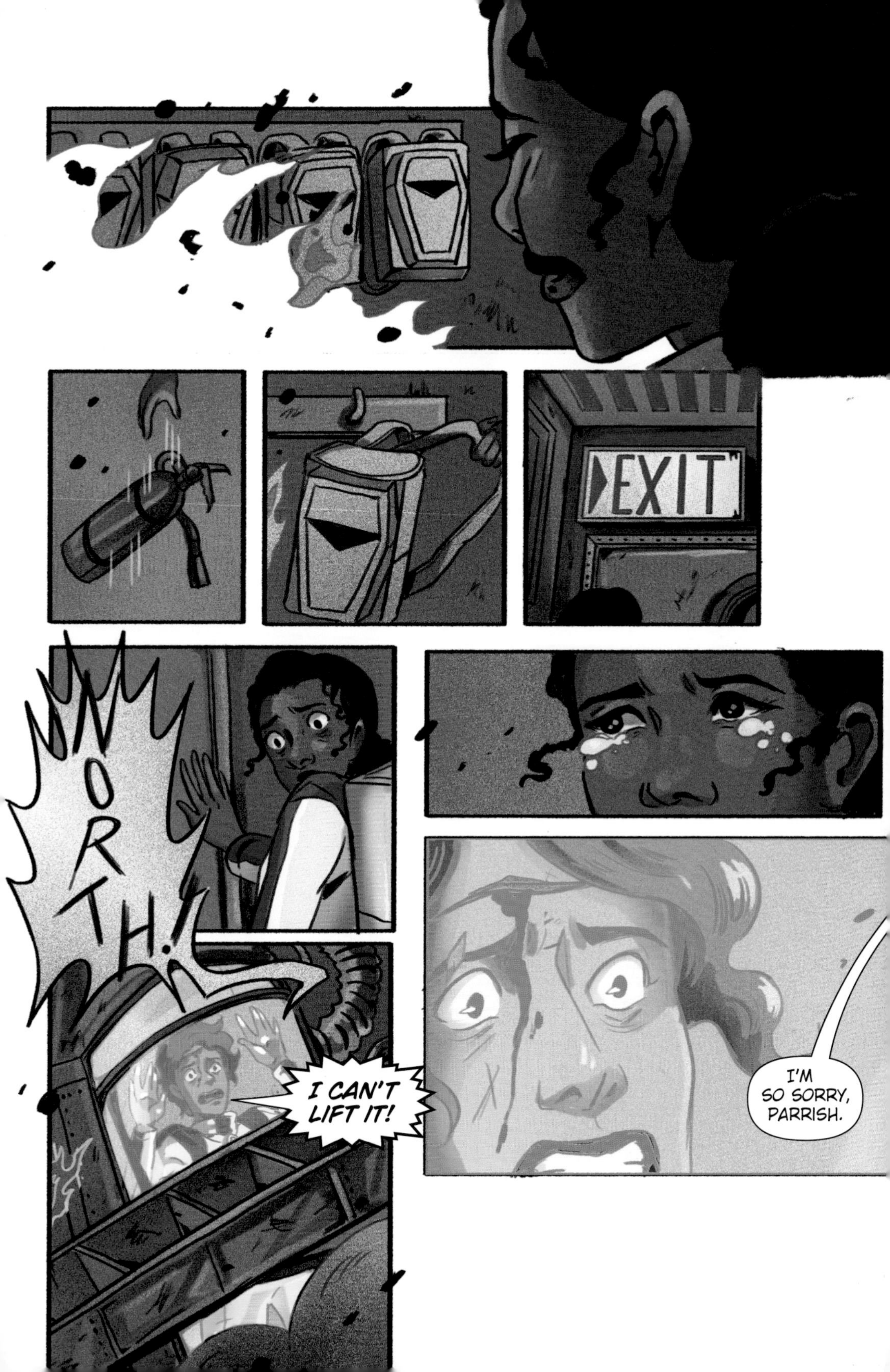
EXIT
NORTH!
I CAN'T LIFT IT!
I'M SO SORRY, PARRISH.

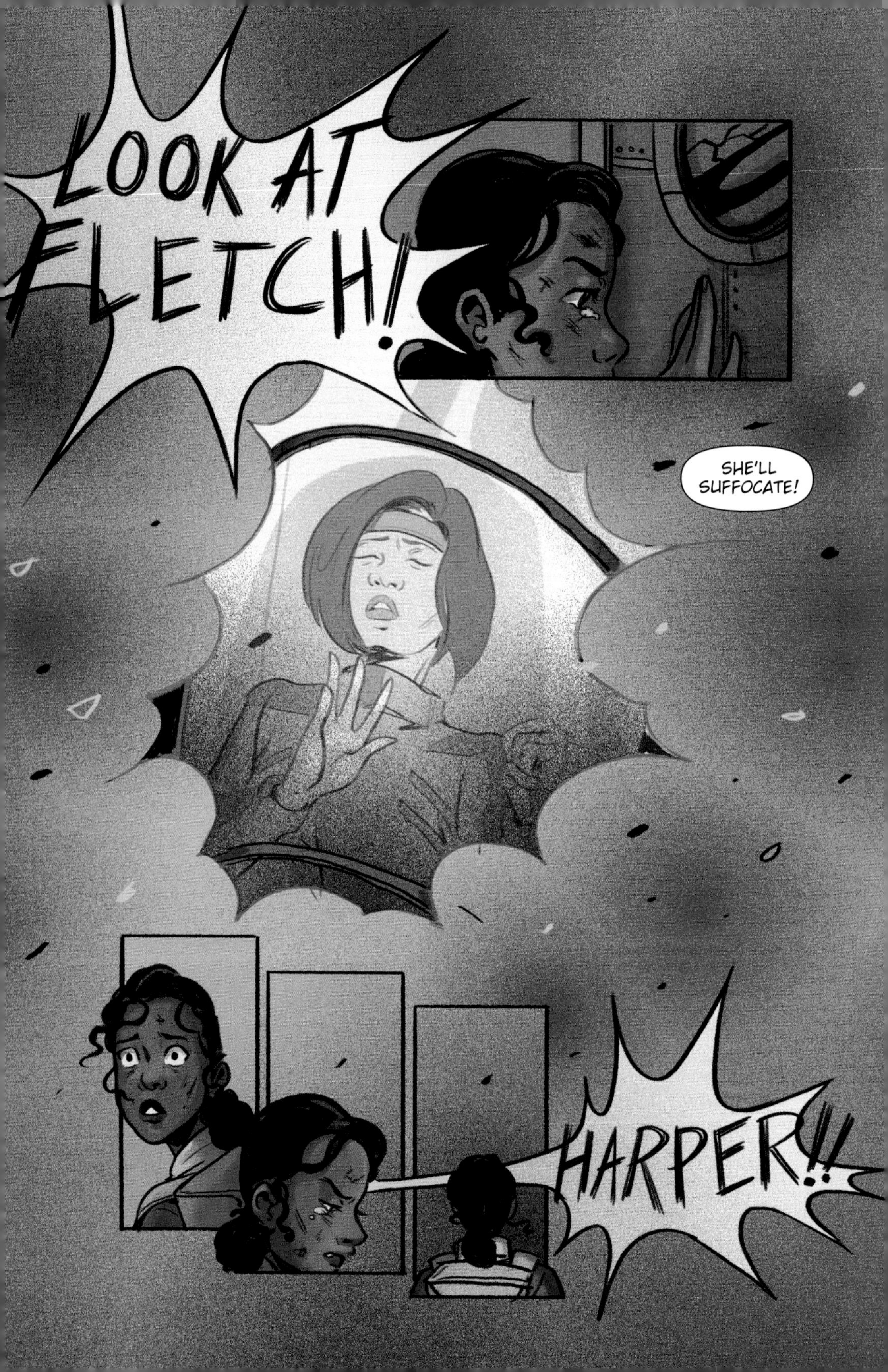
LOOK AT FLETCH!
SHE'LL SUFFOCATE!
HARPER!!

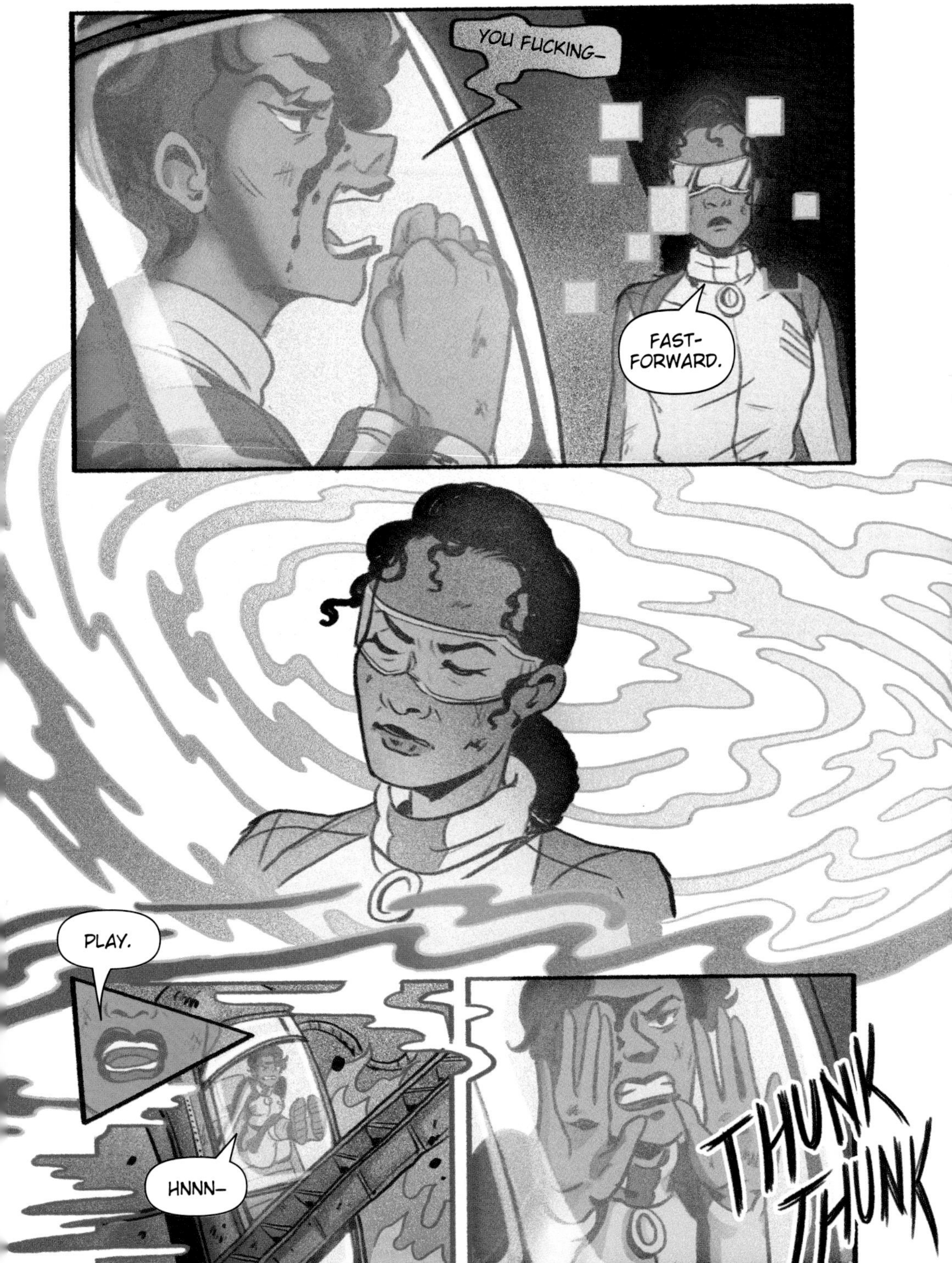
YOU FUCKING–
FAST-FORWARD.
PLAY.
HNNN–
THUNK THUNK

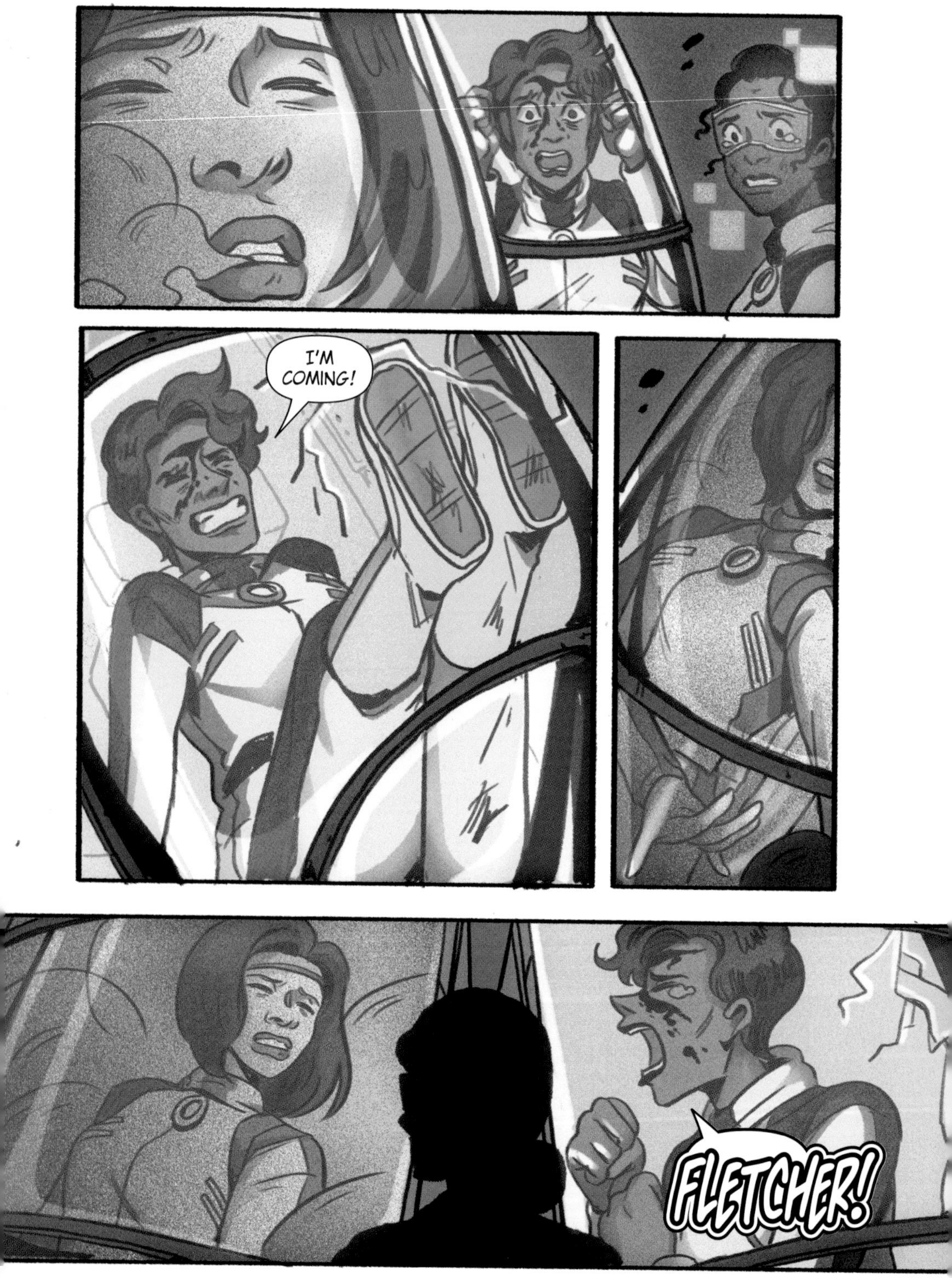
I'M COMING!
FLETCHER!

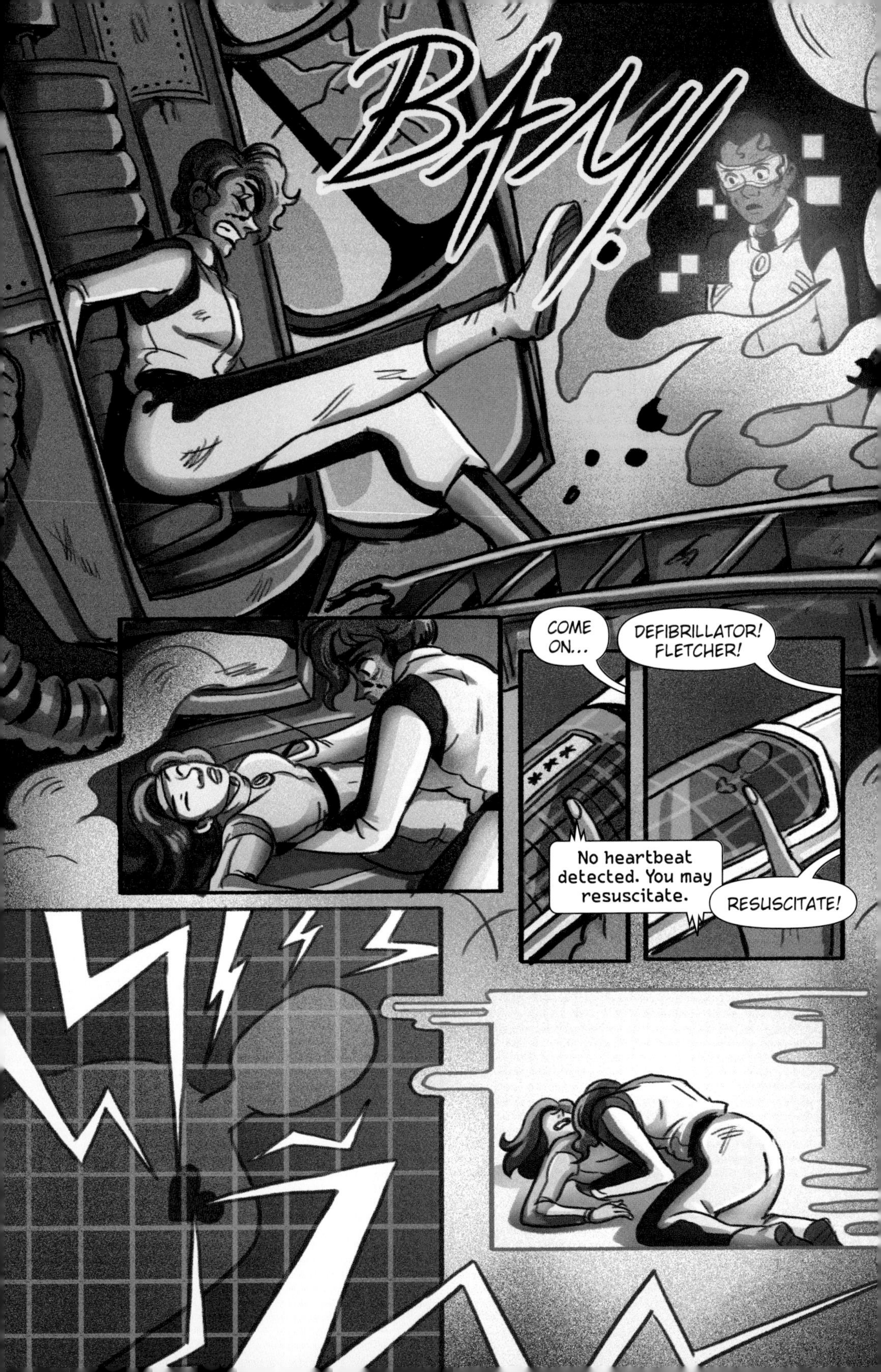
BAM!
COME ON...
DEFIBRILLATOR! FLETCHER!
No heartbeat detected. You may resuscitate.
RESUSCITATE!

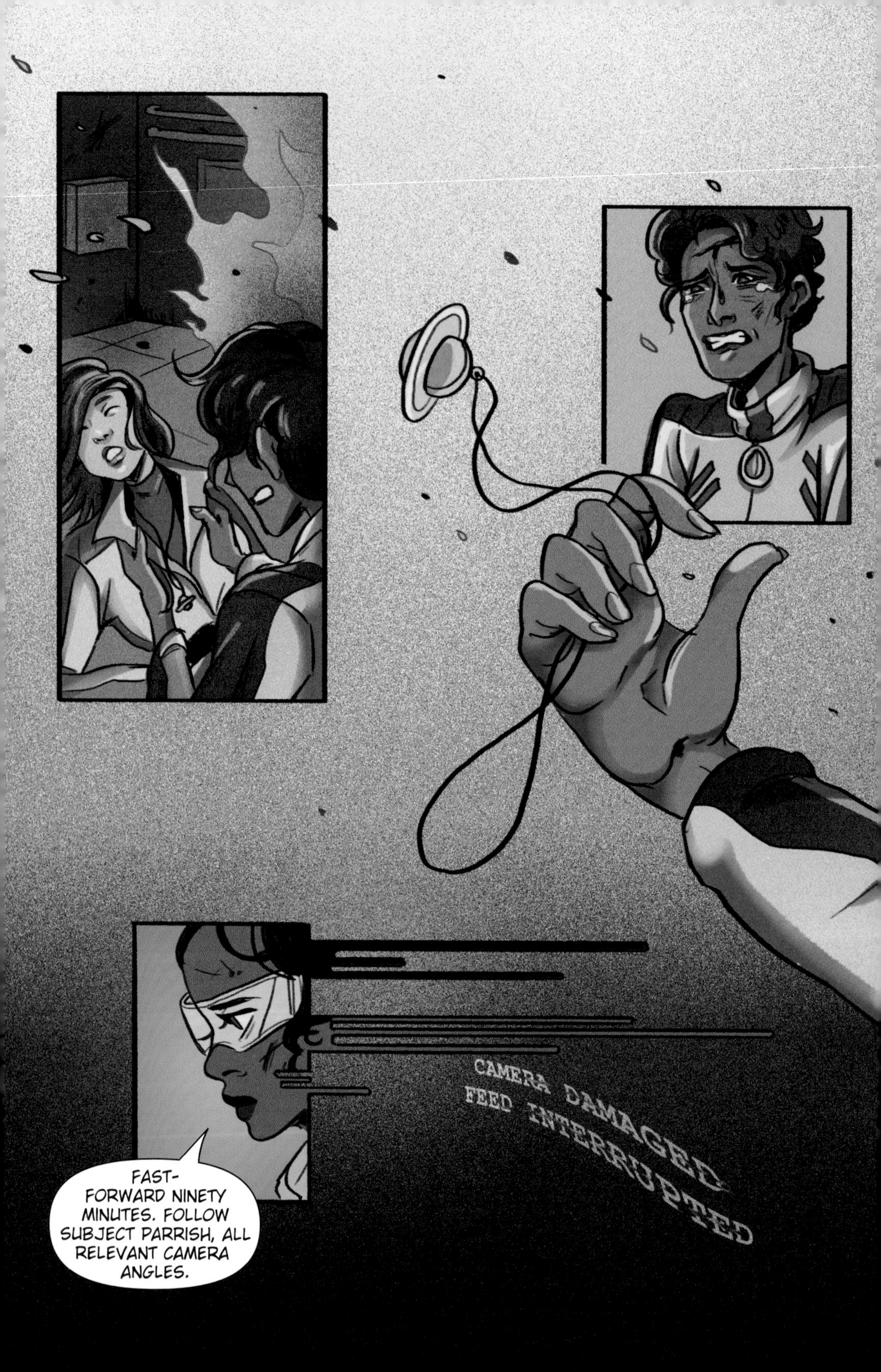
CAMERA DAMAGED
FEED INTERRUPTED
FAST-FORWARD NINETY MINUTES. FOLLOW SUBJECT PARRISH, ALL RELEVANT CAMERA ANGLES.

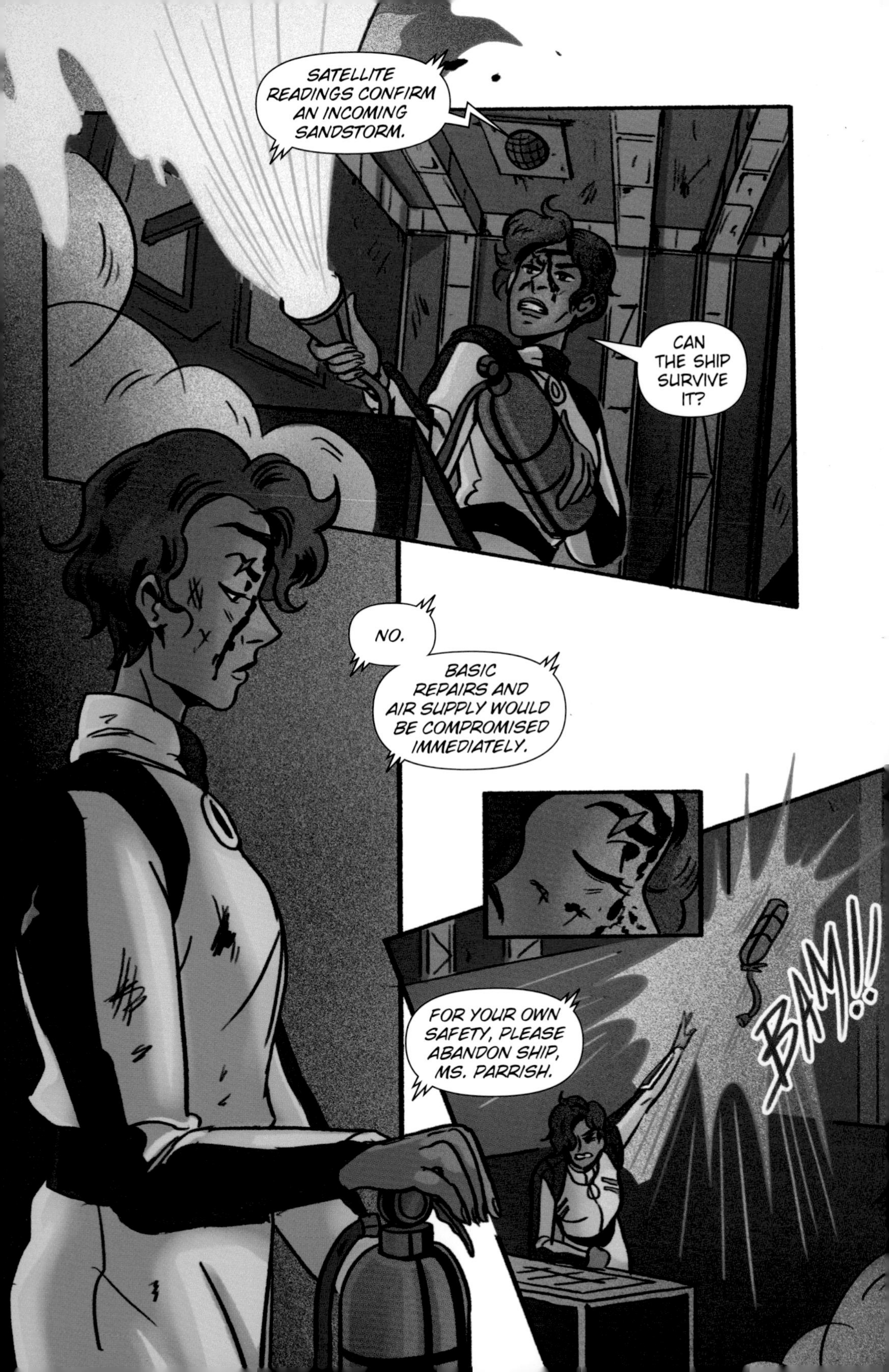
SATELLITE READINGS CONFIRM AN INCOMING SANDSTORM.
CAN THE SHIP SURVIVE IT?
NO.
BASIC REPAIRS AND AIR SUPPLY WOULD BE COMPROMISED IMMEDIATELY.
FOR YOUR OWN SAFETY, PLEASE ABANDON SHIP, MS. PARRISH.
BAM!!

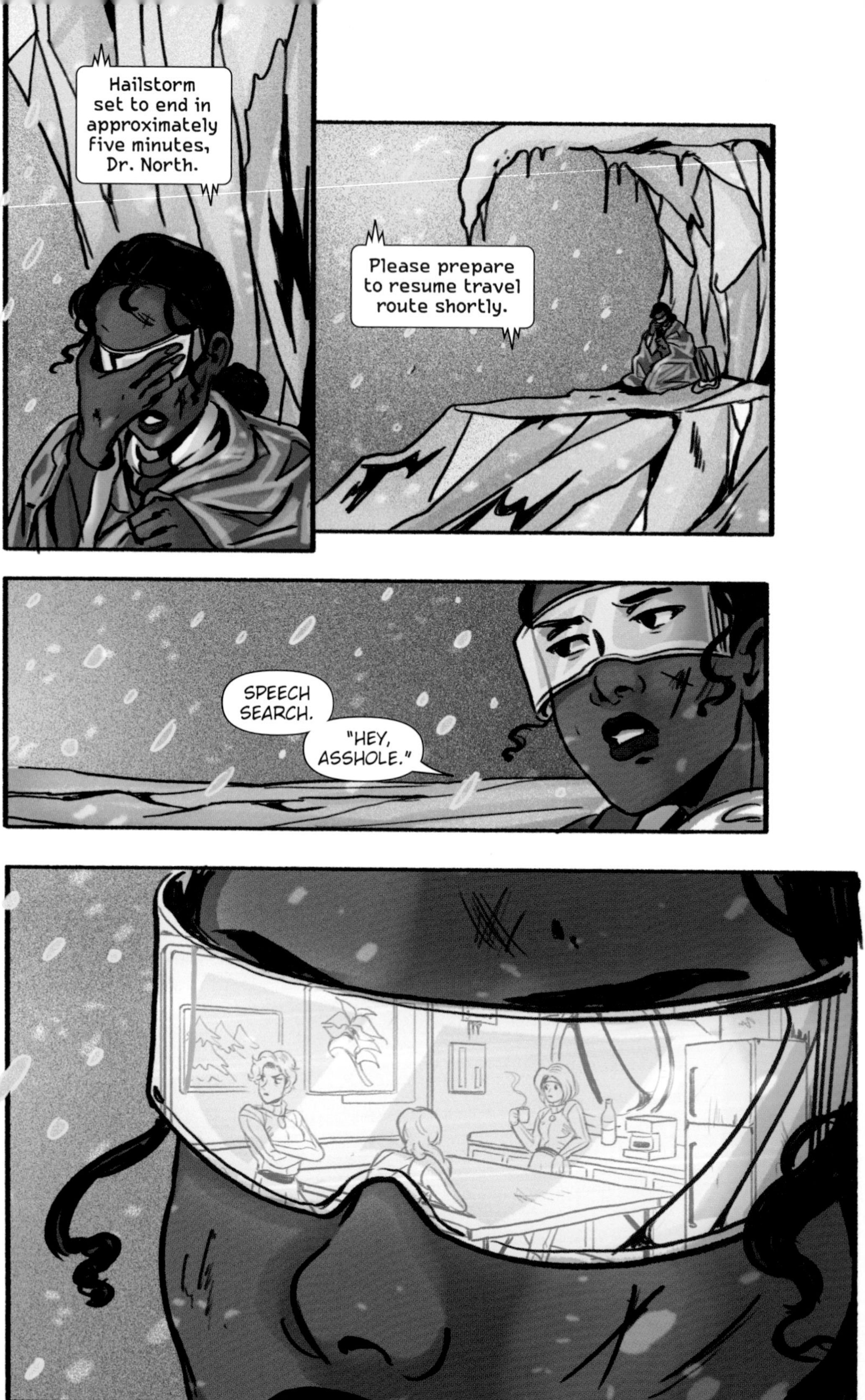
Hailstorm set to end in approximately five minutes, Dr. North.
Please prepare to resume travel route shortly.
SPEECH SEARCH.
"HEY, ASSHOLE."

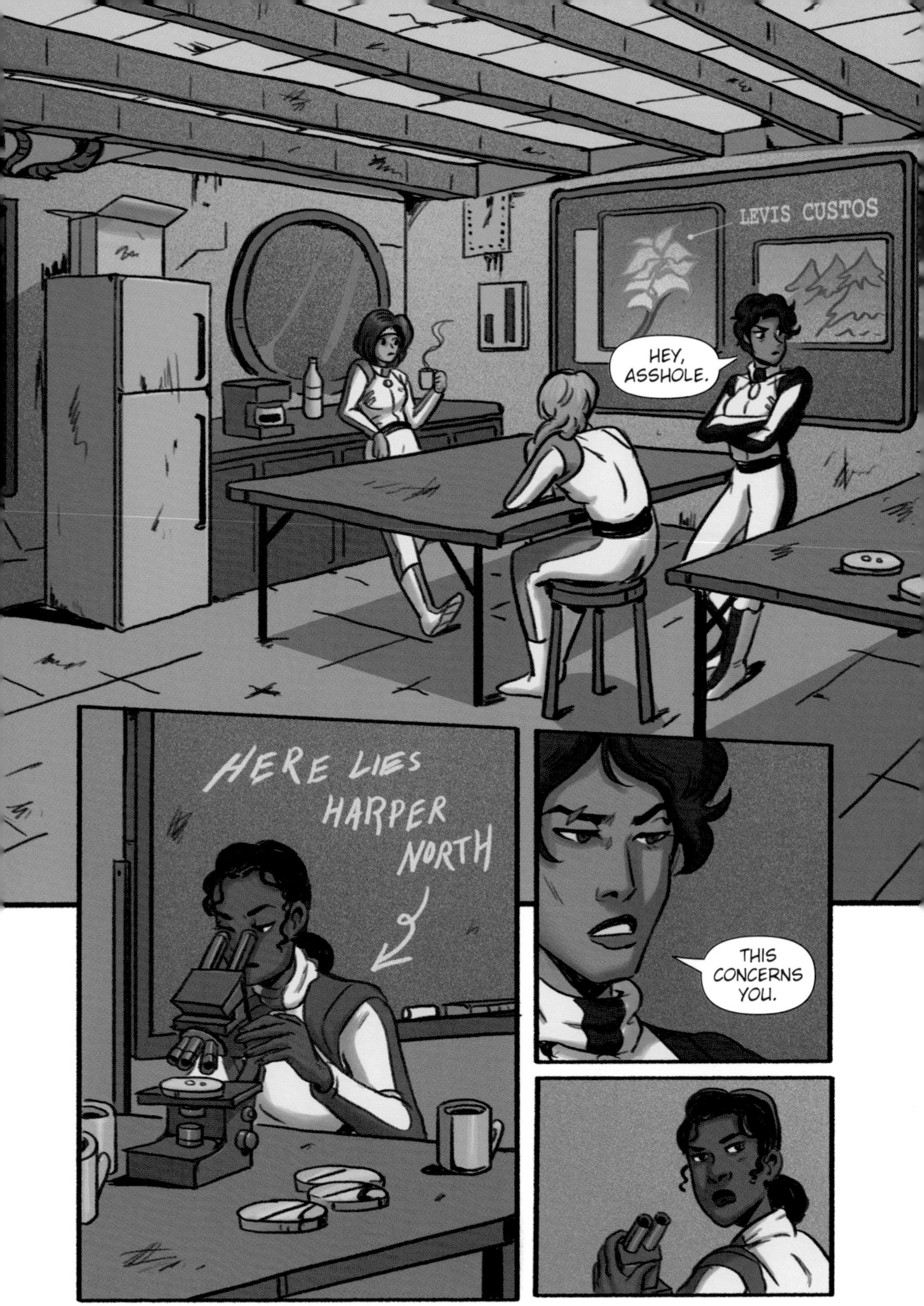
LEVIS CUSTOS
HEY, ASSHOLE.
HERE LIES HARPER NORTH
THIS CONCERNS YOU.

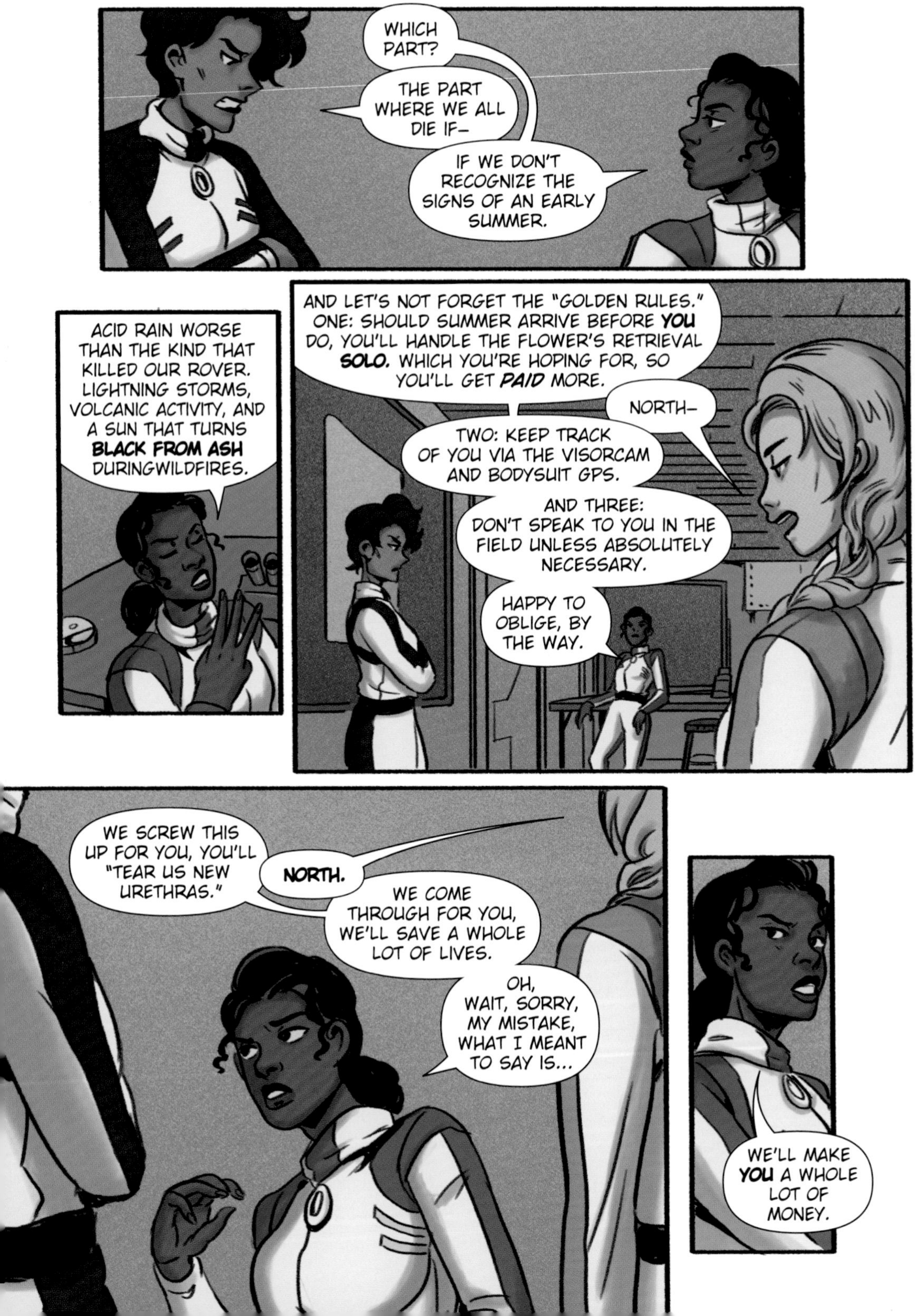
WHICH PART?
THE PART WHERE WE ALL DIE IF—
IF WE DON'T RECOGNIZE THE SIGNS OF AN EARLY SUMMER.
ACID RAIN WORSE THAN THE KIND THAT KILLED OUR ROVER. LIGHTNING STORMS, VOLCANIC ACTIVITY, AND A SUN THAT TURNS **BLACK FROM ASH** DURINGWILDFIRES.
AND LET'S NOT FORGET THE "GOLDEN RULES." ONE: SHOULD SUMMER ARRIVE BEFORE **YOU** DO, YOU'LL HANDLE THE FLOWER'S RETRIEVAL **SOLO.** WHICH YOU'RE HOPING FOR, SO YOU'LL GET ***PAID*** MORE.
NORTH—
TWO: KEEP TRACK OF YOU VIA THE VISORCAM AND BODYSUIT GPS.
AND THREE: DON'T SPEAK TO YOU IN THE FIELD UNLESS ABSOLUTELY NECESSARY.
HAPPY TO OBLIGE, BY THE WAY.
WE SCREW THIS UP FOR YOU, YOU'LL "TEAR US NEW URETHRAS."
NORTH.
WE COME THROUGH FOR YOU, WE'LL SAVE A WHOLE LOT OF LIVES.
OH, WAIT, SORRY, MY MISTAKE, WHAT I MEANT TO SAY IS...
WE'LL MAKE **YOU** A WHOLE LOT OF MONEY.

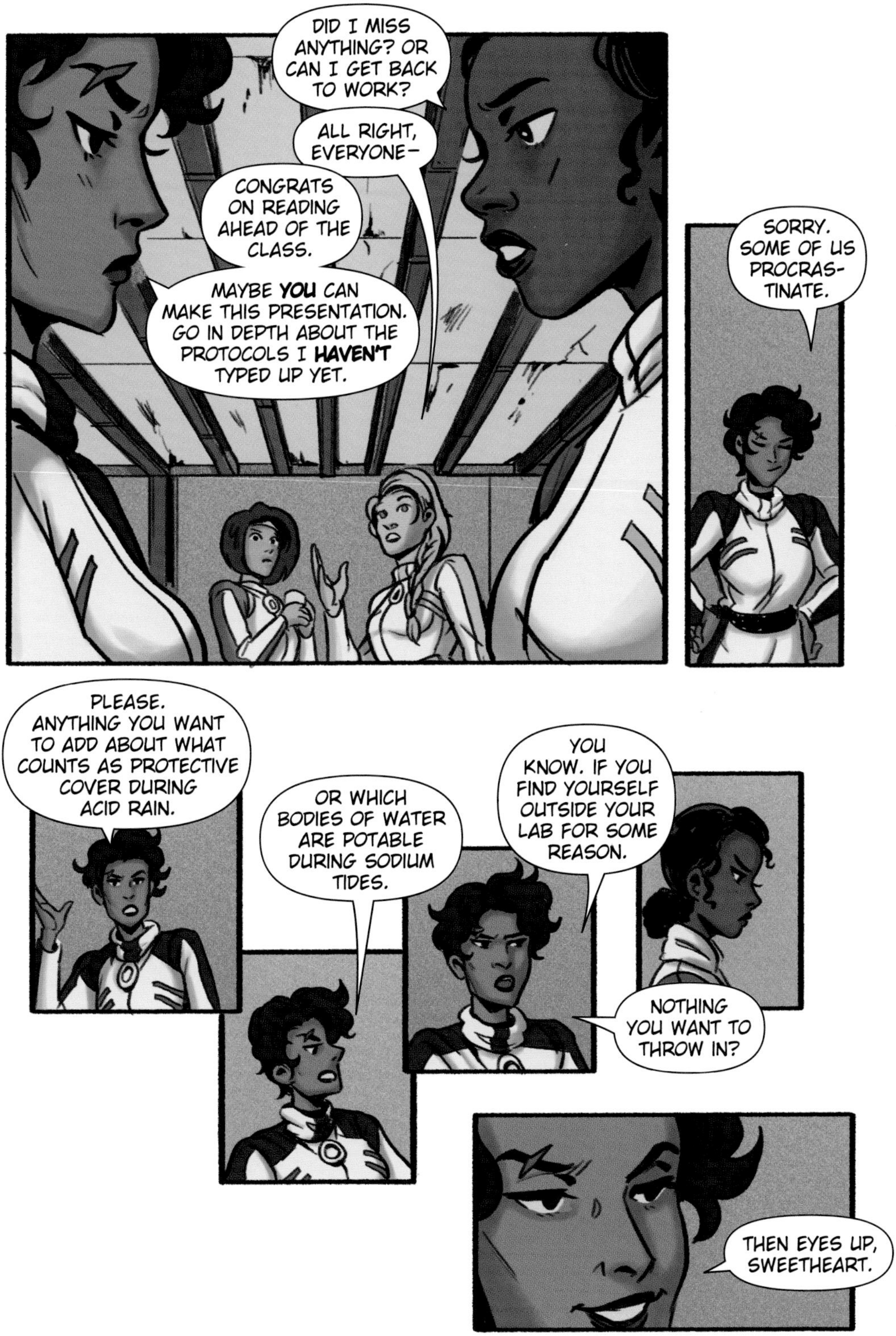
DID I MISS ANYTHING? OR CAN I GET BACK TO WORK?
ALL RIGHT, EVERYONE—
CONGRATS ON READING AHEAD OF THE CLASS.
MAYBE **YOU** CAN MAKE THIS PRESENTATION. GO IN DEPTH ABOUT THE PROTOCOLS I **HAVEN'T** TYPED UP YET.
SORRY. SOME OF US PROCRAS-TINATE.
PLEASE. ANYTHING YOU WANT TO ADD ABOUT WHAT COUNTS AS PROTECTIVE COVER DURING ACID RAIN.
OR WHICH BODIES OF WATER ARE POTABLE DURING SODIUM TIDES.
YOU KNOW. IF YOU FIND YOURSELF OUTSIDE YOUR LAB FOR SOME REASON.
NOTHING YOU WANT TO THROW IN?
THEN EYES UP, SWEETHEART.

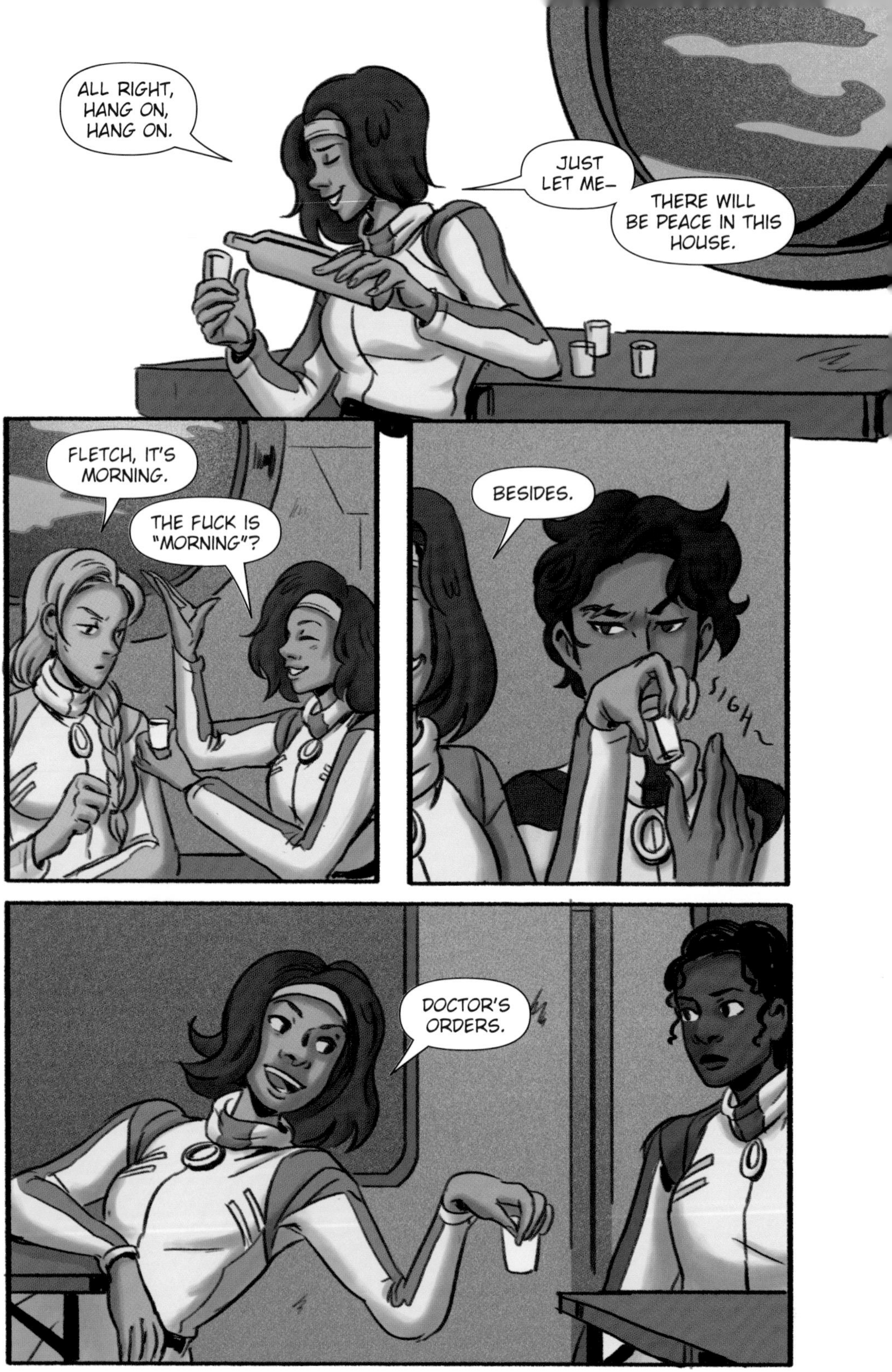
ALL RIGHT, HANG ON, HANG ON.
JUST LET ME–
THERE WILL BE PEACE IN THIS HOUSE.
FLETCH, IT'S MORNING.
THE FUCK IS "MORNING"?
BESIDES.
SIGH~
DOCTOR'S ORDERS.

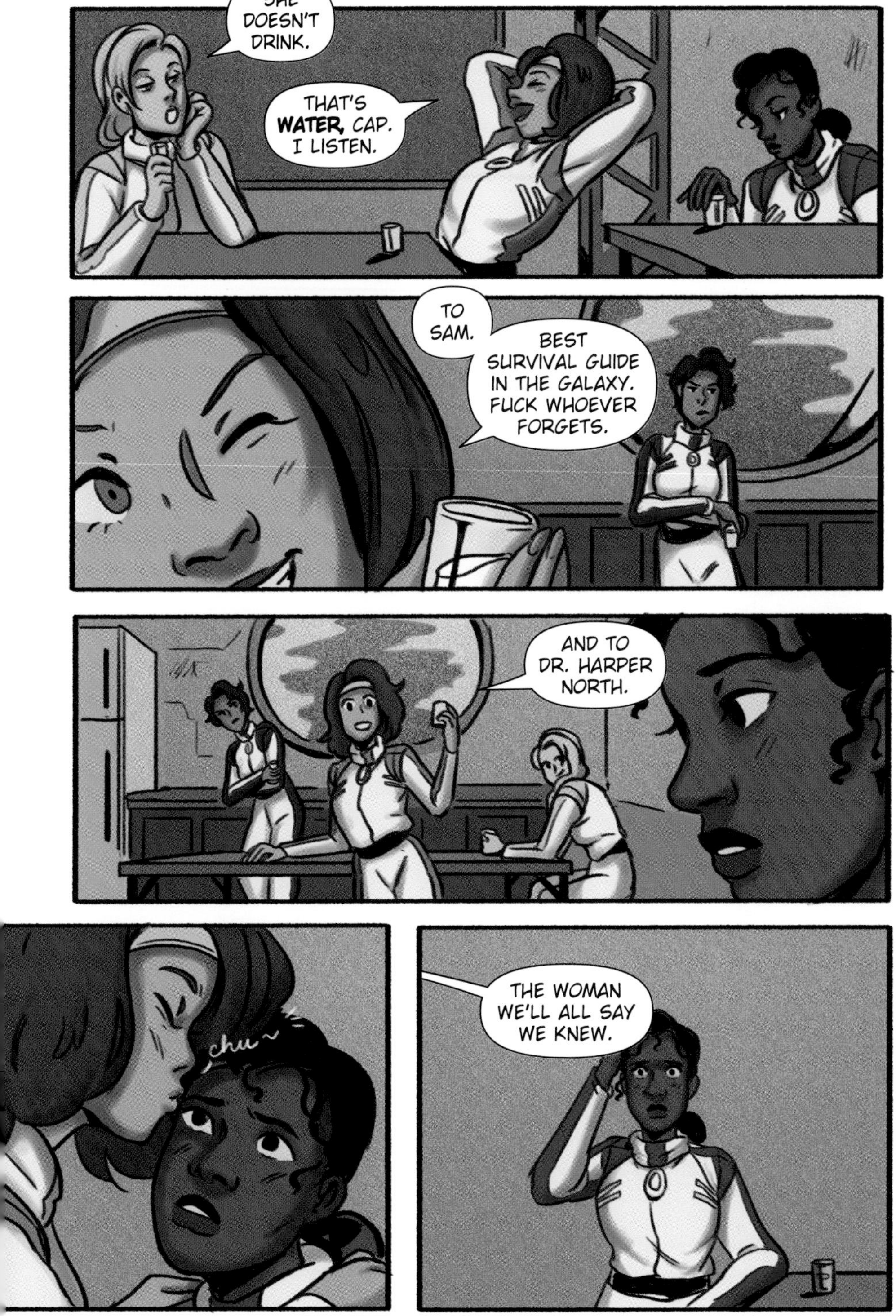
SHE DOESN'T DRINK.
THAT'S **WATER,** CAP. I LISTEN.
TO SAM.
BEST SURVIVAL GUIDE IN THE GALAXY. FUCK WHOEVER FORGETS.
AND TO DR. HARPER NORTH.
chu~
THE WOMAN WE'LL ALL SAY WE KNEW.

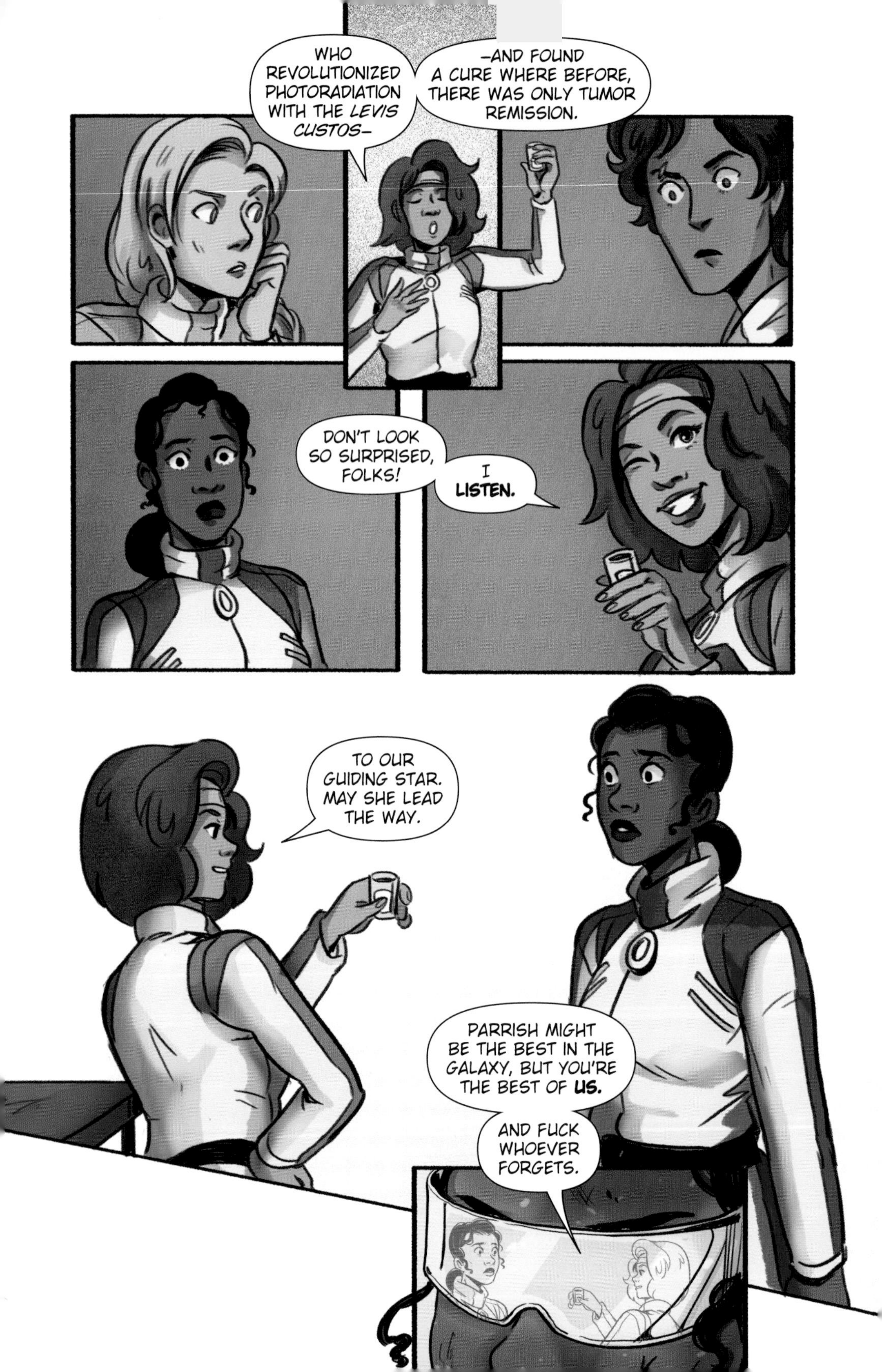
WHO REVOLUTIONIZED PHOTORADIATION WITH THE *LEVIS CUSTOS*–
–AND FOUND A CURE WHERE BEFORE, THERE WAS ONLY TUMOR REMISSION.
DON'T LOOK SO SURPRISED, FOLKS!
I **LISTEN.**
TO OUR GUIDING STAR. MAY SHE LEAD THE WAY.
PARRISH MIGHT BE THE BEST IN THE GALAXY, BUT YOU'RE THE BEST OF **US.**
AND FUCK WHOEVER FORGETS.

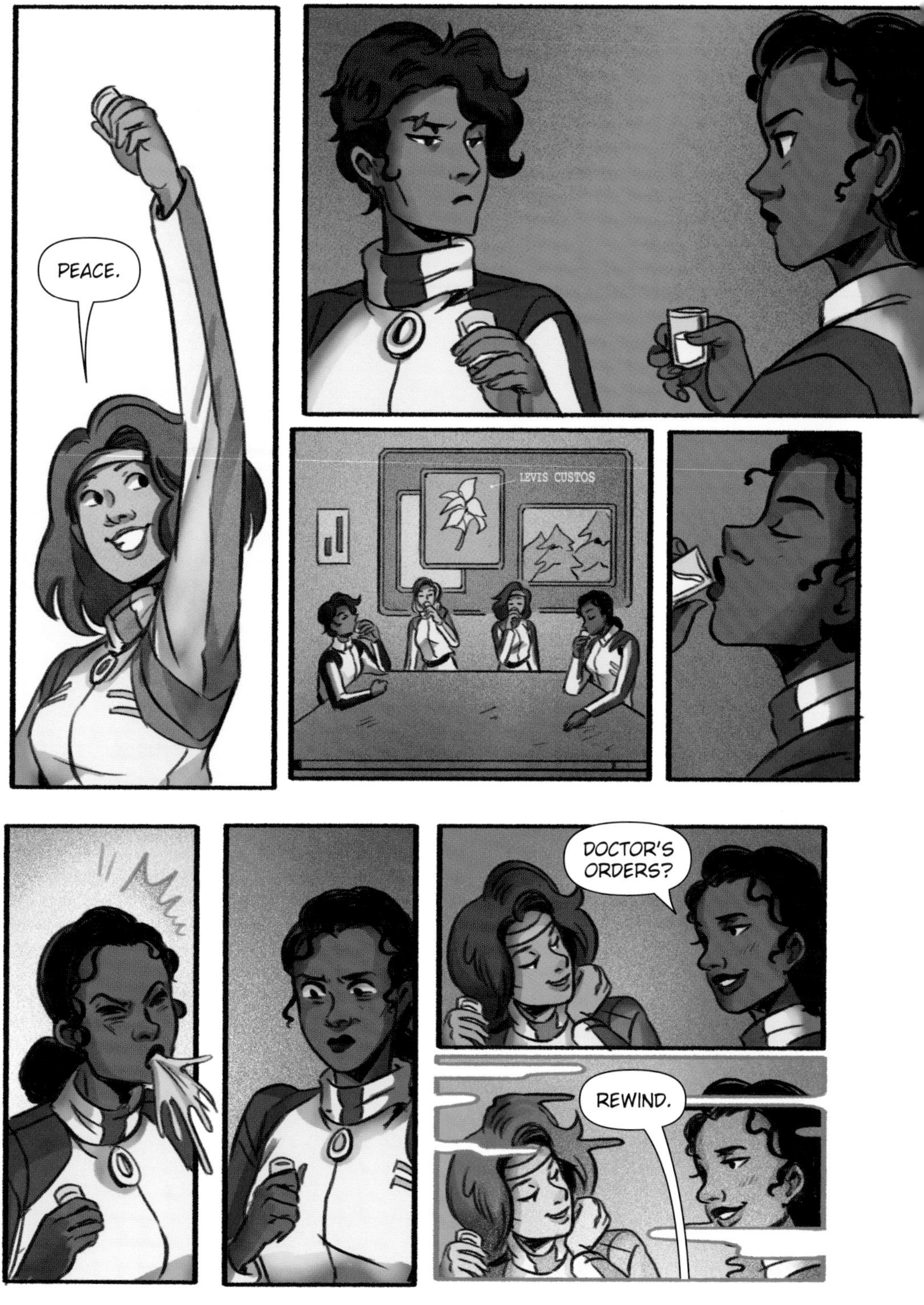
PEACE.
LEVIS CUSTOS
DOCTOR'S ORDERS?
REWIND.

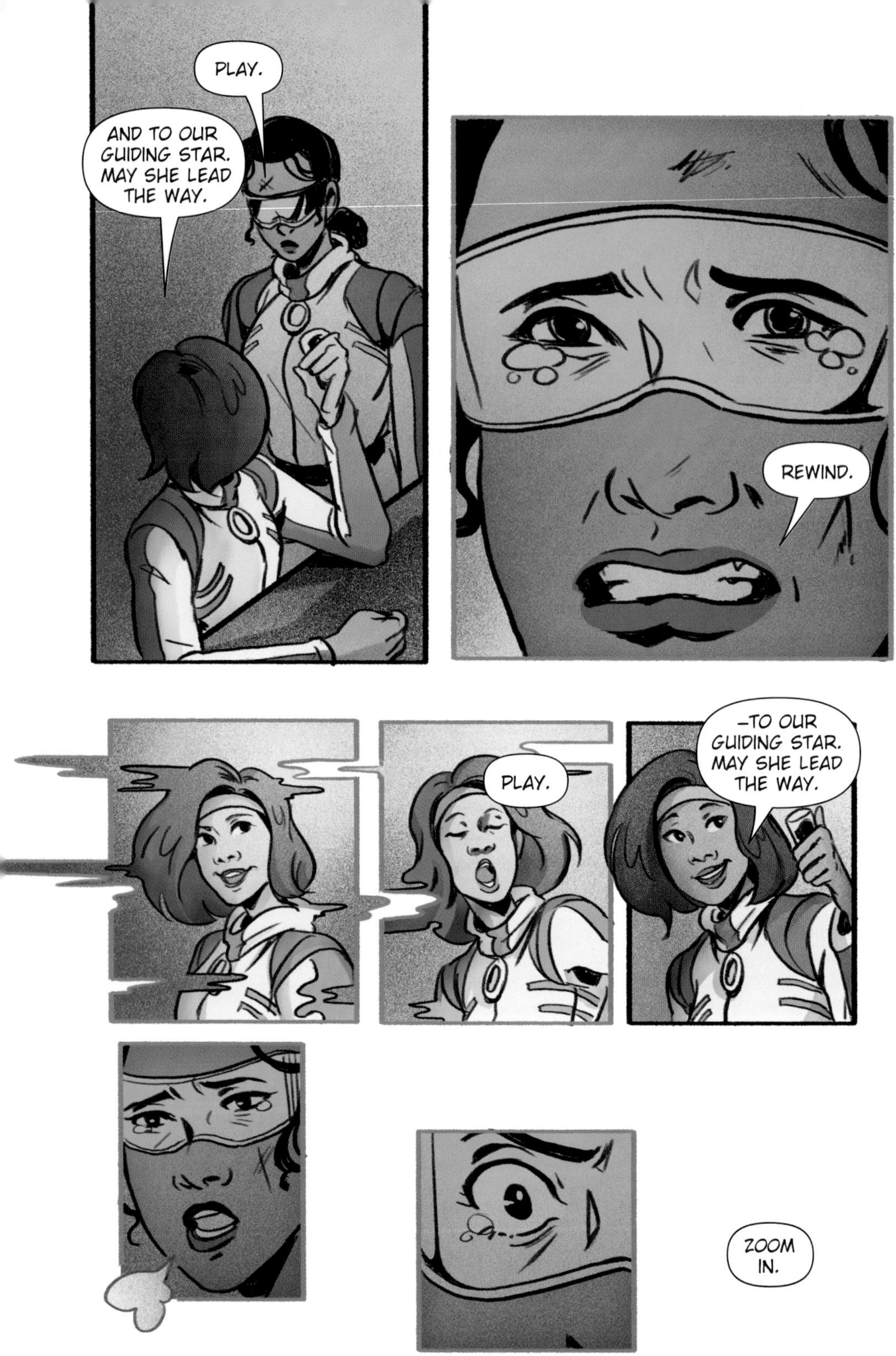
PLAY.
AND TO OUR GUIDING STAR. MAY SHE LEAD THE WAY.
REWIND.
PLAY.
–TO OUR GUIDING STAR. MAY SHE LEAD THE WAY.
ZOOM IN.

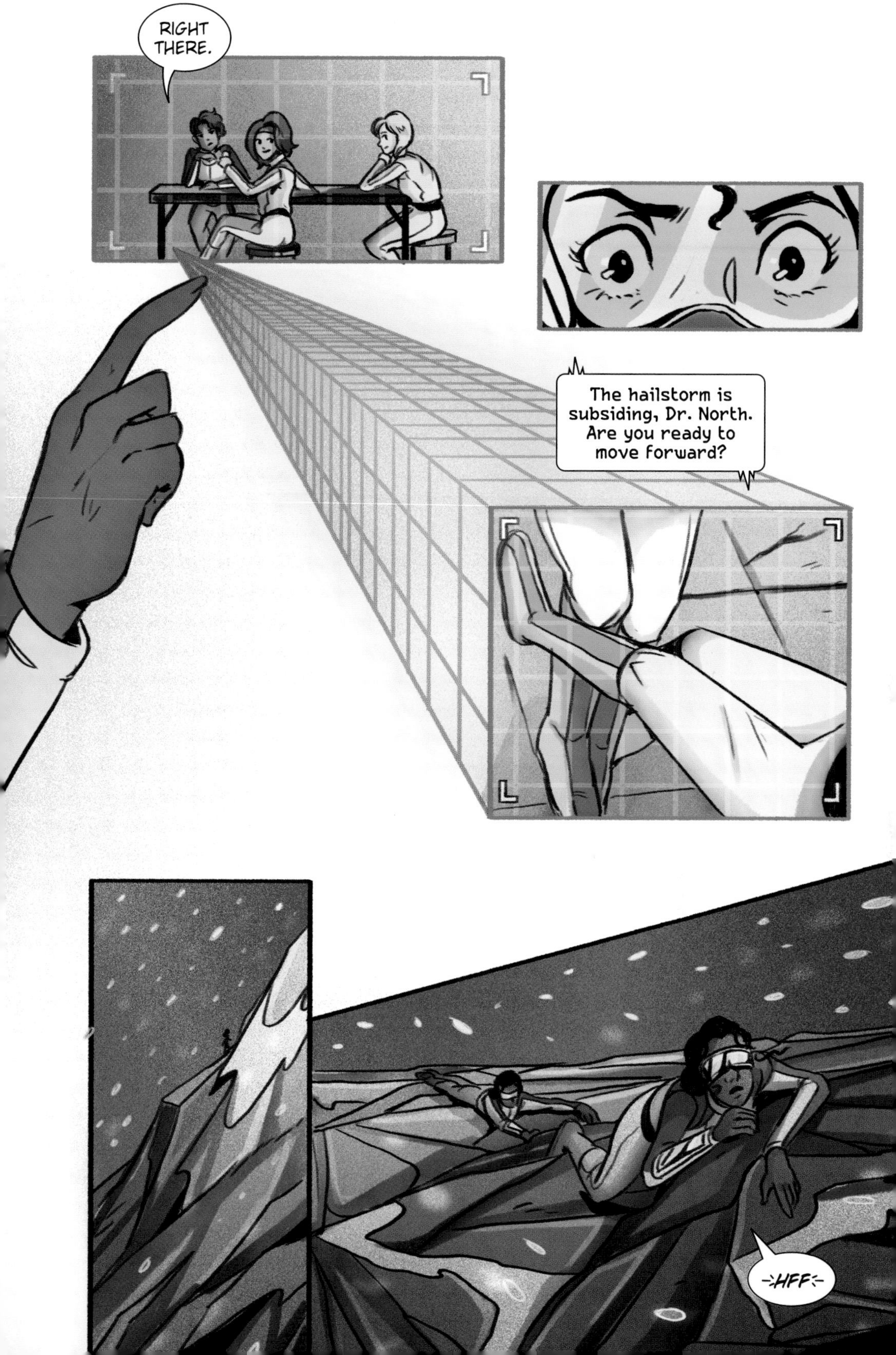
RIGHT THERE.
The hailstorm is subsiding, Dr. North. Are you ready to move forward?
HFF

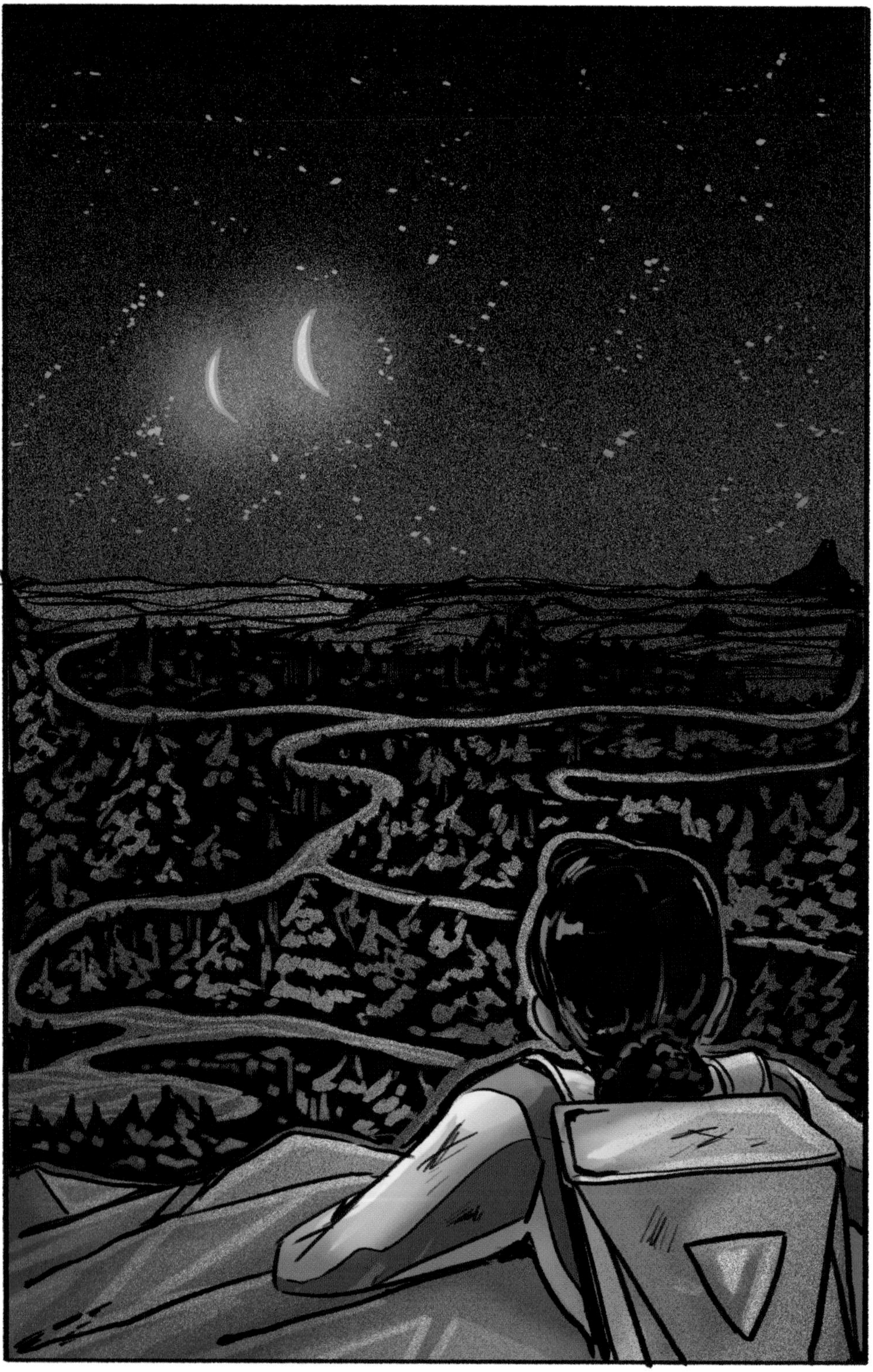

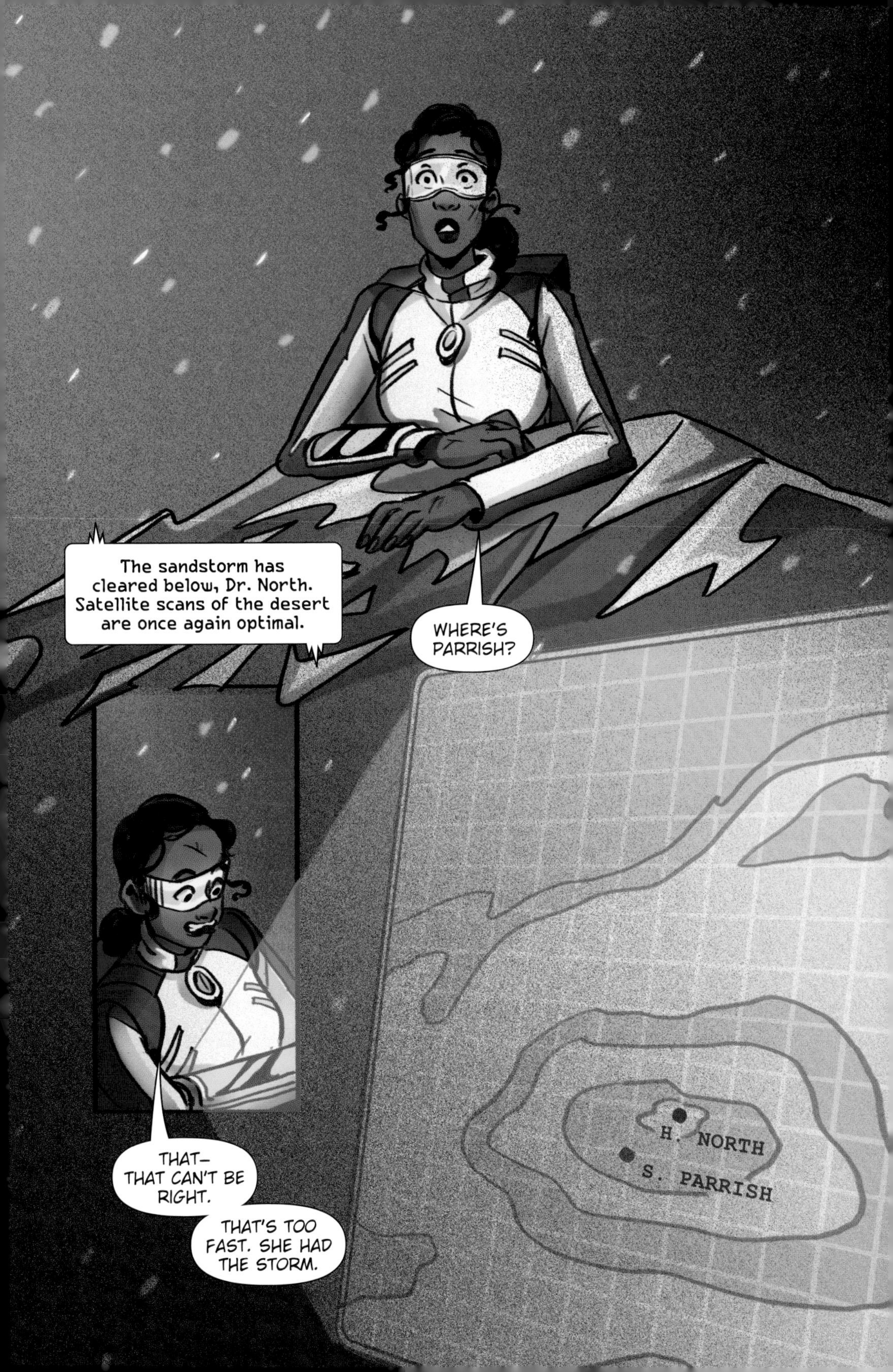
The sandstorm has cleared below, Dr. North. Satellite scans of the desert are once again optimal.
WHERE'S PARRISH?
THAT— THAT CAN'T BE RIGHT.
THAT'S TOO FAST. SHE HAD THE STORM.
H. NORTH
S. PARRISH

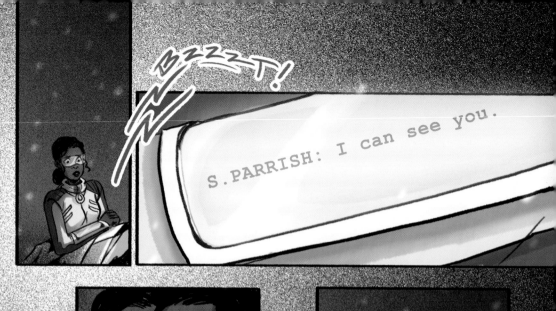

BZZZZT!

S.PARRISH: I can see you.

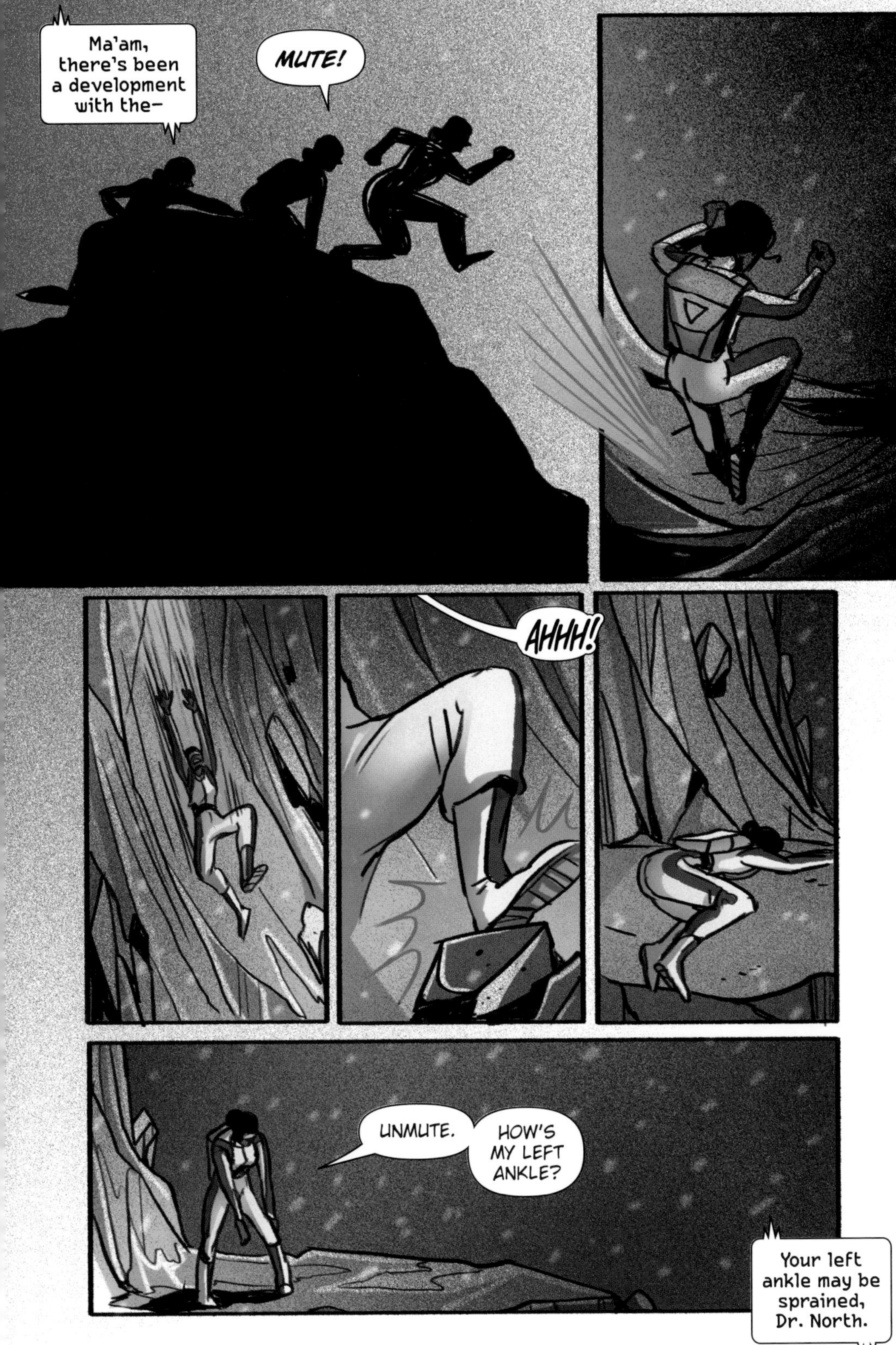
Ma'am, there's been a development with the–
MUTE!
AHHH!
UNMUTE.
HOW'S MY LEFT ANKLE?
Your left ankle may be sprained, Dr. North.

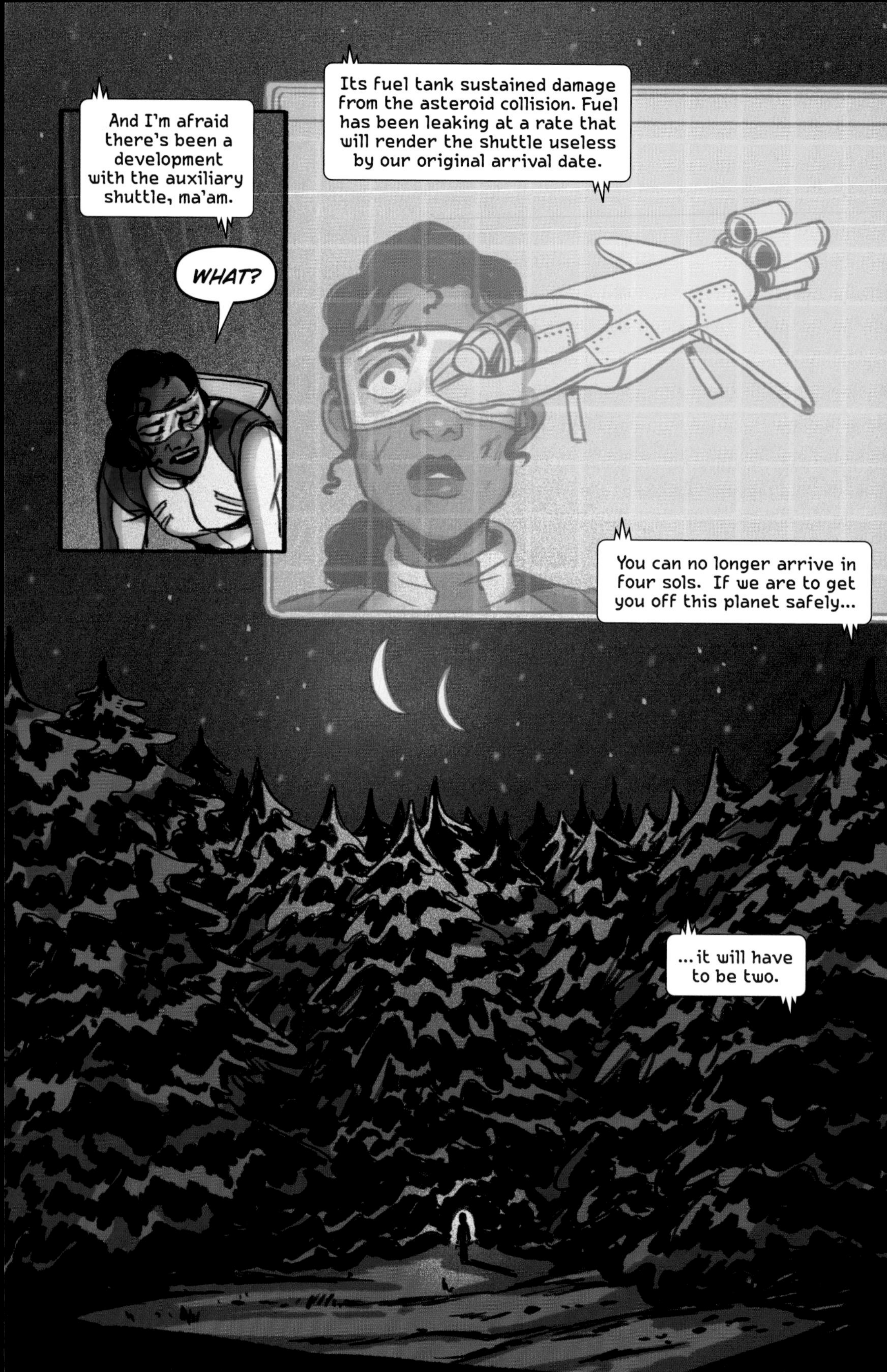
And I'm afraid there's been a development with the auxiliary shuttle, ma'am.
WHAT?
Its fuel tank sustained damage from the asteroid collision. Fuel has been leaking at a rate that will render the shuttle useless by our original arrival date.
You can no longer arrive in four sols. If we are to get you off this planet safely...
...it will have to be two.

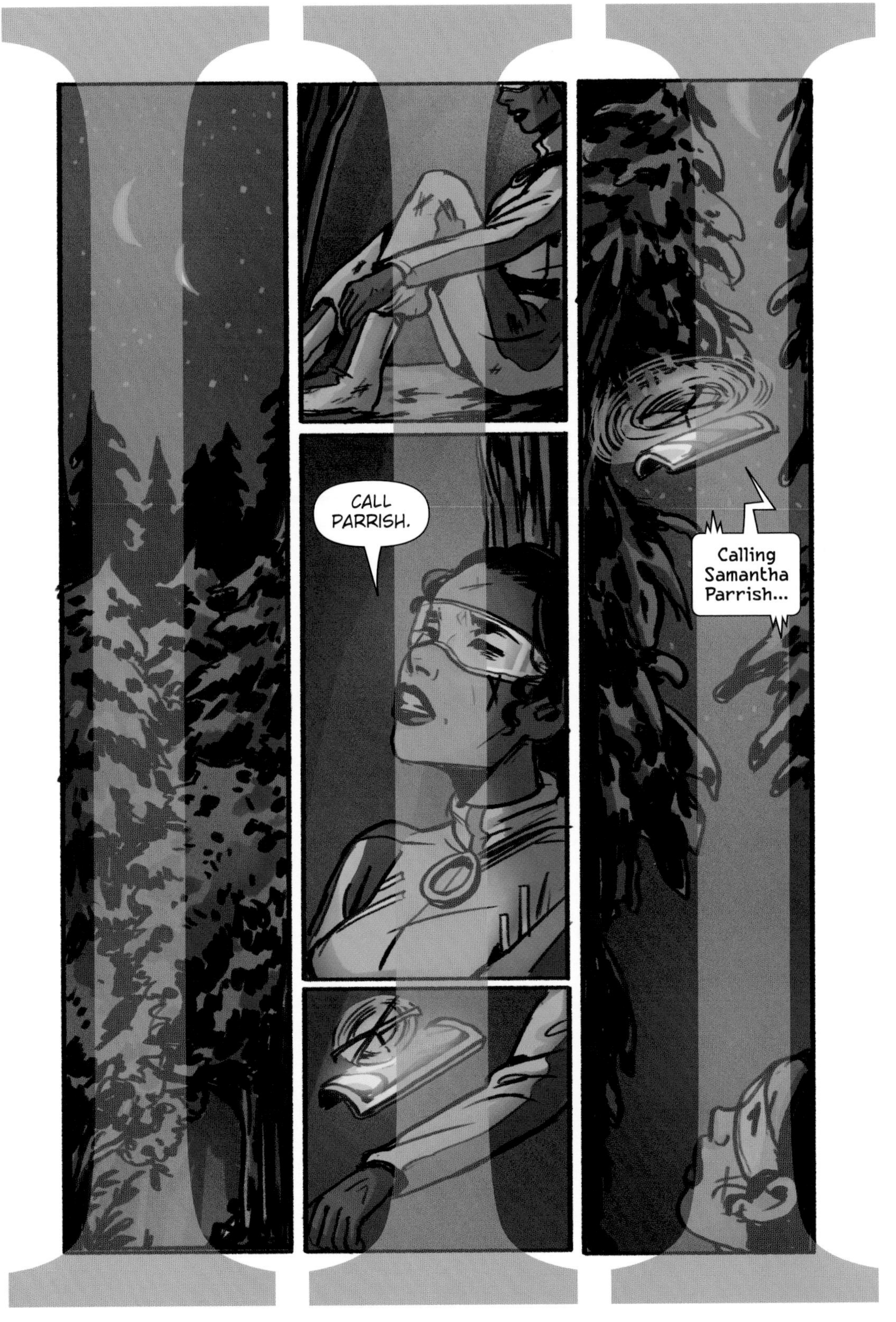
CALL PARRISH.
Calling Samantha Parrish...

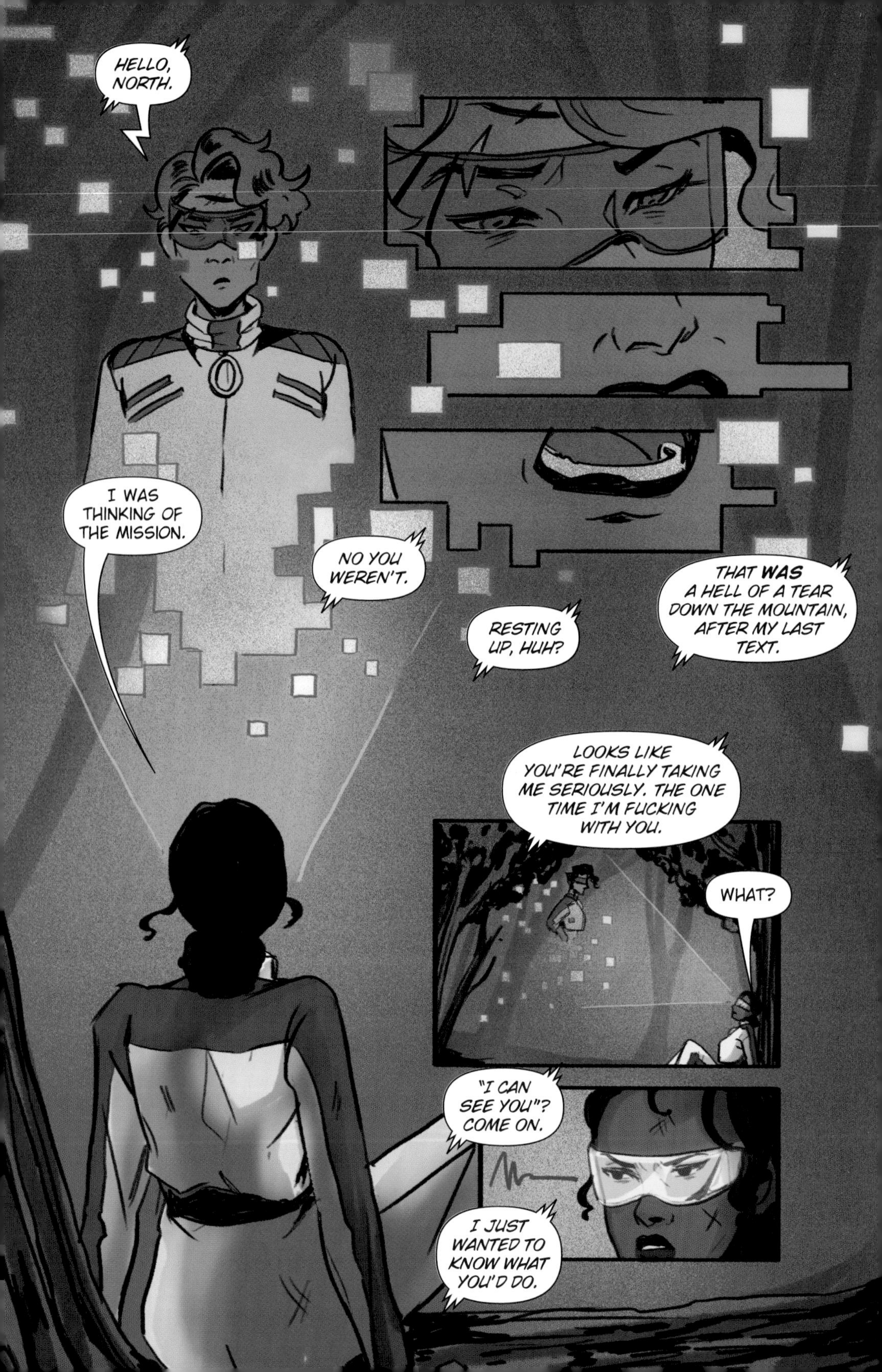
HELLO, NORTH.
I WAS THINKING OF THE MISSION.
NO YOU WEREN'T.
RESTING UP, HUH?
THAT **WAS** A HELL OF A TEAR DOWN THE MOUNTAIN, AFTER MY LAST TEXT.
LOOKS LIKE YOU'RE FINALLY TAKING ME SERIOUSLY. THE ONE TIME I'M FUCKING WITH YOU.
WHAT?
"I CAN SEE YOU"? COME ON.
I JUST WANTED TO KNOW WHAT YOU'D DO.

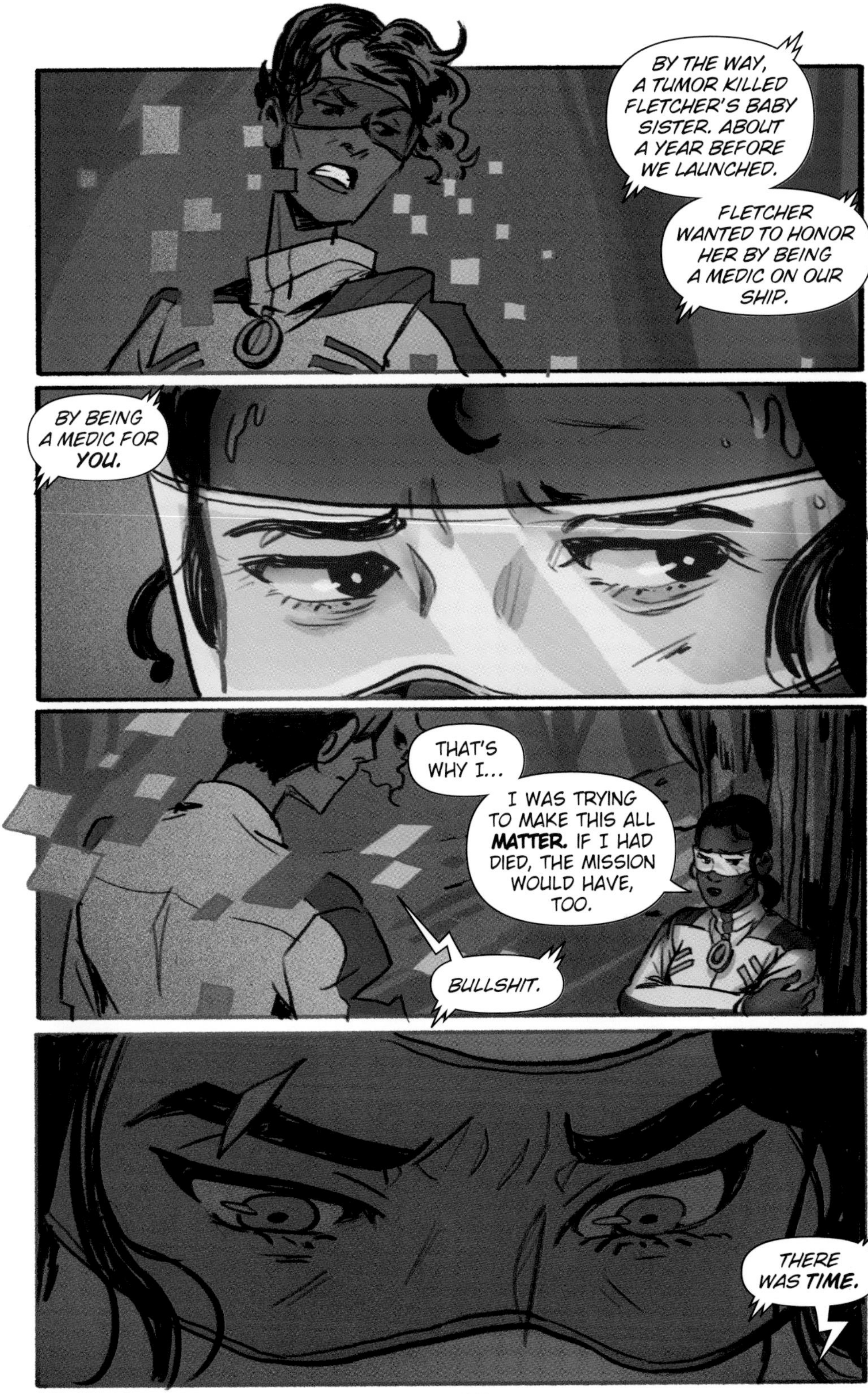
BY THE WAY, A TUMOR KILLED FLETCHER'S BABY SISTER. ABOUT A YEAR BEFORE WE LAUNCHED.
FLETCHER WANTED TO HONOR HER BY BEING A MEDIC ON OUR SHIP.
BY BEING A MEDIC FOR YOU.
THAT'S WHY I...
I WAS TRYING TO MAKE THIS ALL MATTER. IF I HAD DIED, THE MISSION WOULD HAVE, TOO.
BULLSHIT.
THERE WAS TIME.

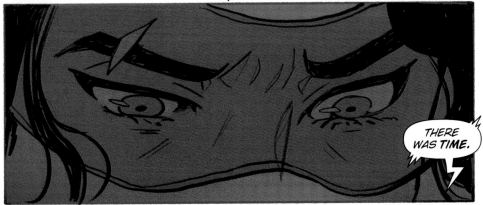

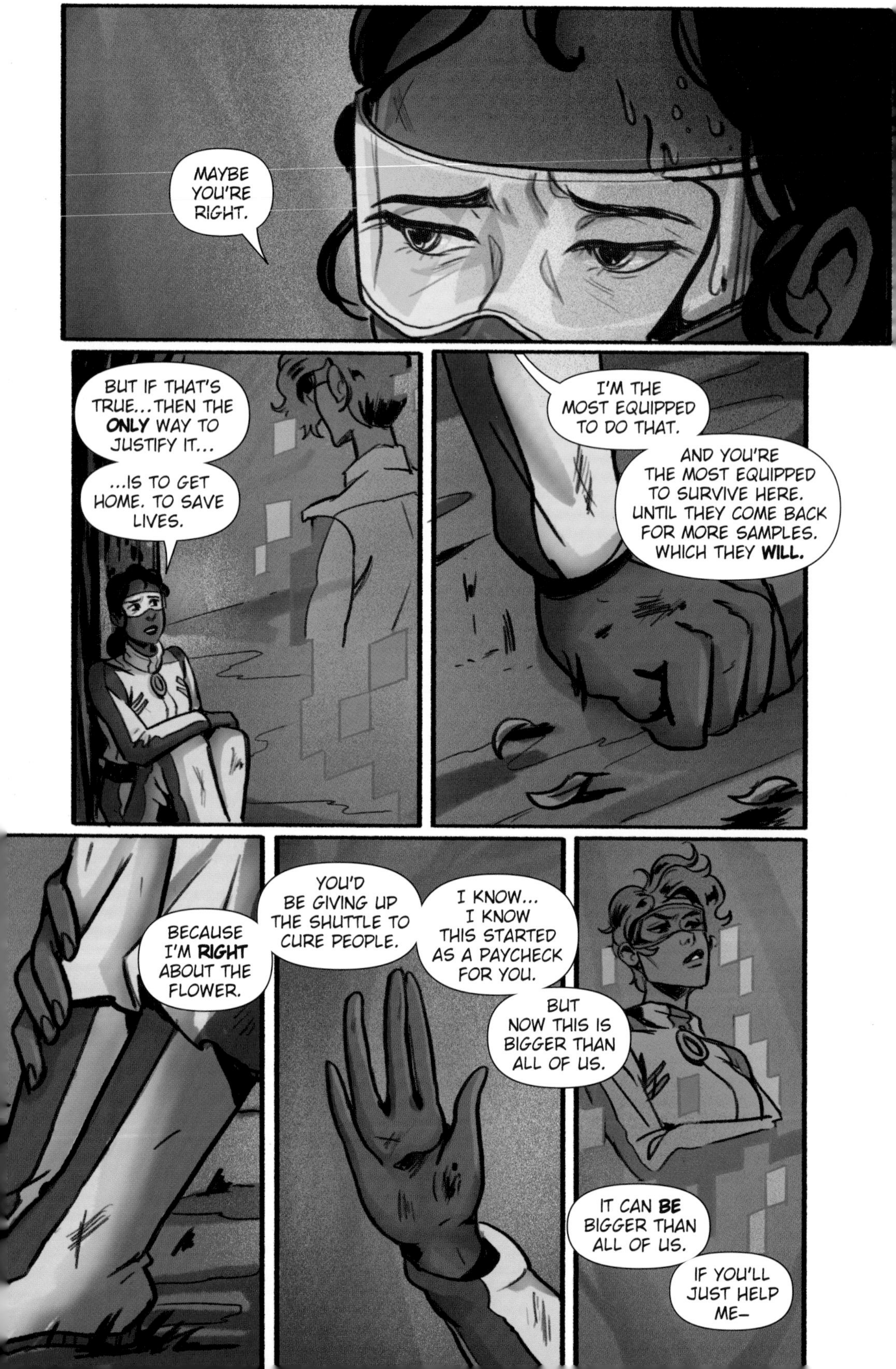
MAYBE YOU'RE RIGHT.
BUT IF THAT'S TRUE...THEN THE **ONLY** WAY TO JUSTIFY IT...
...IS TO GET HOME. TO SAVE LIVES.
I'M THE MOST EQUIPPED TO DO THAT.
AND YOU'RE THE MOST EQUIPPED TO SURVIVE HERE. UNTIL THEY COME BACK FOR MORE SAMPLES. WHICH THEY **WILL.**
BECAUSE I'M **RIGHT** ABOUT THE FLOWER.
YOU'D BE GIVING UP THE SHUTTLE TO CURE PEOPLE.
I KNOW... I KNOW THIS STARTED AS A PAYCHECK FOR YOU.
BUT NOW THIS IS BIGGER THAN ALL OF US.
IT CAN **BE** BIGGER THAN ALL OF US.
IF YOU'LL JUST HELP ME—

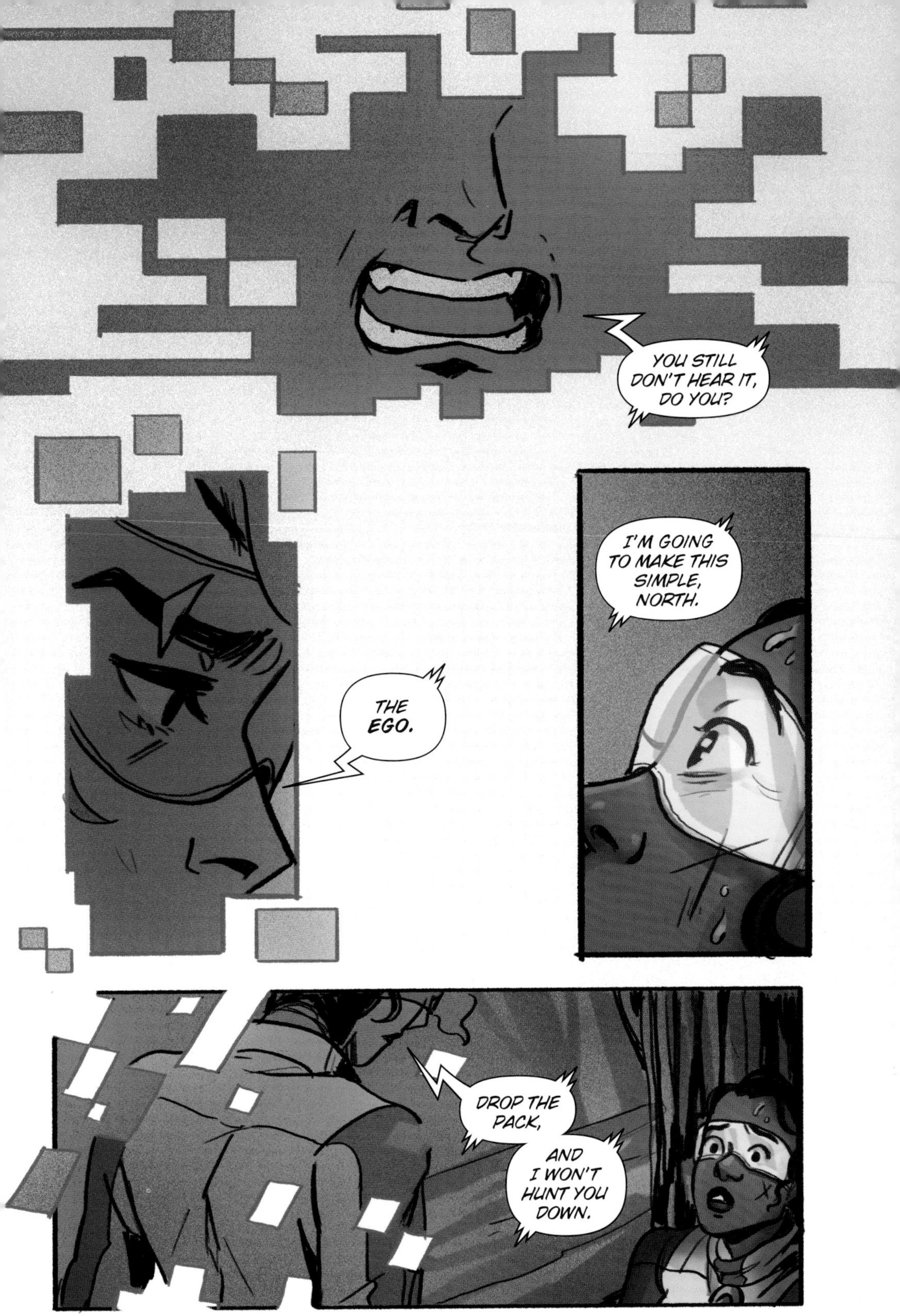
YOU STILL DON'T HEAR IT, DO YOU?
THE EGO.
I'M GOING TO MAKE THIS SIMPLE, NORTH.
DROP THE PACK,
AND I WON'T HUNT YOU DOWN.

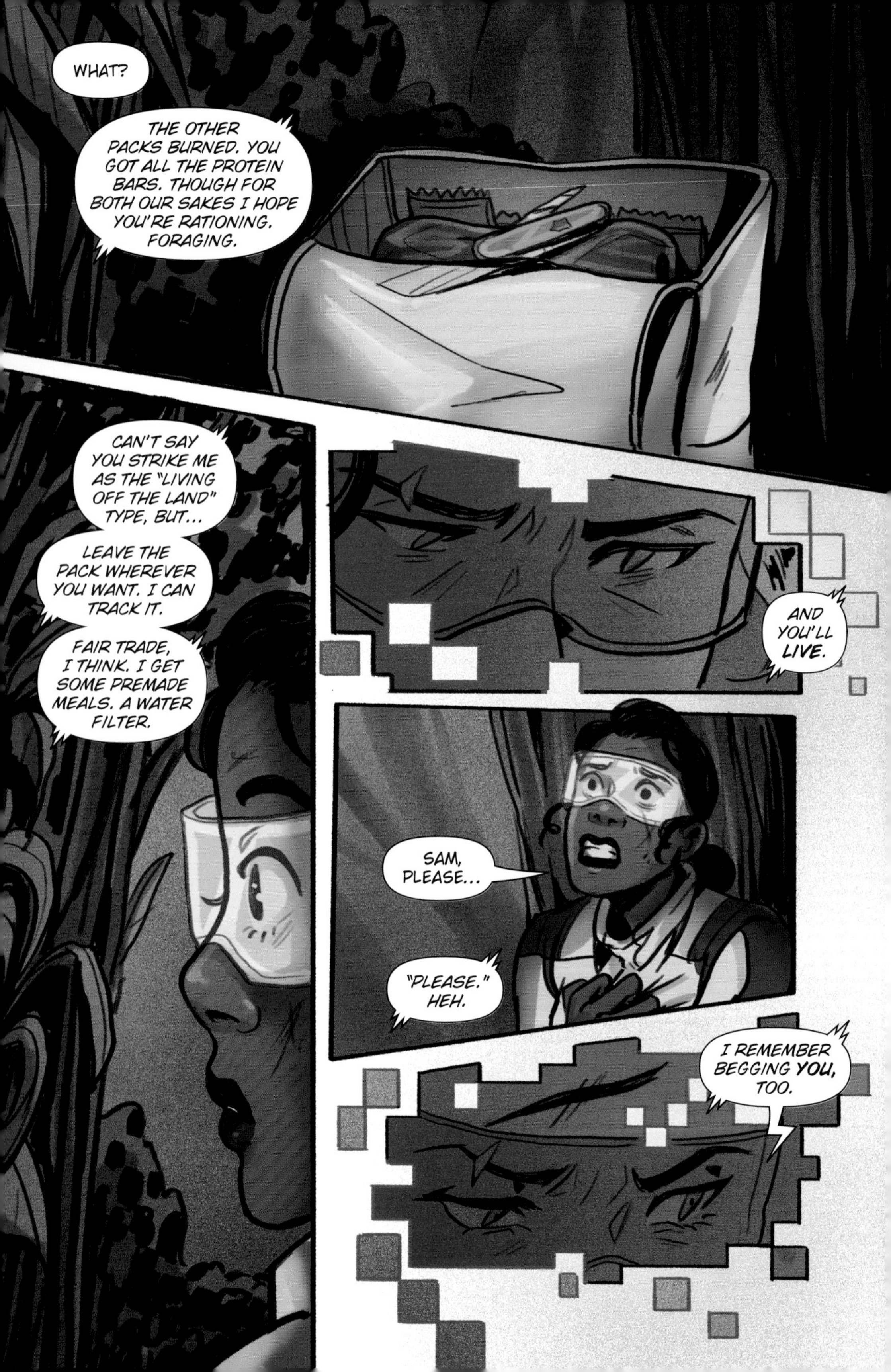
WHAT?
THE OTHER PACKS BURNED. YOU GOT ALL THE PROTEIN BARS. THOUGH FOR BOTH OUR SAKES I HOPE YOU'RE RATIONING. FORAGING.
CAN'T SAY YOU STRIKE ME AS THE "LIVING OFF THE LAND" TYPE, BUT...
LEAVE THE PACK WHEREVER YOU WANT. I CAN TRACK IT.
FAIR TRADE, I THINK. I GET SOME PREMADE MEALS. A WATER FILTER.
AND YOU'LL **LIVE**.
SAM, PLEASE...
"PLEASE." HEH.
I REMEMBER BEGGING **YOU**, TOO.

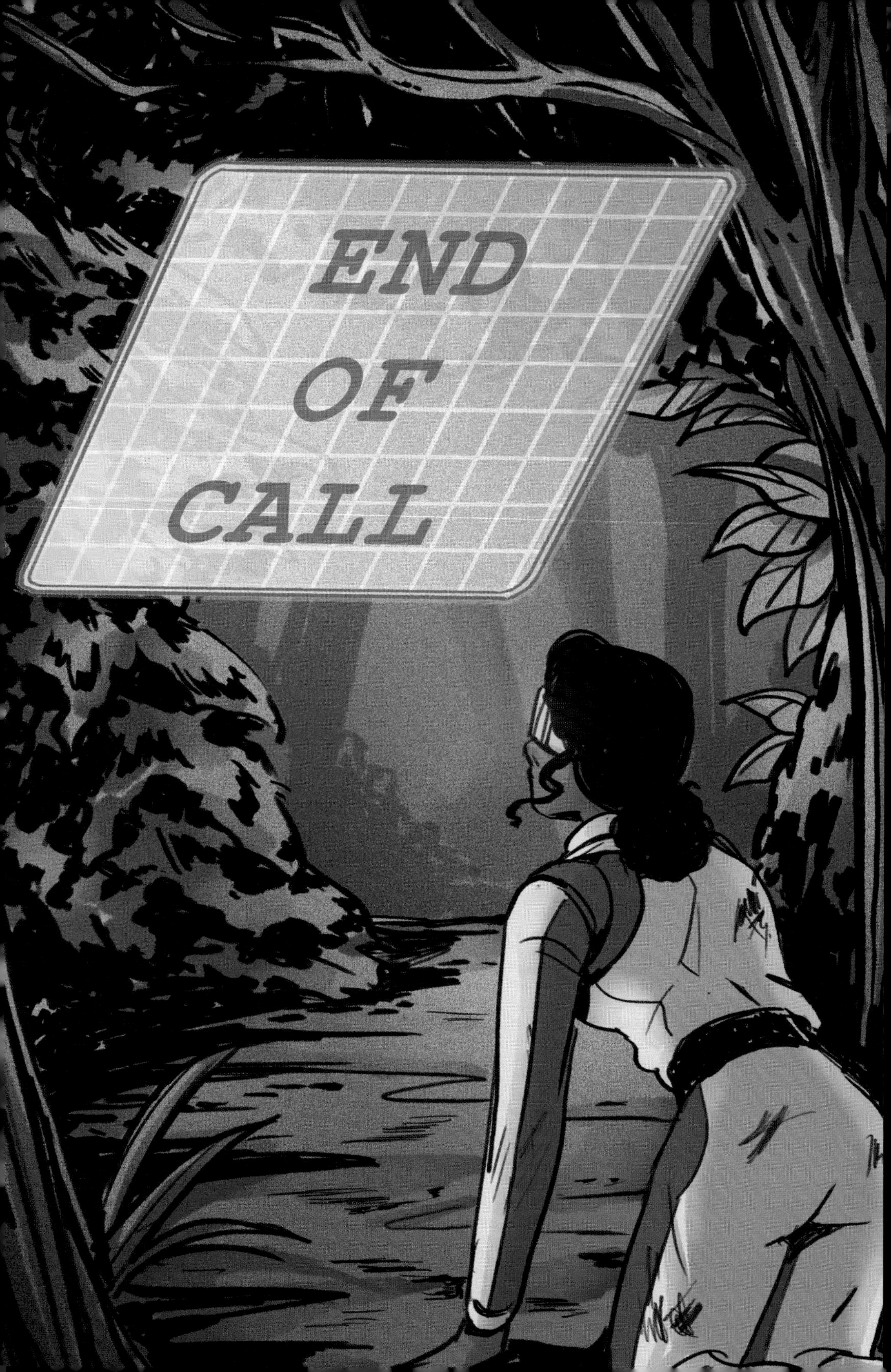
END
OF
CALL

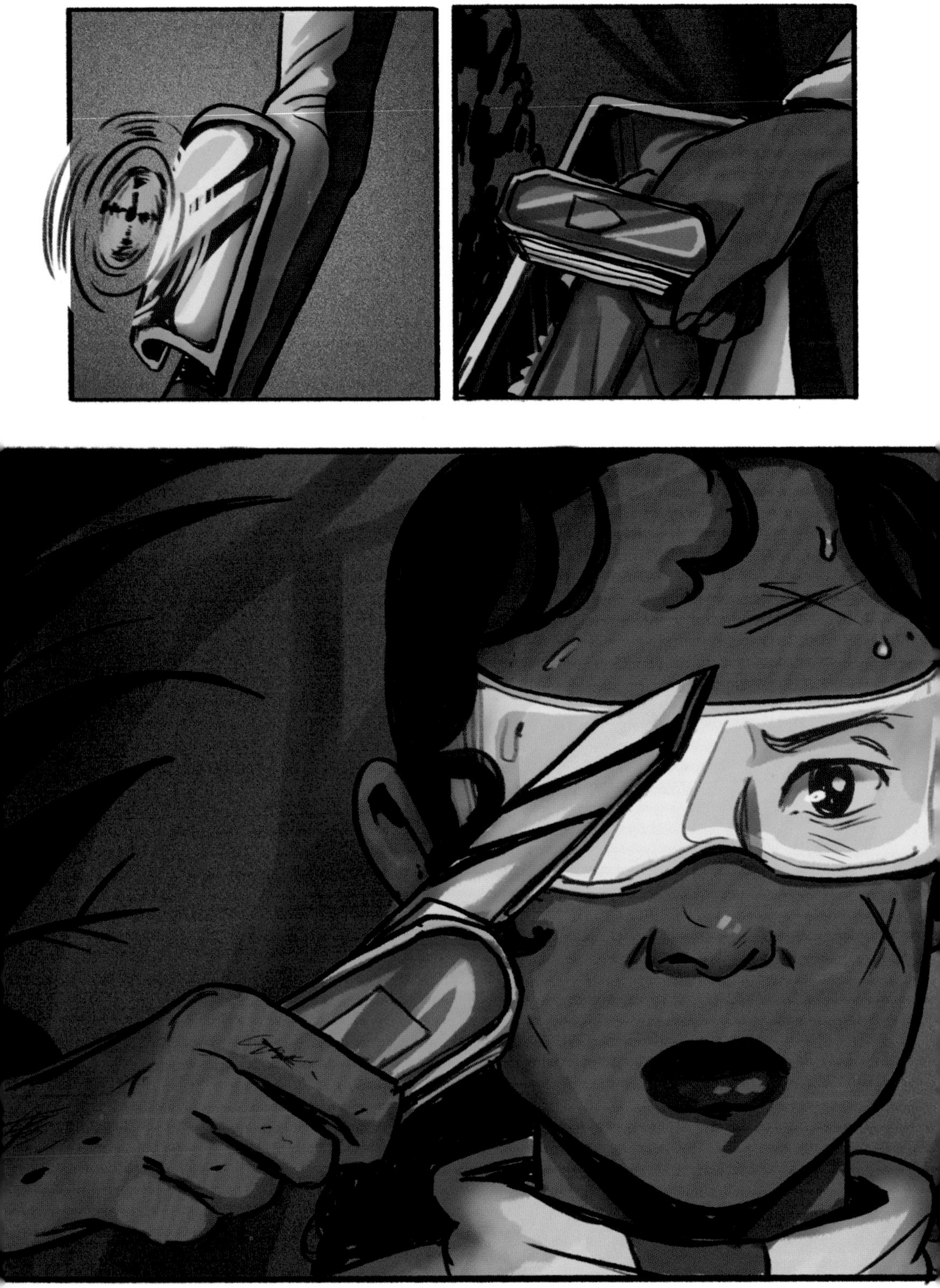

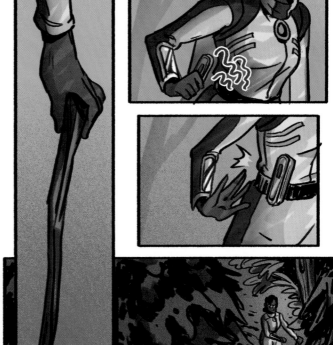

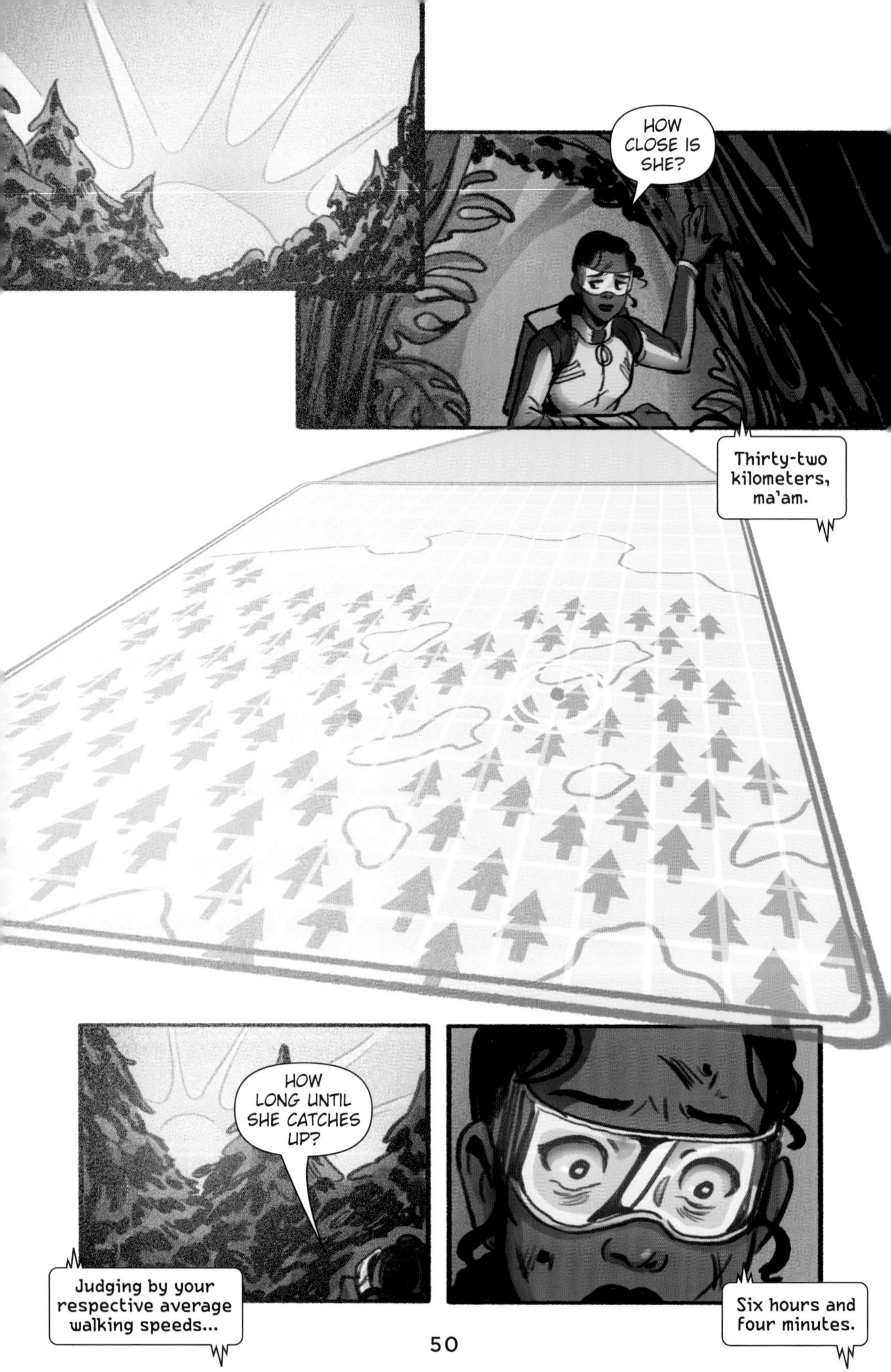
HOW CLOSE IS SHE?
Thirty-two kilometers, ma'am.
HOW LONG UNTIL SHE CATCHES UP?
Judging by your respective average walking speeds...
Six hours and four minutes.

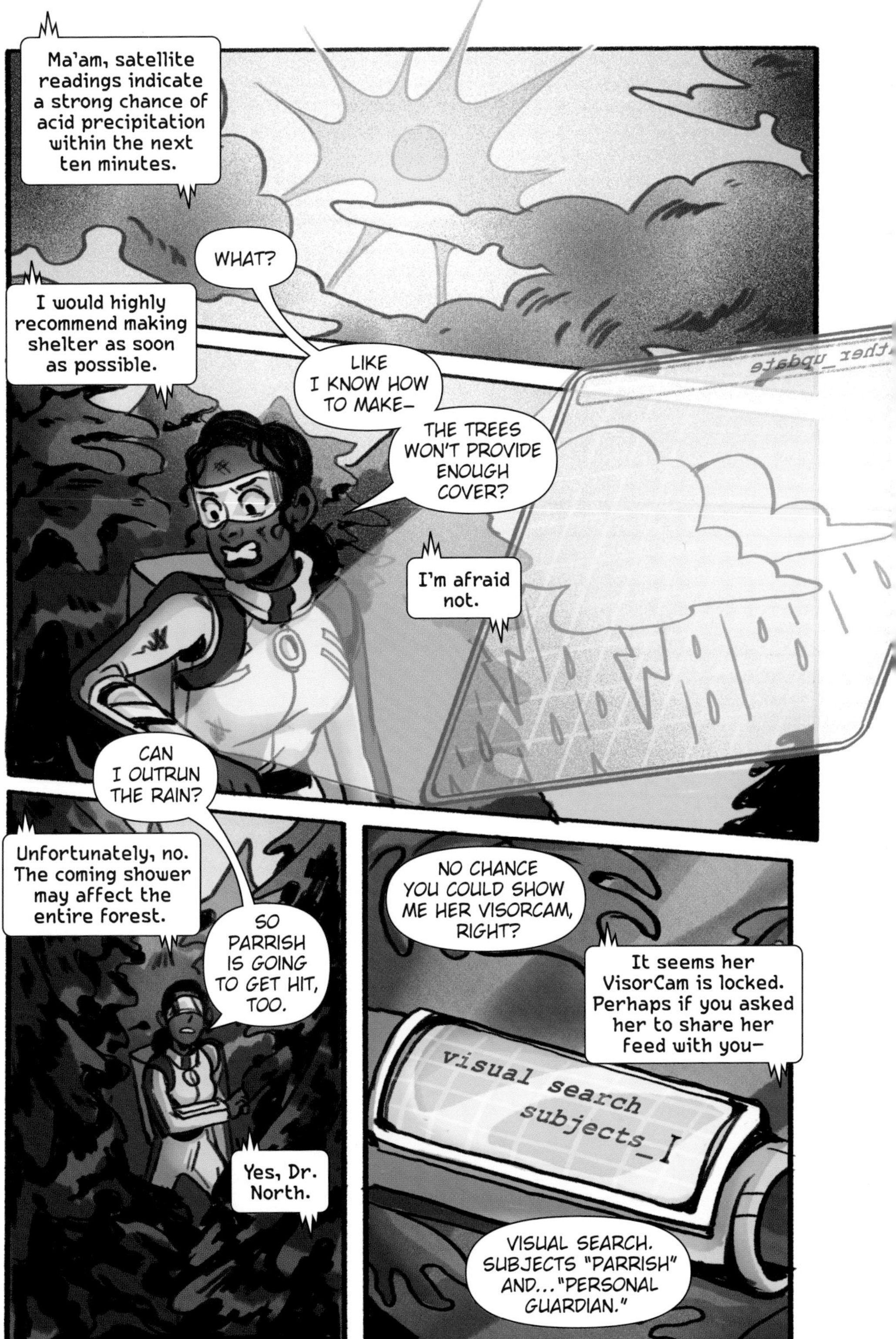

Ma'am, satellite readings indicate a strong chance of acid precipitation within the next ten minutes.
WHAT?
I would highly recommend making shelter as soon as possible.
LIKE I KNOW HOW TO MAKE—
THE TREES WON'T PROVIDE ENOUGH COVER?
I'm afraid not.
CAN I OUTRUN THE RAIN?
Unfortunately, no. The coming shower may affect the entire forest.
SO PARRISH IS GOING TO GET HIT, TOO.
Yes, Dr. North.
NO CHANCE YOU COULD SHOW ME HER VISORCAM, RIGHT?
It seems her VisorCam is locked. Perhaps if you asked her to share her feed with you—
visual search
subjects_I
VISUAL SEARCH. SUBJECTS "PARRISH" AND... "PERSONAL GUARDIAN."

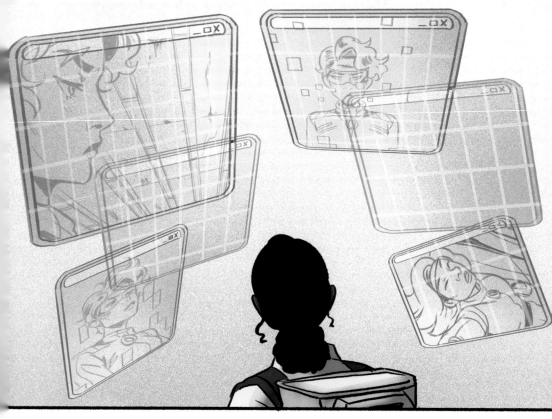

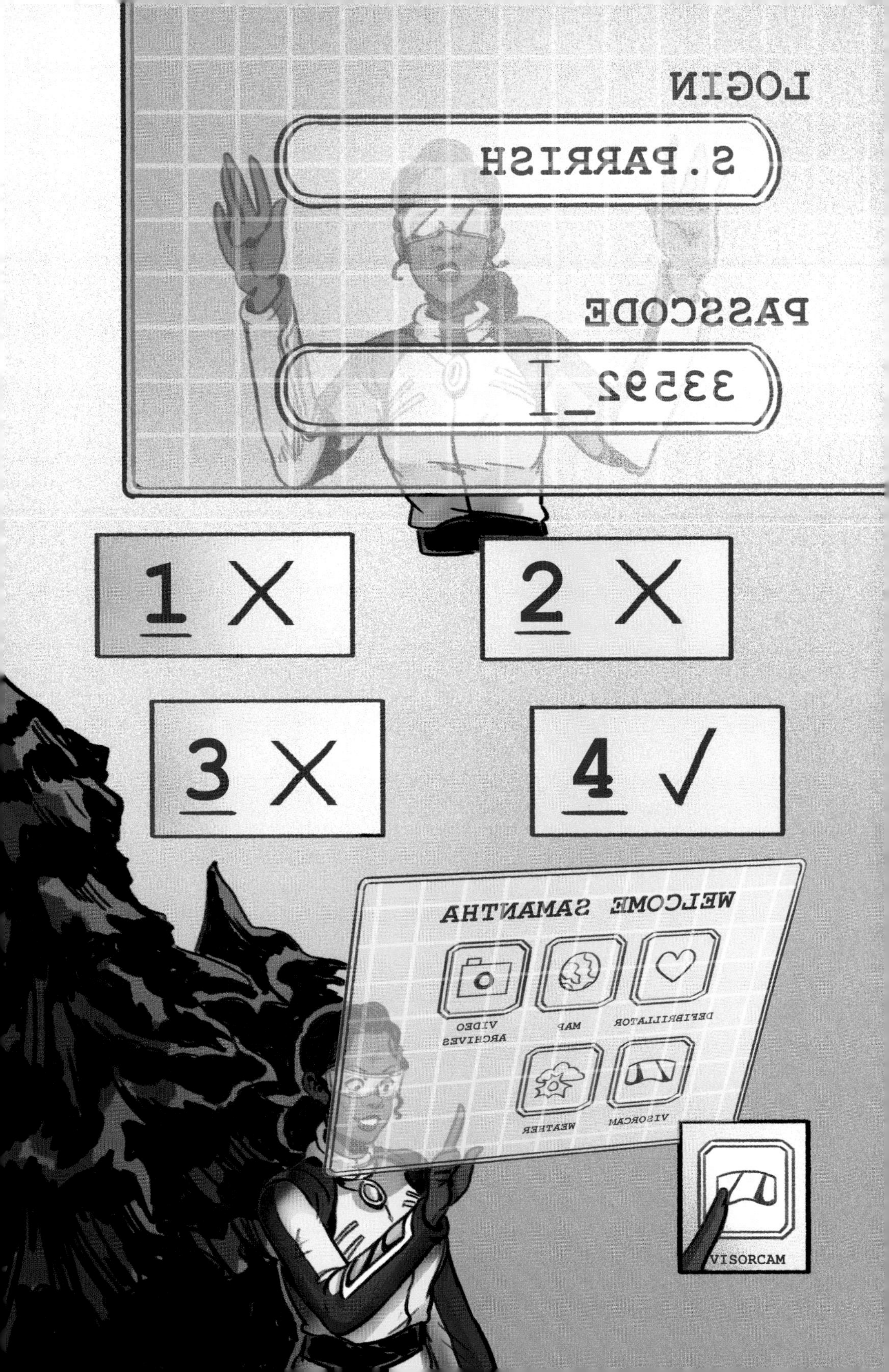

LOGIN
S.PARRISH
PASSCODE
33592_
1 X
2 X
3 X
4 ✓
WELCOME SAMANTHA
VIDEO ARCHIVES
MAP
DEFIBRILLATOR
WEATHER
VISORCAM
VISORCAM

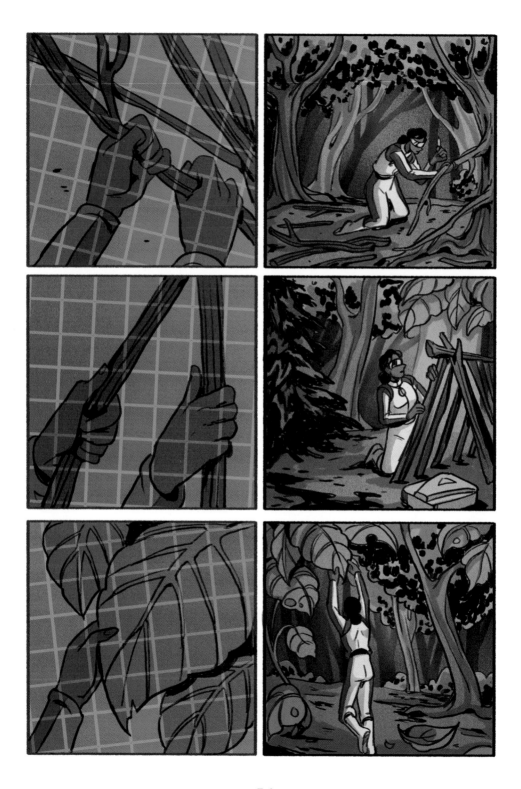

HSSSS
HSSSS
HSSSS
HSSSS
HSSSS
HSSSS
S.PARRISH
DEFIBRILLATOR
VISORCAM
DEFIBRILLATOR. PARRISH.
...RESUSCITATE.
HEARTBEAT DETECTED. DEFIBRILLATION PROHIBITED.

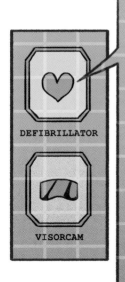

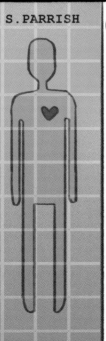

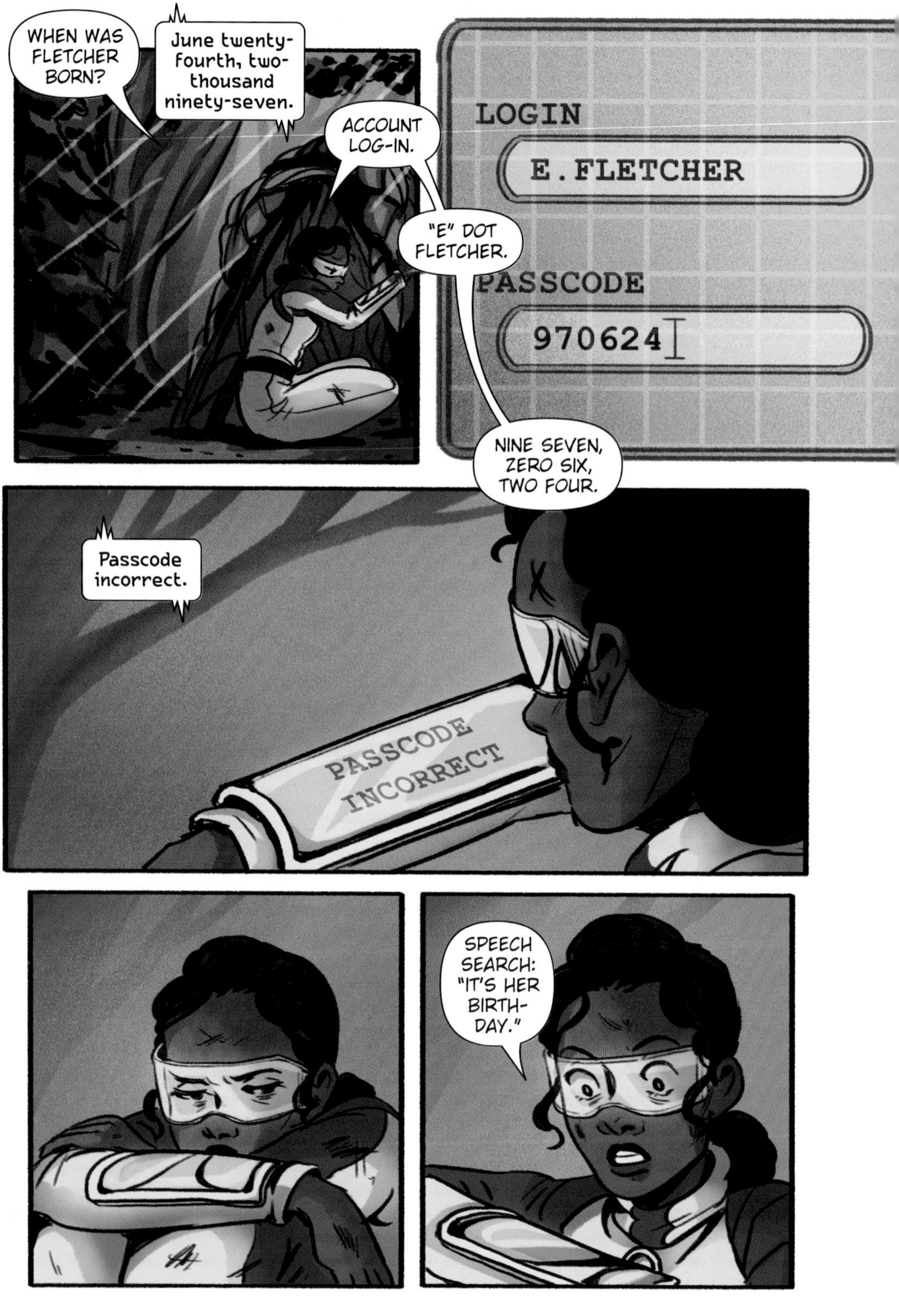
WHEN WAS FLETCHER BORN?
June twenty-fourth, two-thousand ninety-seven.
ACCOUNT LOG-IN.
"E" DOT FLETCHER.
LOGIN
E.FLETCHER
PASSCODE
970624
NINE SEVEN, ZERO SIX, TWO FOUR.
Passcode incorrect.
PASSCODE INCORRECT
SPEECH SEARCH: "IT'S HER BIRTH-DAY."

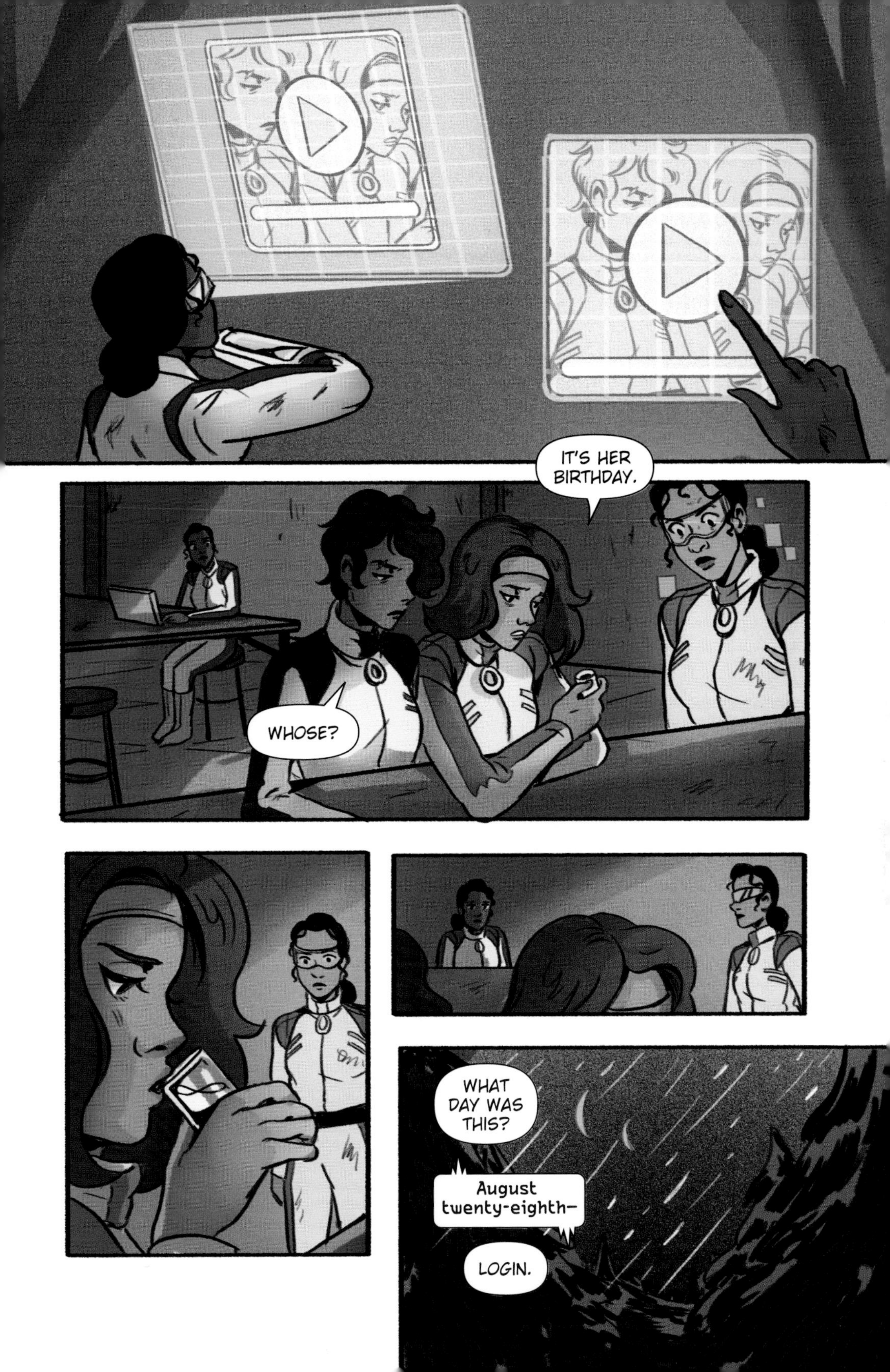
IT'S HER BIRTHDAY.
WHOSE?
WHAT DAY WAS THIS?
August twenty-eighth—
LOGIN.

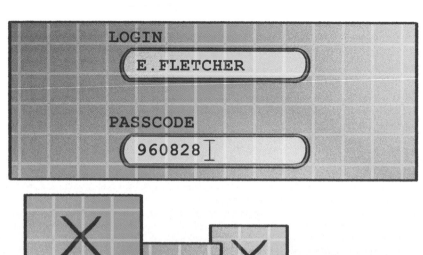

LOGIN

E.FLETCHER

PASSCODE

960828

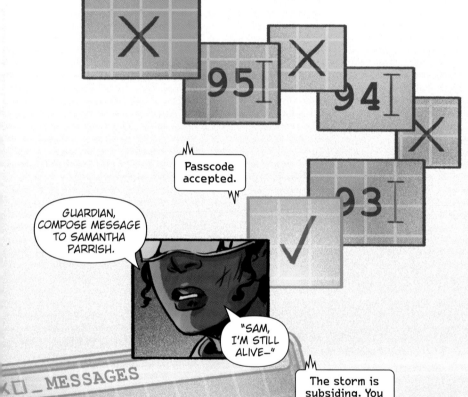

Passcode accepted.

GUARDIAN, COMPOSE MESSAGE TO SAMANTHA PARRISH.

"SAM, I'M STILL ALIVE—"

The storm is subsiding. You will be free to continue walking within a few minutes.

X□_MESSAGES

TO: SAMANTHA PARRISH
FR: ELIZABETH FLETCHER

SAM, I'M STILL ALI

EXIT MESSAGES.

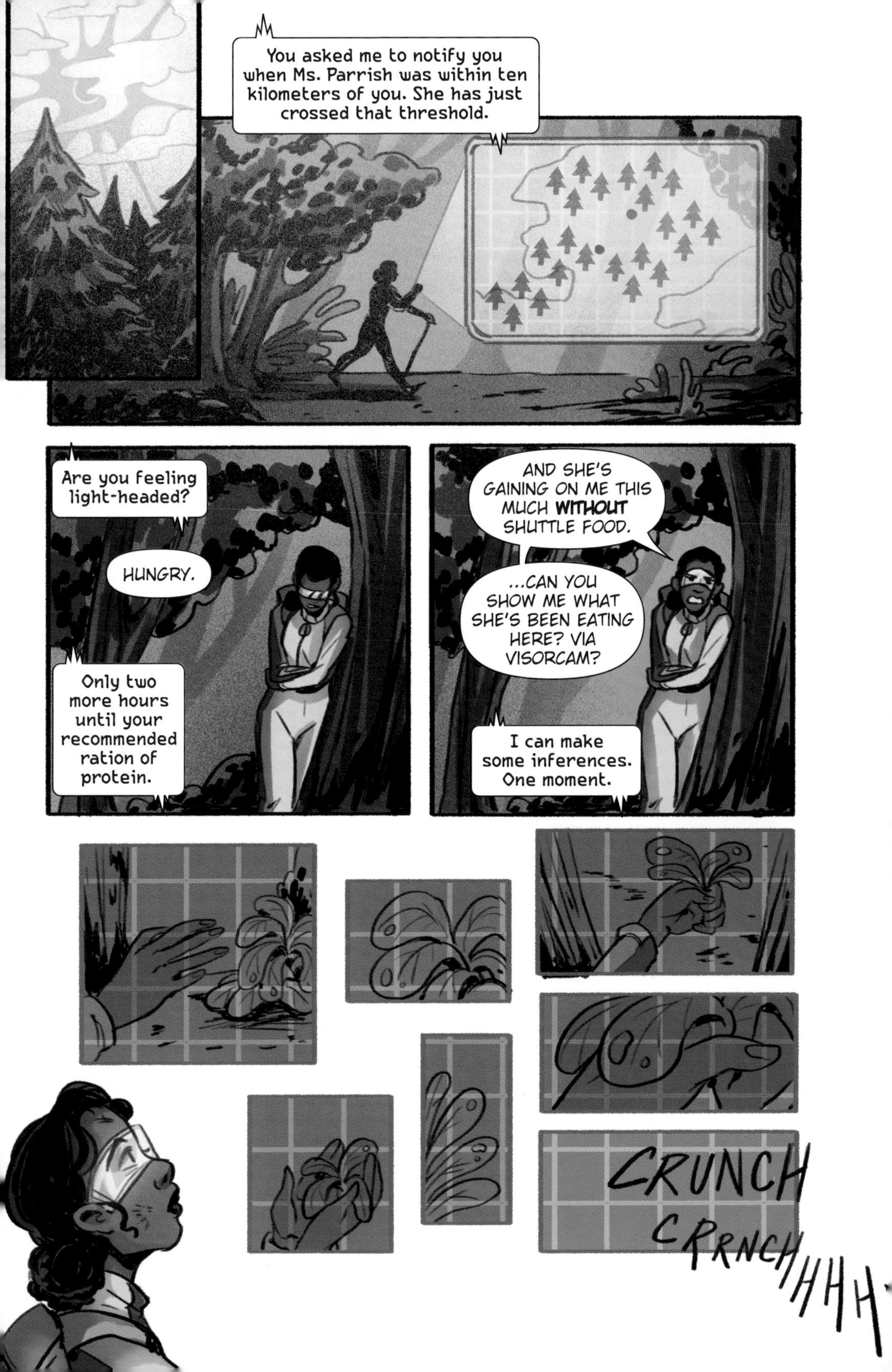
You asked me to notify you when Ms. Parrish was within ten kilometers of you. She has just crossed that threshold.
Are you feeling light-headed?
HUNGRY.
Only two more hours until your recommended ration of protein.
AND SHE'S GAINING ON ME THIS MUCH **WITHOUT** SHUTTLE FOOD.
...CAN YOU SHOW ME WHAT SHE'S BEEN EATING HERE? VIA VISORCAM?
I can make some inferences. One moment.
CRUNCH
CRRNCHHHHH

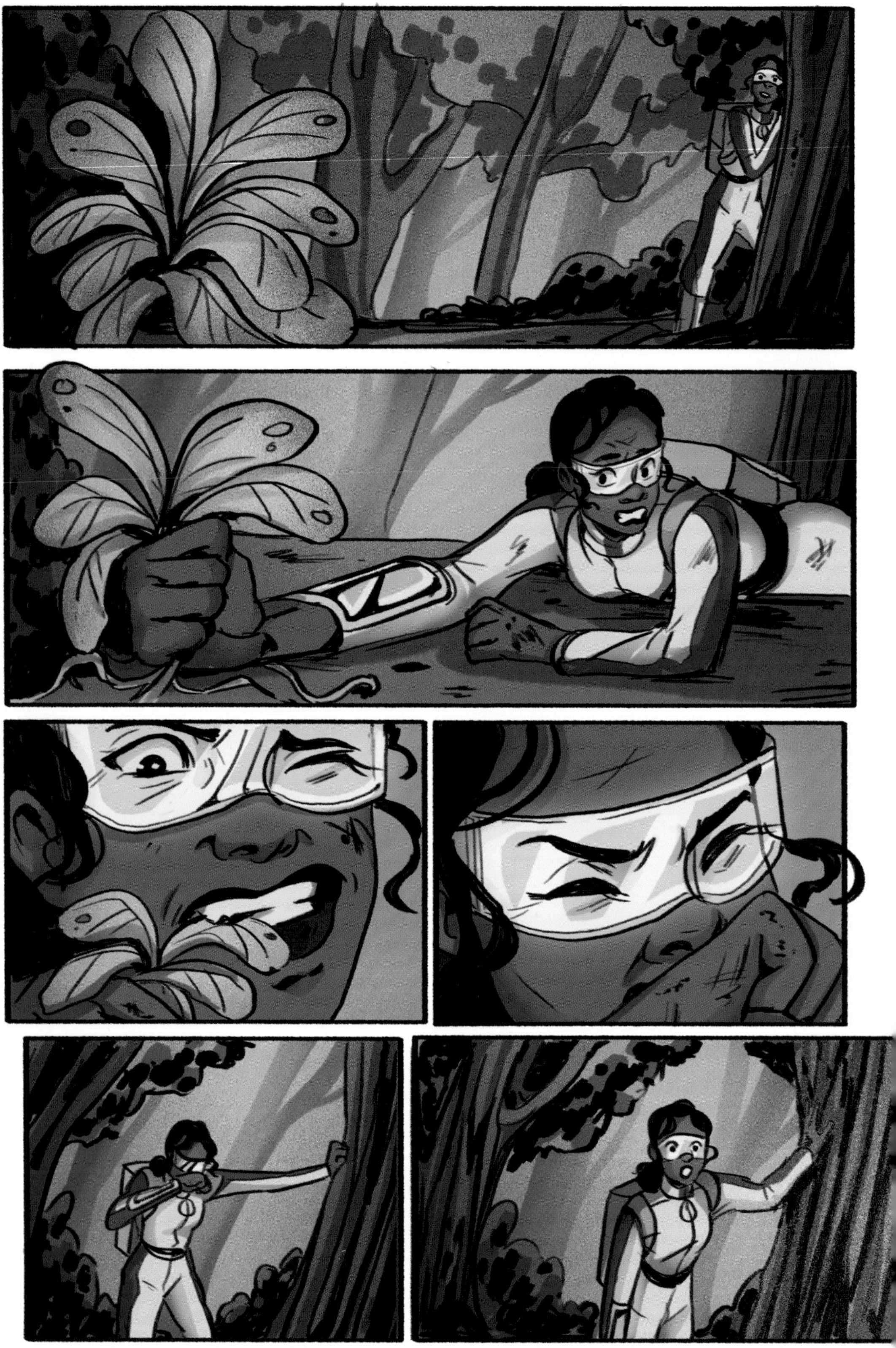

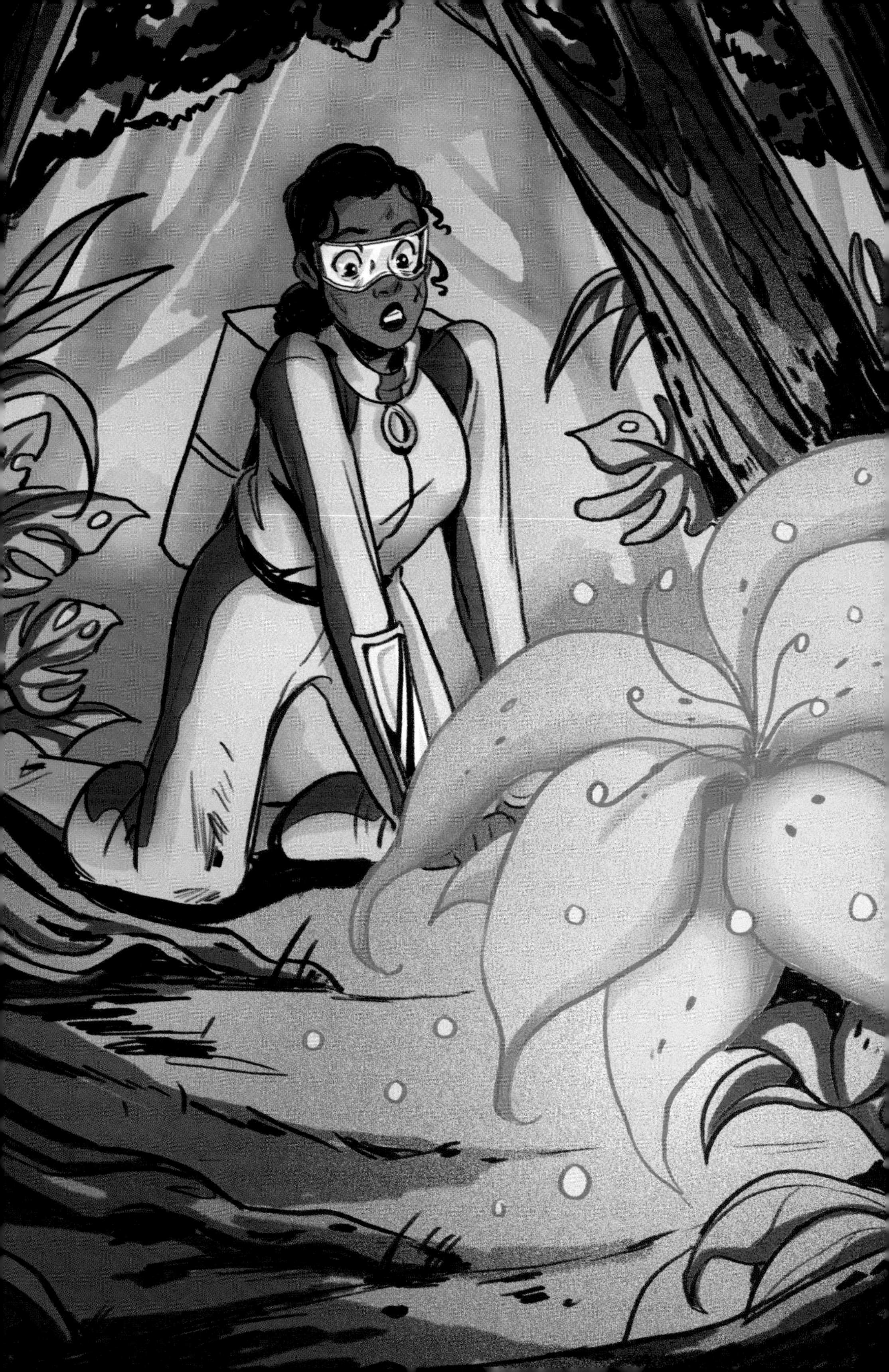

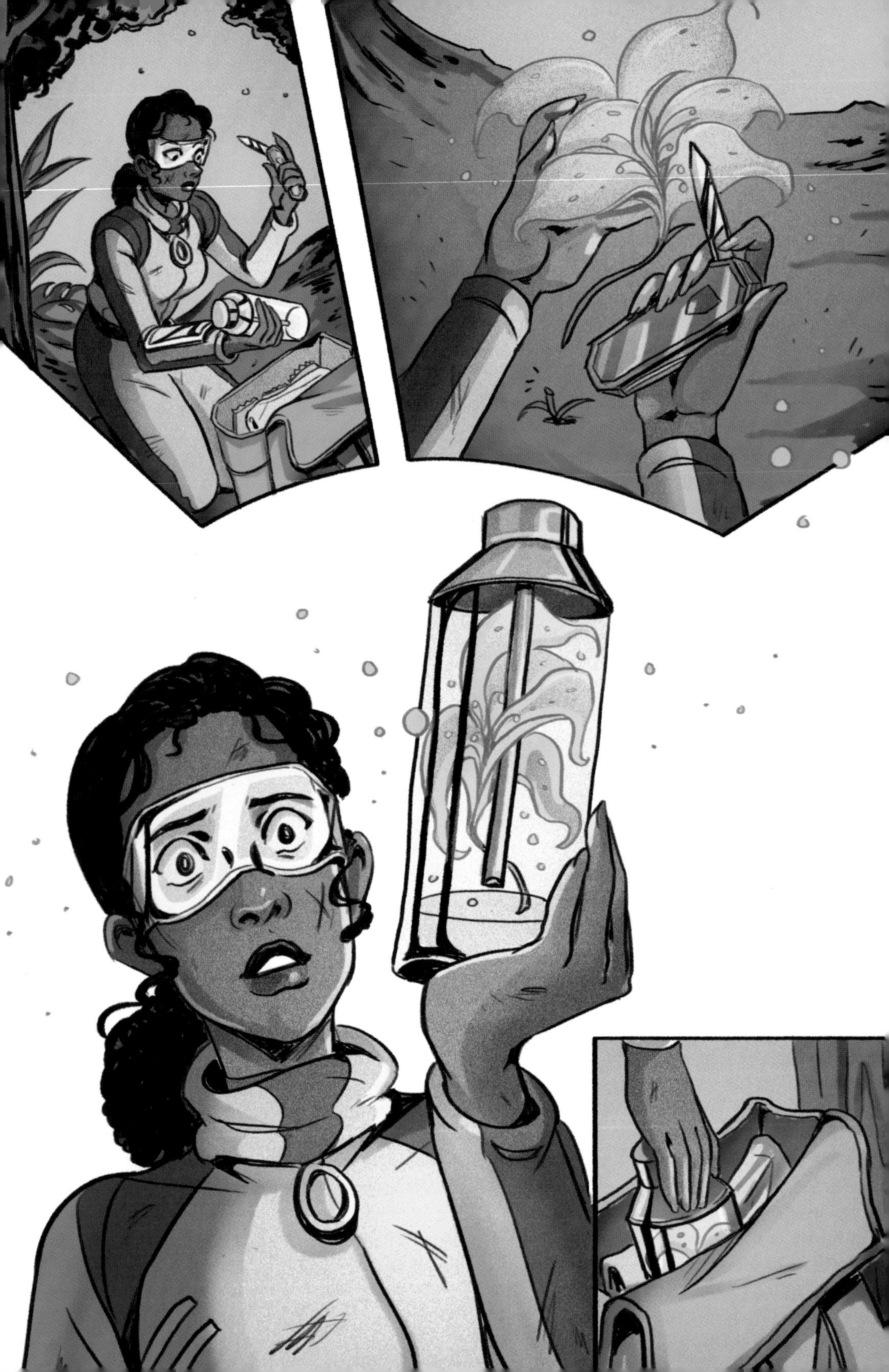

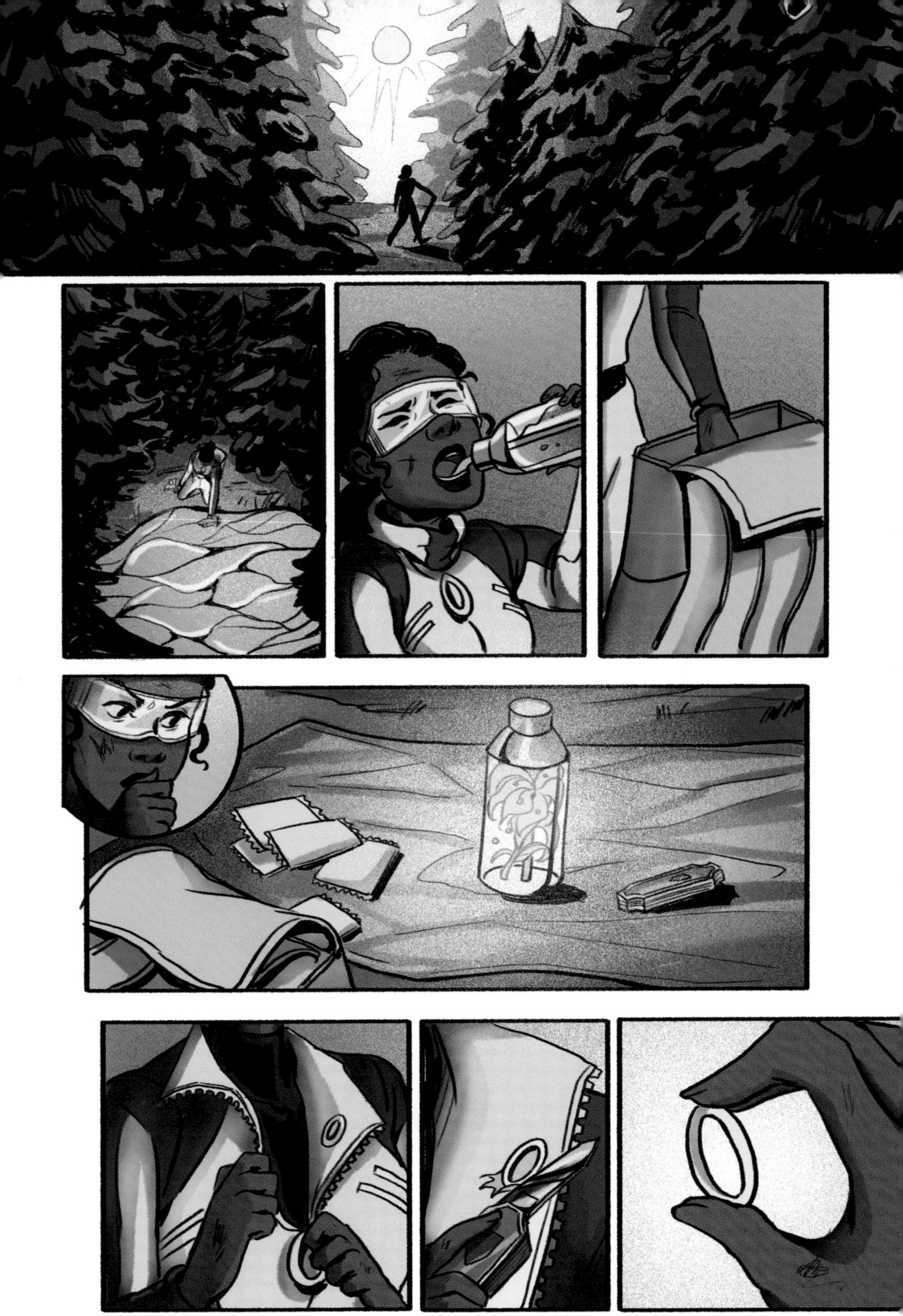

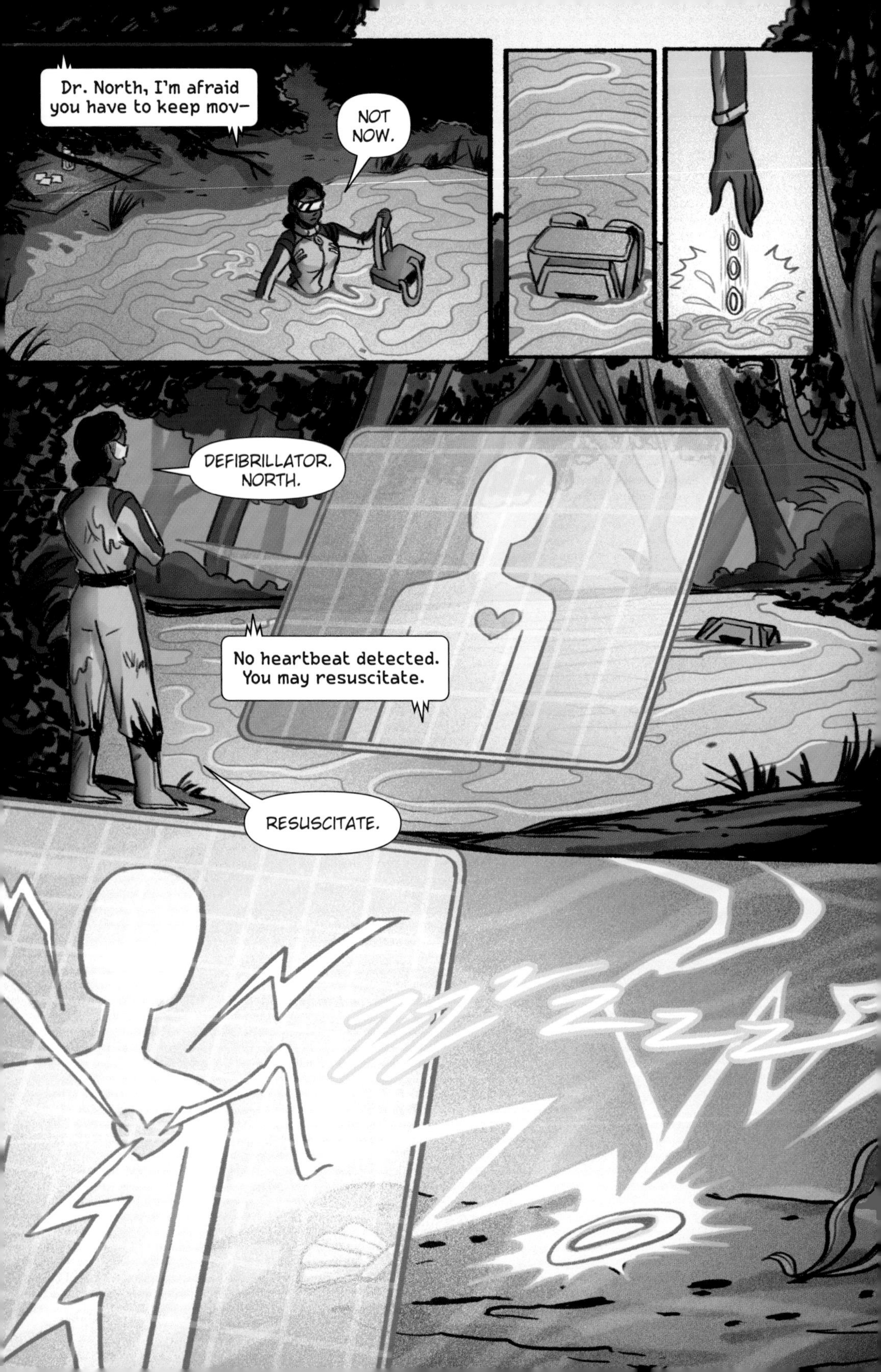

Dr. North, I'm afraid you have to keep mov–
NOT NOW.
DEFIBRILLATOR. NORTH.
No heartbeat detected. You may resuscitate.
RESUSCITATE.
ZZZZZAP

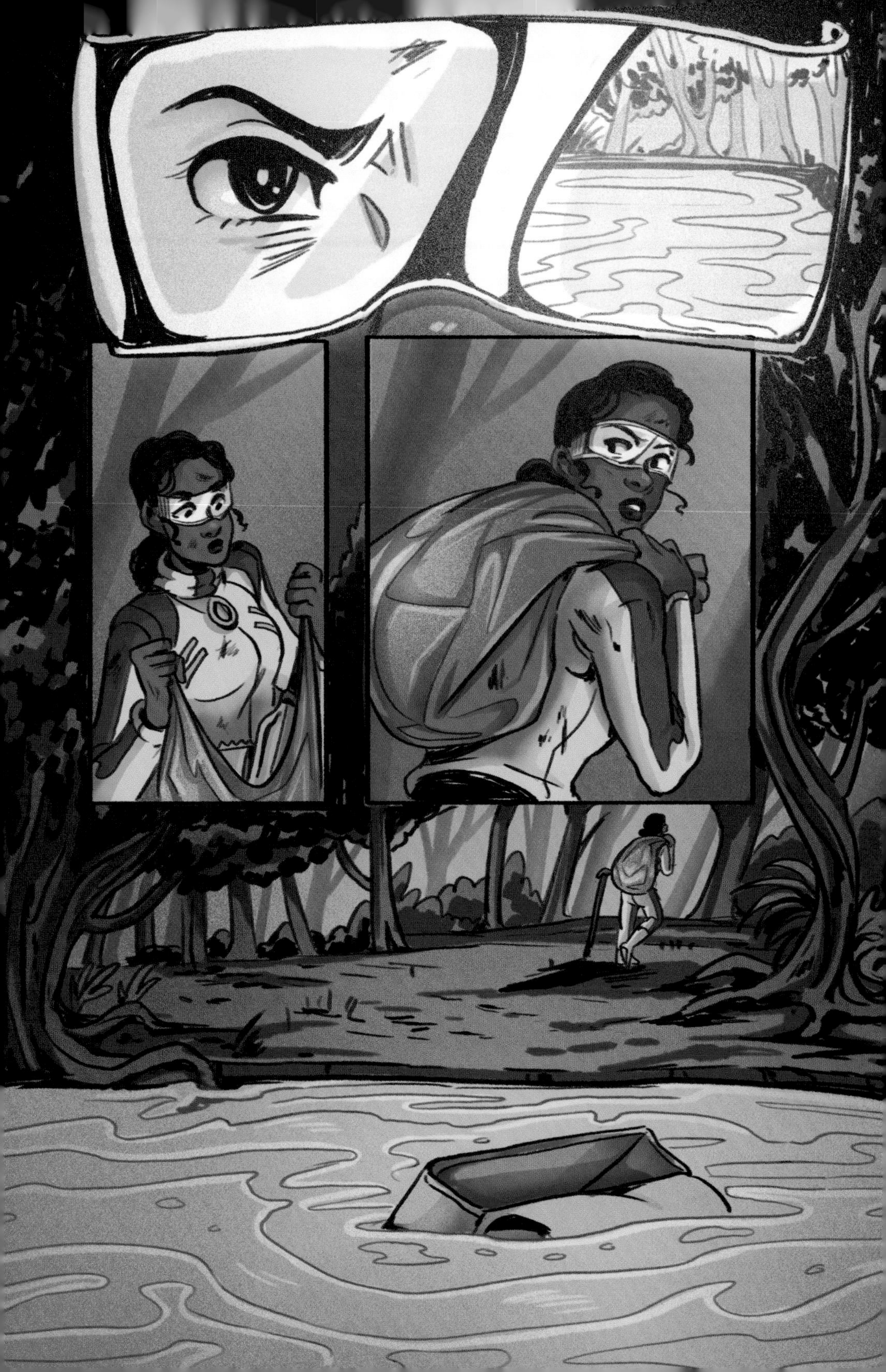

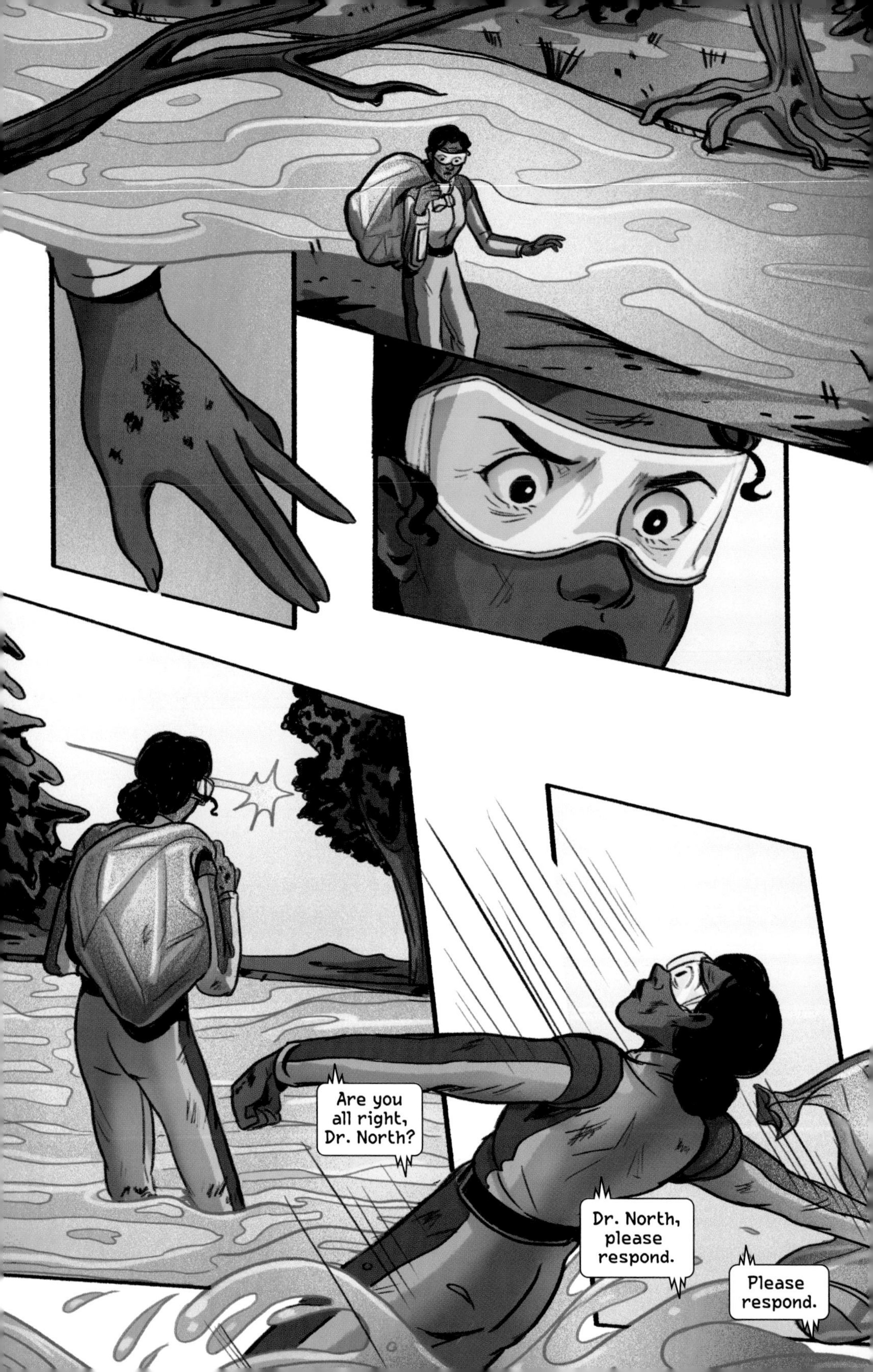
Are you all right, Dr. North?
Dr. North, please respond.
Please respond.

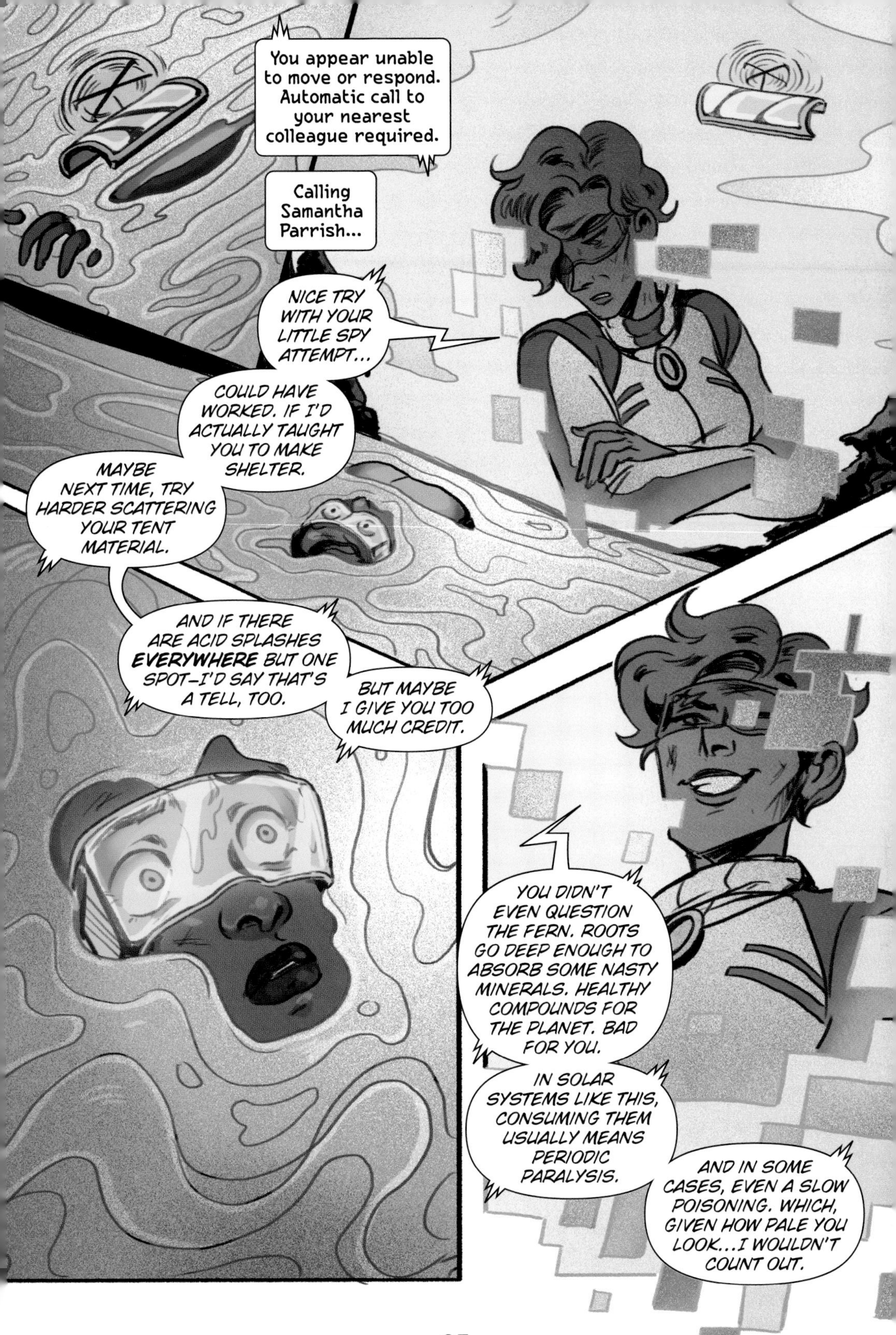
You appear unable to move or respond. Automatic call to your nearest colleague required.
Calling Samantha Parrish...
NICE TRY WITH YOUR LITTLE SPY ATTEMPT...
COULD HAVE WORKED. IF I'D ACTUALLY TAUGHT YOU TO MAKE SHELTER.
MAYBE NEXT TIME, TRY HARDER SCATTERING YOUR TENT MATERIAL.
AND IF THERE ARE ACID SPLASHES **EVERYWHERE** BUT ONE SPOT—I'D SAY THAT'S A TELL, TOO.
BUT MAYBE I GIVE YOU TOO MUCH CREDIT.
YOU DIDN'T EVEN QUESTION THE FERN. ROOTS GO DEEP ENOUGH TO ABSORB SOME NASTY MINERALS. HEALTHY COMPOUNDS FOR THE PLANET. BAD FOR YOU.
IN SOLAR SYSTEMS LIKE THIS, CONSUMING THEM USUALLY MEANS PERIODIC PARALYSIS.
AND IN SOME CASES, EVEN A SLOW POISONING. WHICH, GIVEN HOW PALE YOU LOOK...I WOULDN'T COUNT OUT.

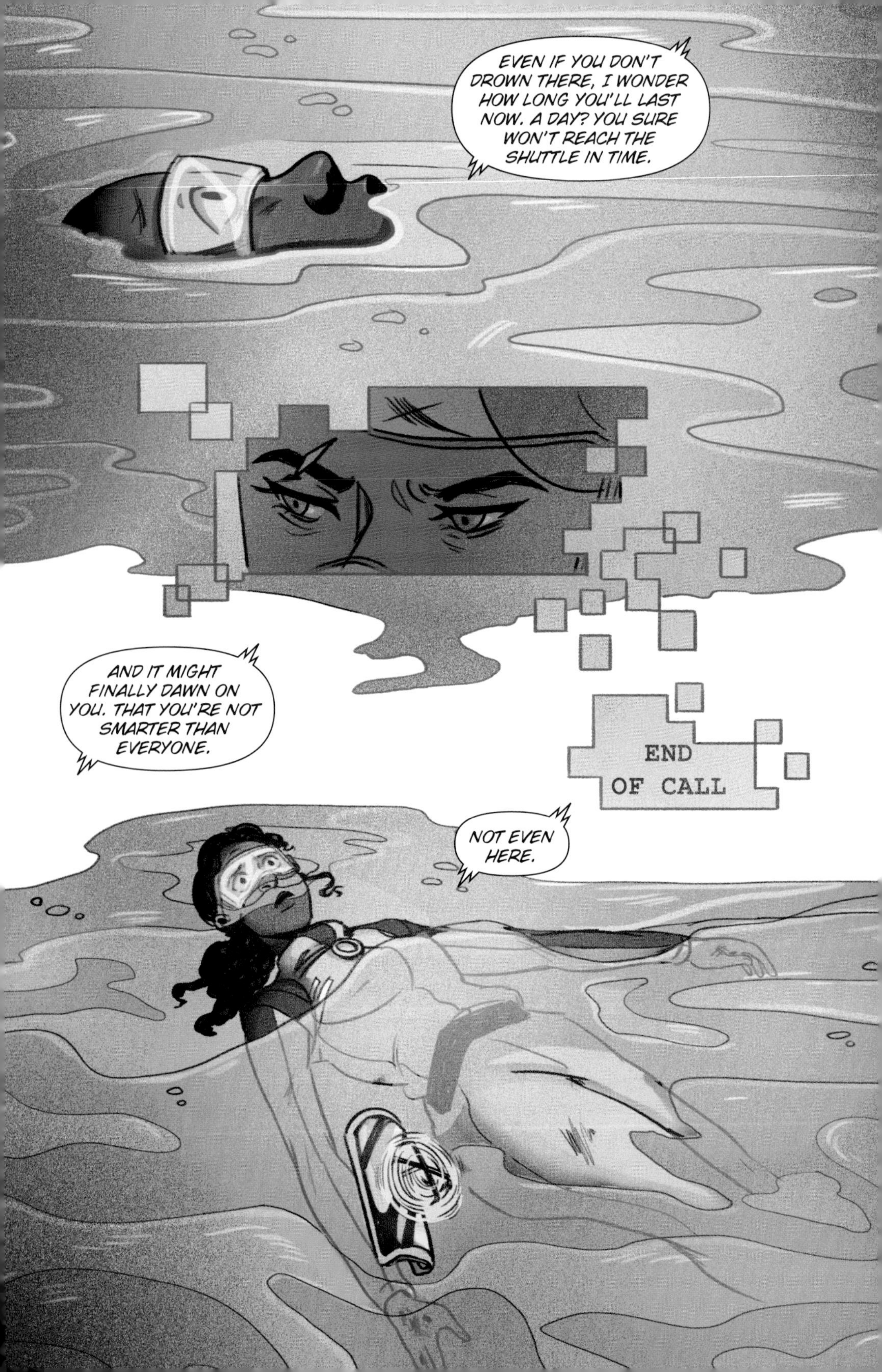
EVEN IF YOU DON'T DROWN THERE, I WONDER HOW LONG YOU'LL LAST NOW. A DAY? YOU SURE WON'T REACH THE SHUTTLE IN TIME.
AND IT MIGHT FINALLY DAWN ON YOU. THAT YOU'RE NOT SMARTER THAN EVERYONE.
END OF CALL
NOT EVEN HERE.

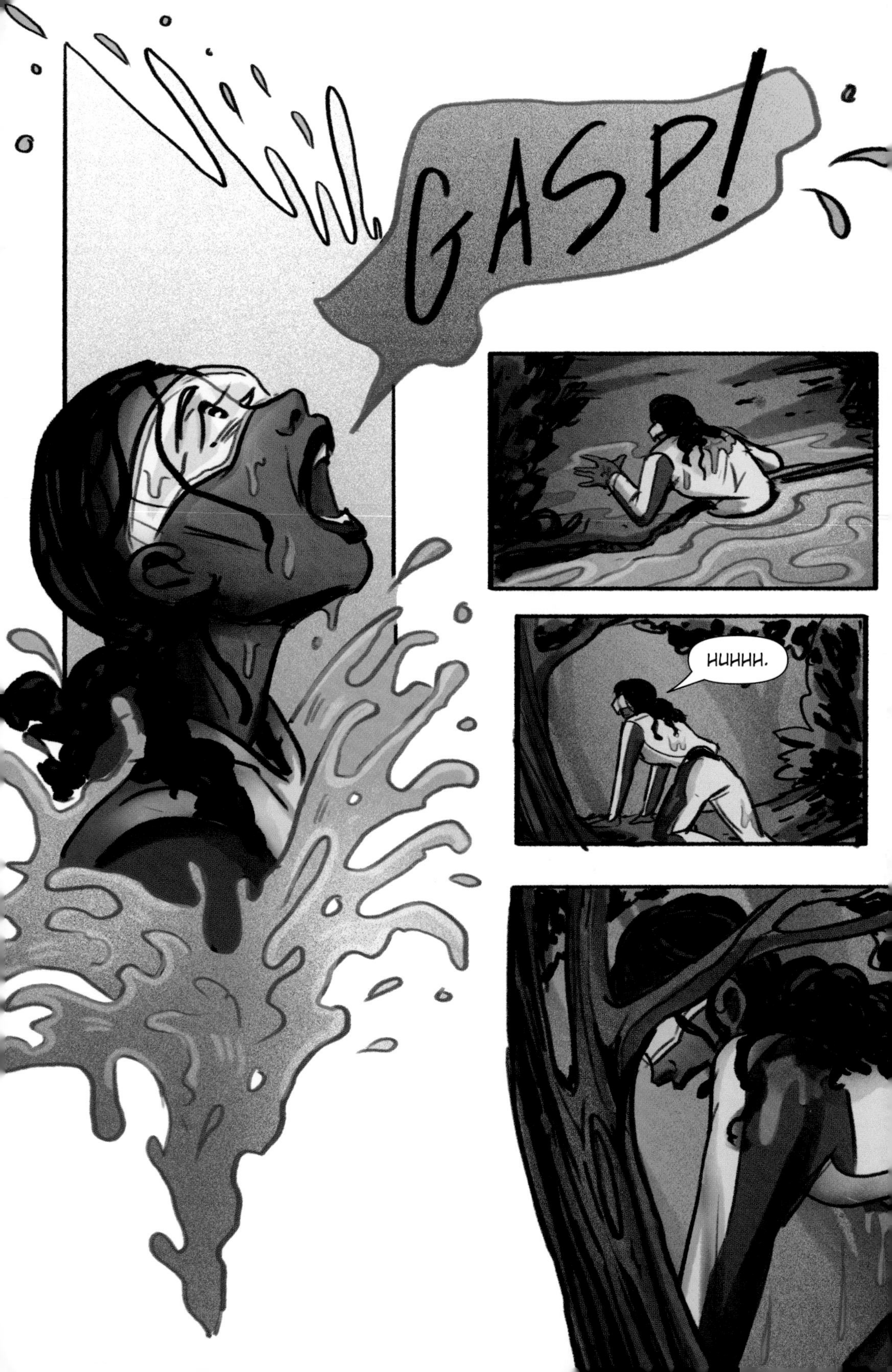
GASP!
HUHHH.

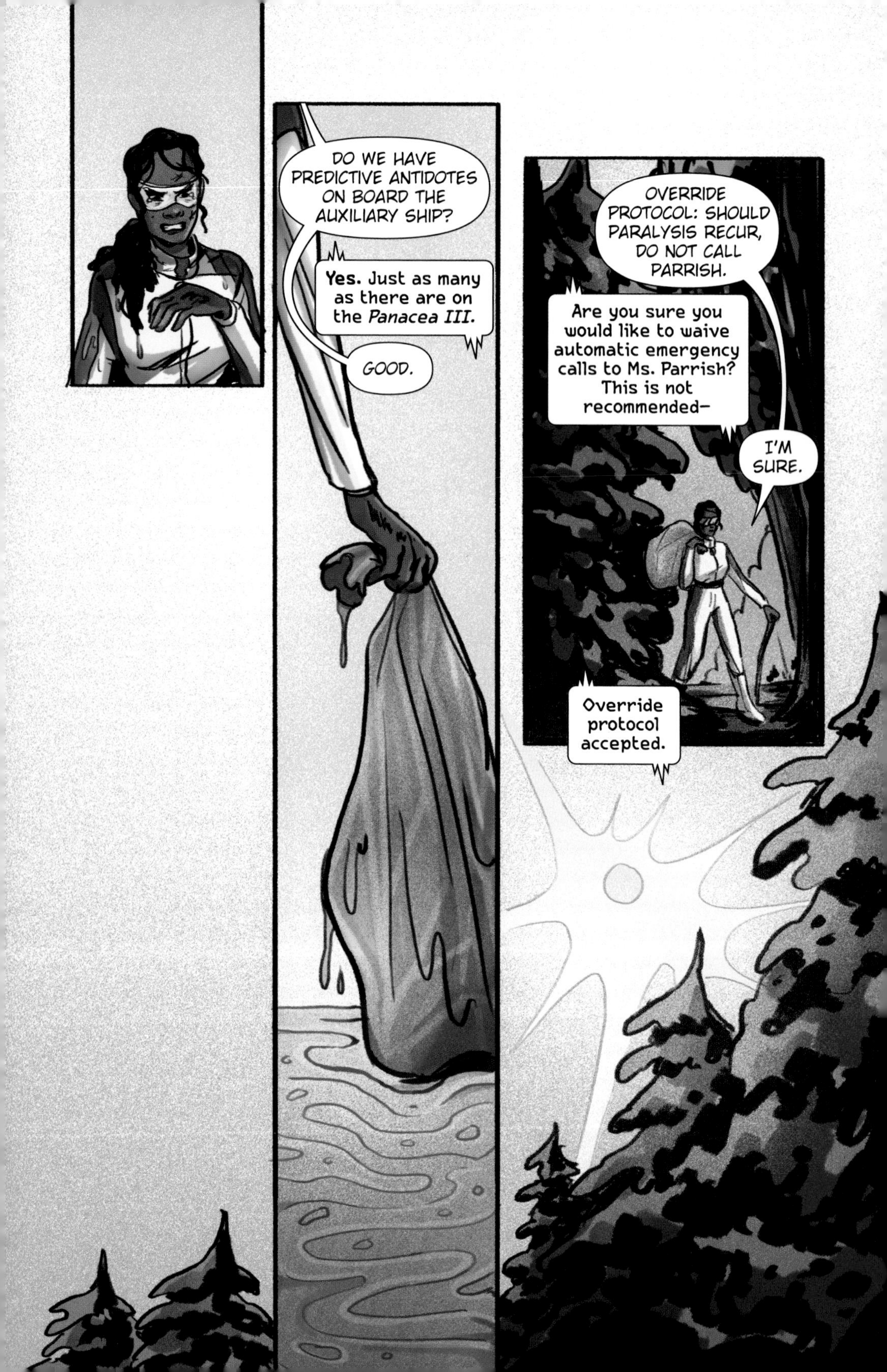

DO WE HAVE PREDICTIVE ANTIDOTES ON BOARD THE AUXILIARY SHIP?
Yes. Just as many as there are on the *Panacea III*.
GOOD.
OVERRIDE PROTOCOL: SHOULD PARALYSIS RECUR, DO NOT CALL PARRISH.
Are you sure you would like to waive automatic emergency calls to Ms. Parrish? This is not recommended–
I'M SURE.
Override protocol accepted.

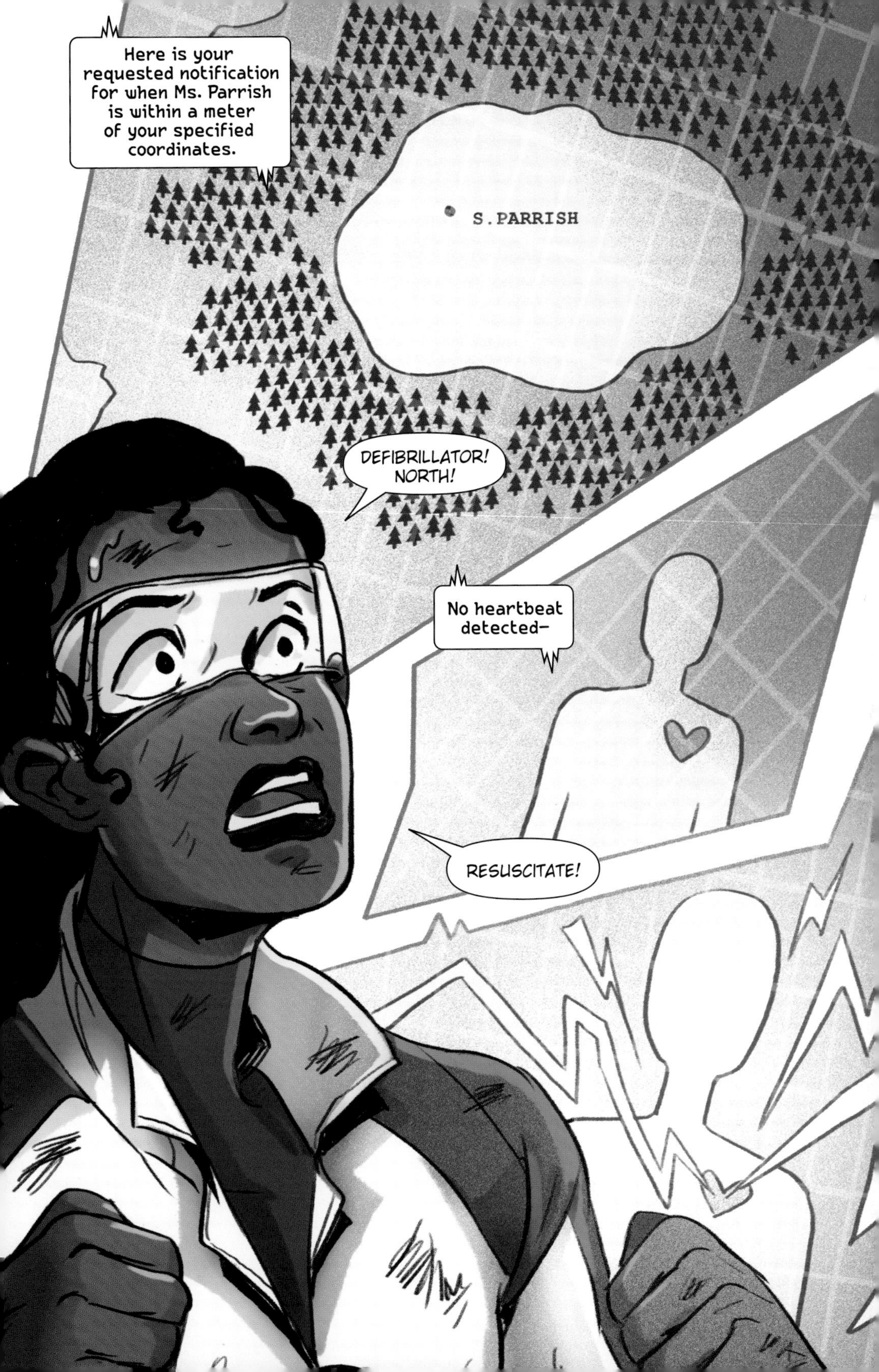
Here is your requested notification for when Ms. Parrish is within a meter of your specified coordinates.
S.PARRISH
DEFIBRILLATOR! NORTH!
No heartbeat detected—
RESUSCITATE!

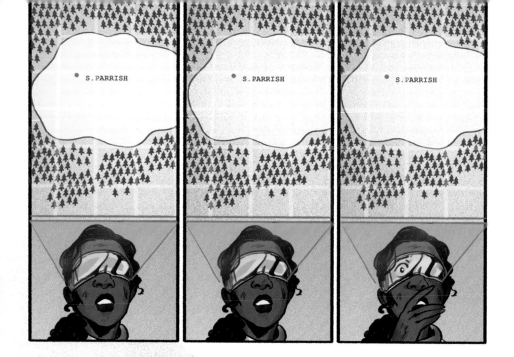

S.PARRISH

S.PARRISH

S.PARRISH

SPEECH
SEARCH:
"YOU'RE THE
BEST OF
US."

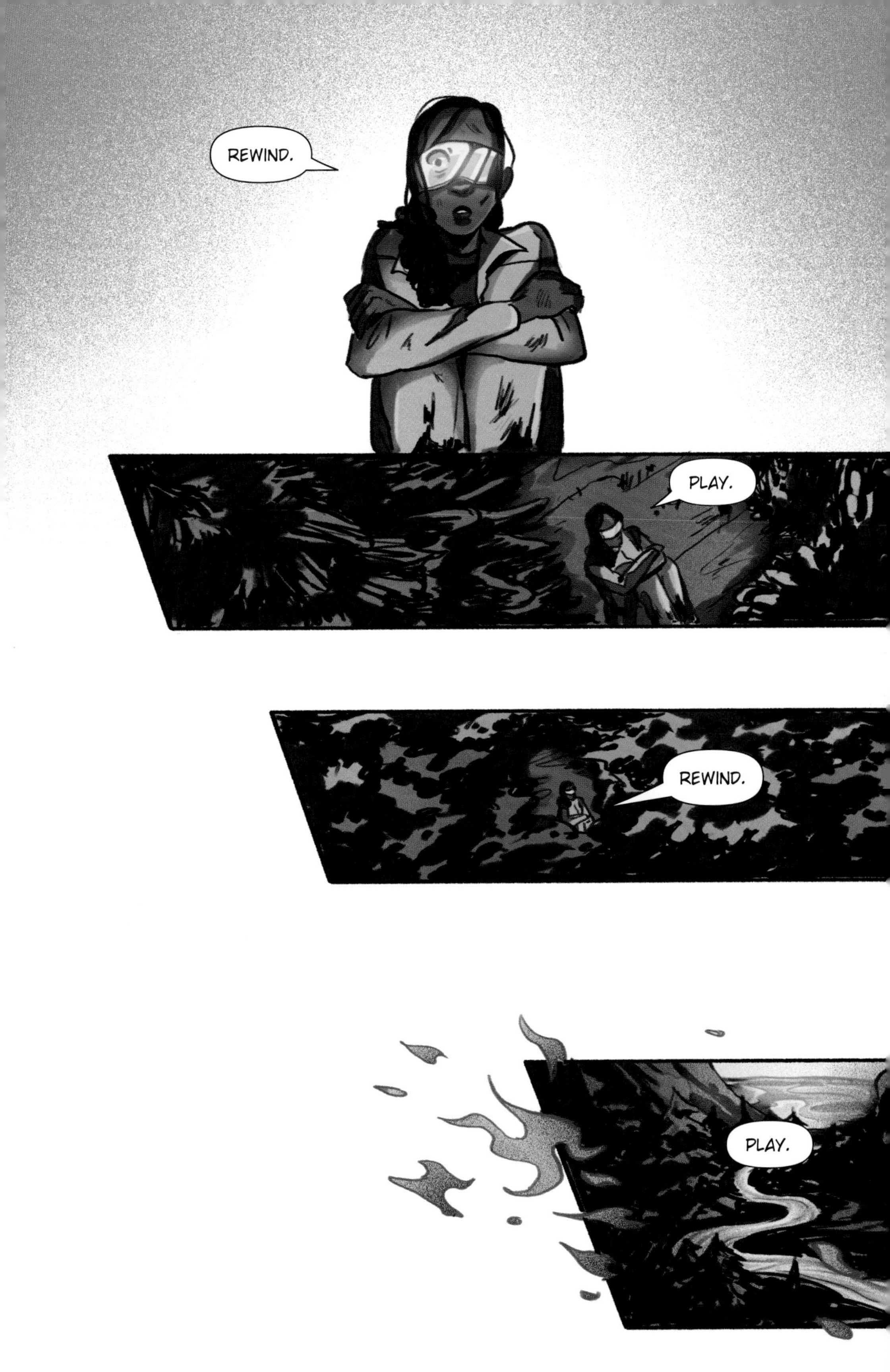
REWIND.
PLAY.
REWIND.
PLAY.

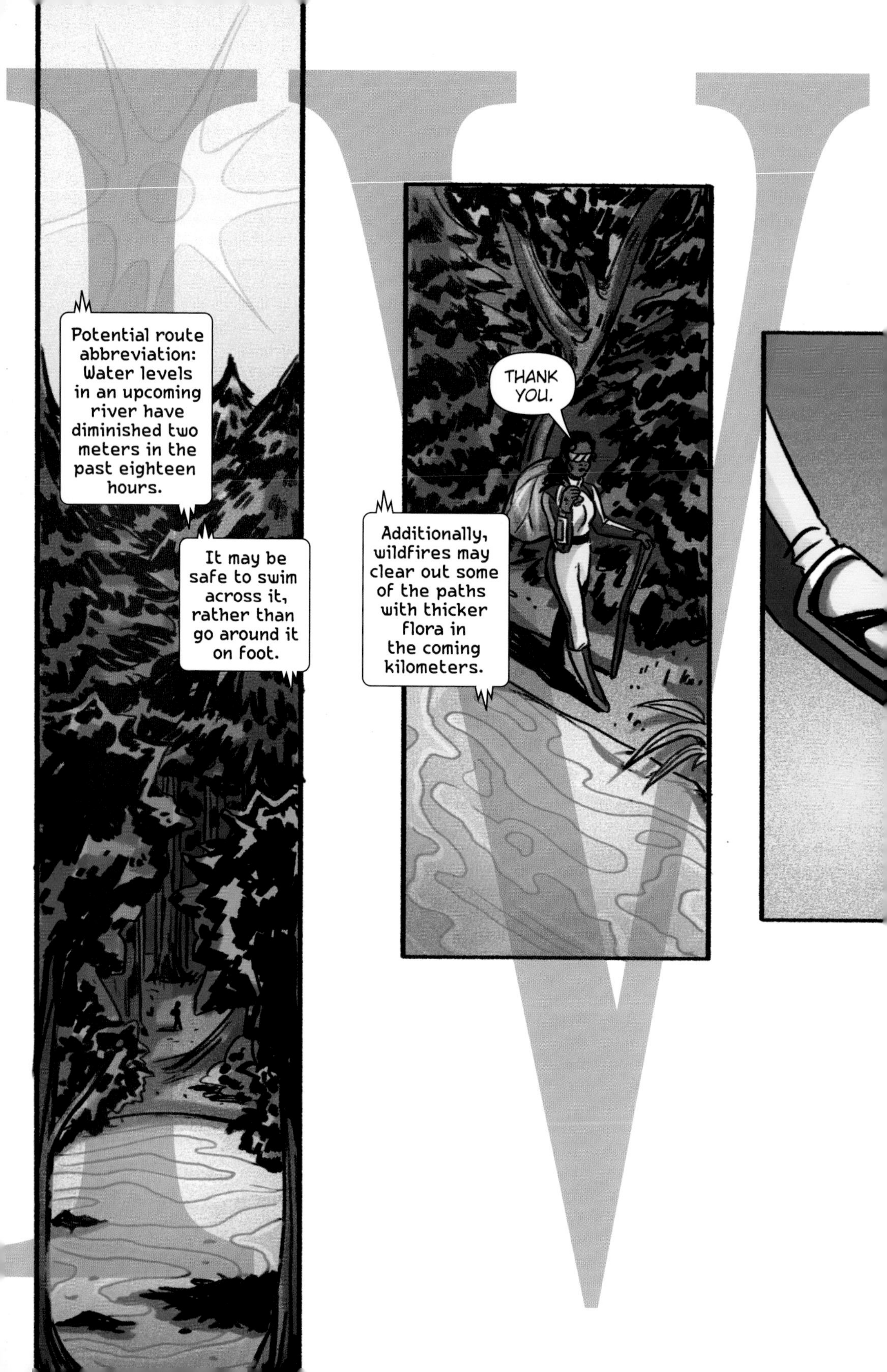
Potential route abbreviation: Water levels in an upcoming river have diminished two meters in the past eighteen hours.
It may be safe to swim across it, rather than go around it on foot.
THANK YOU.
Additionally, wildfires may clear out some of the paths with thicker flora in the coming kilometers.

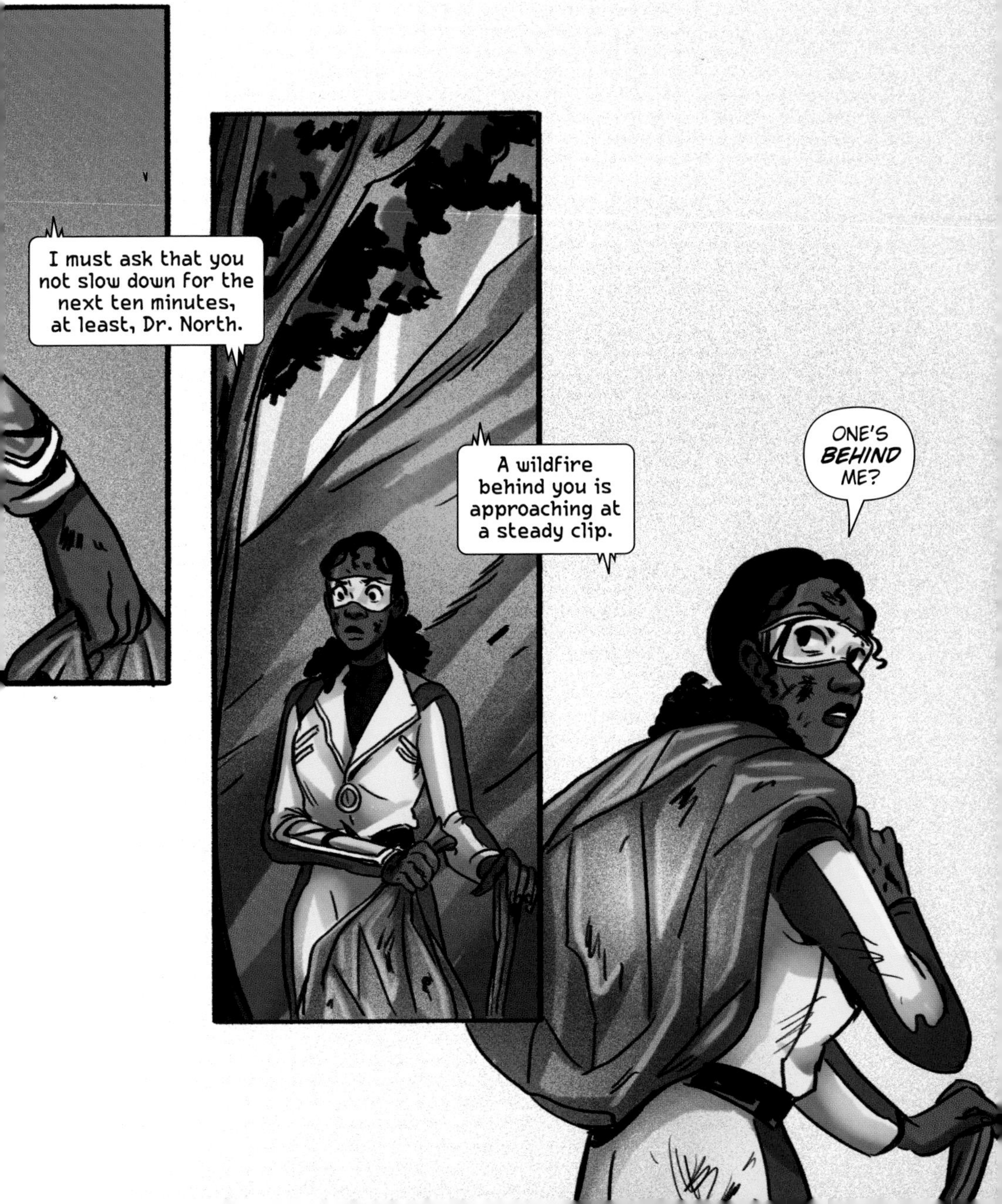
I must ask that you not slow down for the next ten minutes, at least, Dr. North.
A wildfire behind you is approaching at a steady clip.
ONE'S *BEHIND* ME?

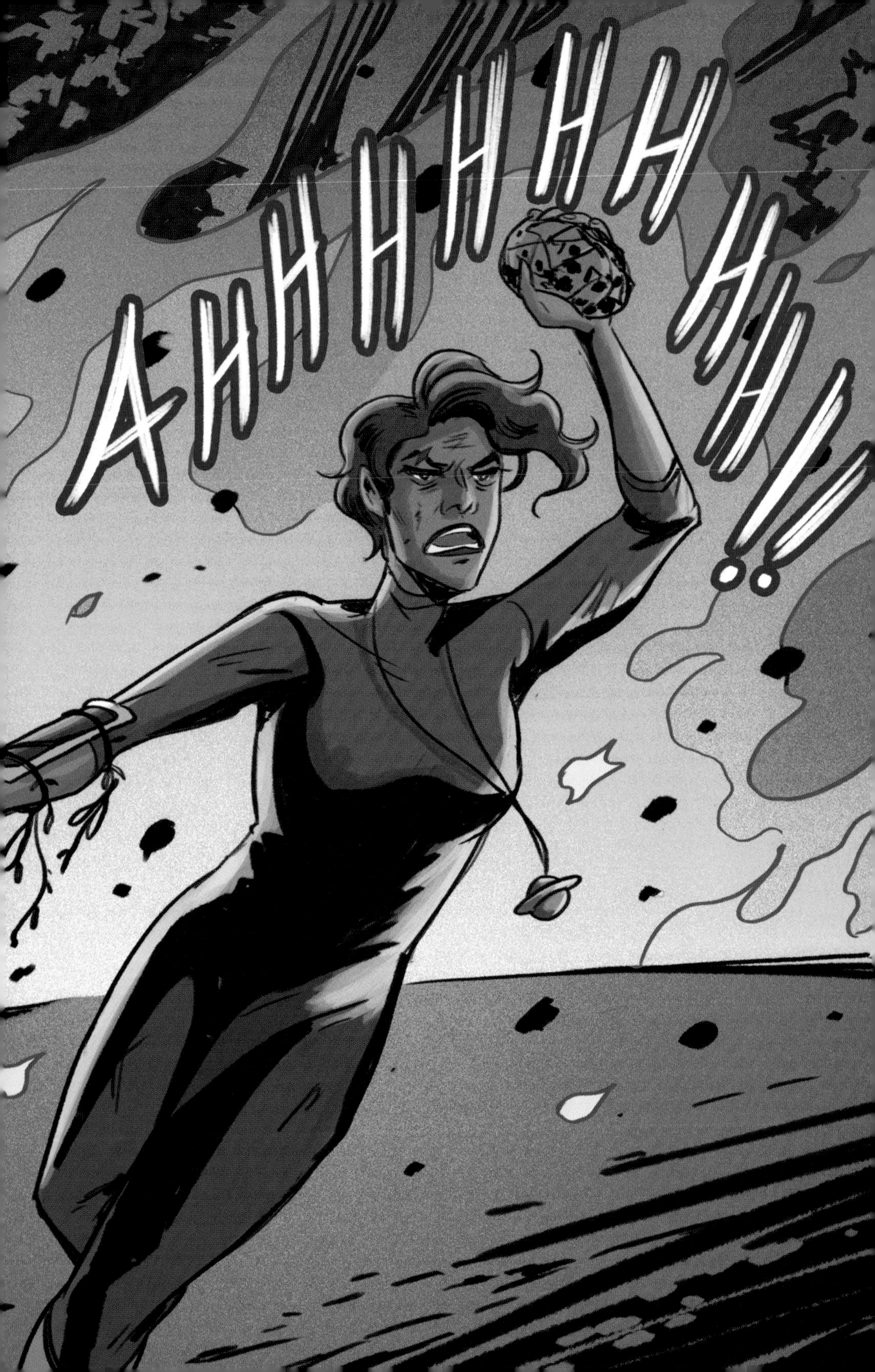
AHHHHHHHHH!!

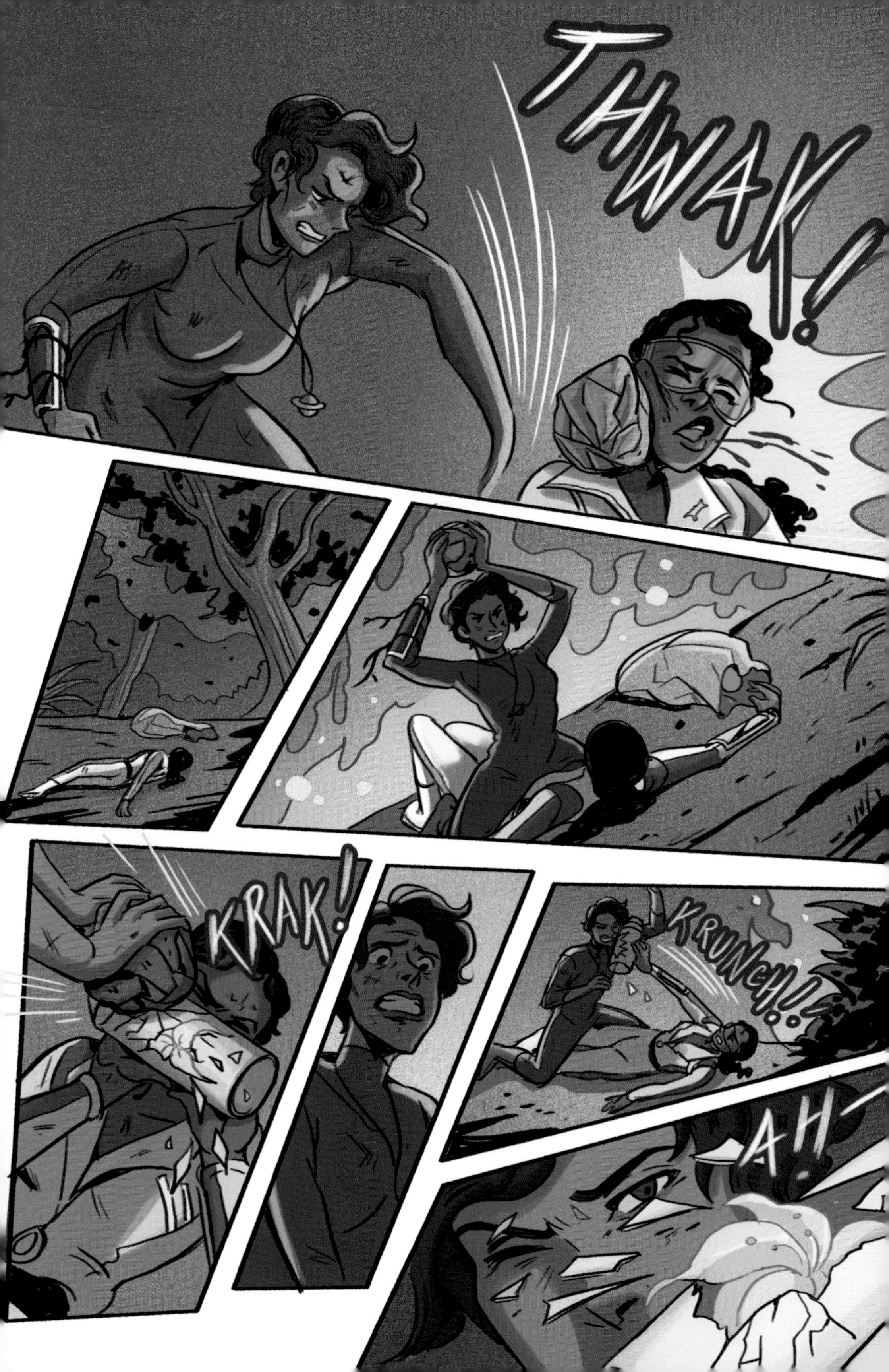
THWAK!
KRAK!
KRUNCH!!
AH-

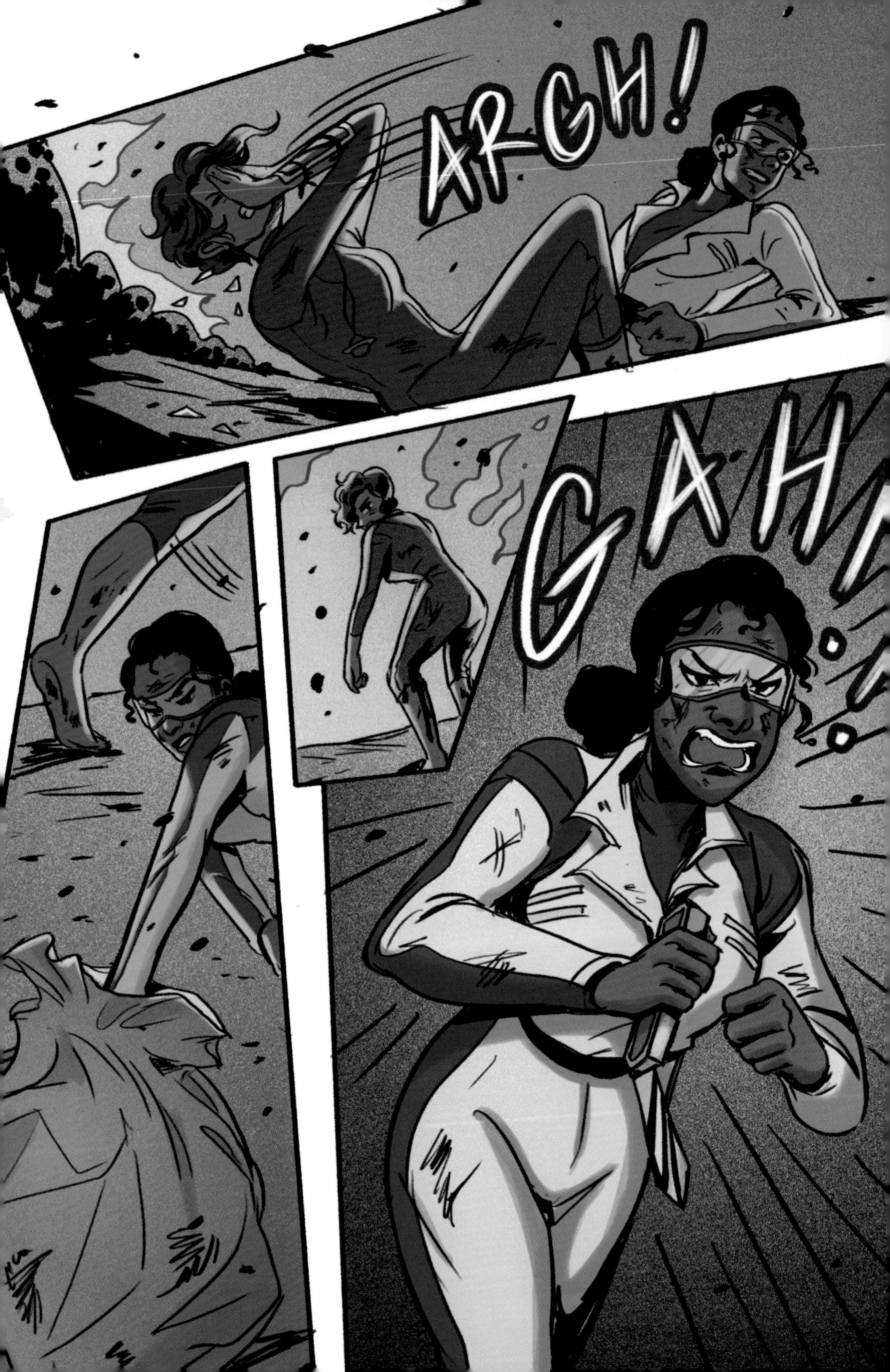
ARGH!
GAH

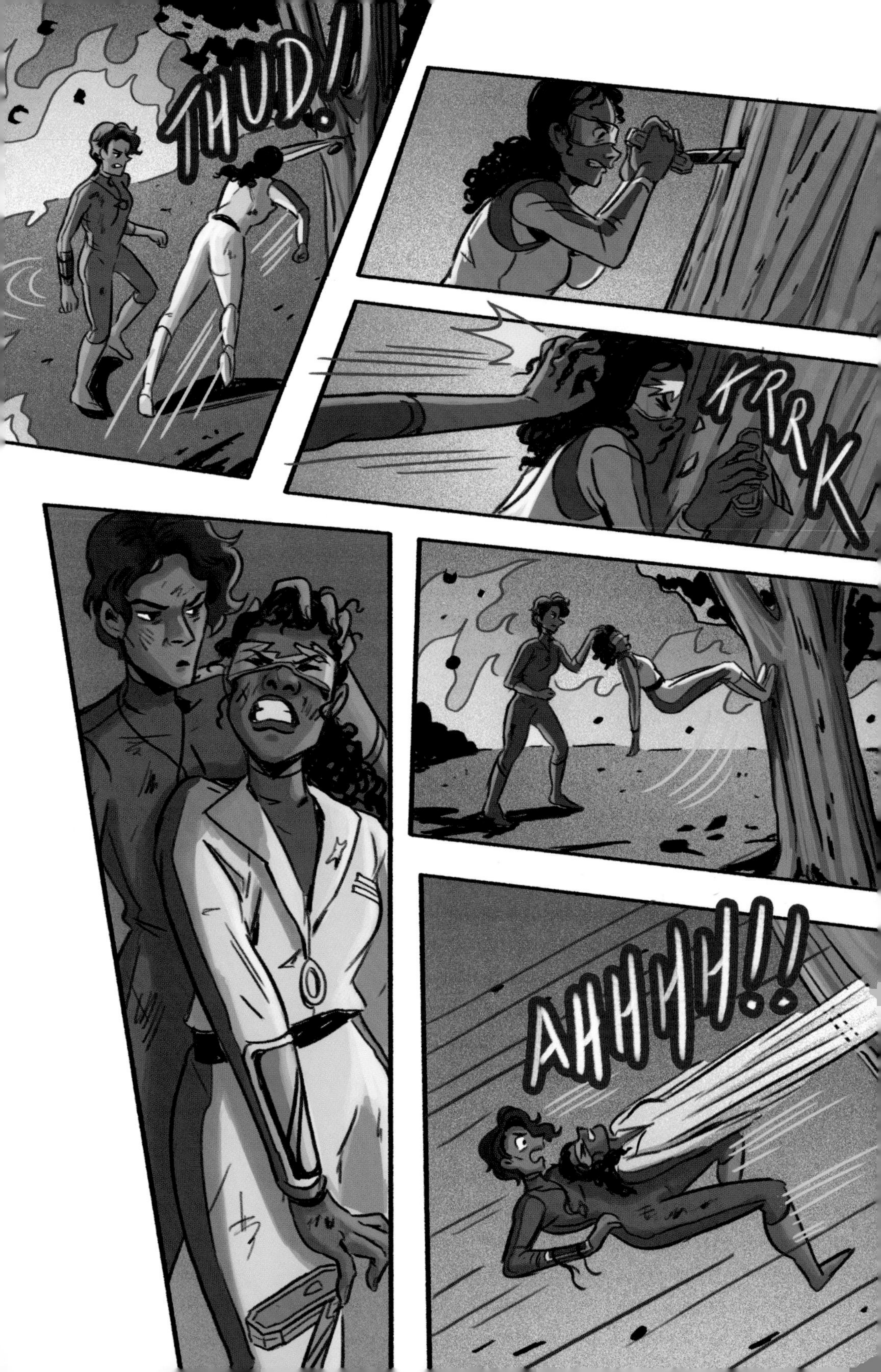
THUD!!
KRRRK
AHHHH!!

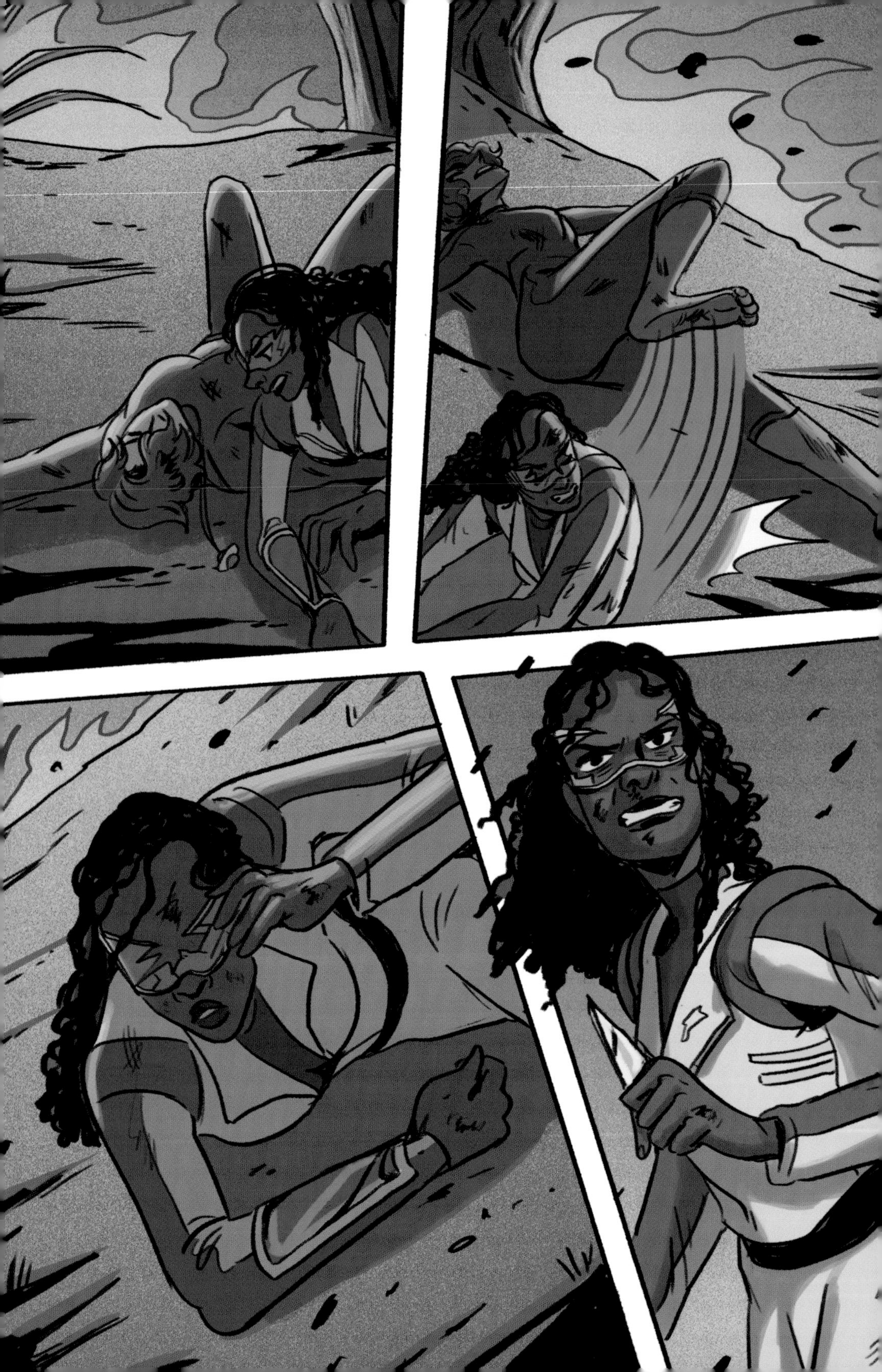

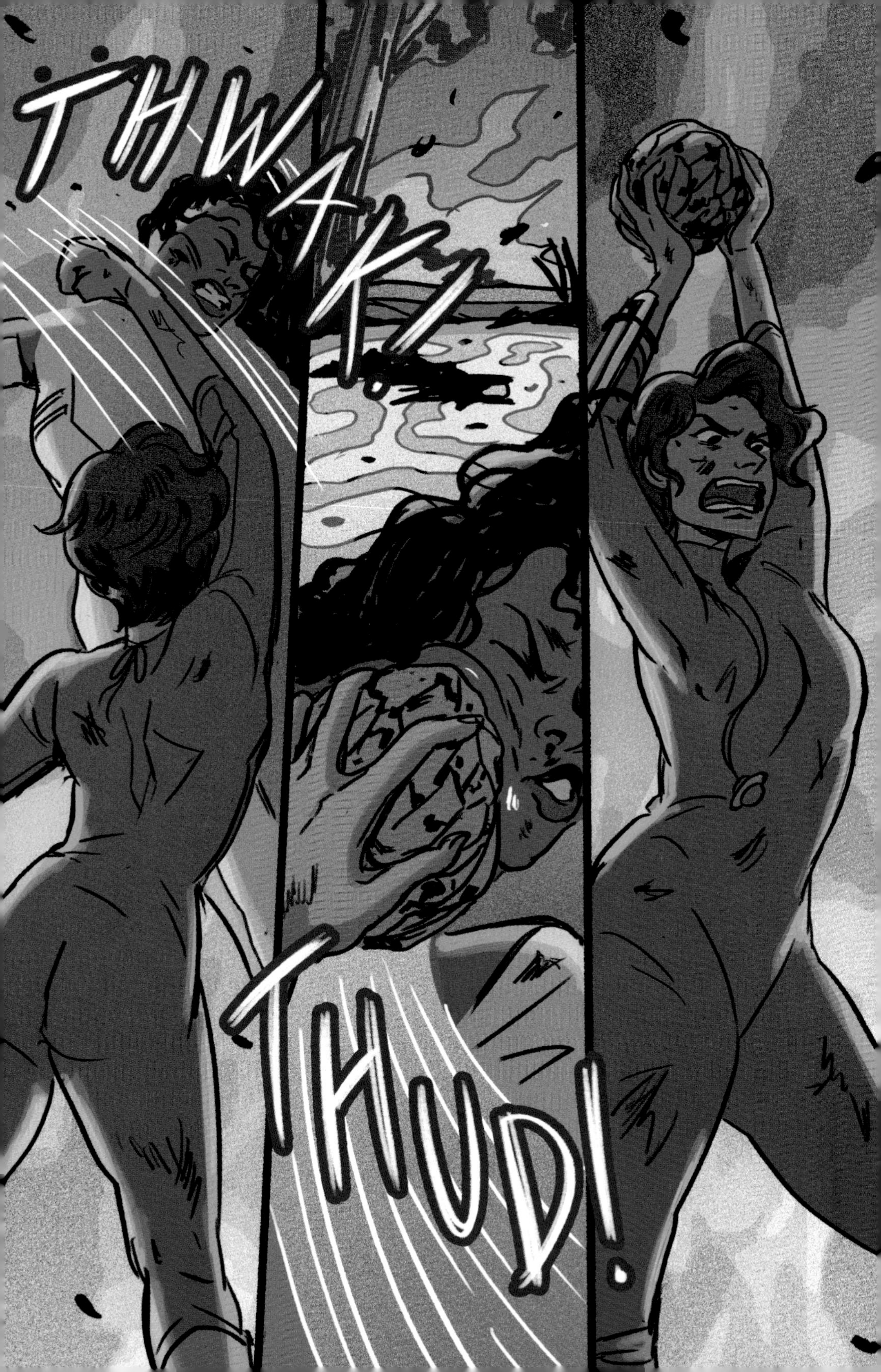
THWAK!
THUD!

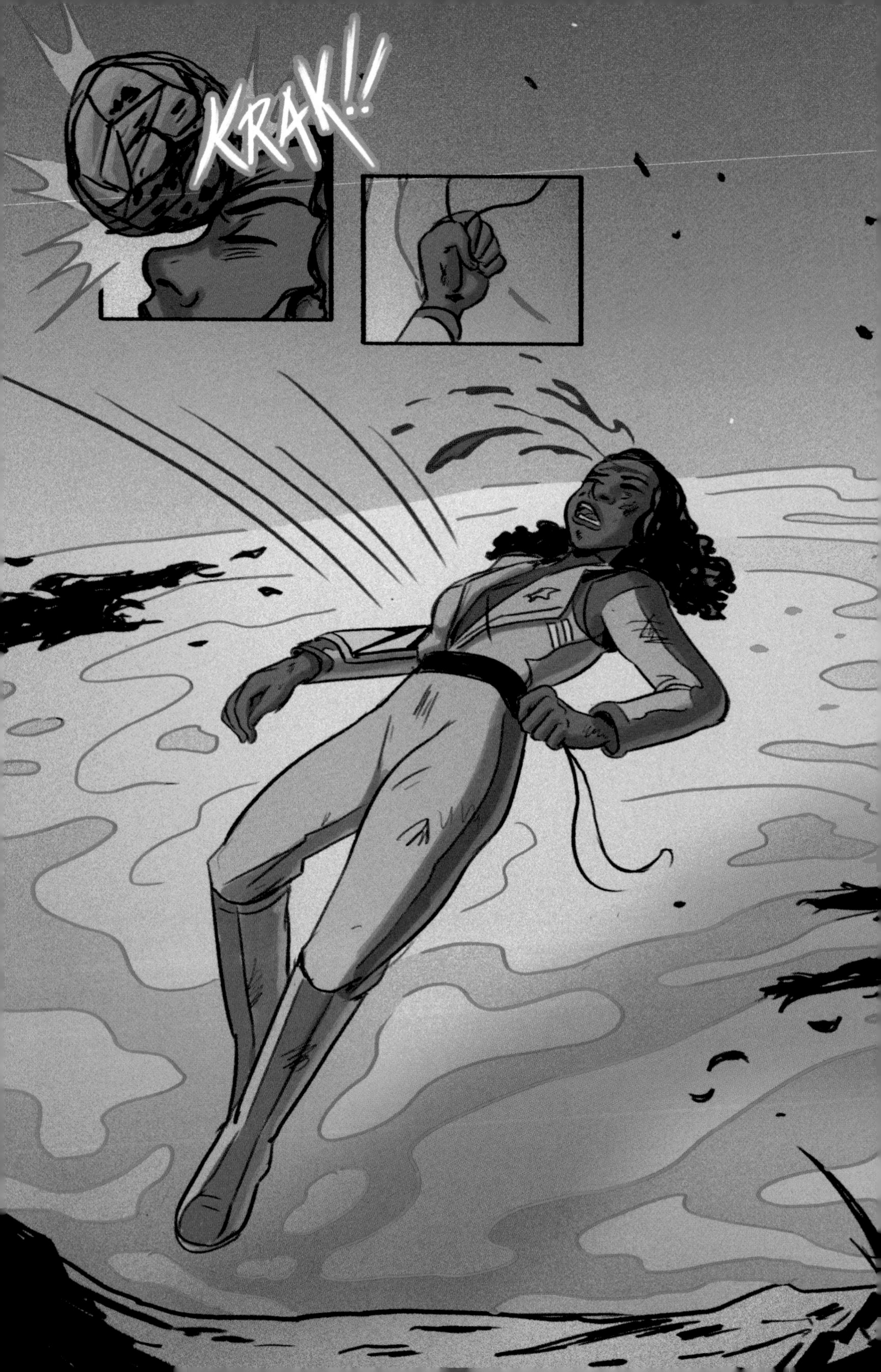
KRAK!!

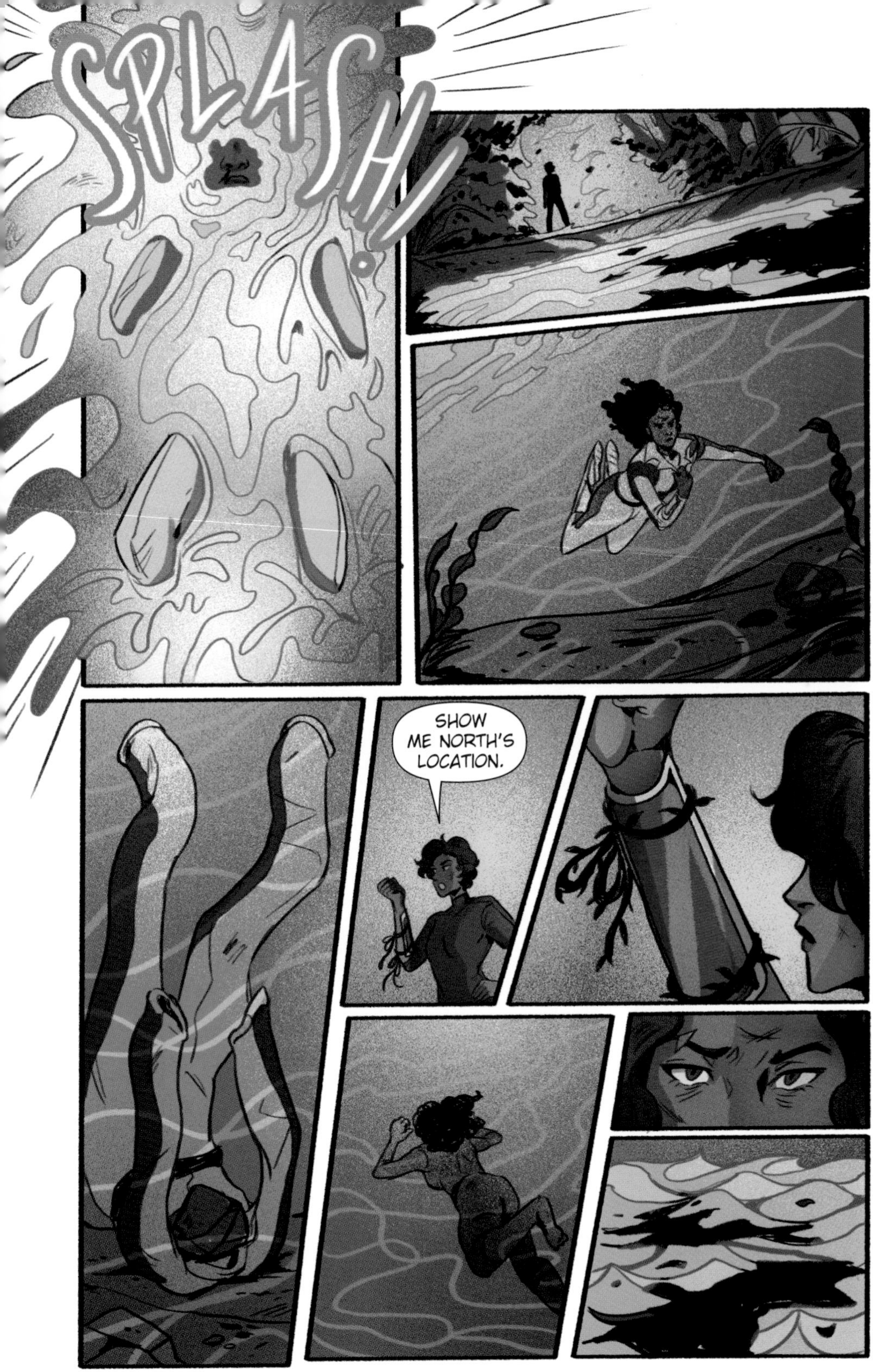
SPLASH!
SHOW ME NORTH'S LOCATION.

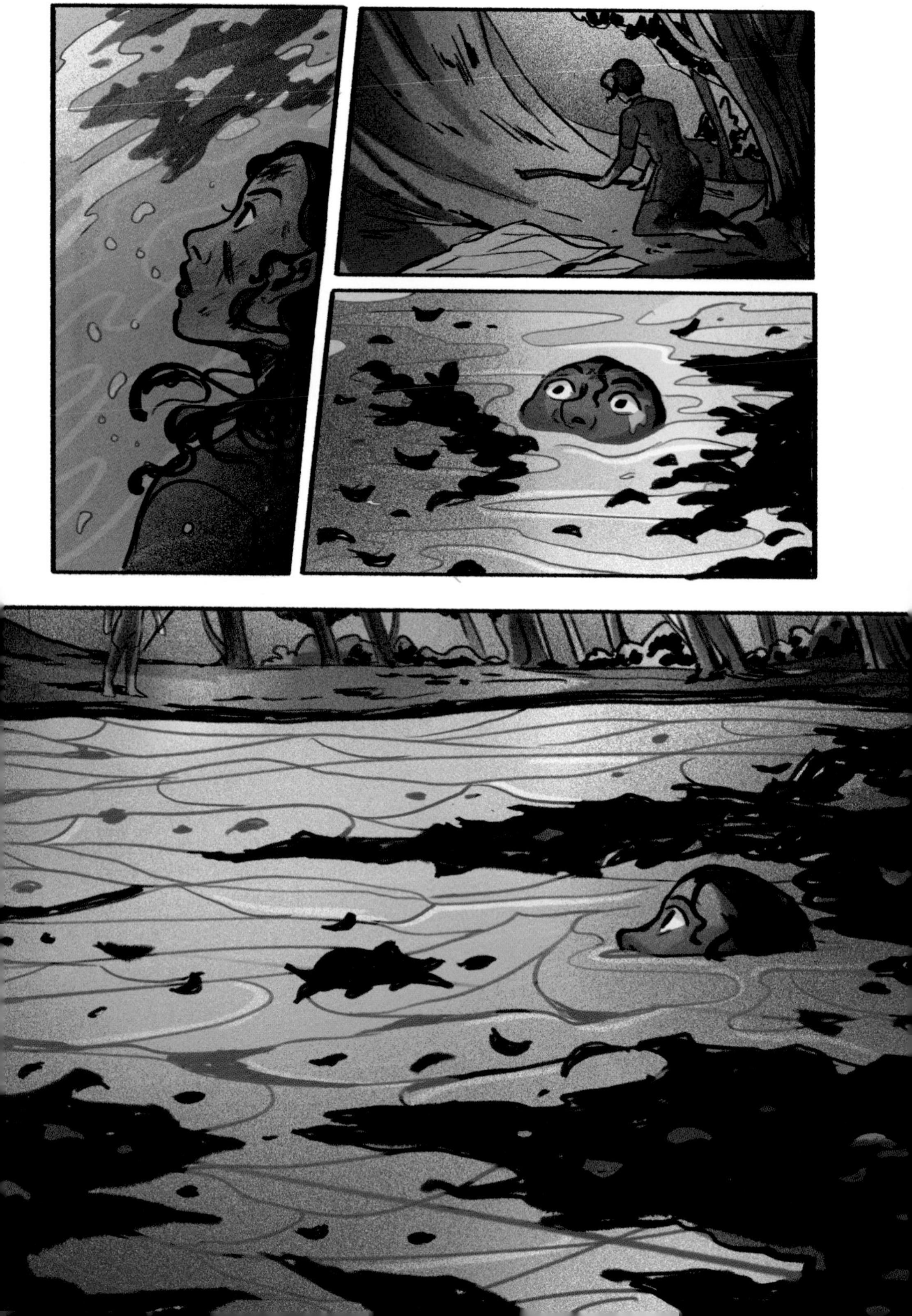

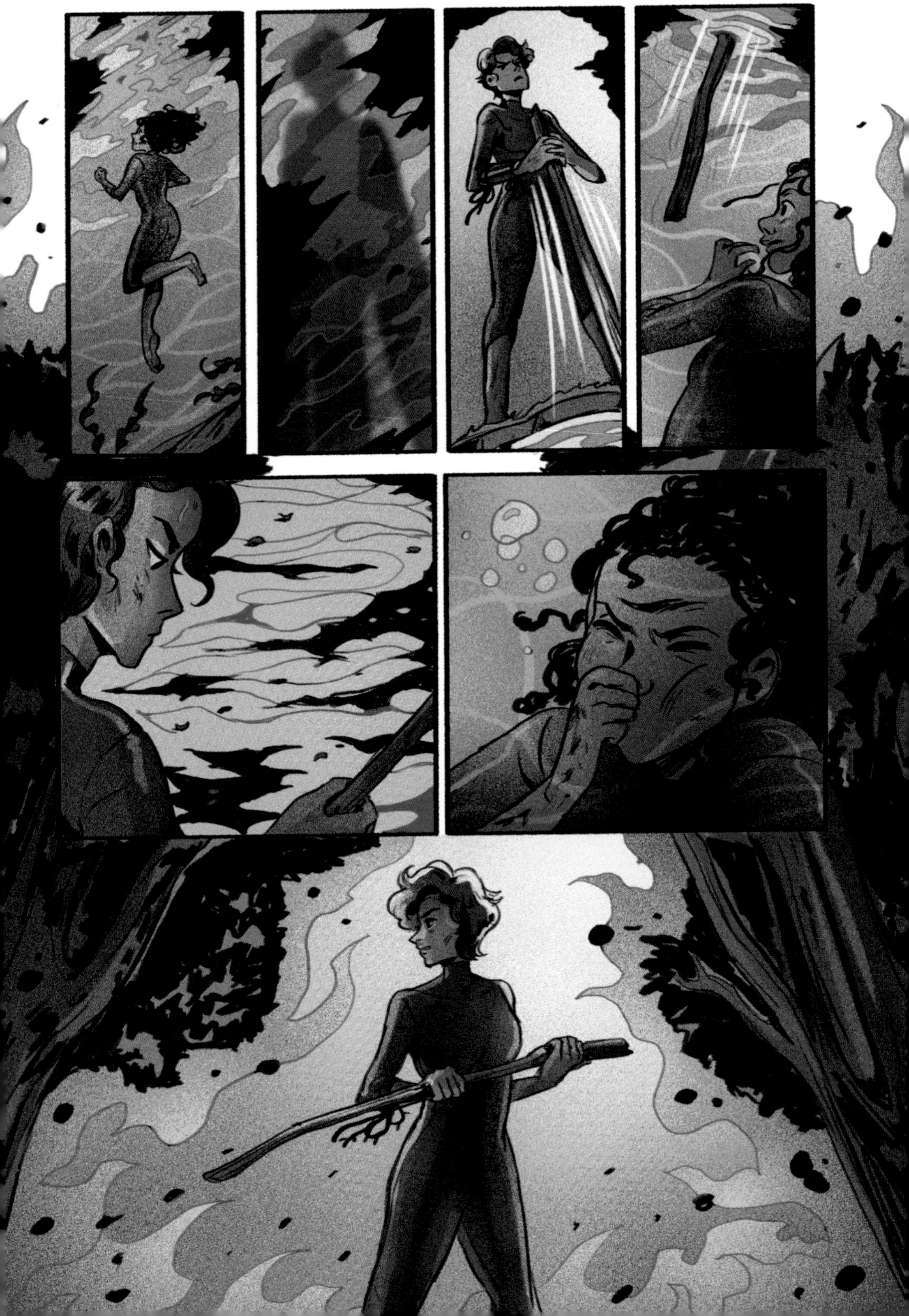

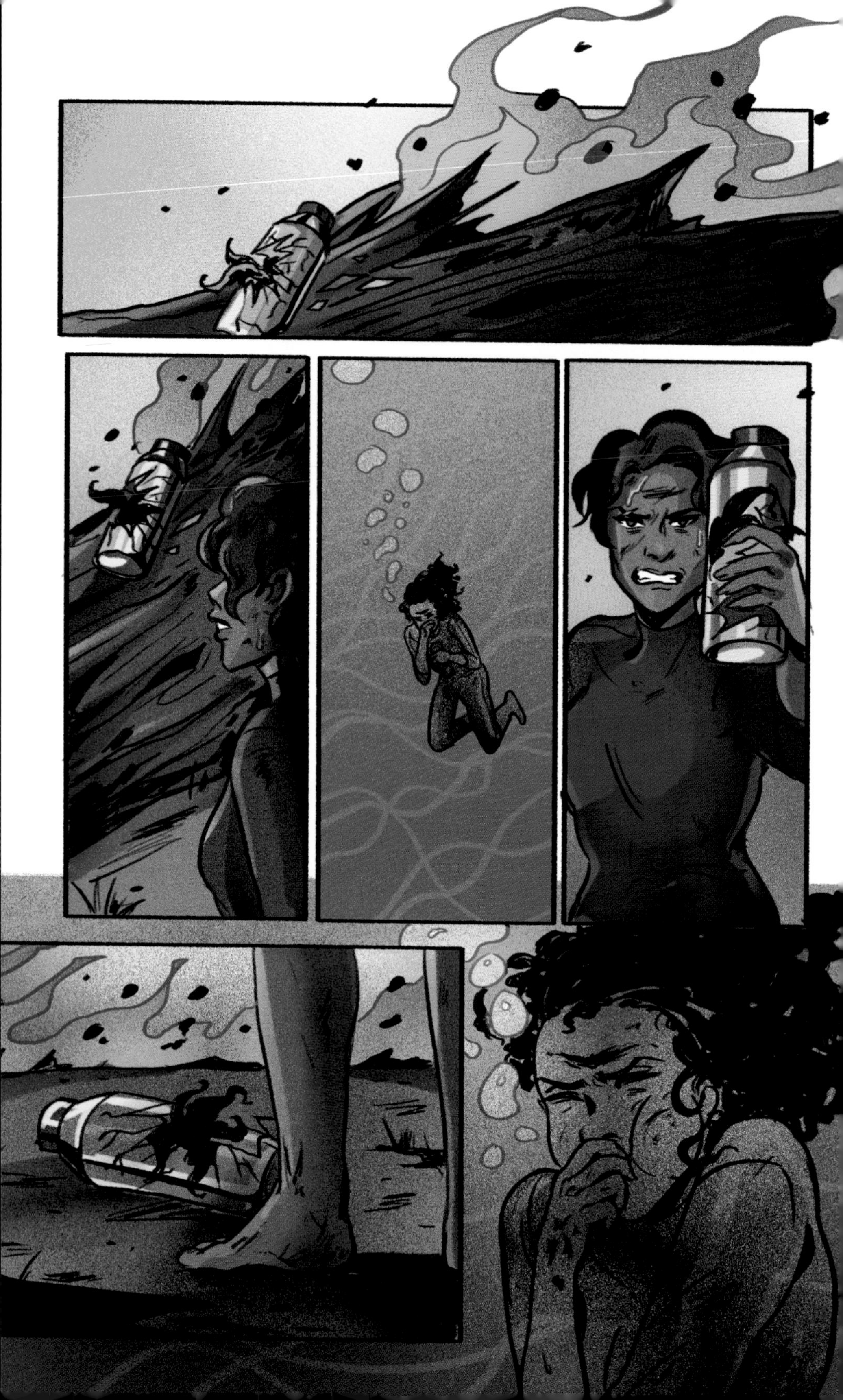

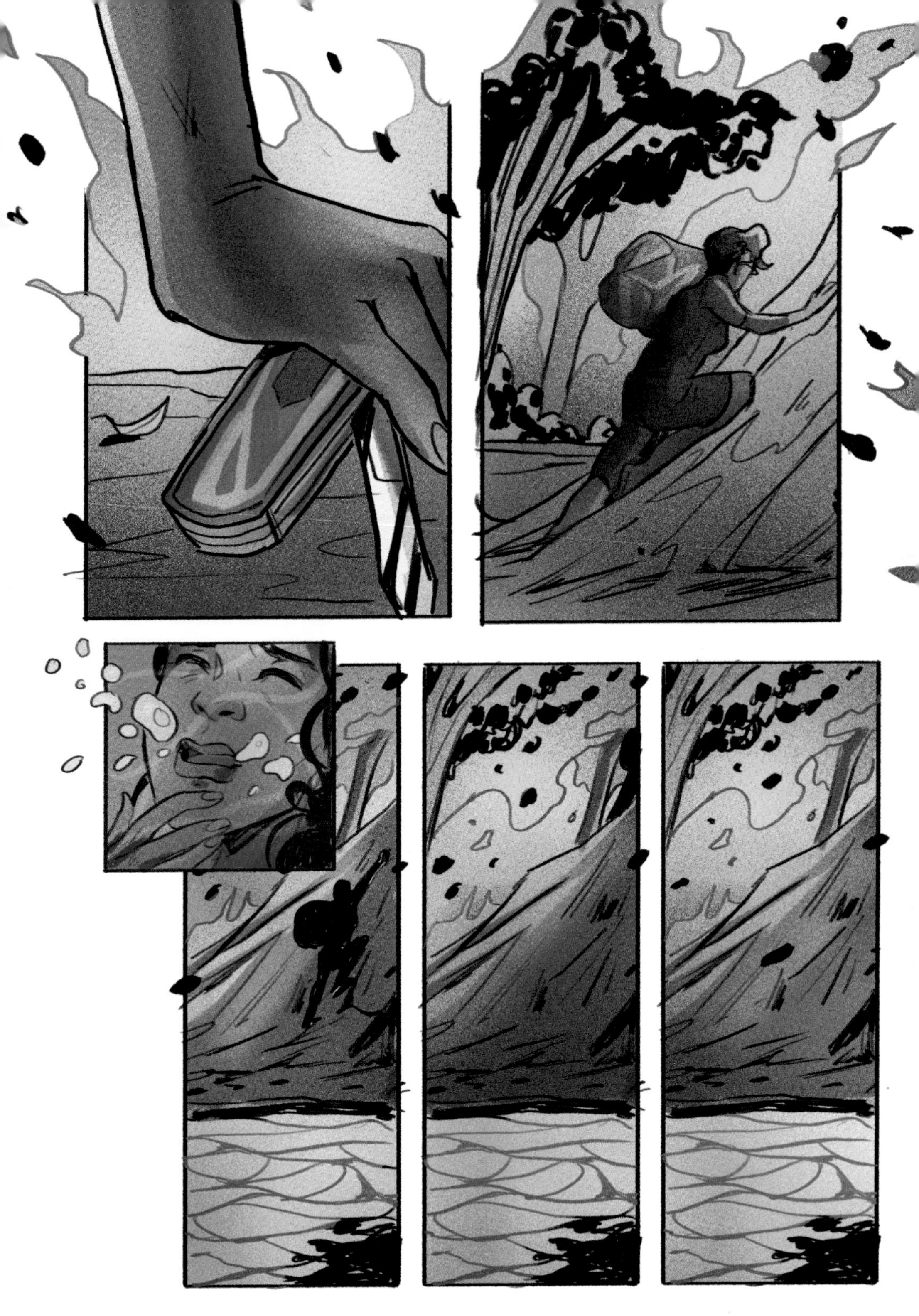

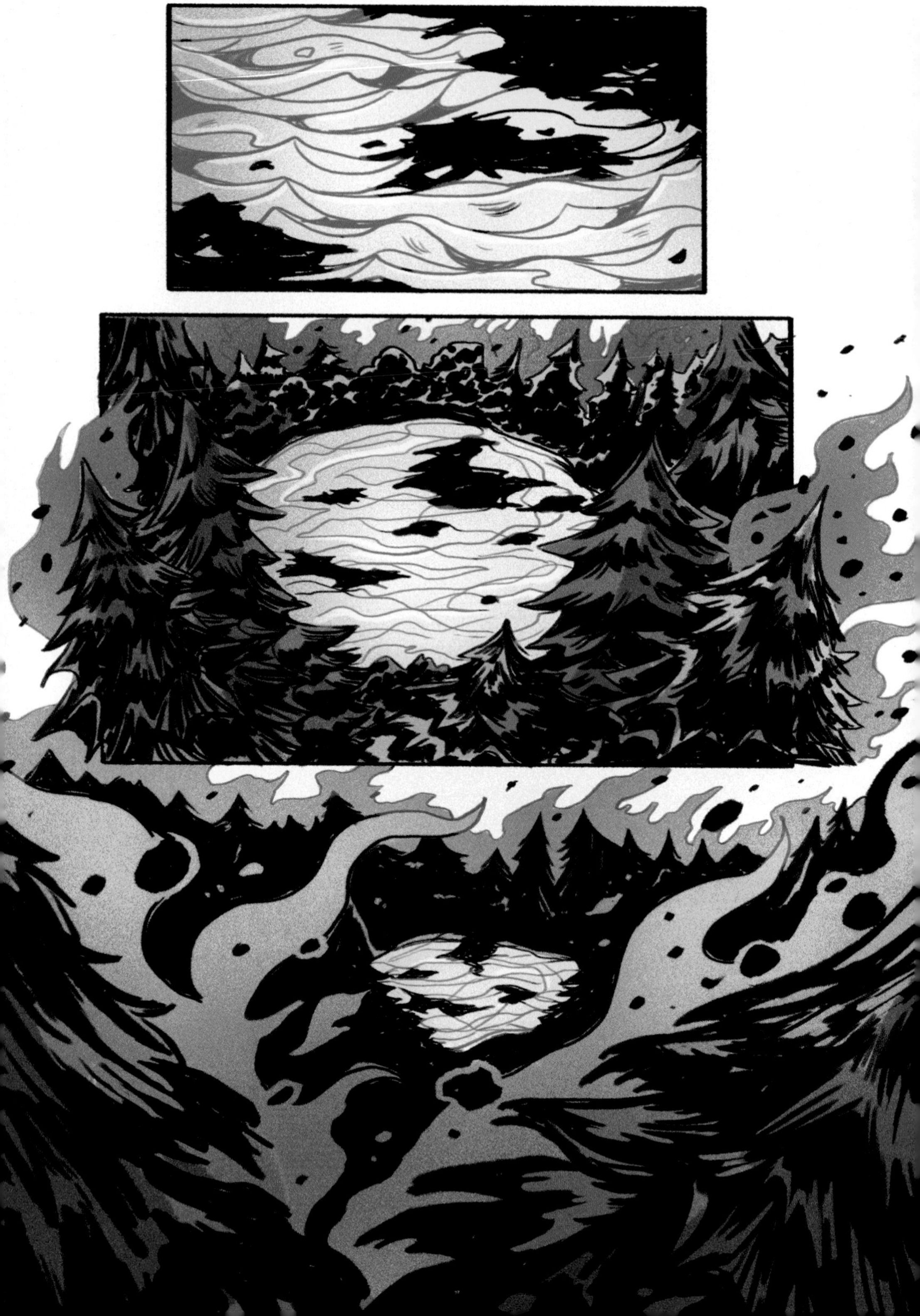

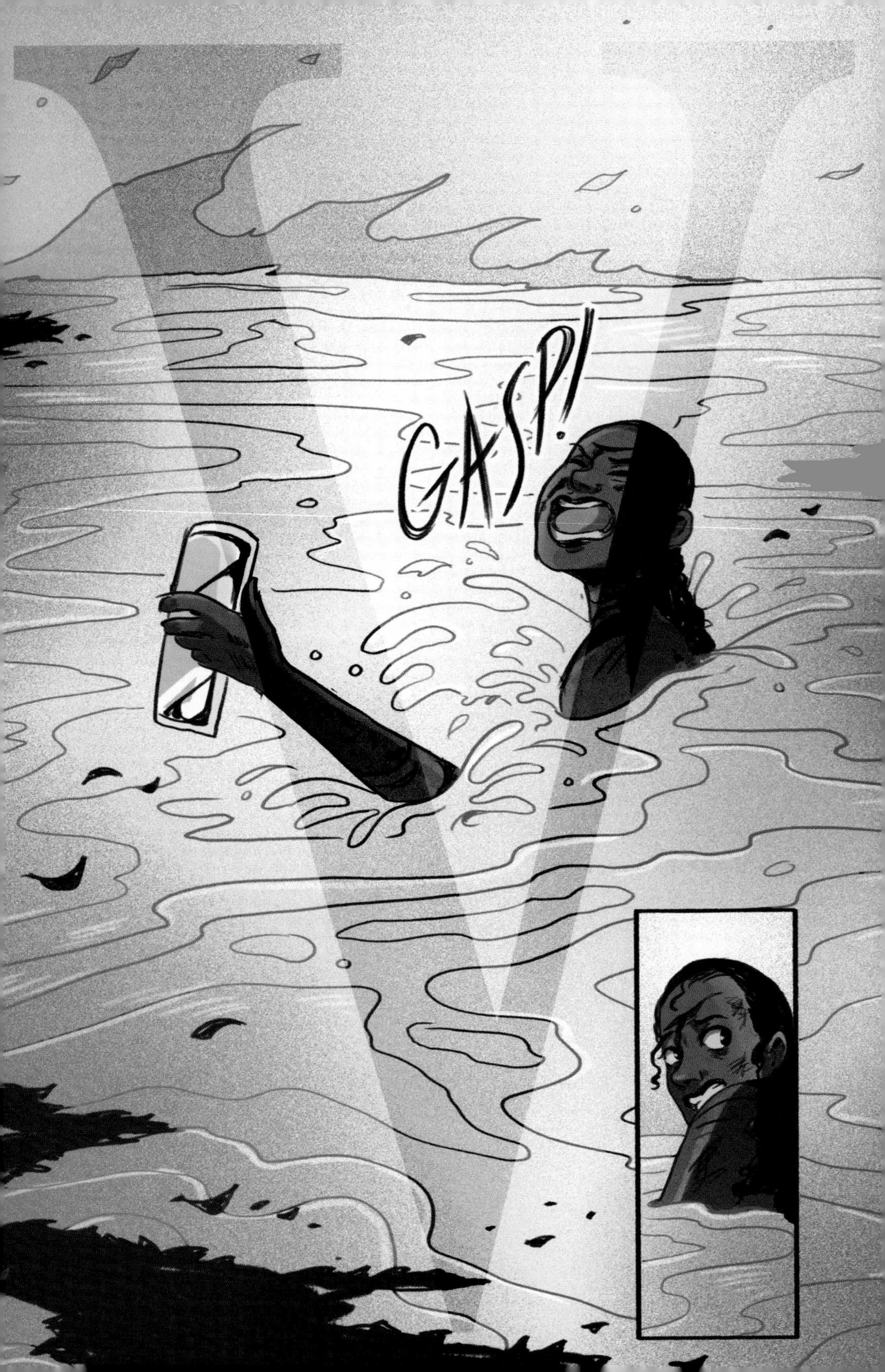
GASP!

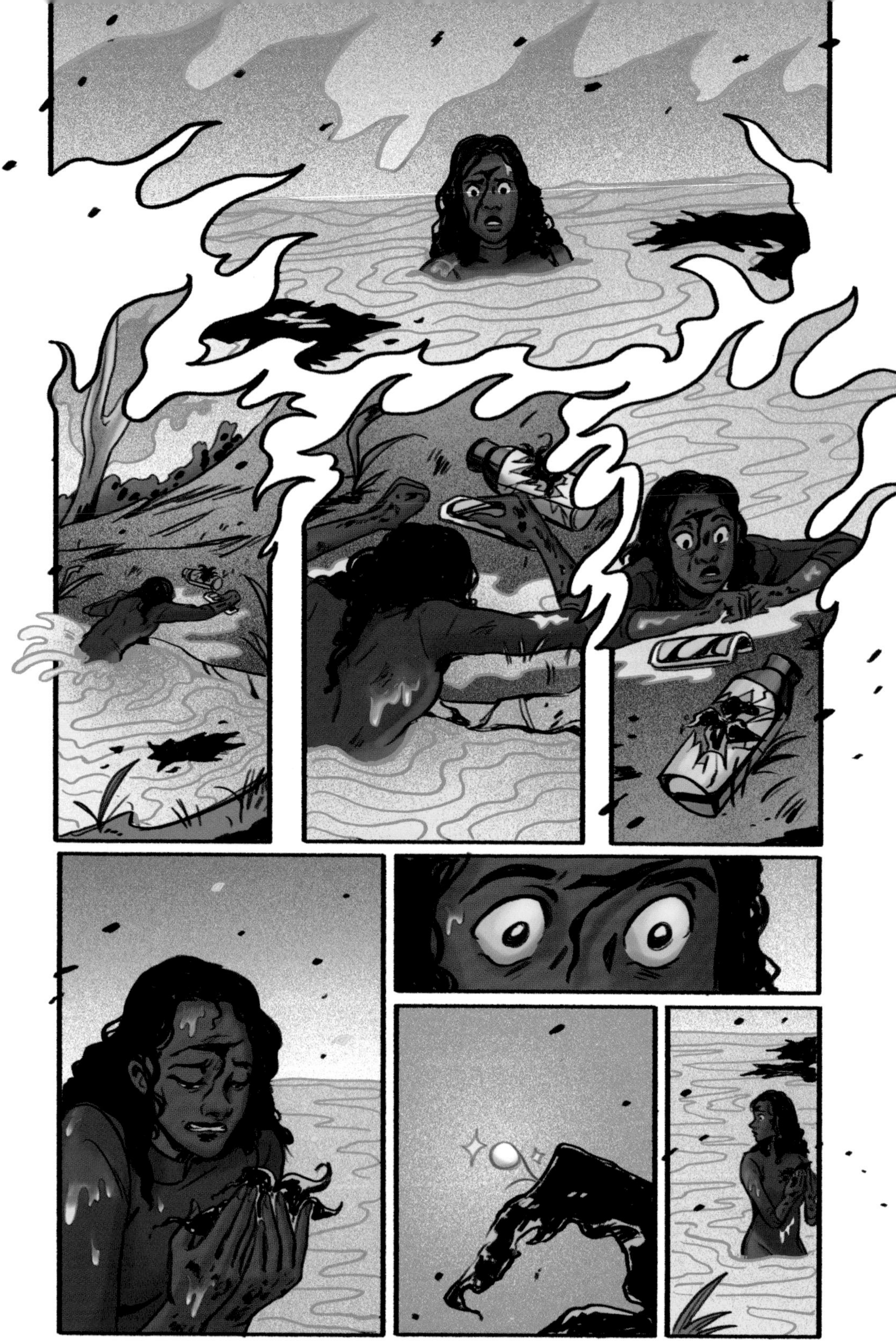

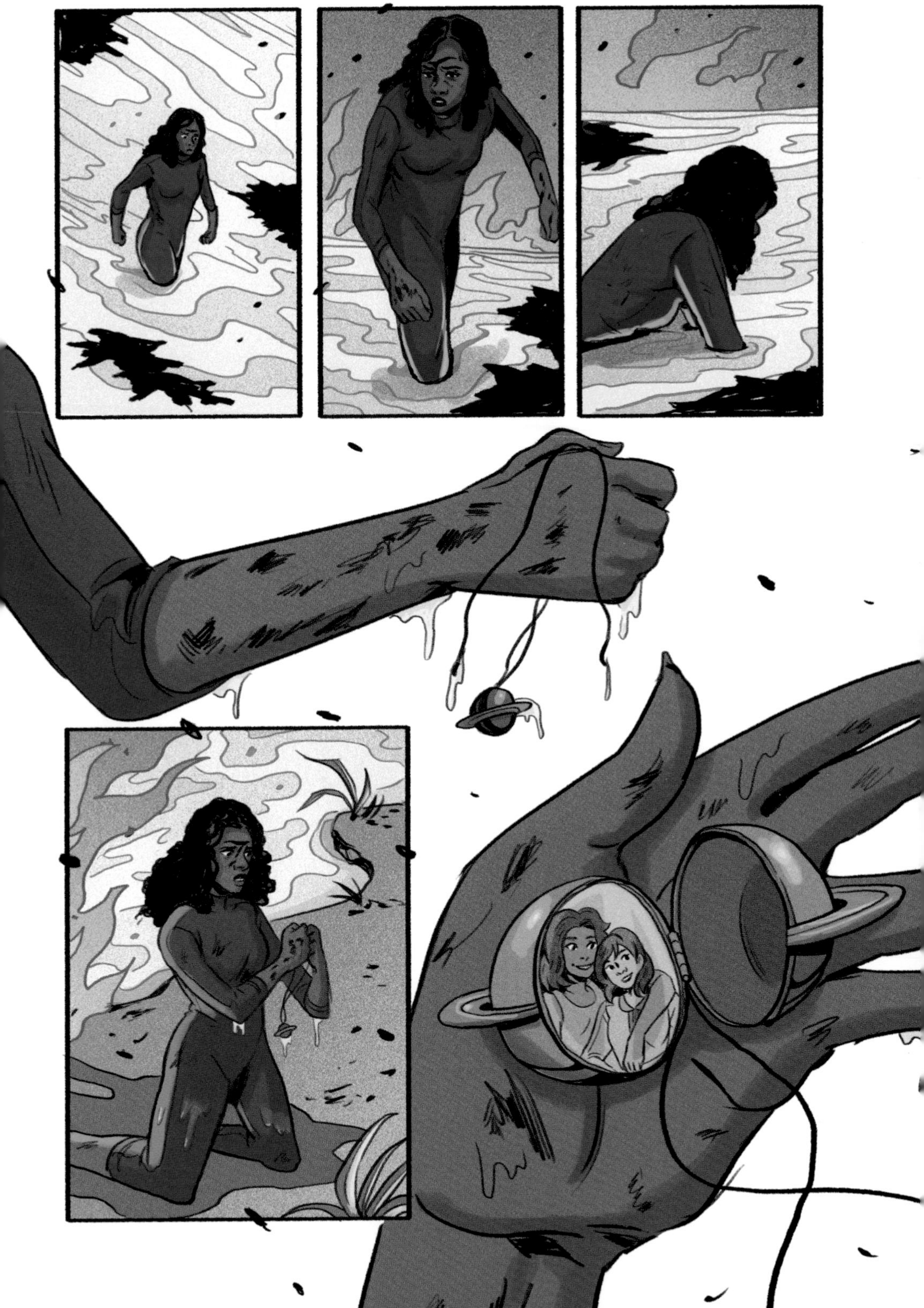

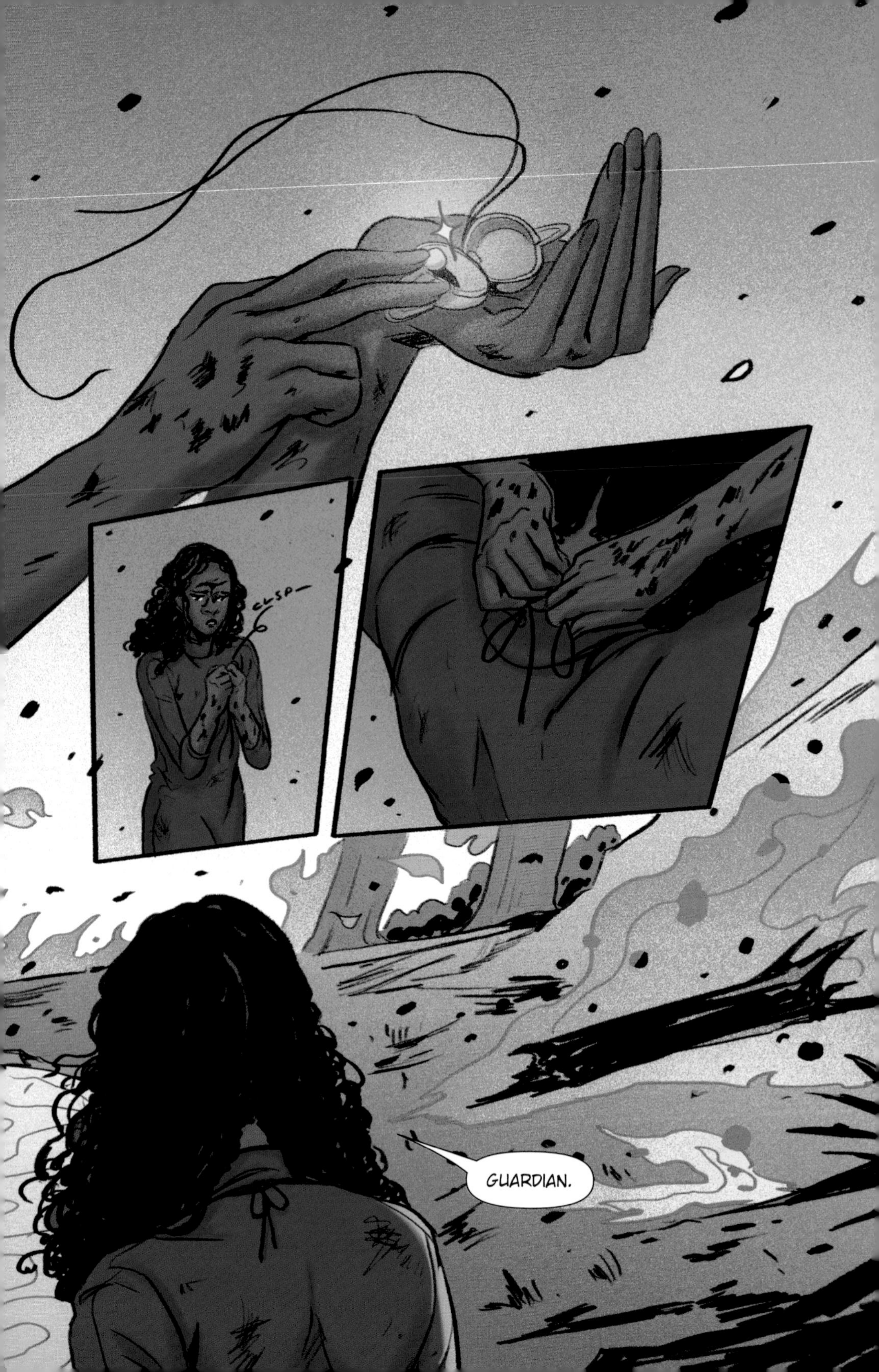
CLSP—
GUARDIAN.

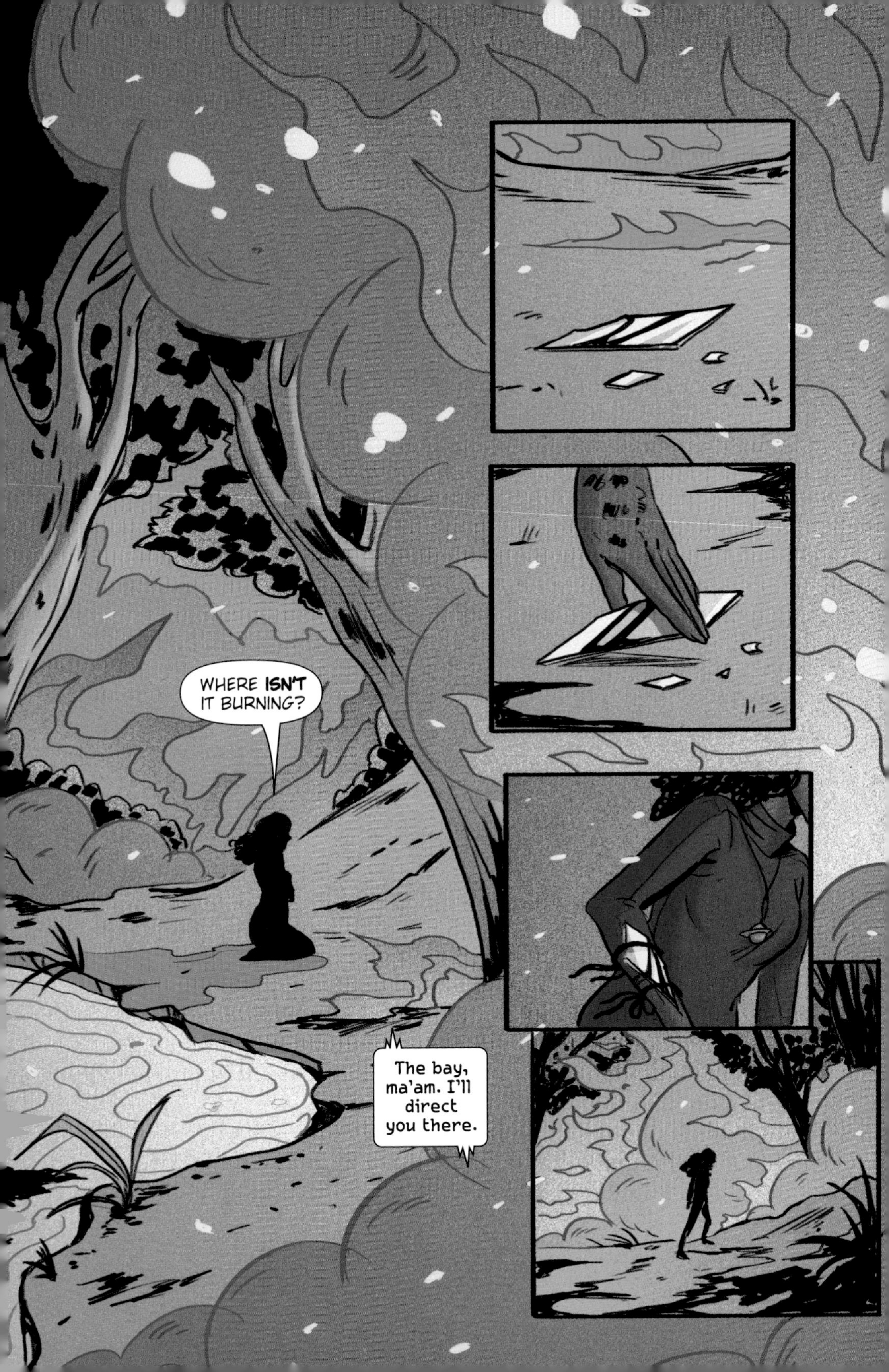
WHERE **ISN'T** IT BURNING?
The bay, ma'am. I'll direct you there.

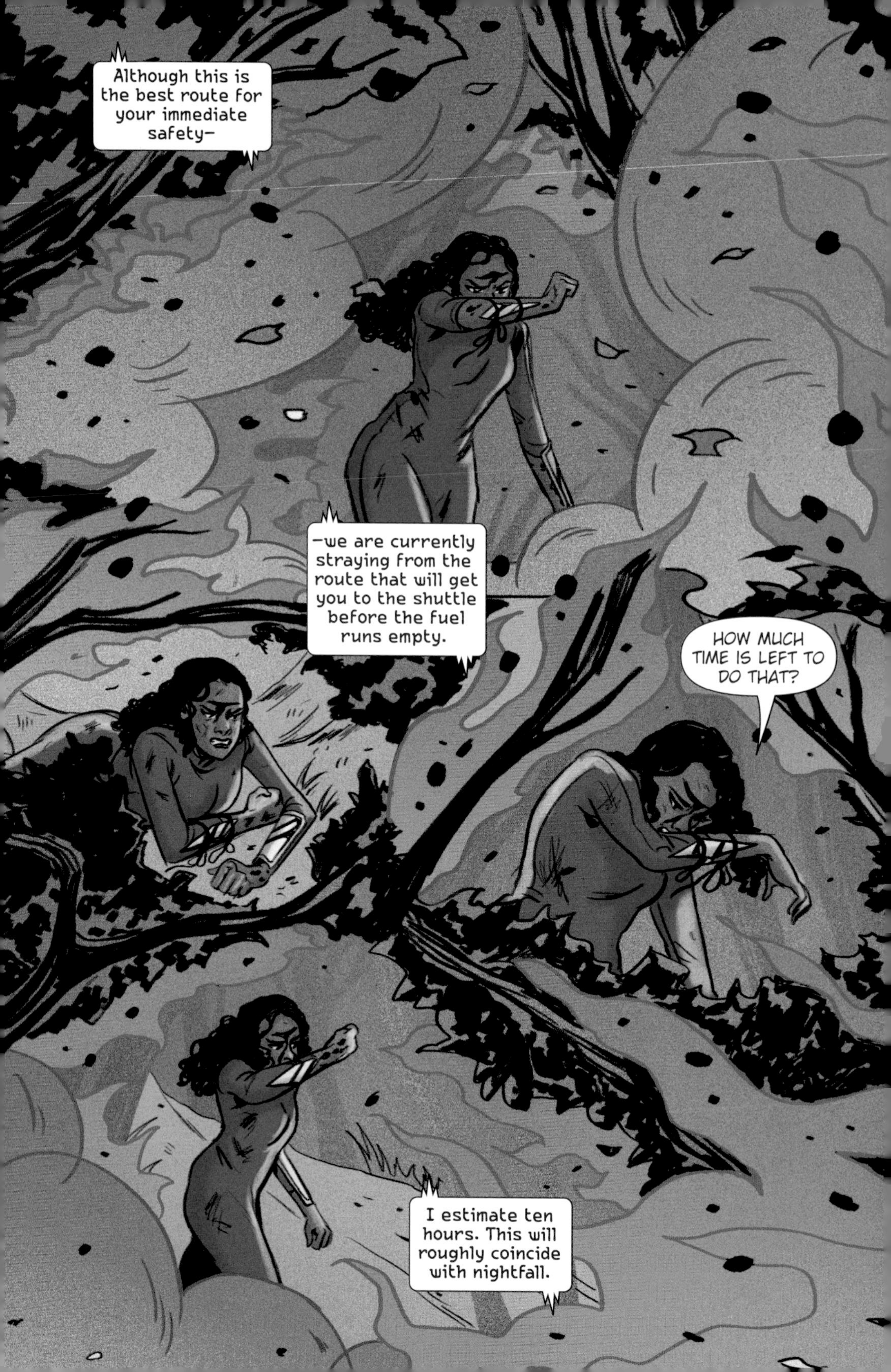
Although this is the best route for your immediate safety—
—we are currently straying from the route that will get you to the shuttle before the fuel runs empty.
HOW MUCH TIME IS LEFT TO DO THAT?
I estimate ten hours. This will roughly coincide with nightfall.

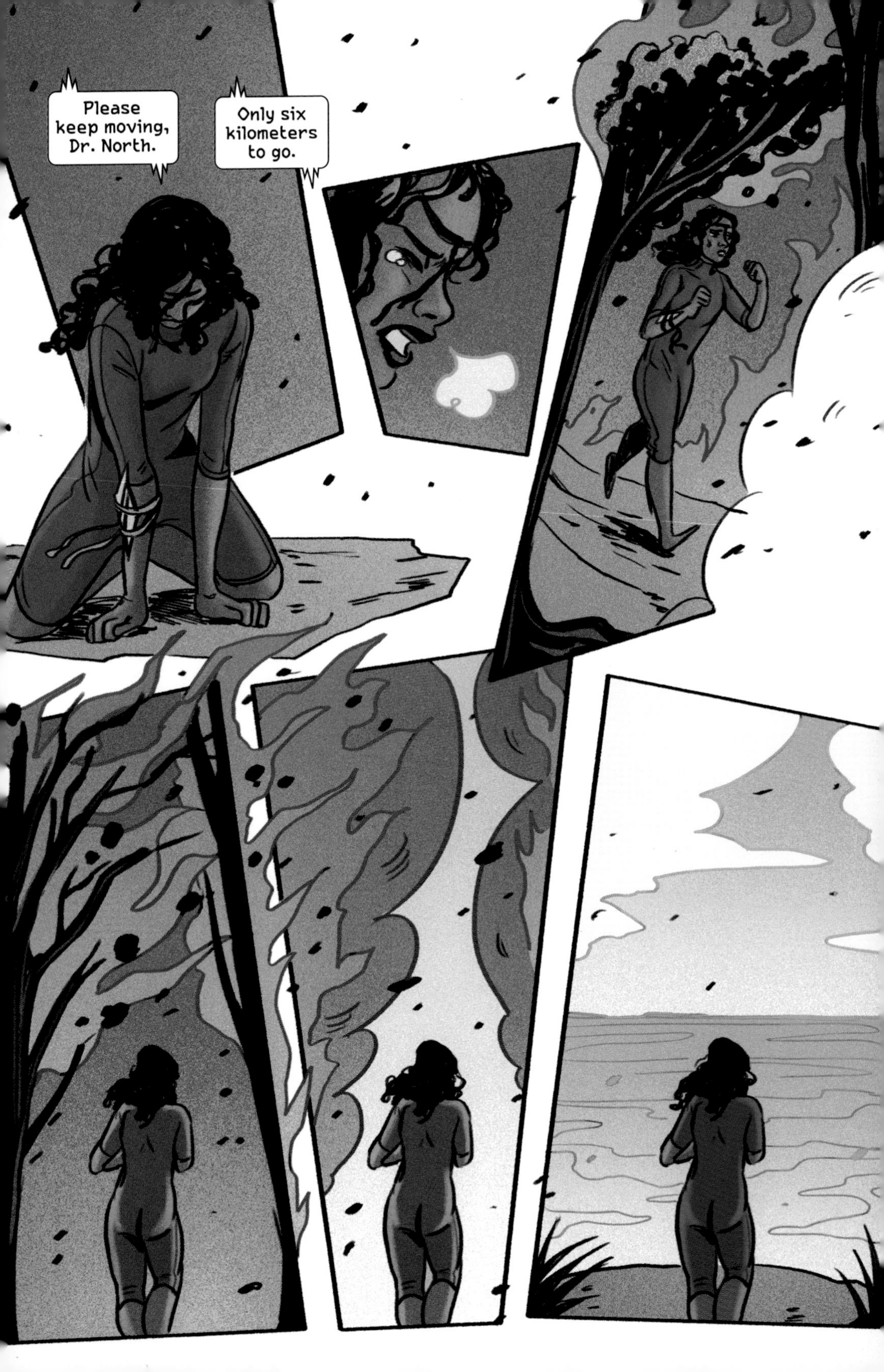
Please keep moving, Dr. North.
Only six kilometers to go.

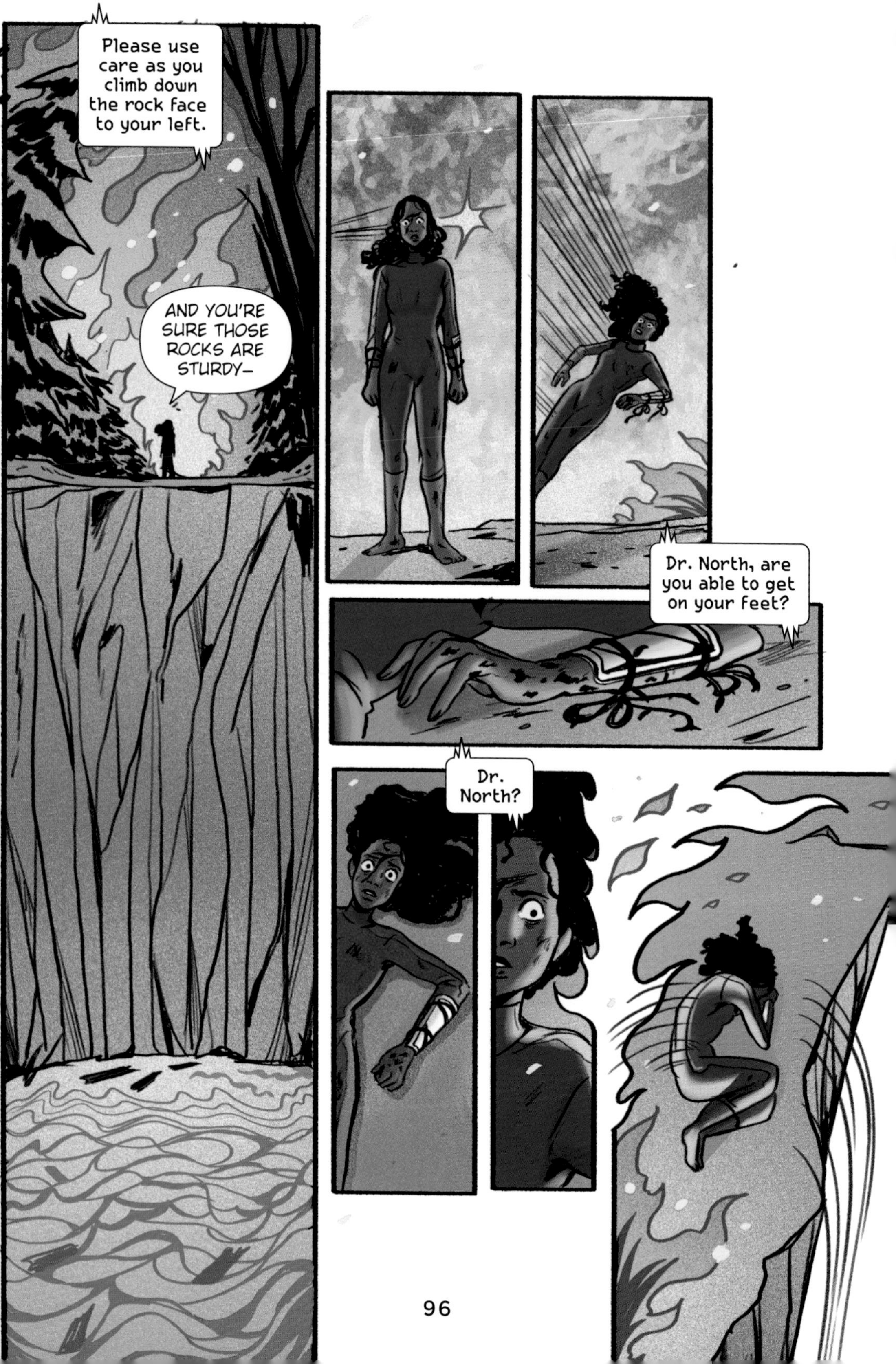
Please use care as you climb down the rock face to your left.
AND YOU'RE SURE THOSE ROCKS ARE STURDY—
Dr. North, are you able to get on your feet?
Dr. North?

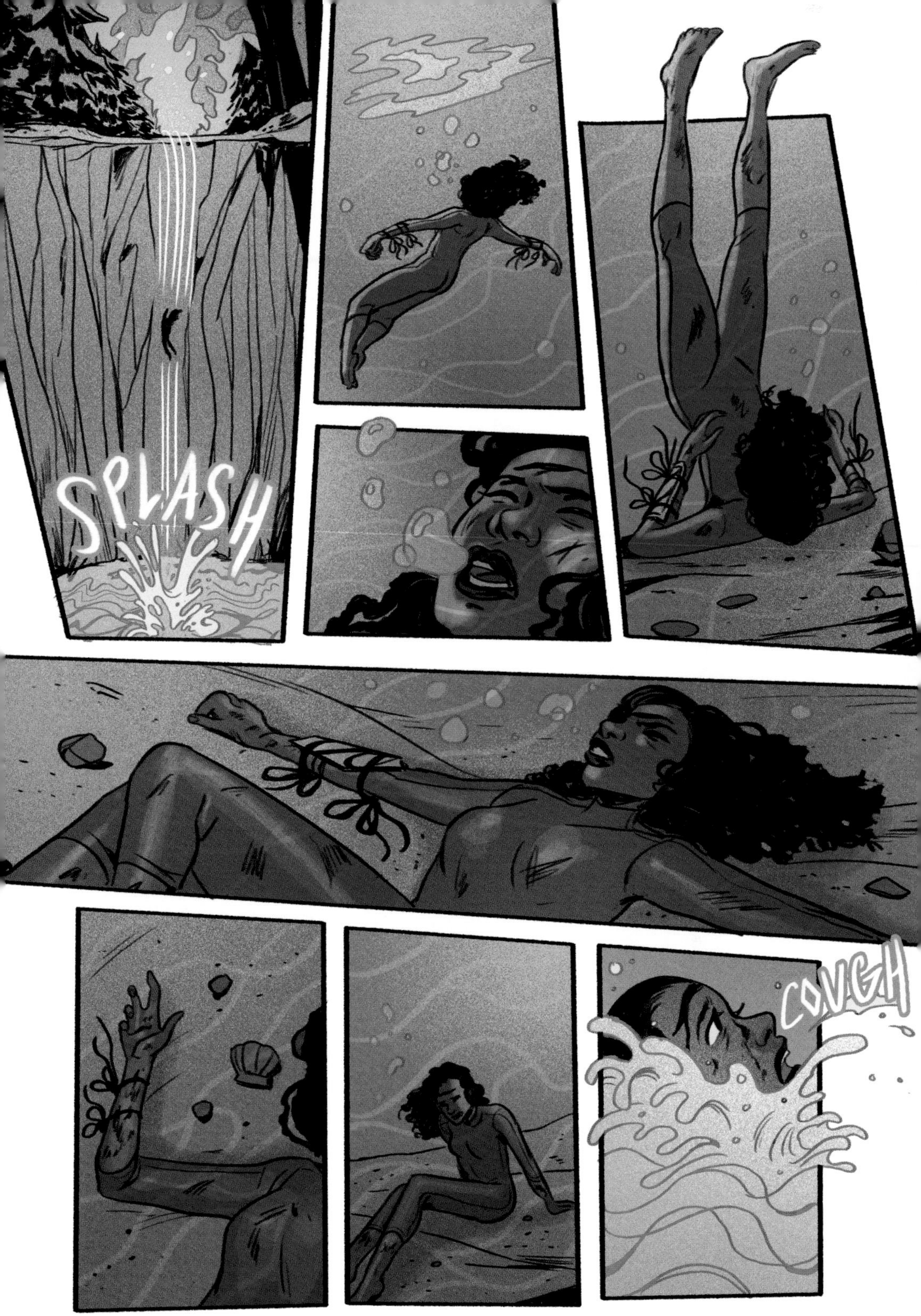
SPLASH
COUGH

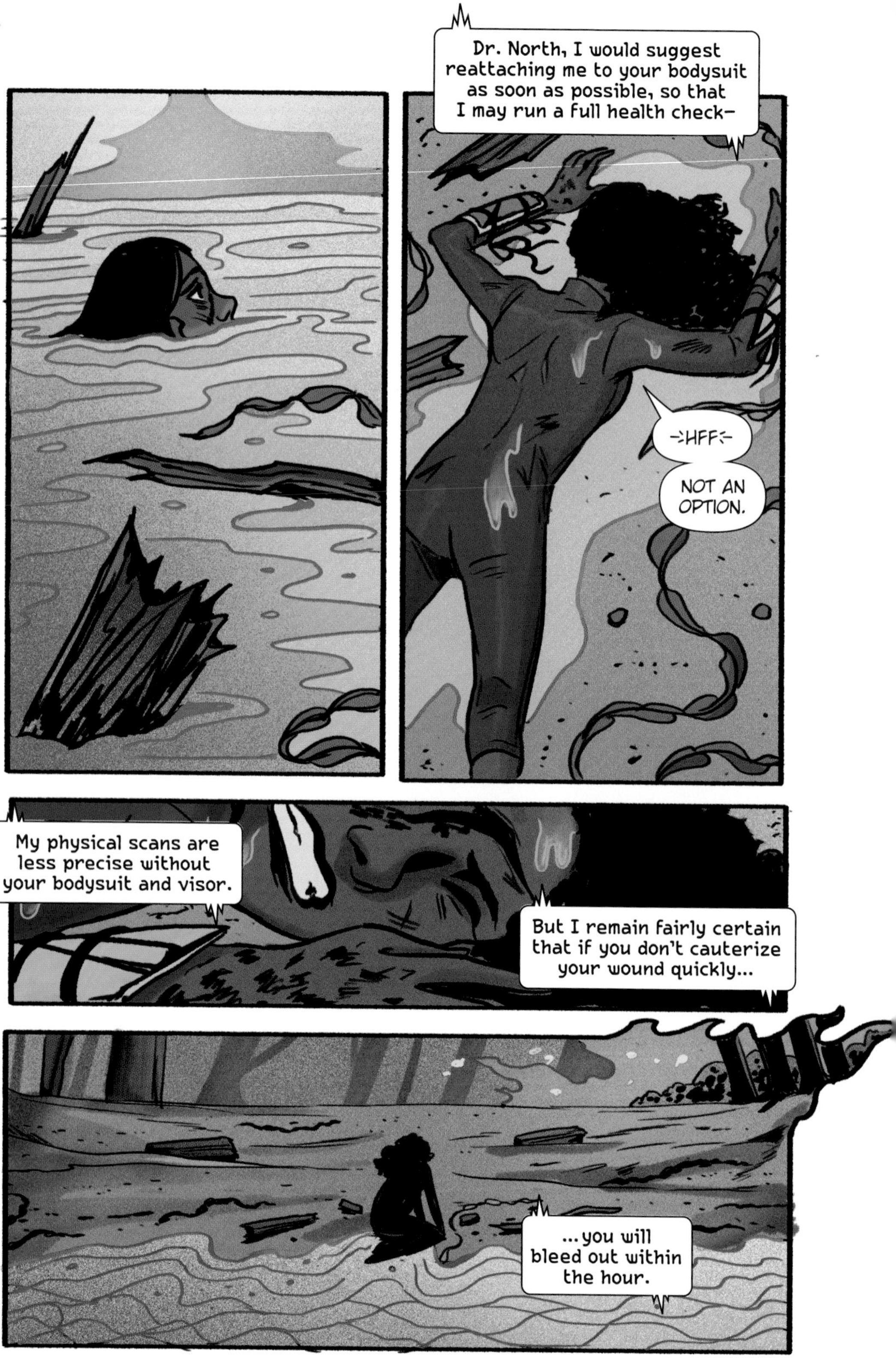
Dr. North, I would suggest reattaching me to your bodysuit as soon as possible, so that I may run a full health check–
HFF
NOT AN OPTION.
My physical scans are less precise without your bodysuit and visor.
But I remain fairly certain that if you don't cauterize your wound quickly...
...you will bleed out within the hour.

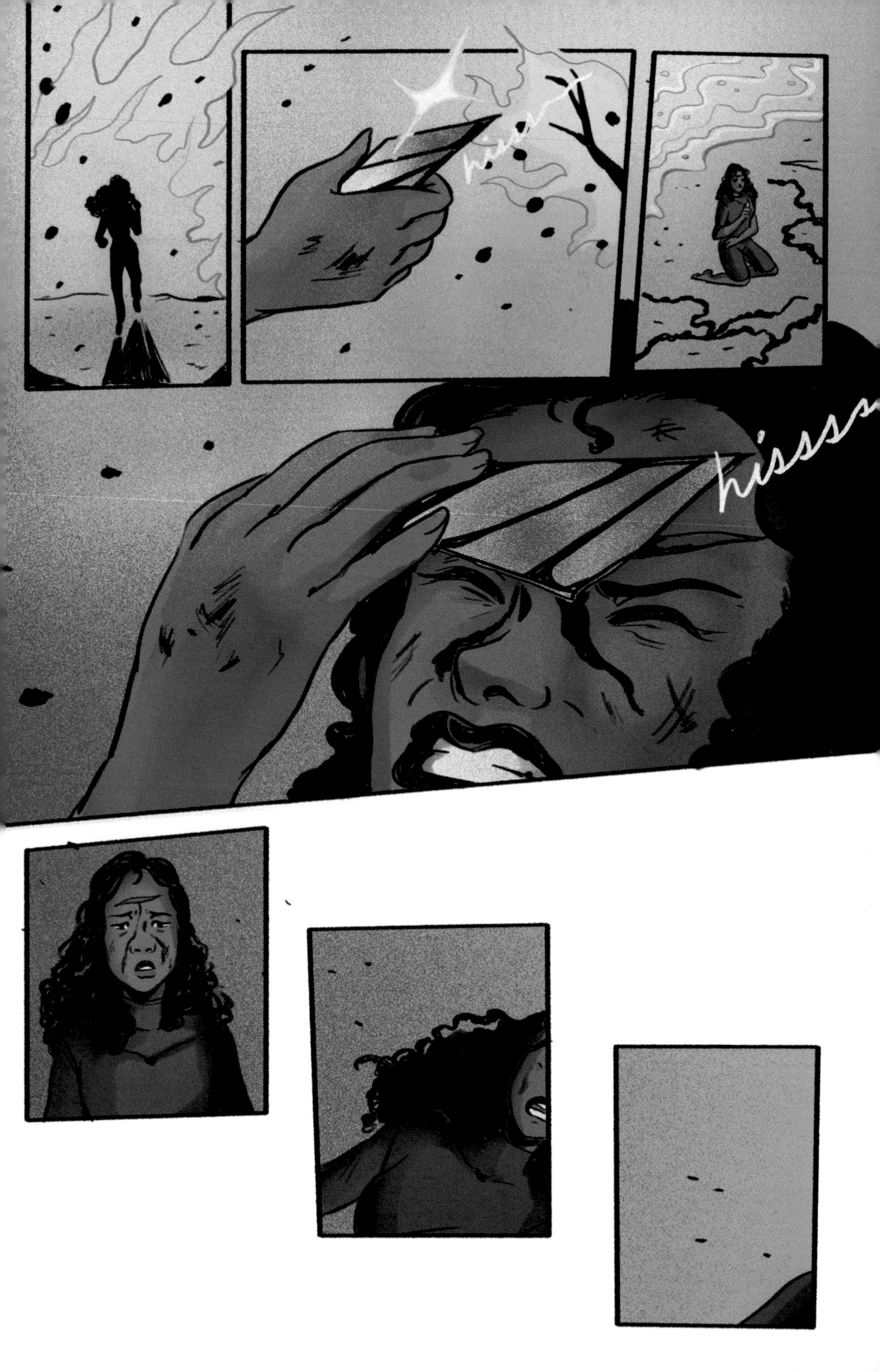

hiss
hissss

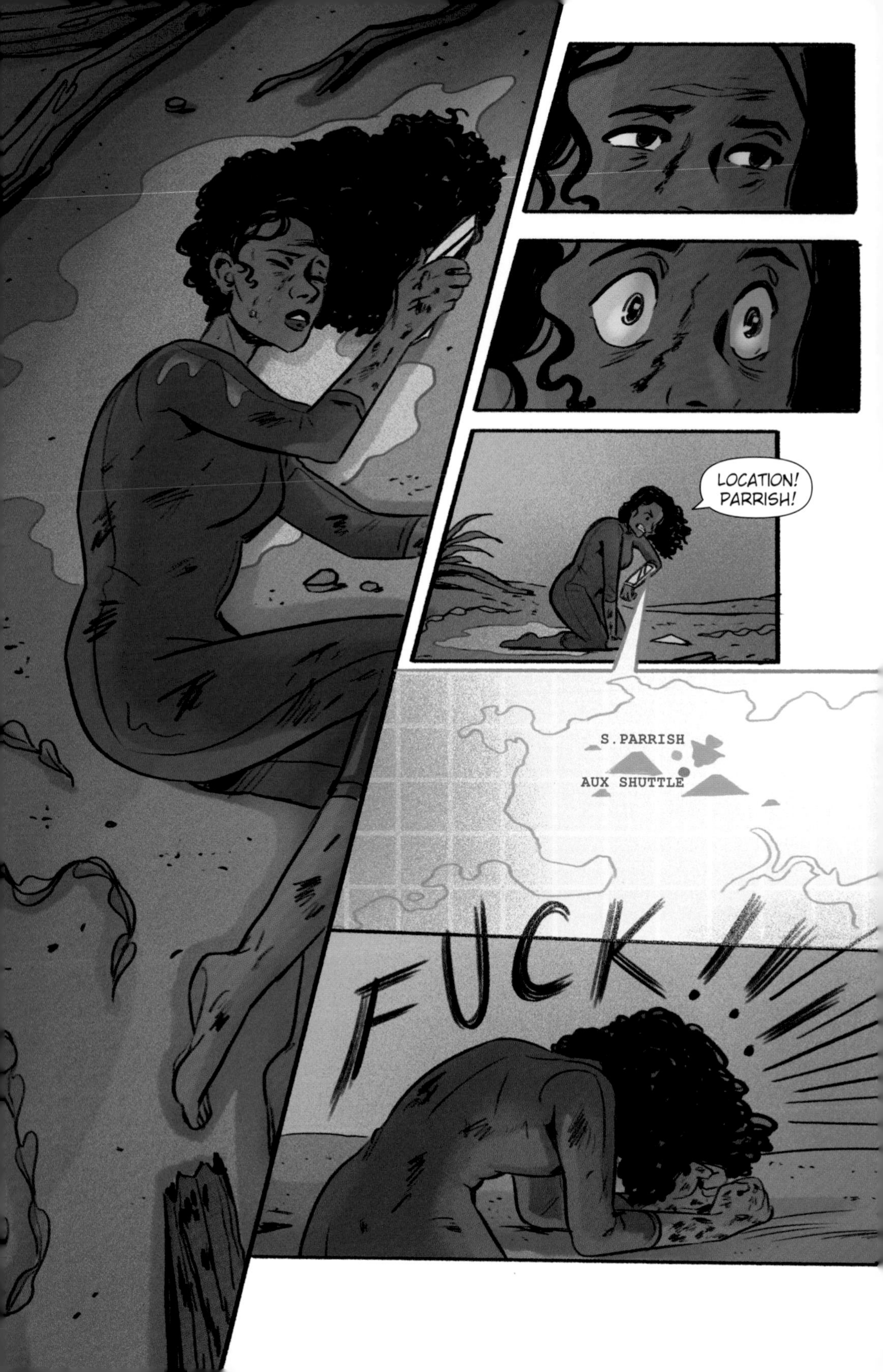
LOCATION!
PARRISH!
S.PARRISH
AUX SHUTTLE
FUCK!!!

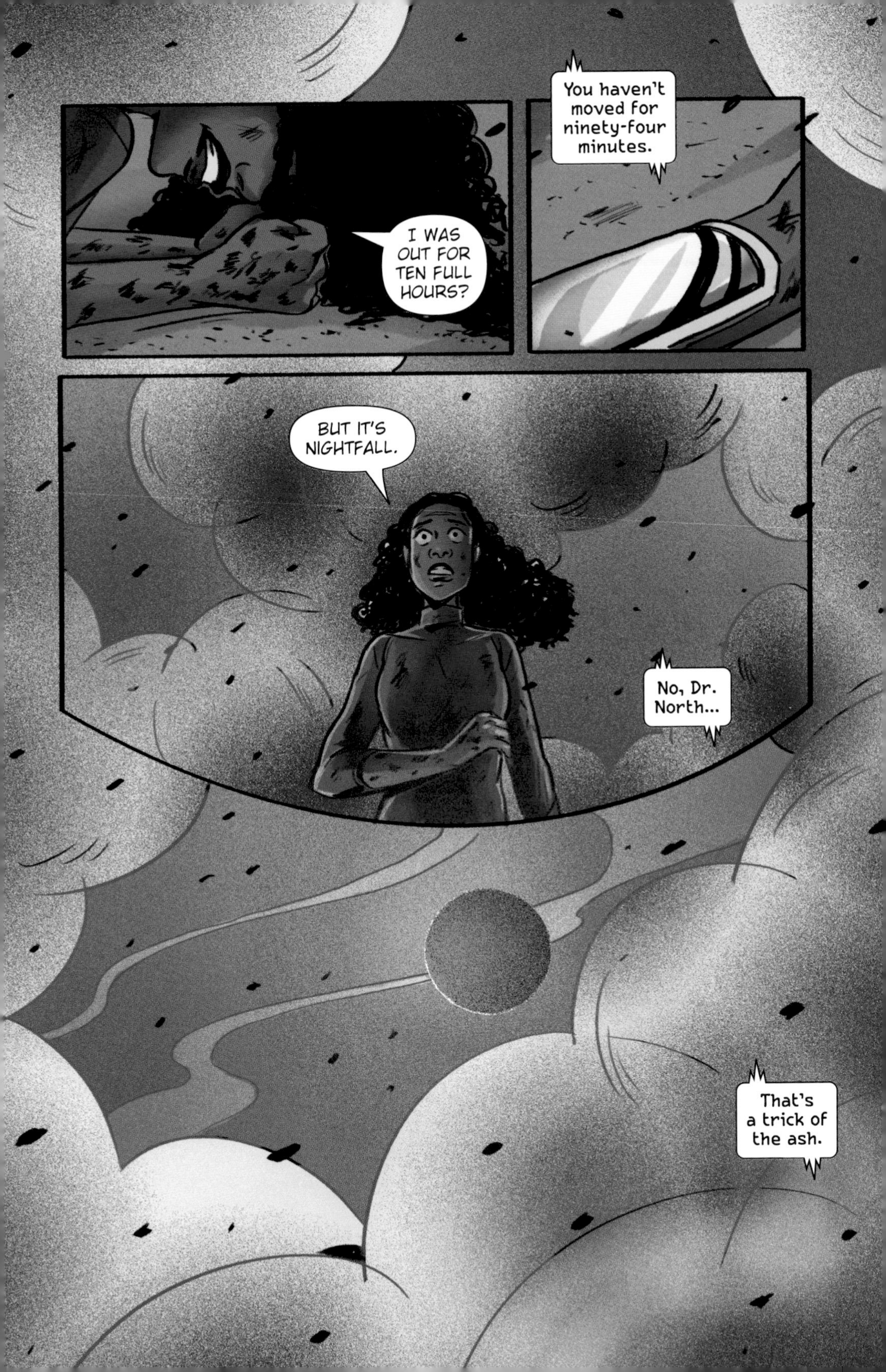
I WAS OUT FOR TEN FULL HOURS?
You haven't moved for ninety-four minutes.
BUT IT'S NIGHTFALL.
No, Dr. North...
That's a trick of the ash.

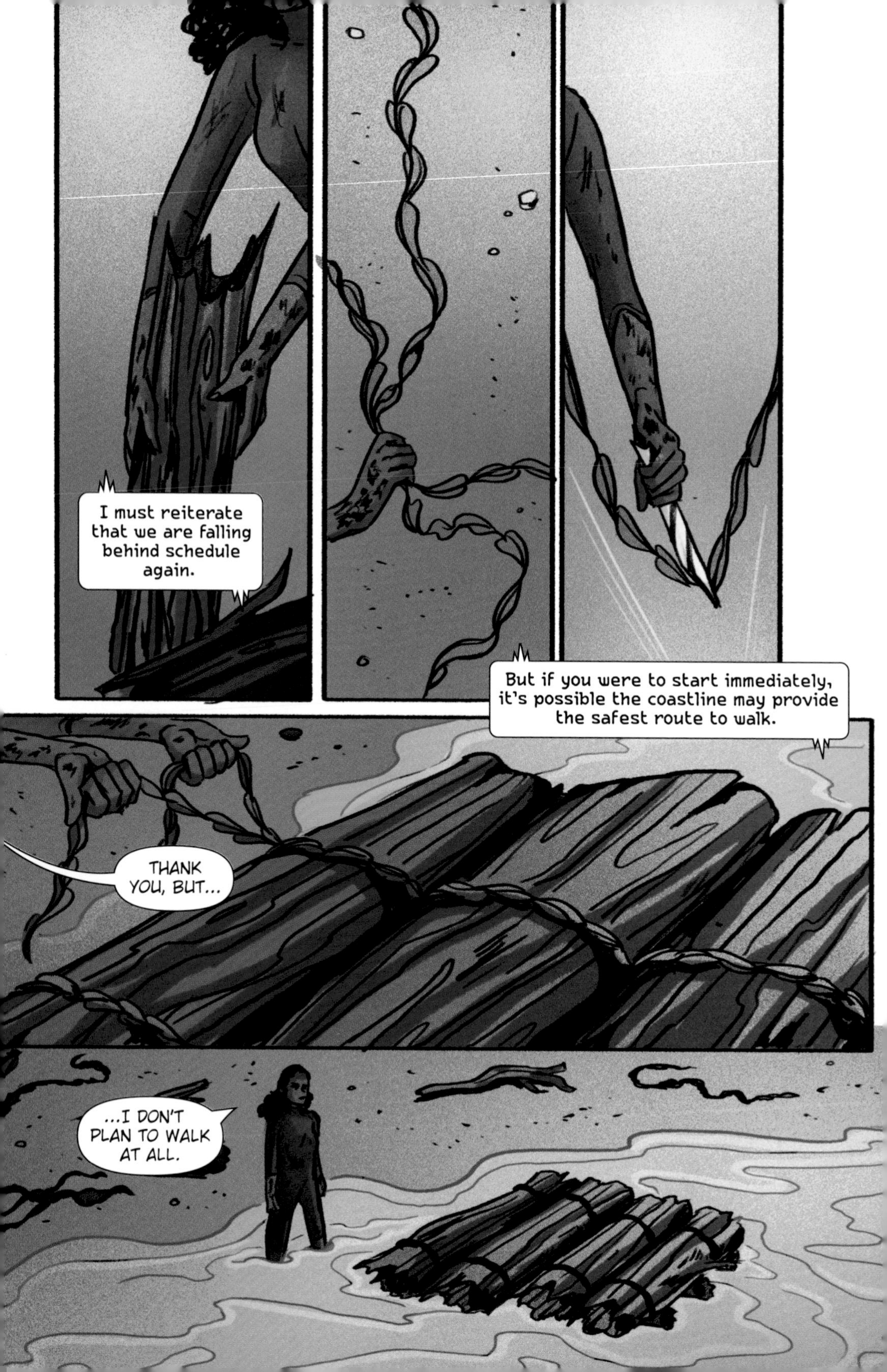

I must reiterate that we are falling behind schedule again.
But if you were to start immediately, it's possible the coastline may provide the safest route to walk.
THANK YOU, BUT...
...I DON'T PLAN TO WALK AT ALL.

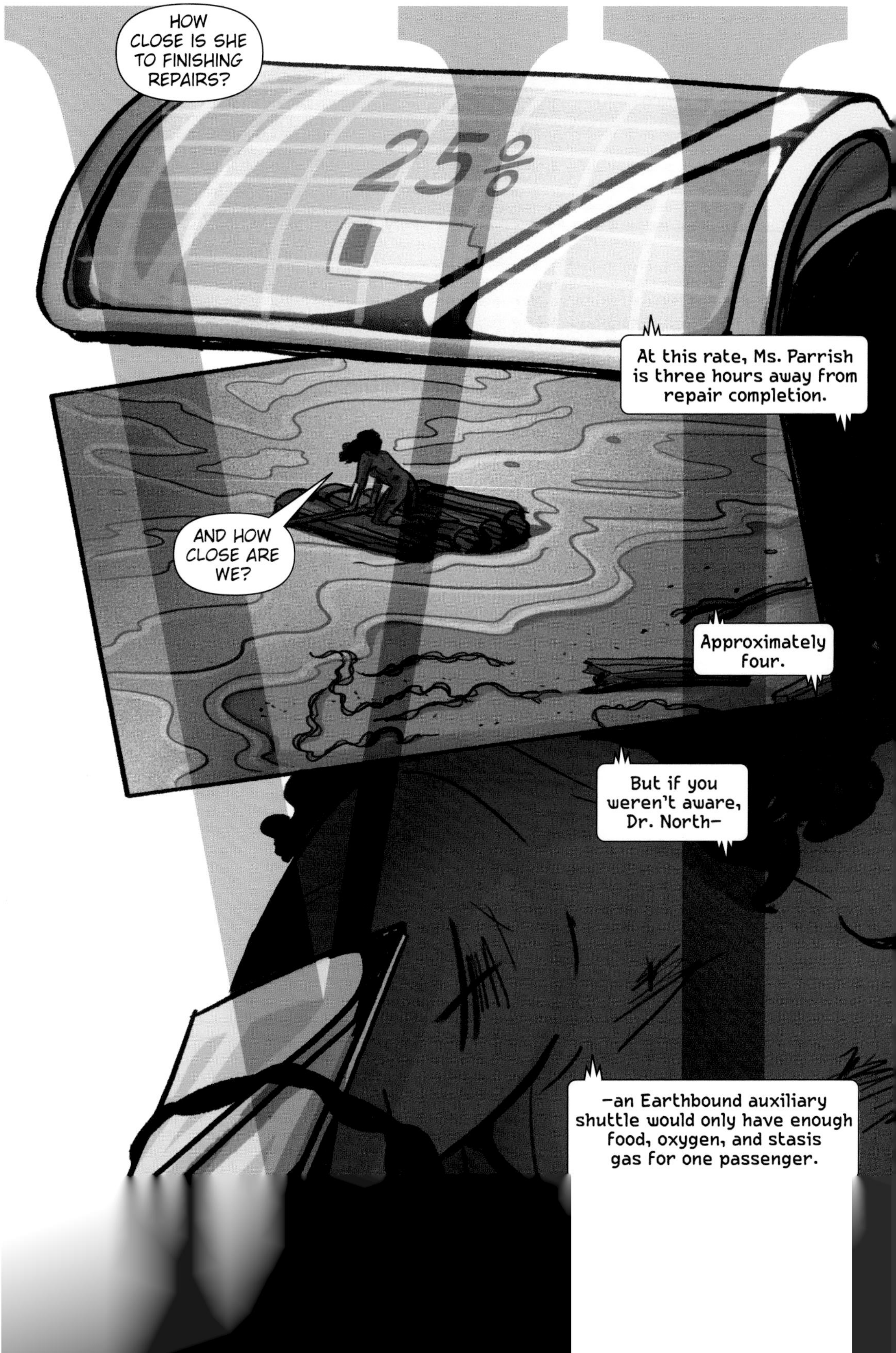
HOW CLOSE IS SHE TO FINISHING REPAIRS?
25%
At this rate, Ms. Parrish is three hours away from repair completion.
AND HOW CLOSE ARE WE?
Approximately four.
But if you weren't aware, Dr. North—
—an Earthbound auxiliary shuttle would only have enough food, oxygen, and stasis gas for one passenger.

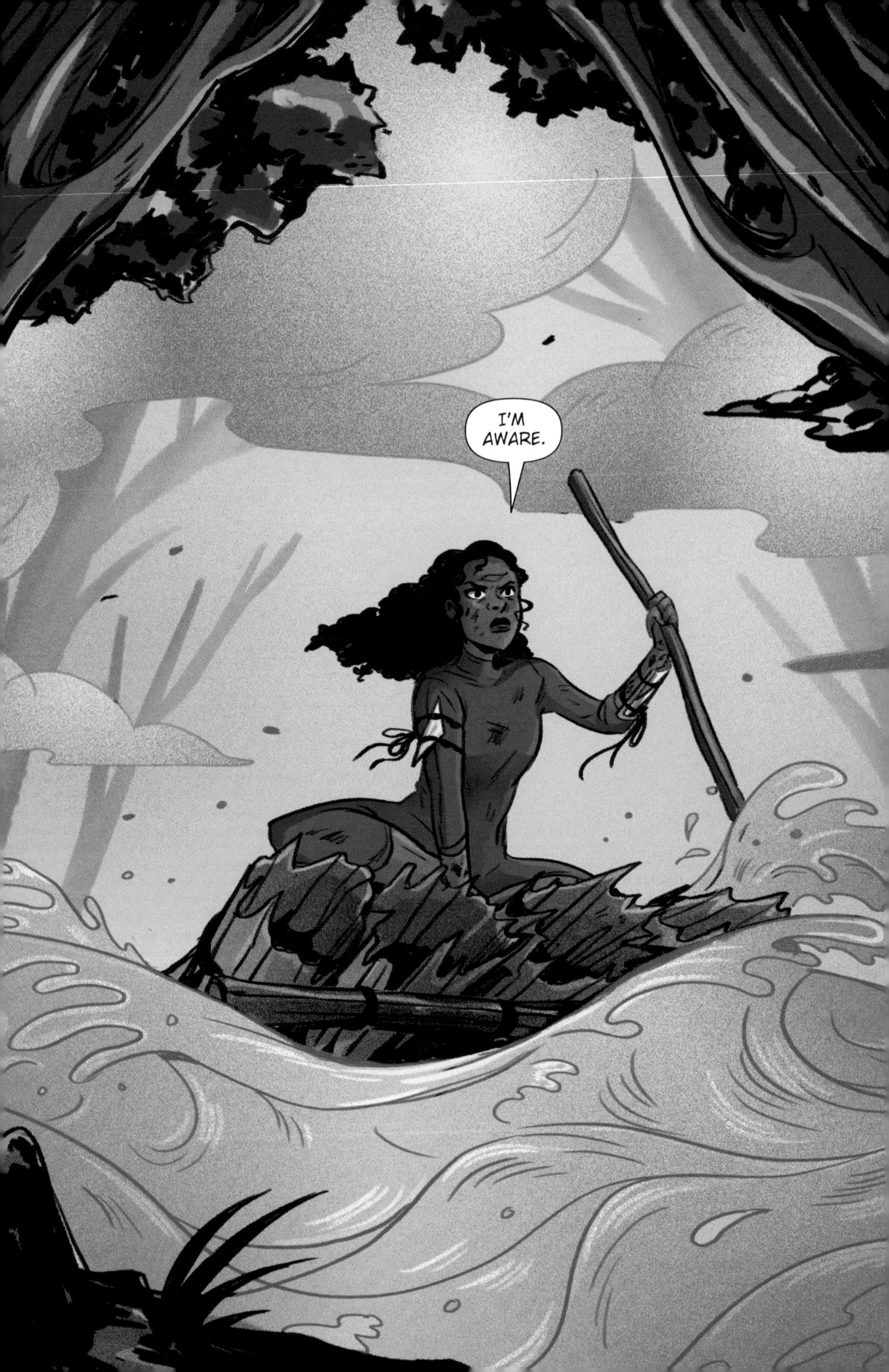
I'M AWARE.

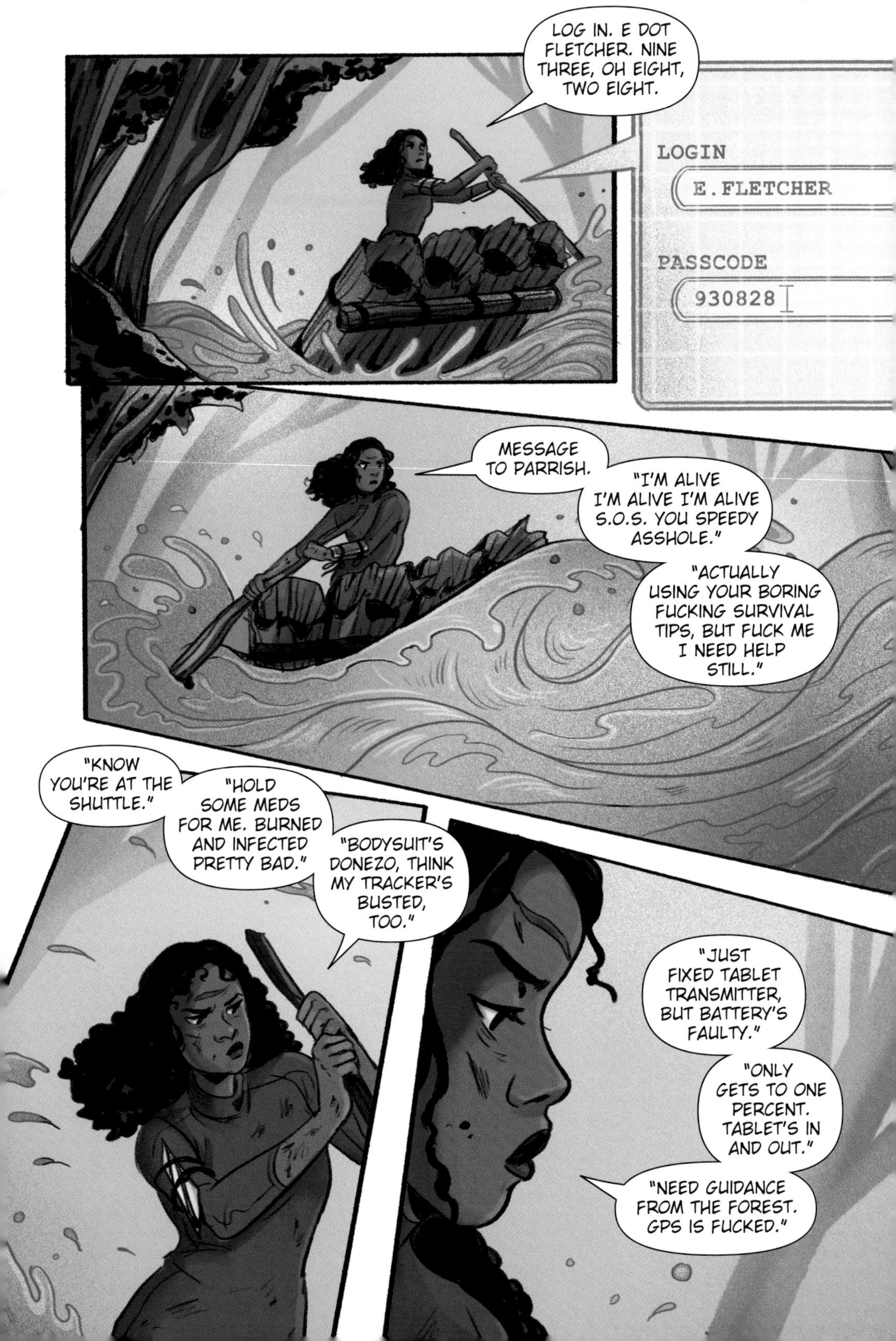
LOG IN. E DOT FLETCHER. NINE THREE, OH EIGHT, TWO EIGHT.
LOGIN
E.FLETCHER
PASSCODE
930828
MESSAGE TO PARRISH.
"I'M ALIVE I'M ALIVE I'M ALIVE S.O.S. YOU SPEEDY ASSHOLE."
"ACTUALLY USING YOUR BORING FUCKING SURVIVAL TIPS, BUT FUCK ME I NEED HELP STILL."
"KNOW YOU'RE AT THE SHUTTLE."
"HOLD SOME MEDS FOR ME. BURNED AND INFECTED PRETTY BAD."
"BODYSUIT'S DONEZO, THINK MY TRACKER'S BUSTED, TOO."
"JUST FIXED TABLET TRANSMITTER, BUT BATTERY'S FAULTY."
"ONLY GETS TO ONE PERCENT. TABLET'S IN AND OUT."
"NEED GUIDANCE FROM THE FOREST. GPS IS FUCKED."

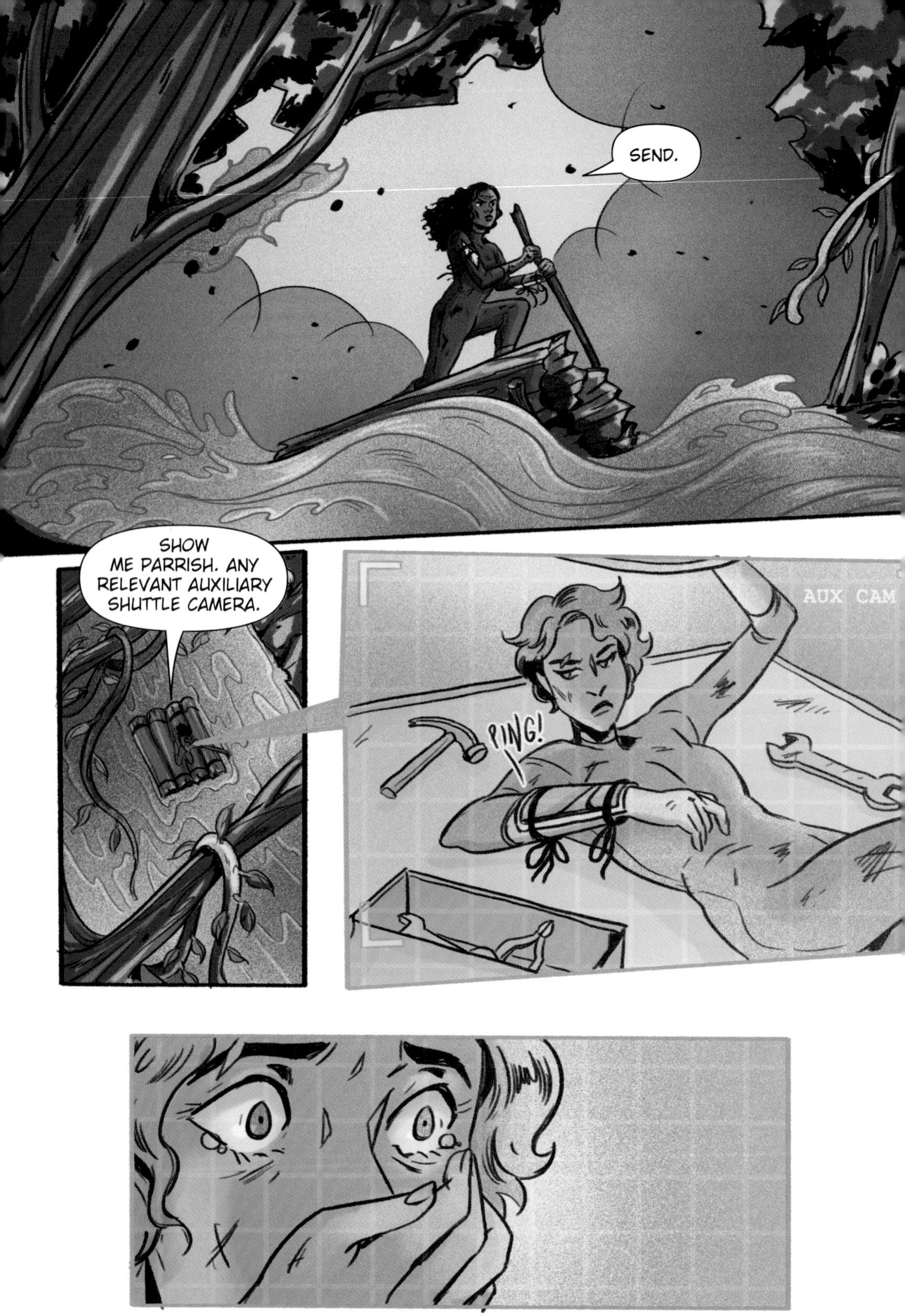
SEND.
SHOW ME PARRISH. ANY RELEVANT AUXILIARY SHUTTLE CAMERA.
AUX CAM
PING!

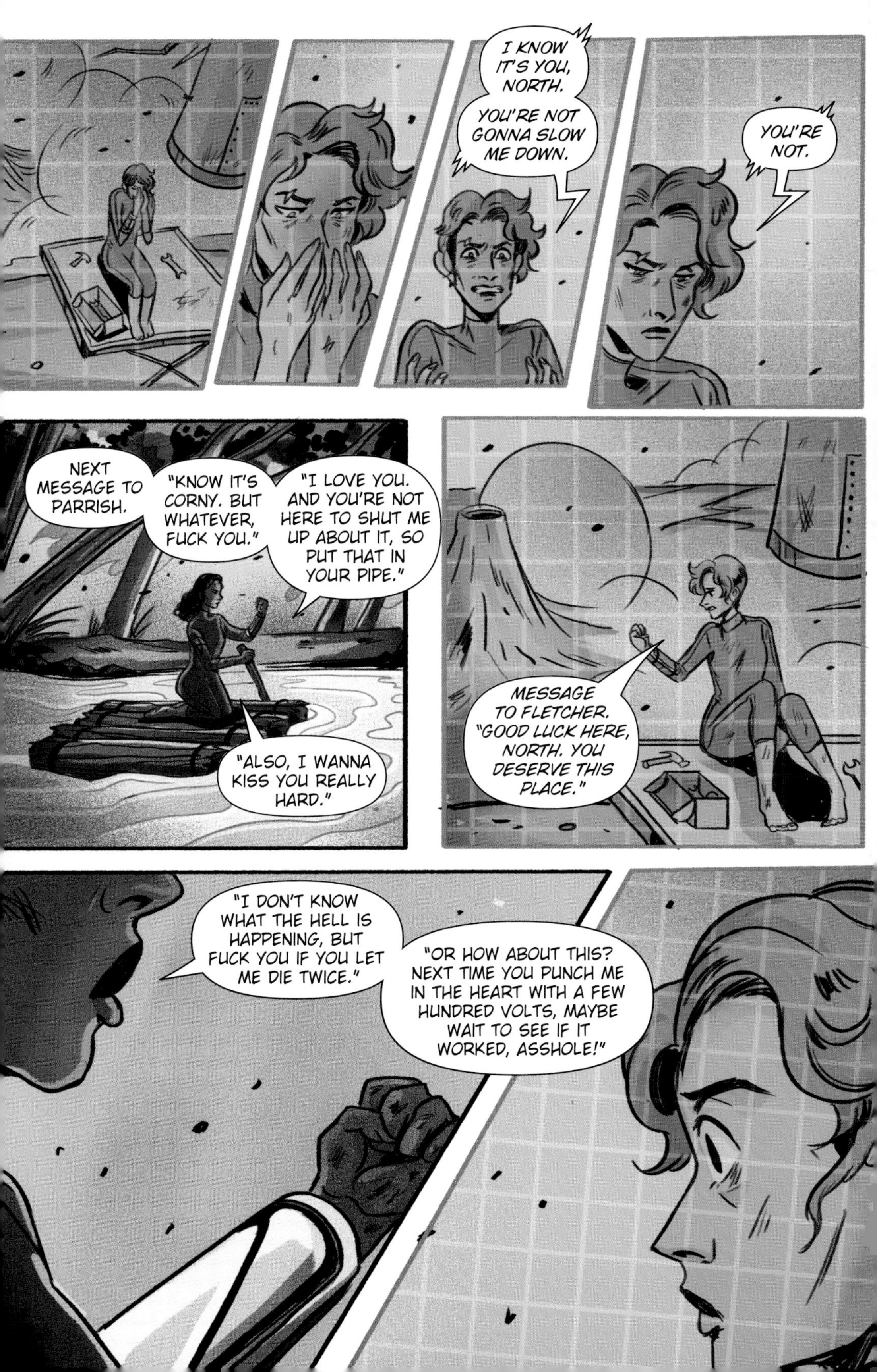
I KNOW IT'S YOU, NORTH.
YOU'RE NOT GONNA SLOW ME DOWN.
YOU'RE NOT.
NEXT MESSAGE TO PARRISH.
"KNOW IT'S CORNY. BUT WHATEVER, FUCK YOU."
"I LOVE YOU. AND YOU'RE NOT HERE TO SHUT ME UP ABOUT IT, SO PUT THAT IN YOUR PIPE."
"ALSO, I WANNA KISS YOU REALLY HARD."
MESSAGE TO FLETCHER. "GOOD LUCK HERE, NORTH. YOU DESERVE THIS PLACE."
"I DON'T KNOW WHAT THE HELL IS HAPPENING, BUT FUCK YOU IF YOU LET ME DIE TWICE."
"OR HOW ABOUT THIS? NEXT TIME YOU PUNCH ME IN THE HEART WITH A FEW HUNDRED VOLTS, MAYBE WAIT TO SEE IF IT WORKED, ASSHOLE!"

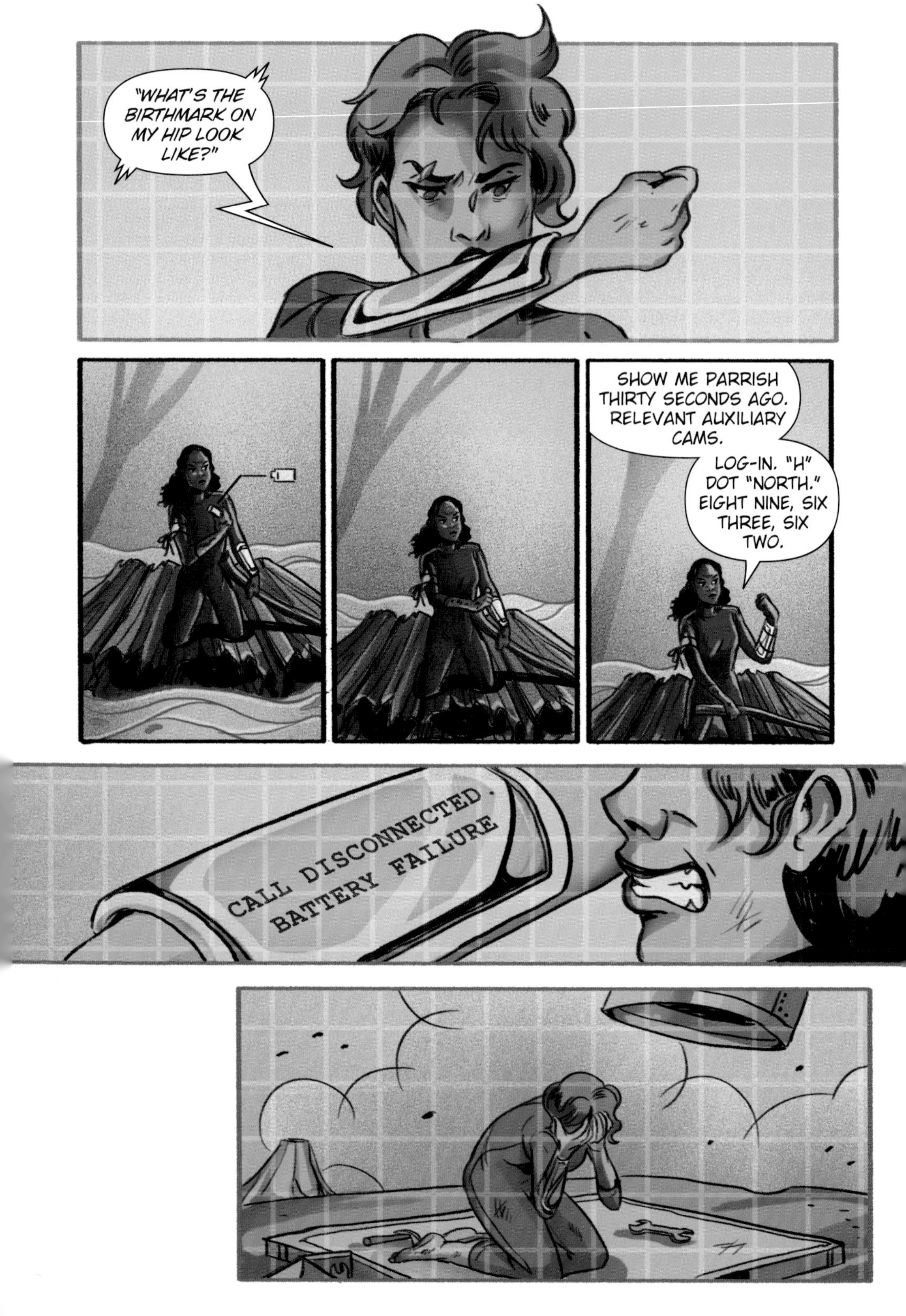
"WHAT'S THE BIRTHMARK ON MY HIP LOOK LIKE?"
SHOW ME PARRISH THIRTY SECONDS AGO. RELEVANT AUXILIARY CAMS.
LOG-IN. "H" DOT "NORTH." EIGHT NINE, SIX THREE, SIX TWO.
CALL DISCONNECTED.
BATTERY FAILURE

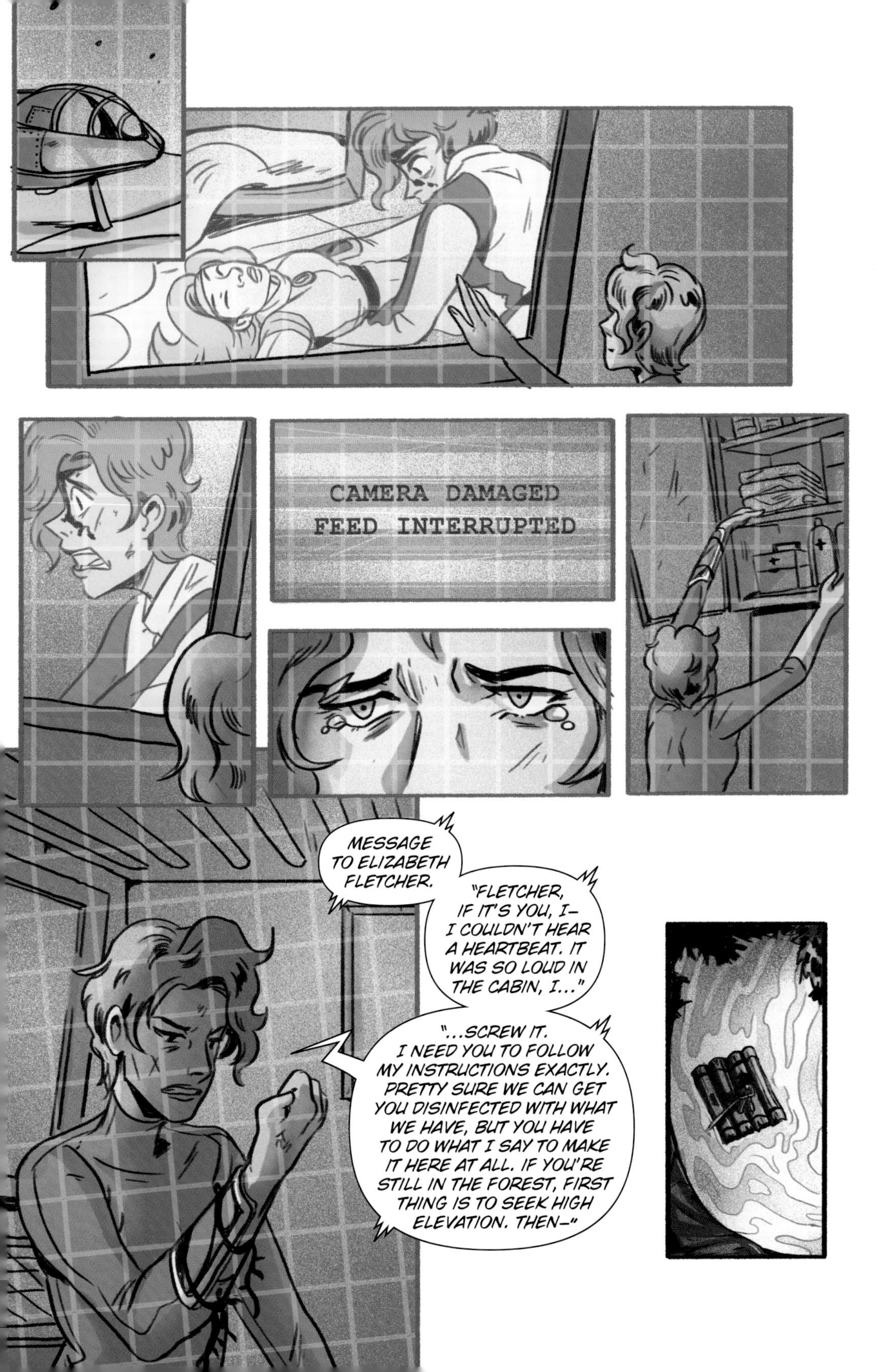
CAMERA DAMAGED
FEED INTERRUPTED
MESSAGE TO ELIZABETH FLETCHER.
"FLETCHER, IF IT'S YOU, I— I COULDN'T HEAR A HEARTBEAT. IT WAS SO LOUD IN THE CABIN, I..."
"...SCREW IT. I NEED YOU TO FOLLOW MY INSTRUCTIONS EXACTLY. PRETTY SURE WE CAN GET YOU DISINFECTED WITH WHAT WE HAVE, BUT YOU HAVE TO DO WHAT I SAY TO MAKE IT HERE AT ALL. IF YOU'RE STILL IN THE FOREST, FIRST THING IS TO SEEK HIGH ELEVATION. THEN—"

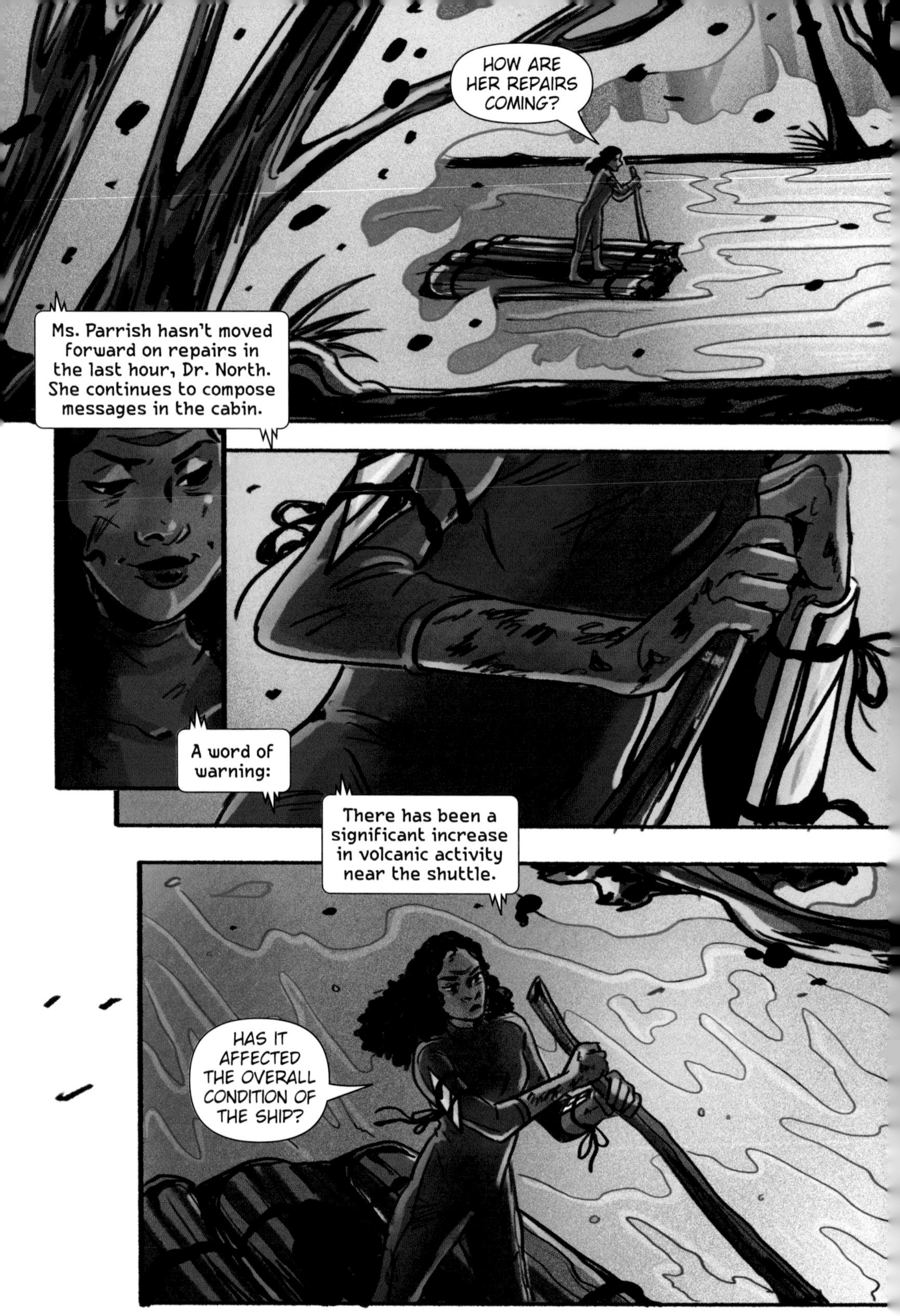
HOW ARE HER REPAIRS COMING?
Ms. Parrish hasn't moved forward on repairs in the last hour, Dr. North. She continues to compose messages in the cabin.
A word of warning:
There has been a significant increase in volcanic activity near the shuttle.
HAS IT AFFECTED THE OVERALL CONDITION OF THE SHIP?

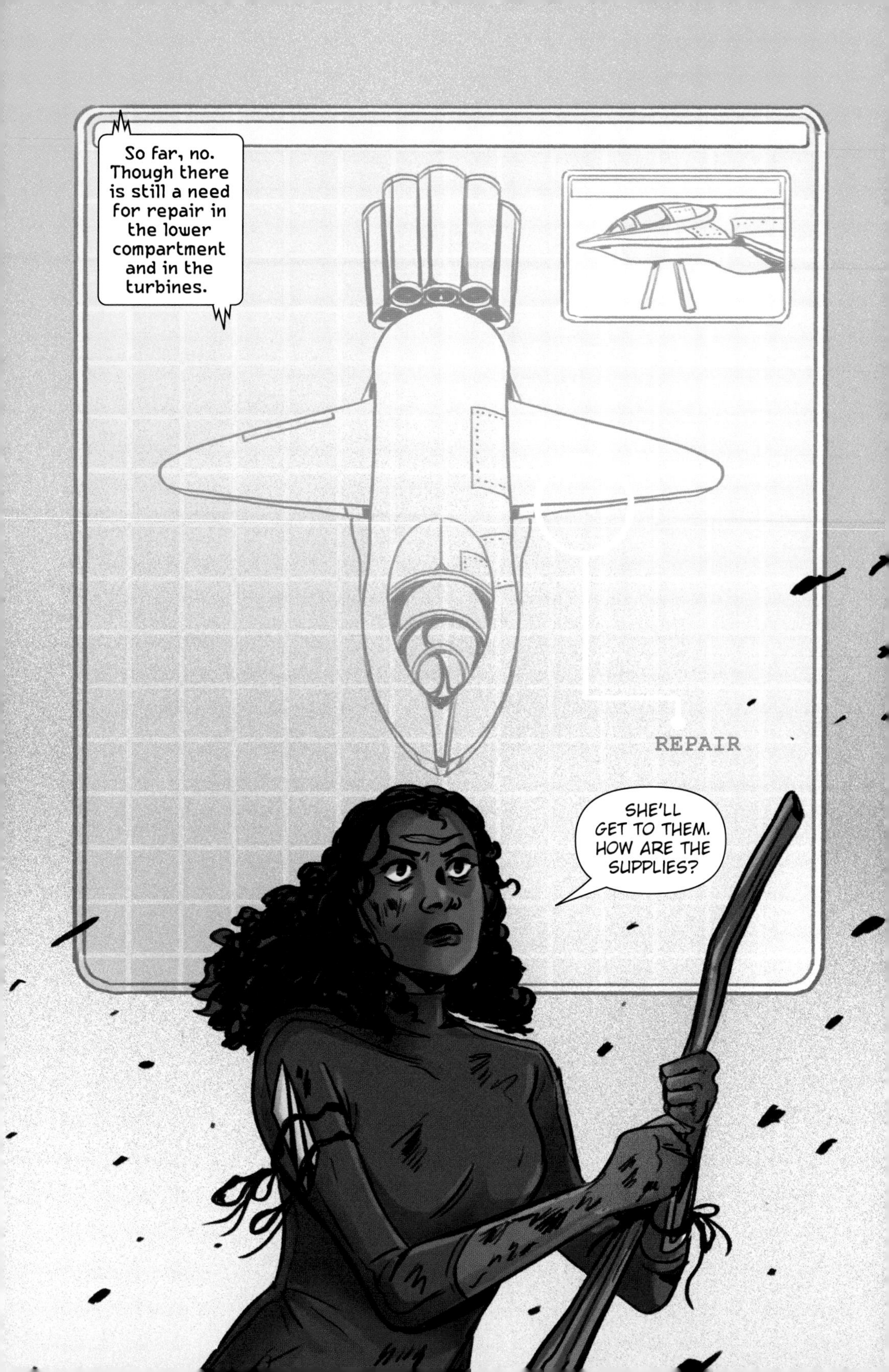
So far, no. Though there is still a need for repair in the lower compartment and in the turbines.
REPAIR
SHE'LL GET TO THEM. HOW ARE THE SUPPLIES?

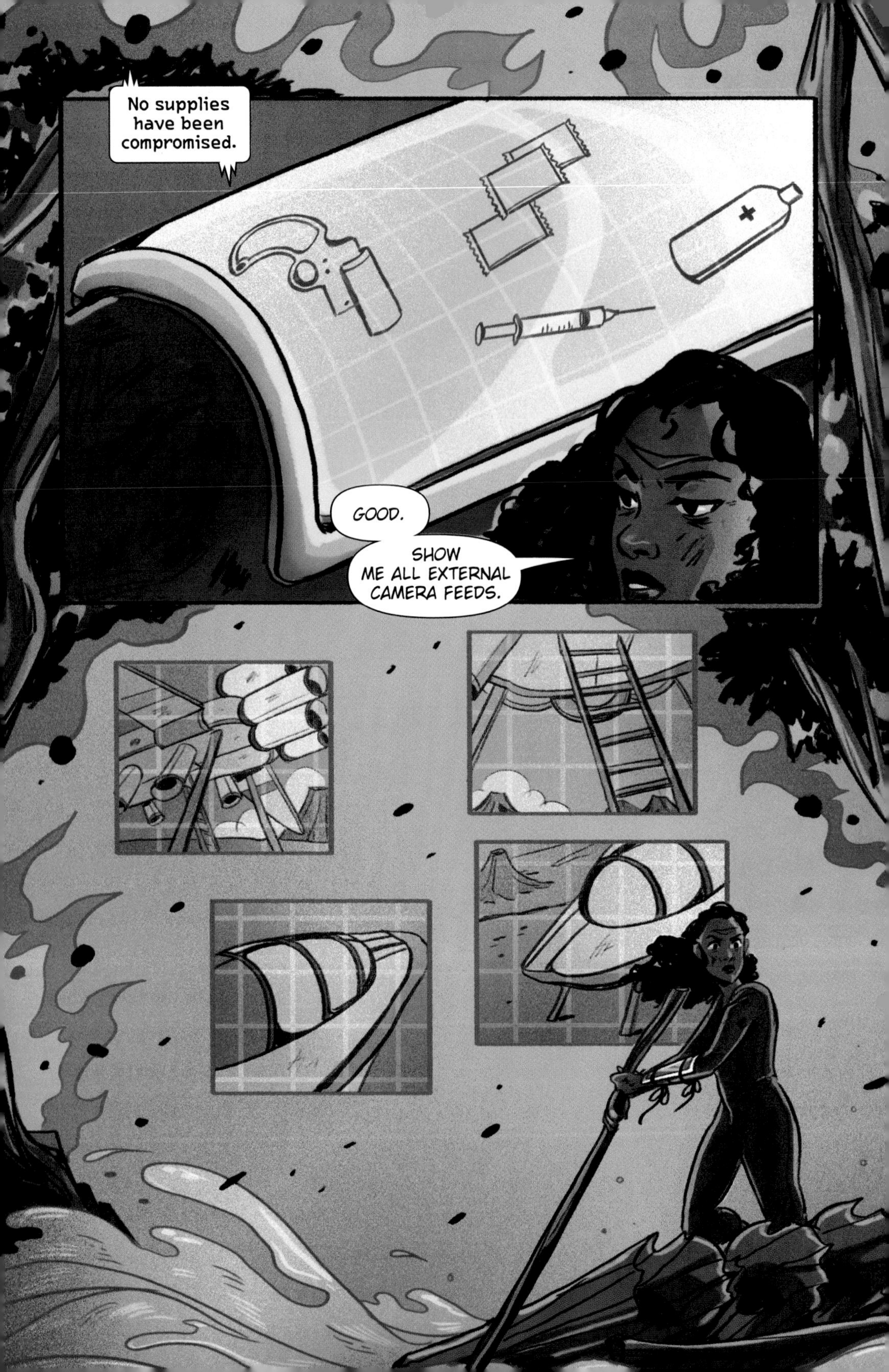
No supplies have been compromised.
GOOD.
SHOW ME ALL EXTERNAL CAMERA FEEDS.

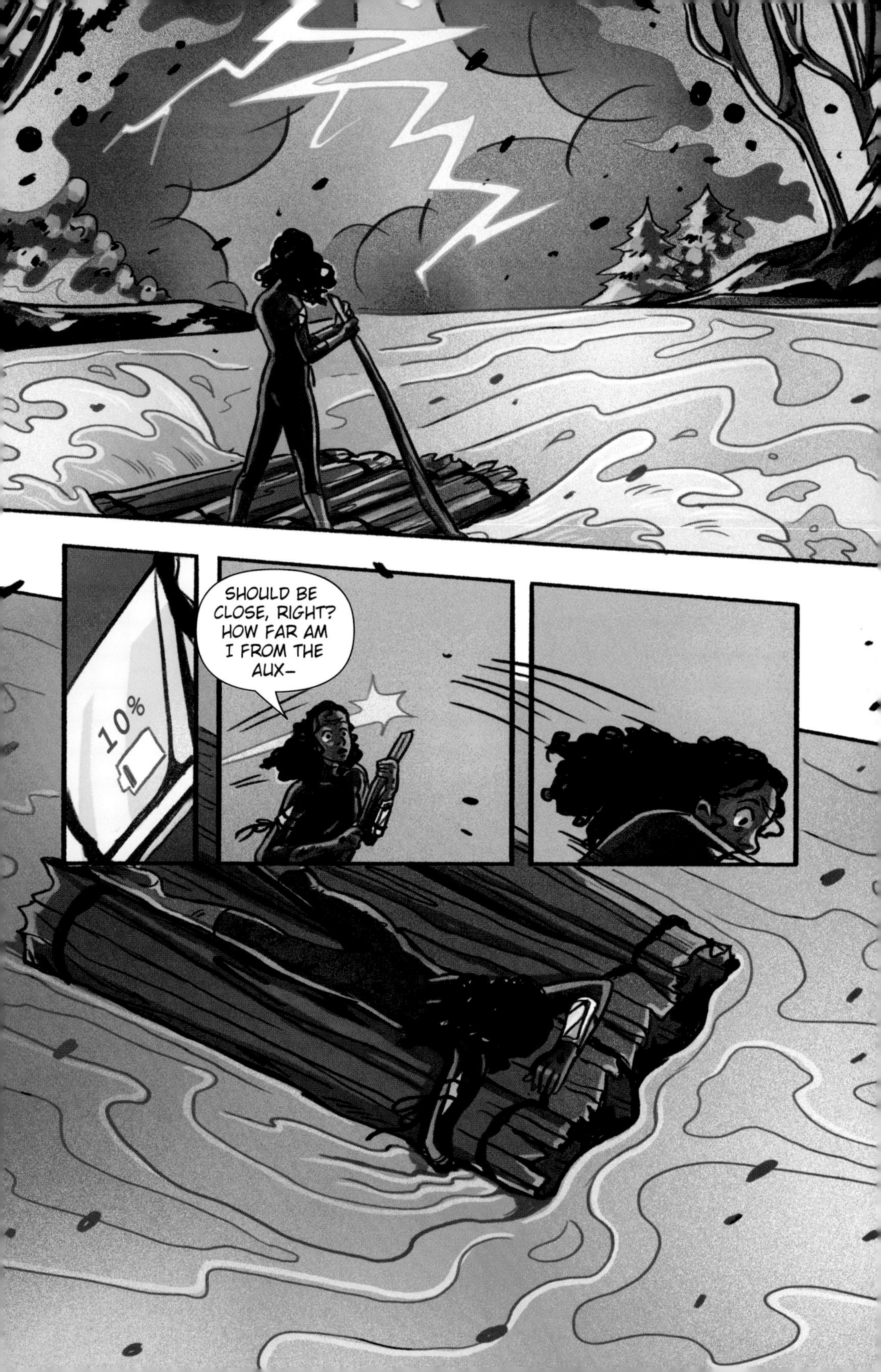
10%
SHOULD BE CLOSE, RIGHT? HOW FAR AM I FROM THE AUX—

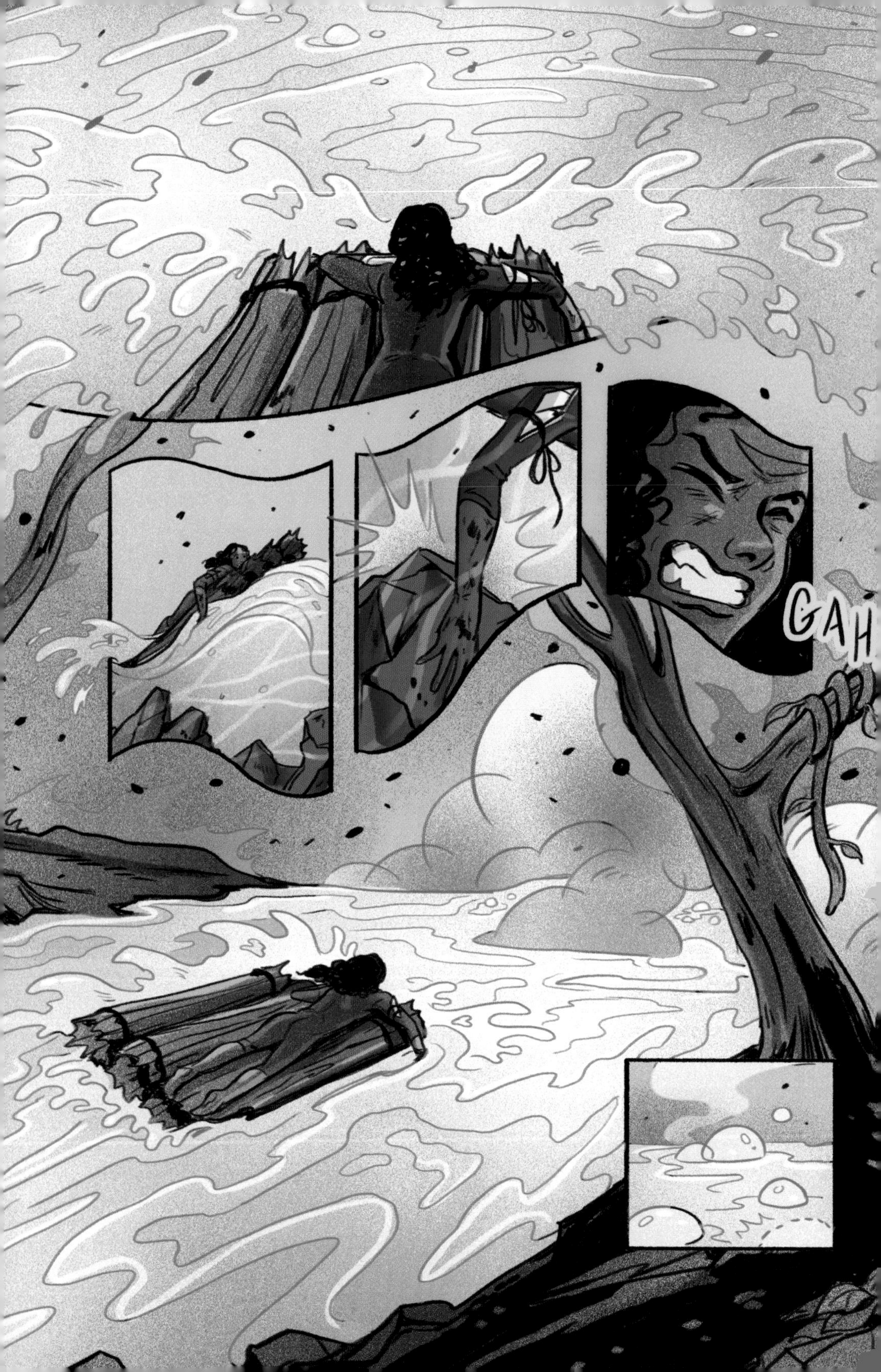
GAH

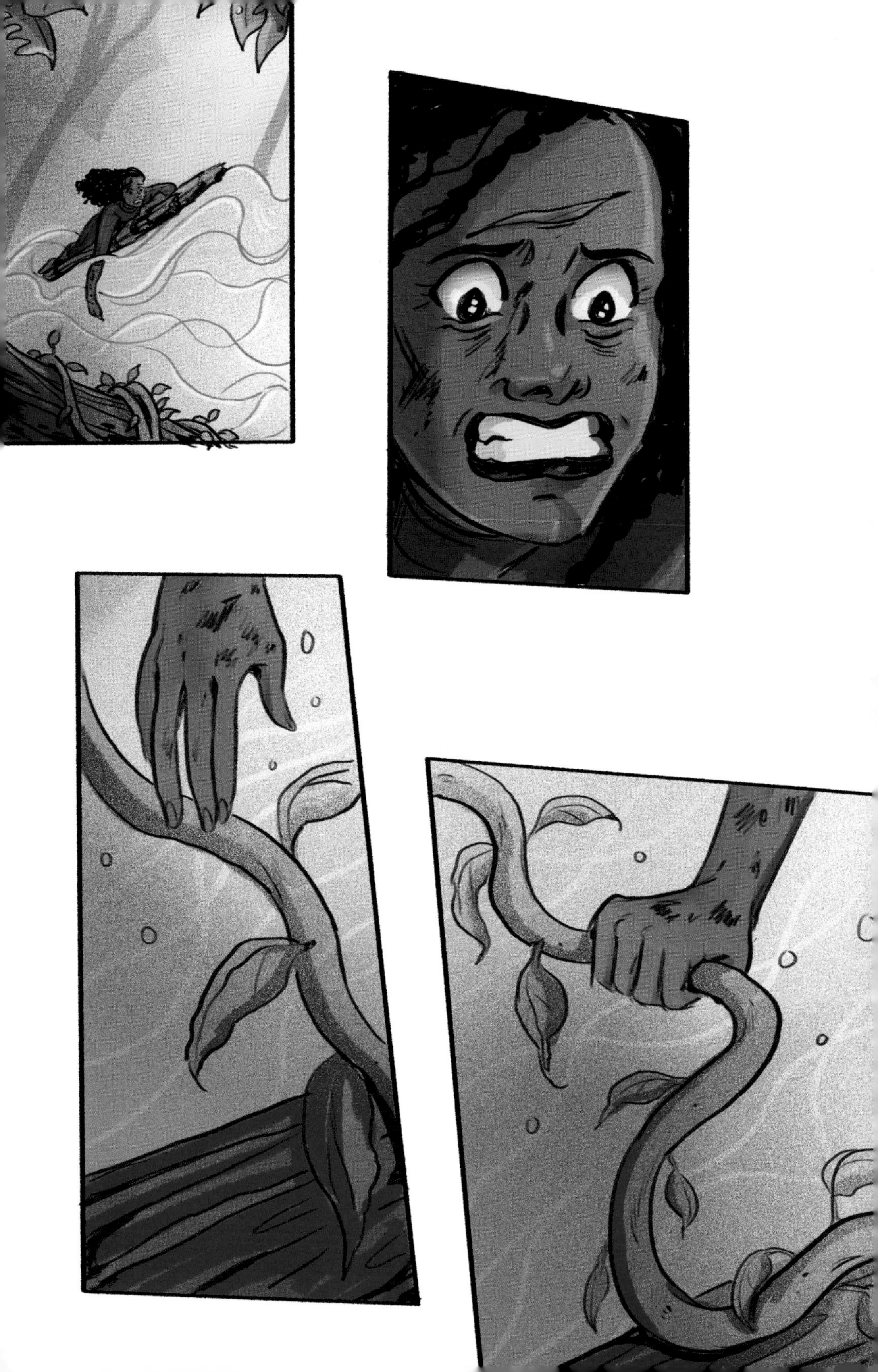

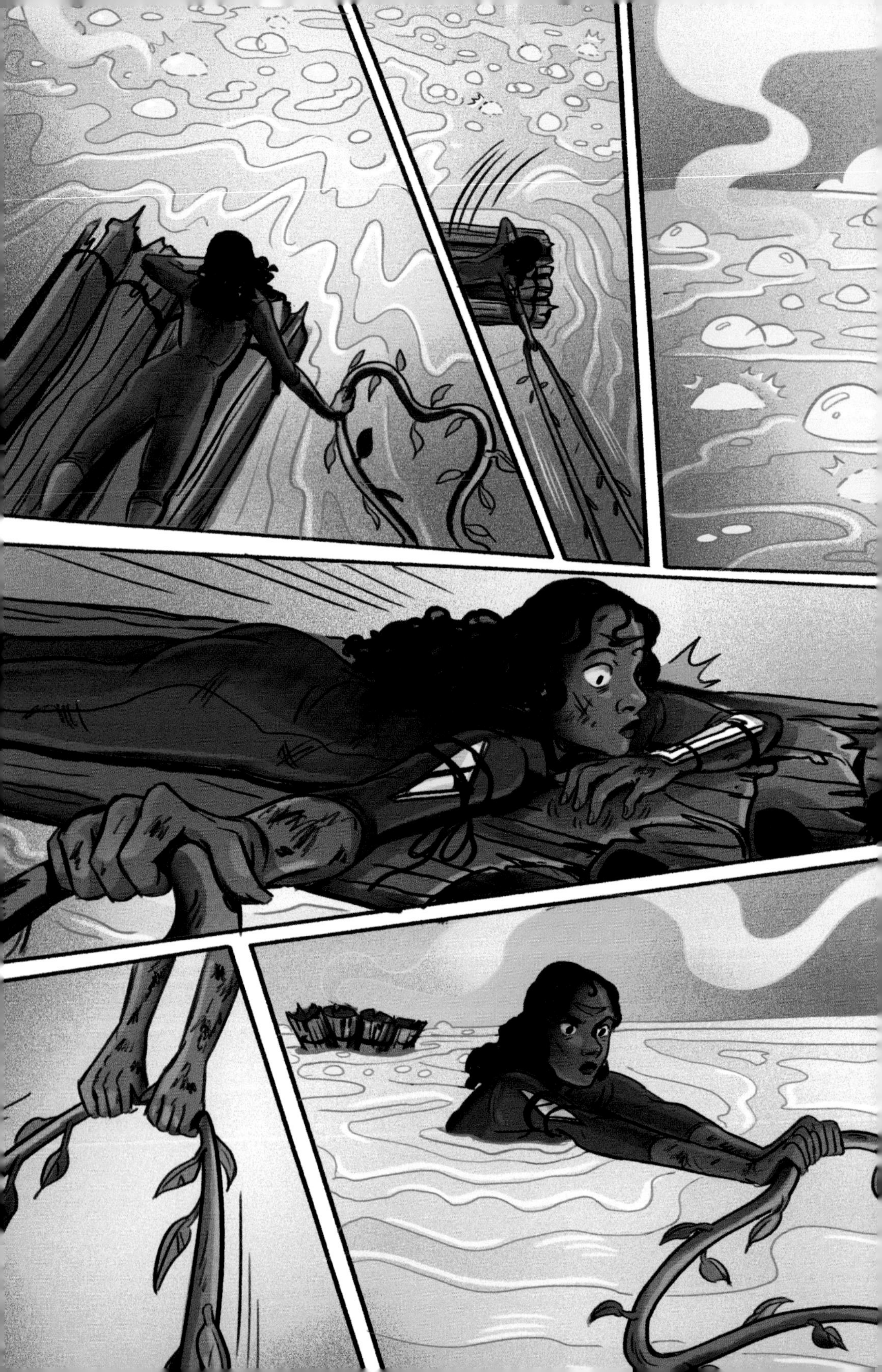

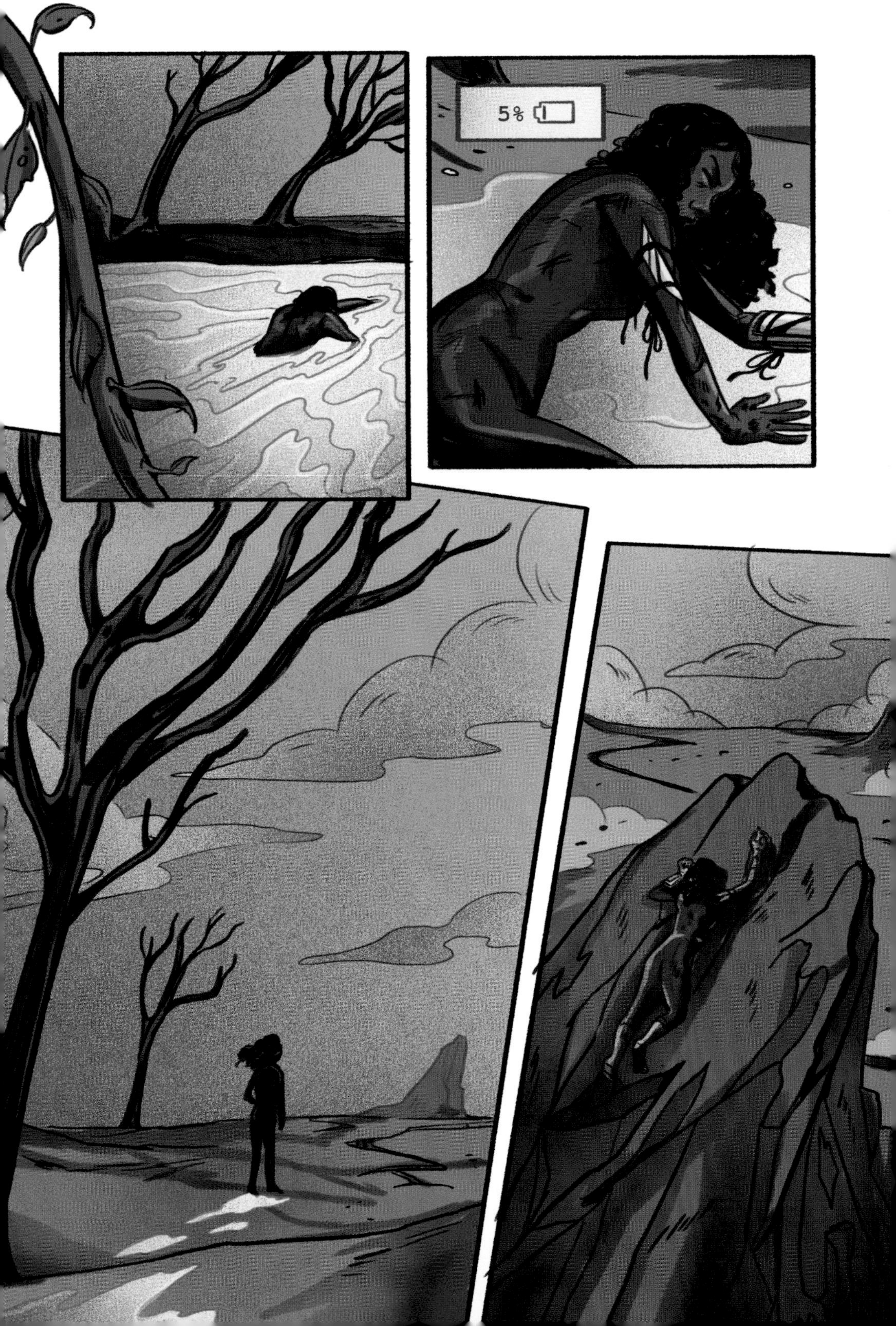
5%

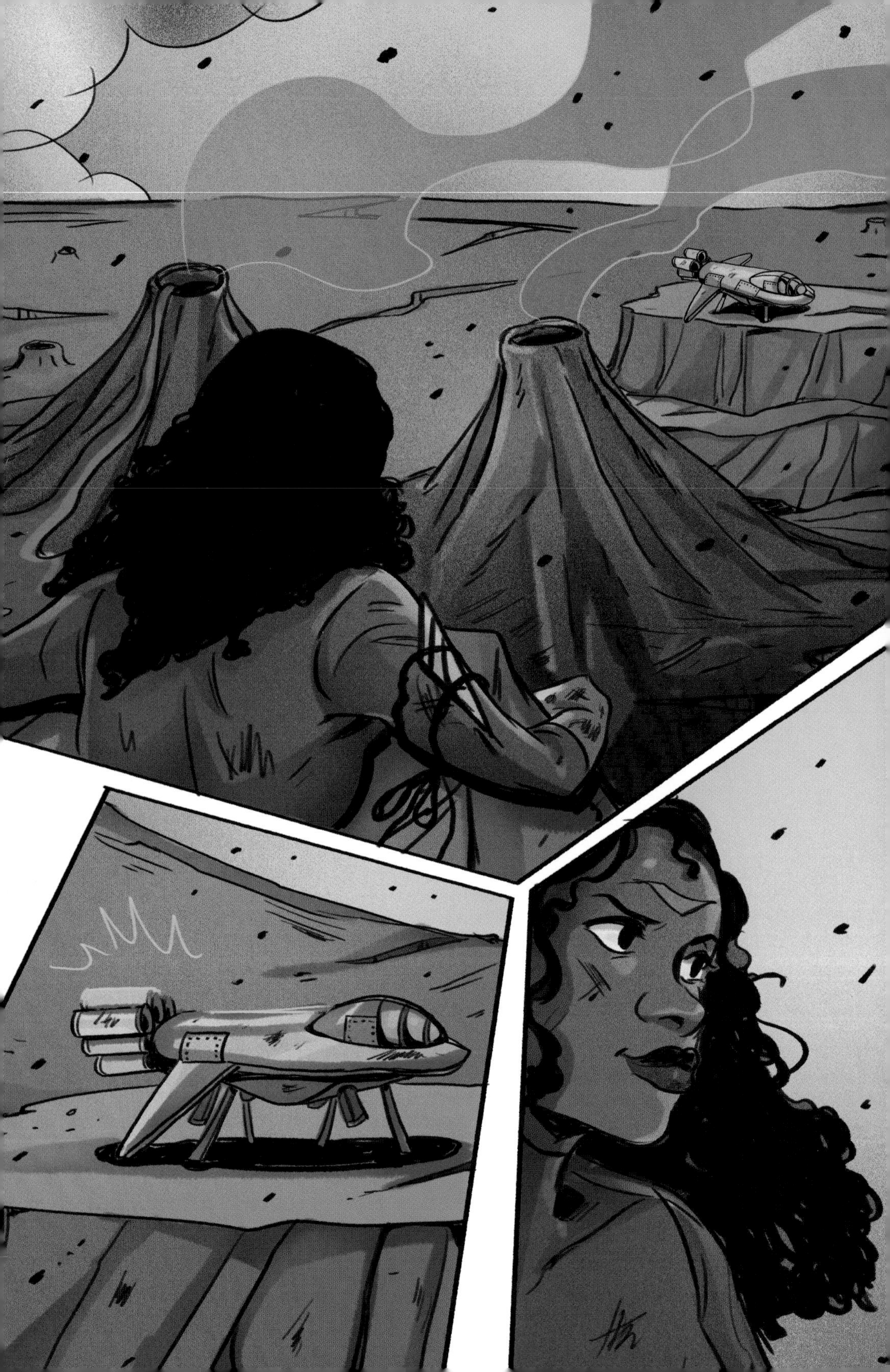

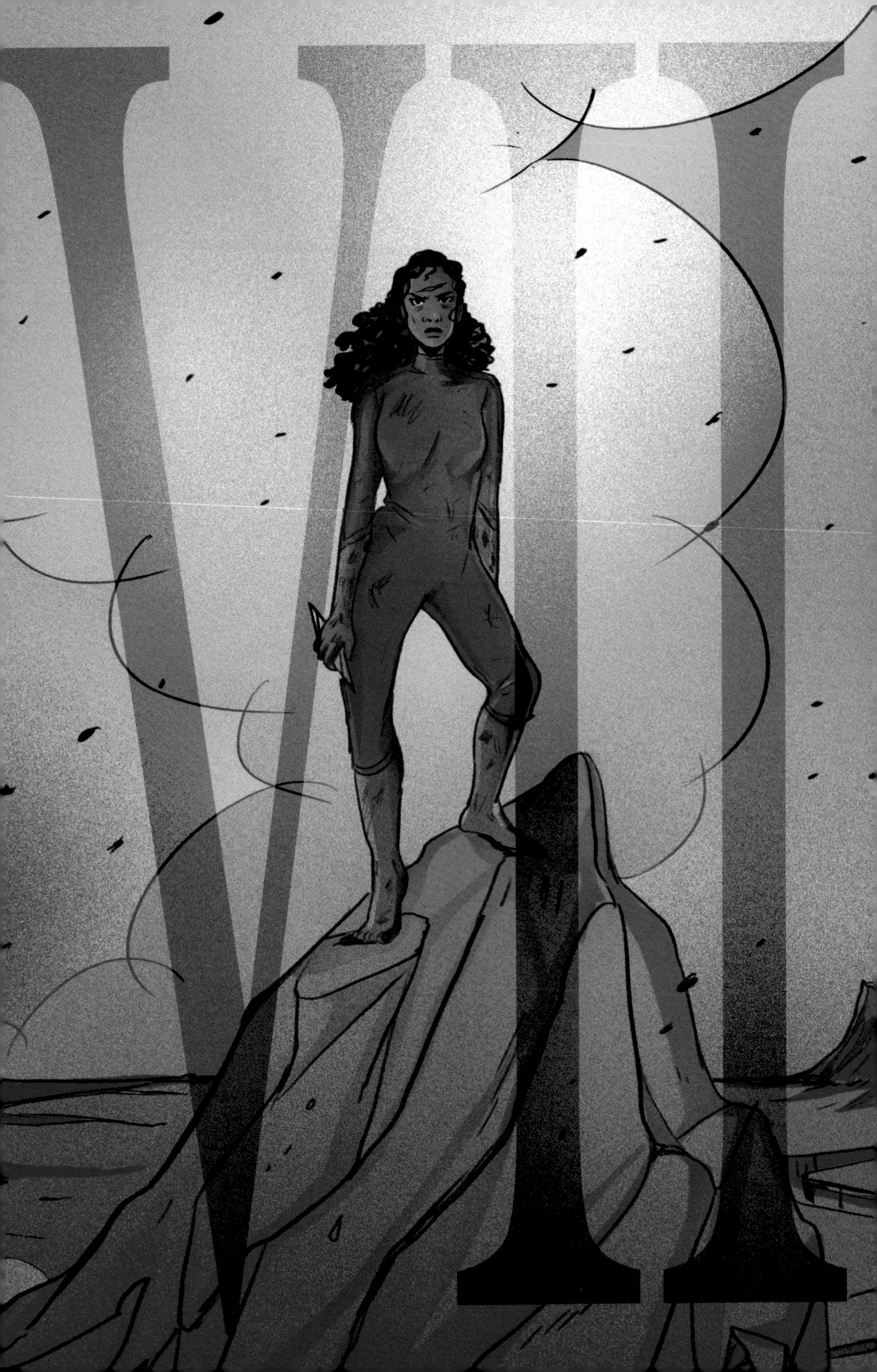
VII

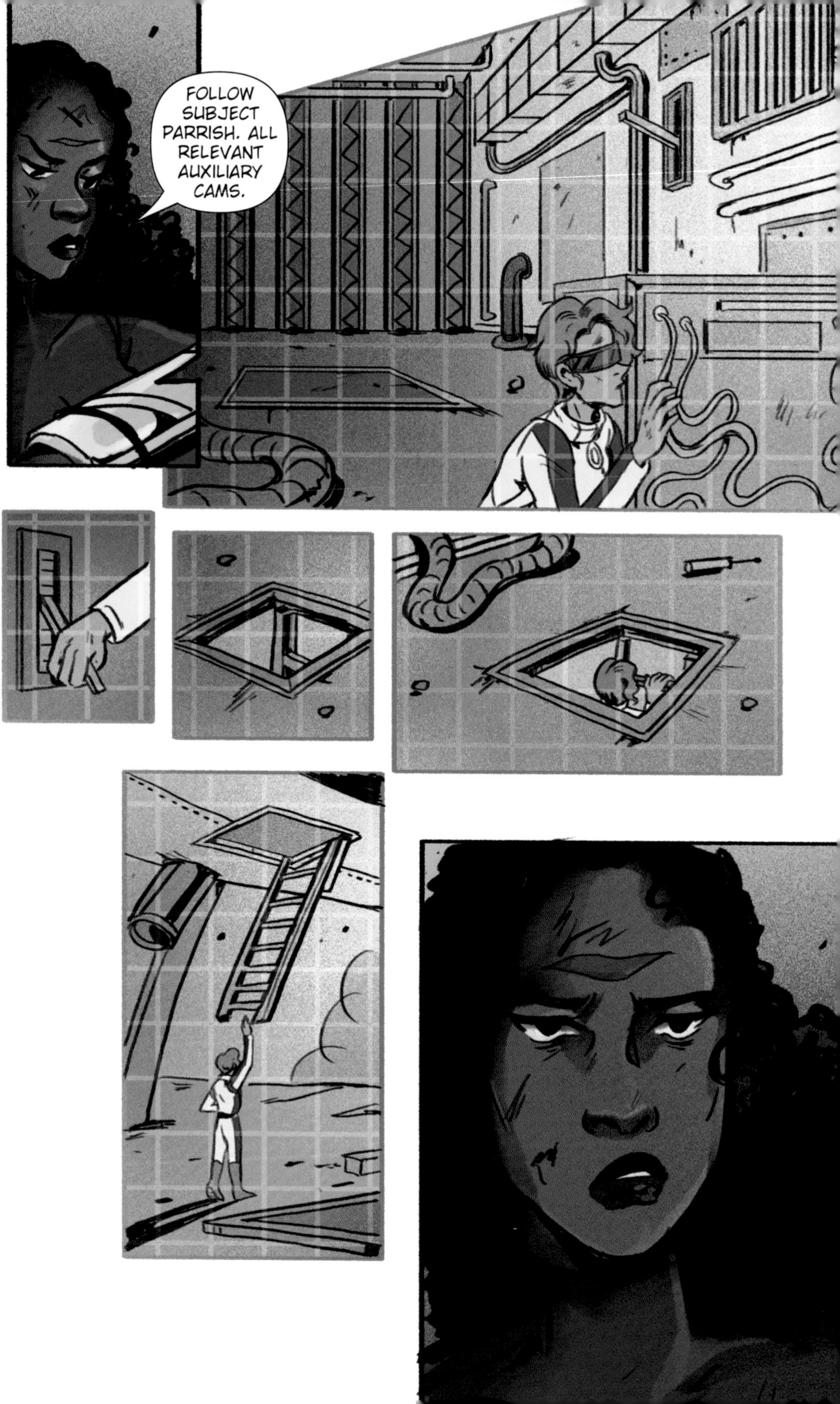
FOLLOW SUBJECT PARRISH. ALL RELEVANT AUXILIARY CAMS.

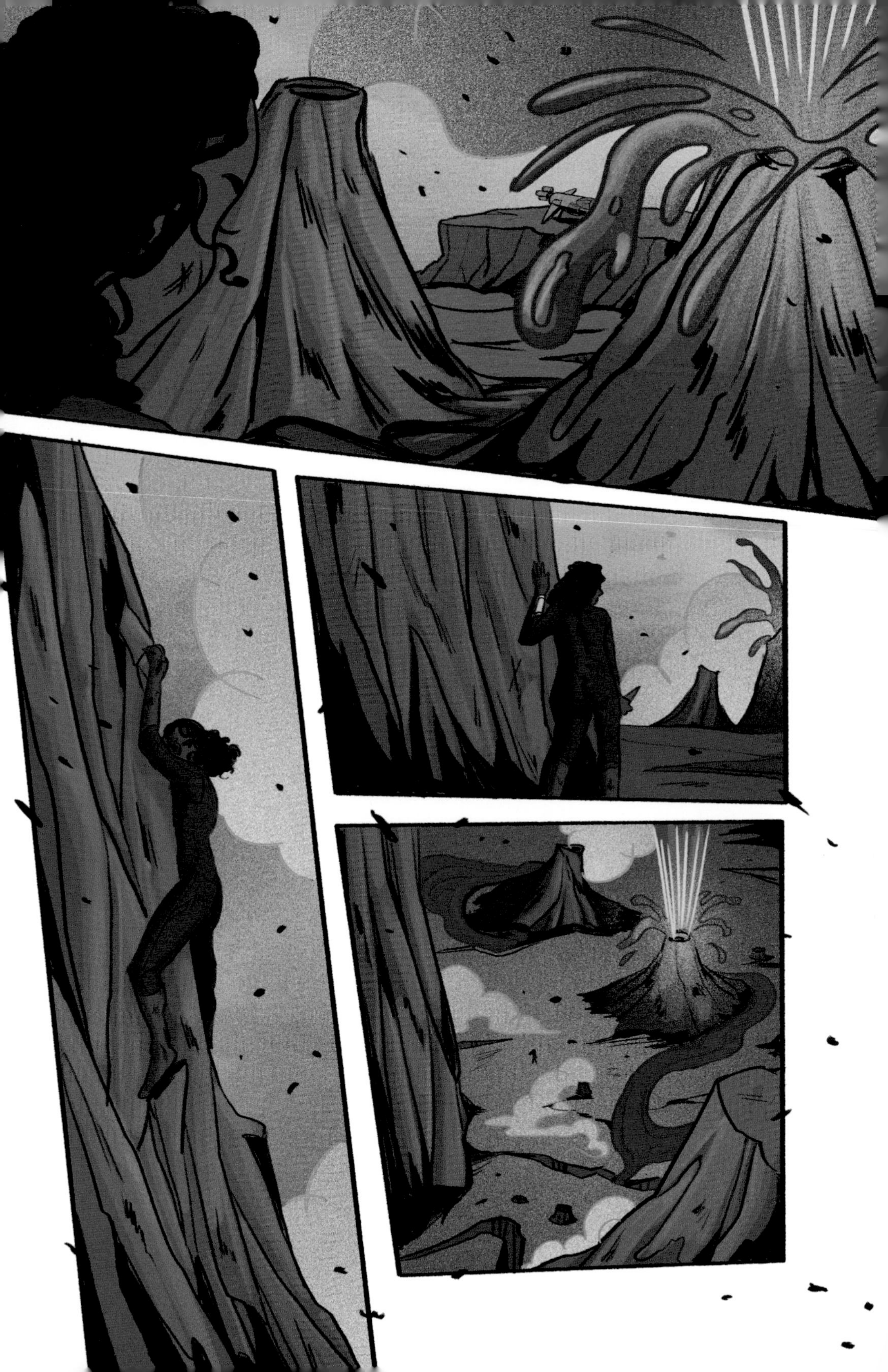

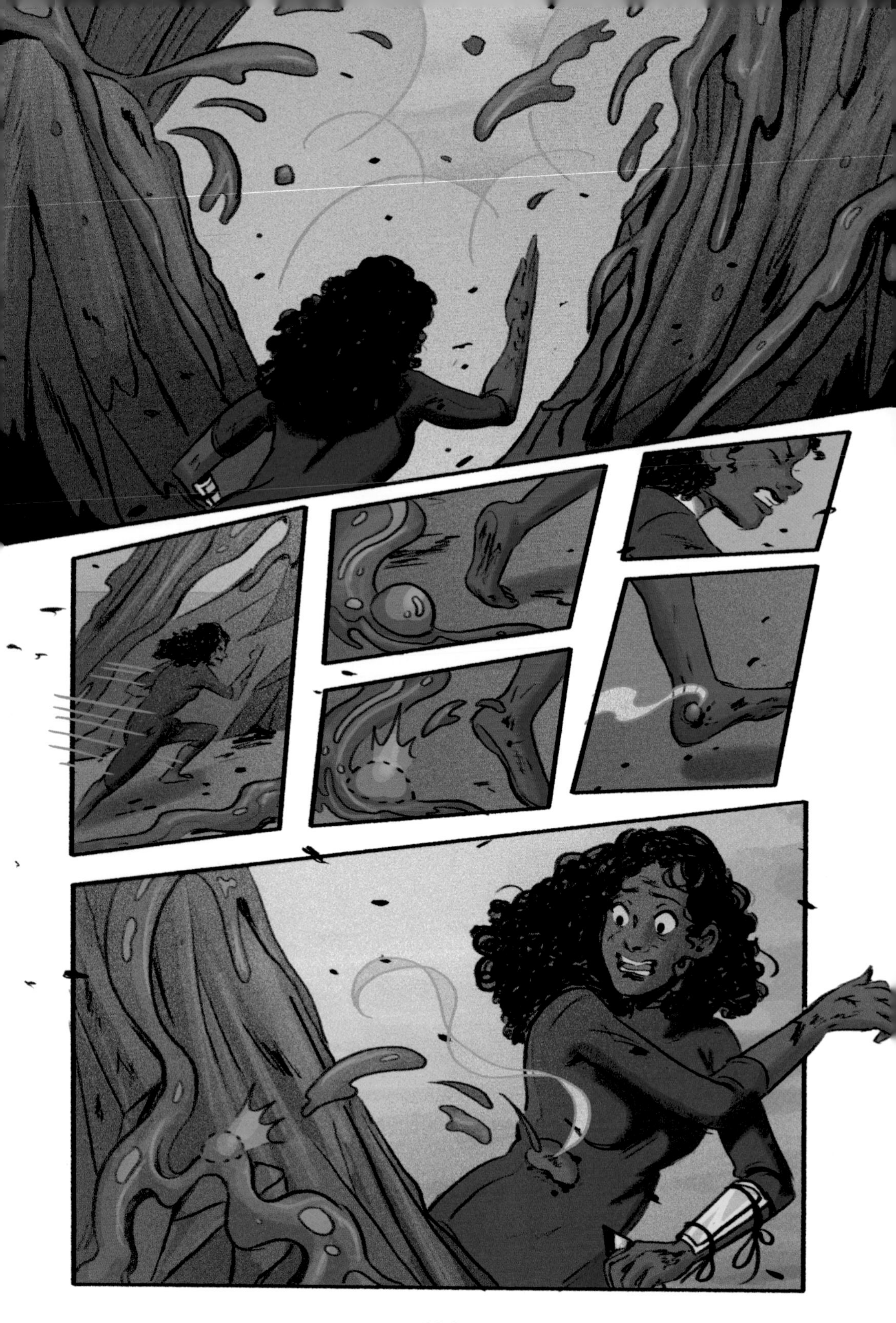

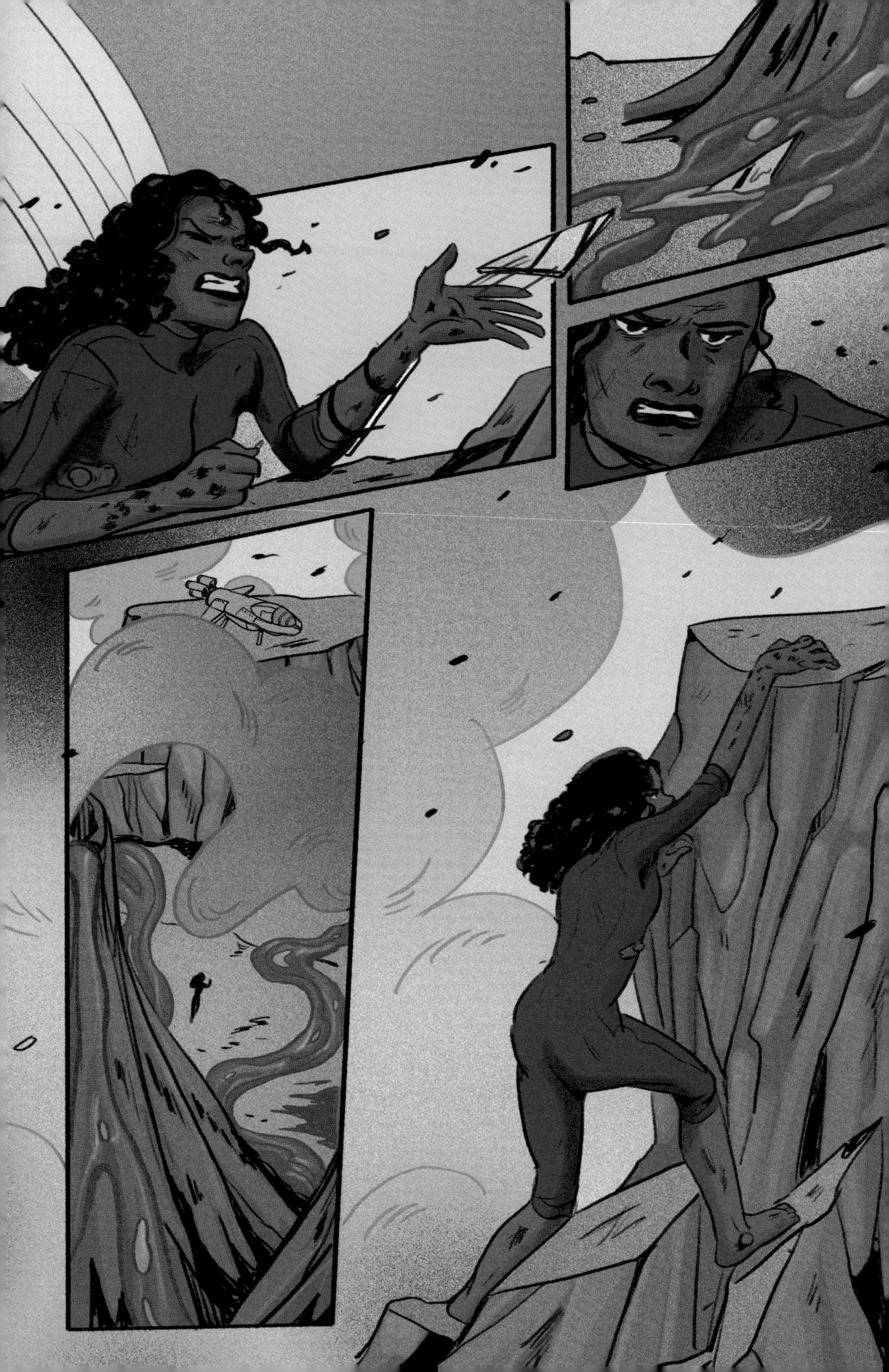

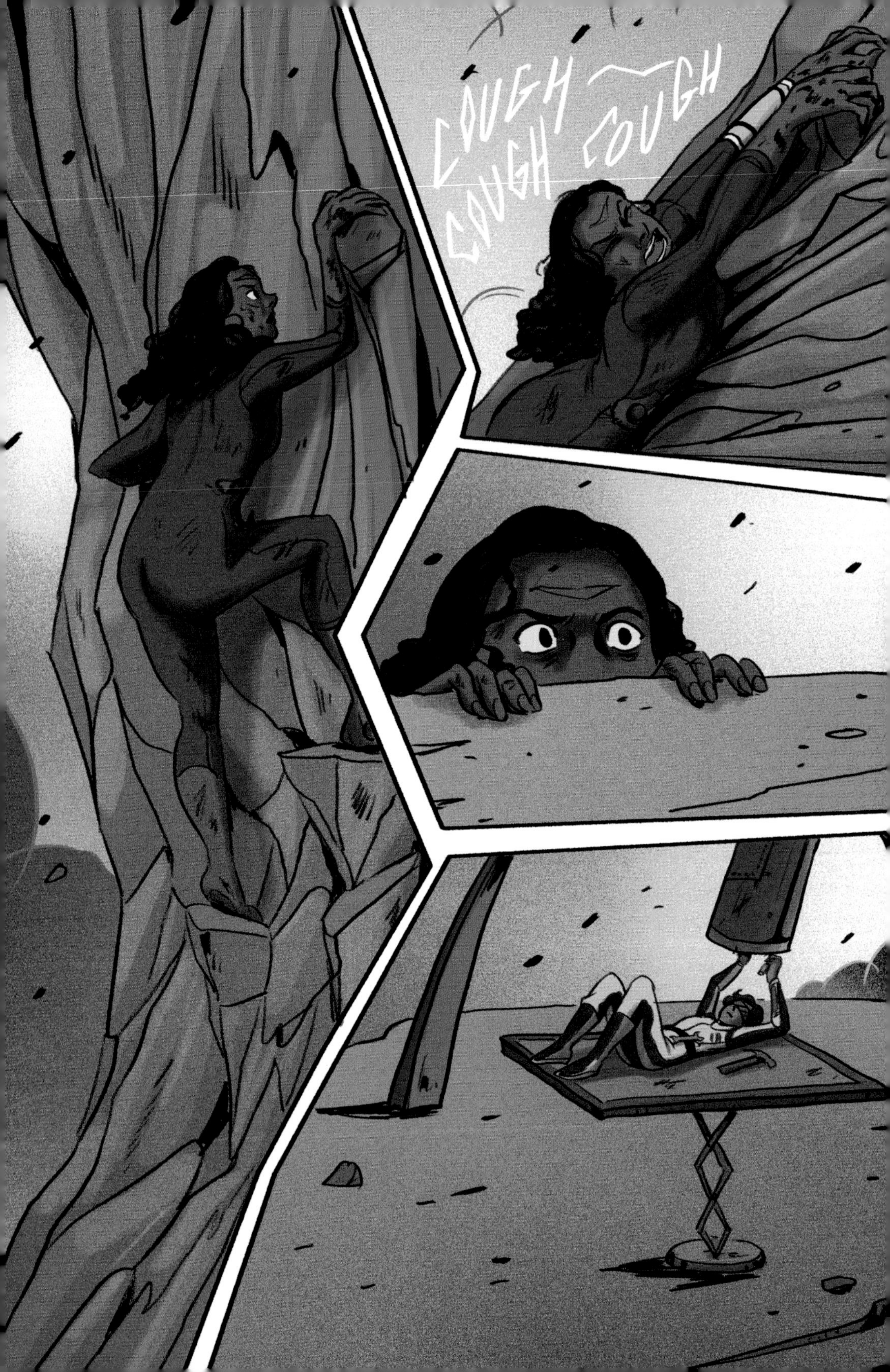
COUGH COUGH COUGH

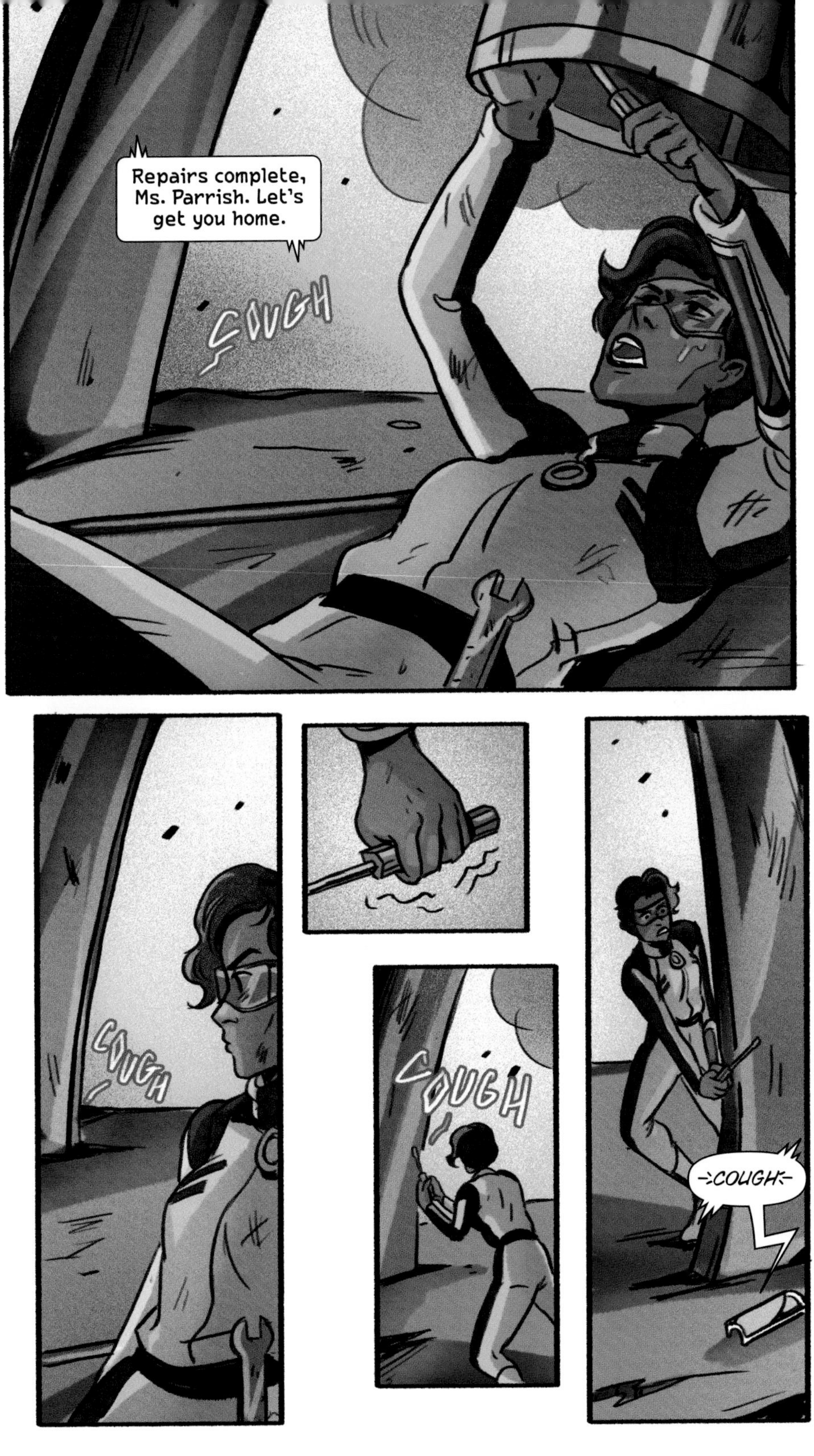

Repairs complete, Ms. Parrish. Let's get you home.
COUGH
COUGH
COUGH
COUGH

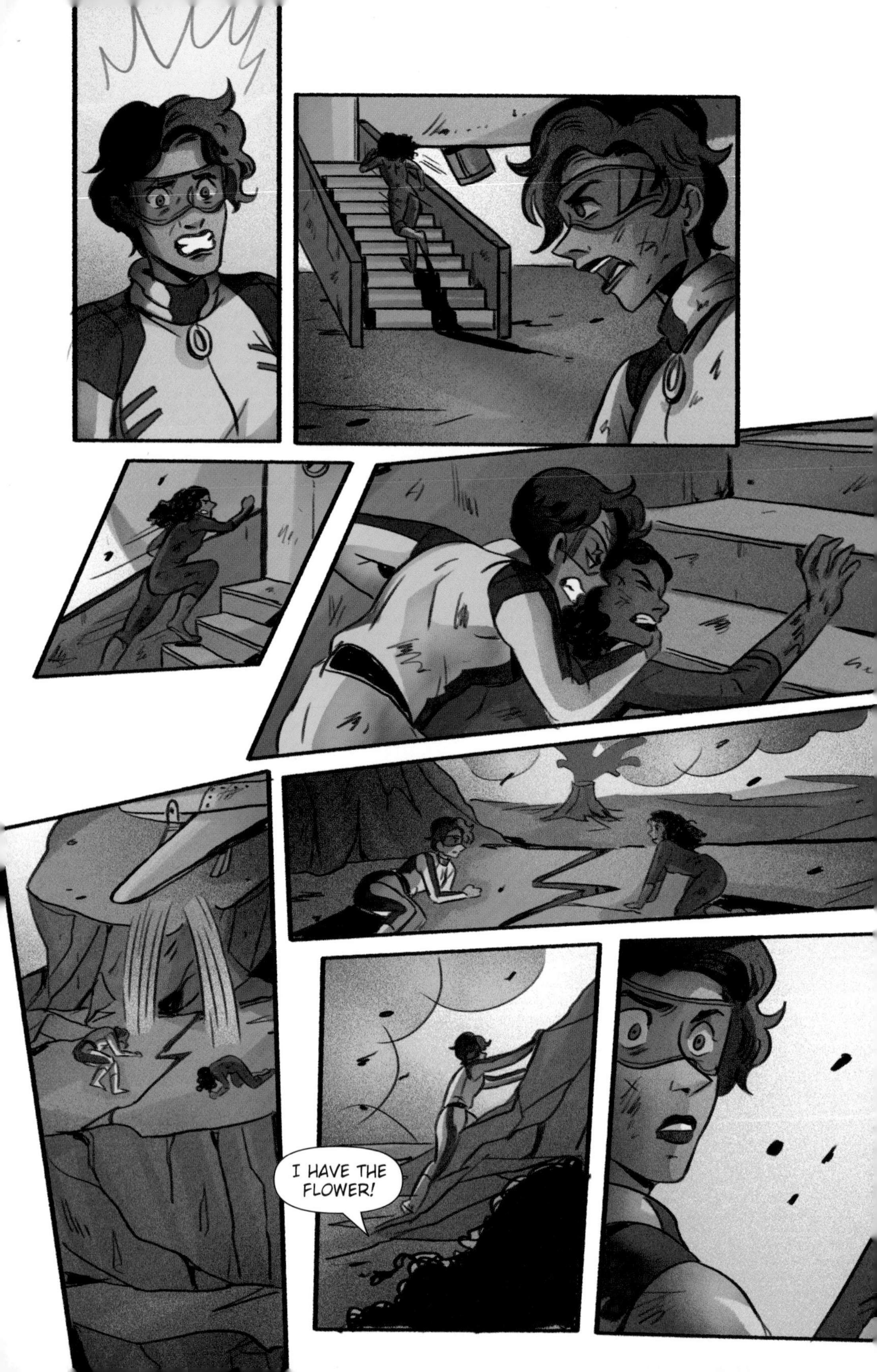
I HAVE THE FLOWER!

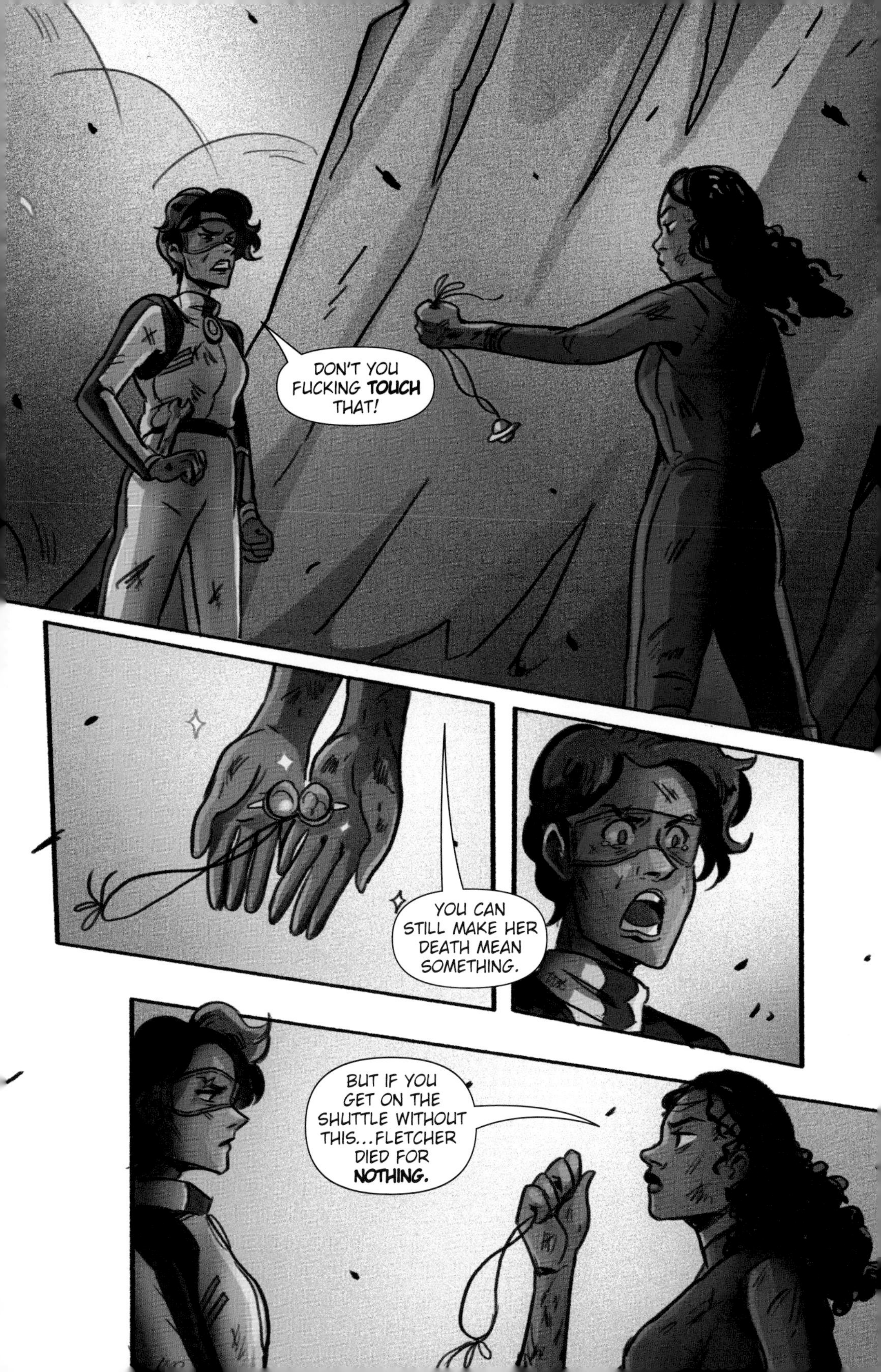
DON'T YOU FUCKING **TOUCH** THAT!
YOU CAN STILL MAKE HER DEATH MEAN SOMETHING.
BUT IF YOU GET ON THE SHUTTLE WITHOUT THIS...FLETCHER DIED FOR **NOTHING.**

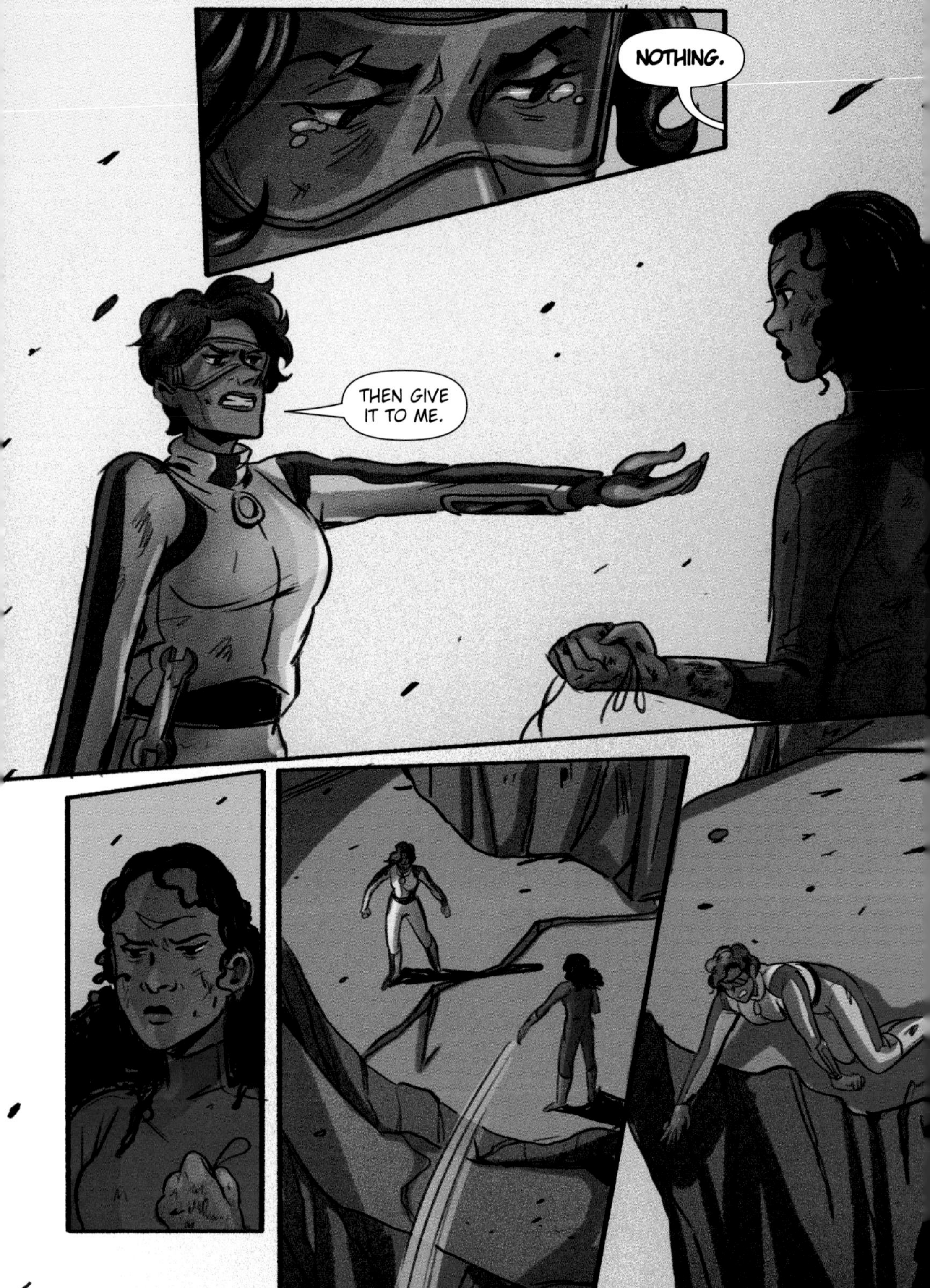
NOTHING.
THEN GIVE IT TO ME.

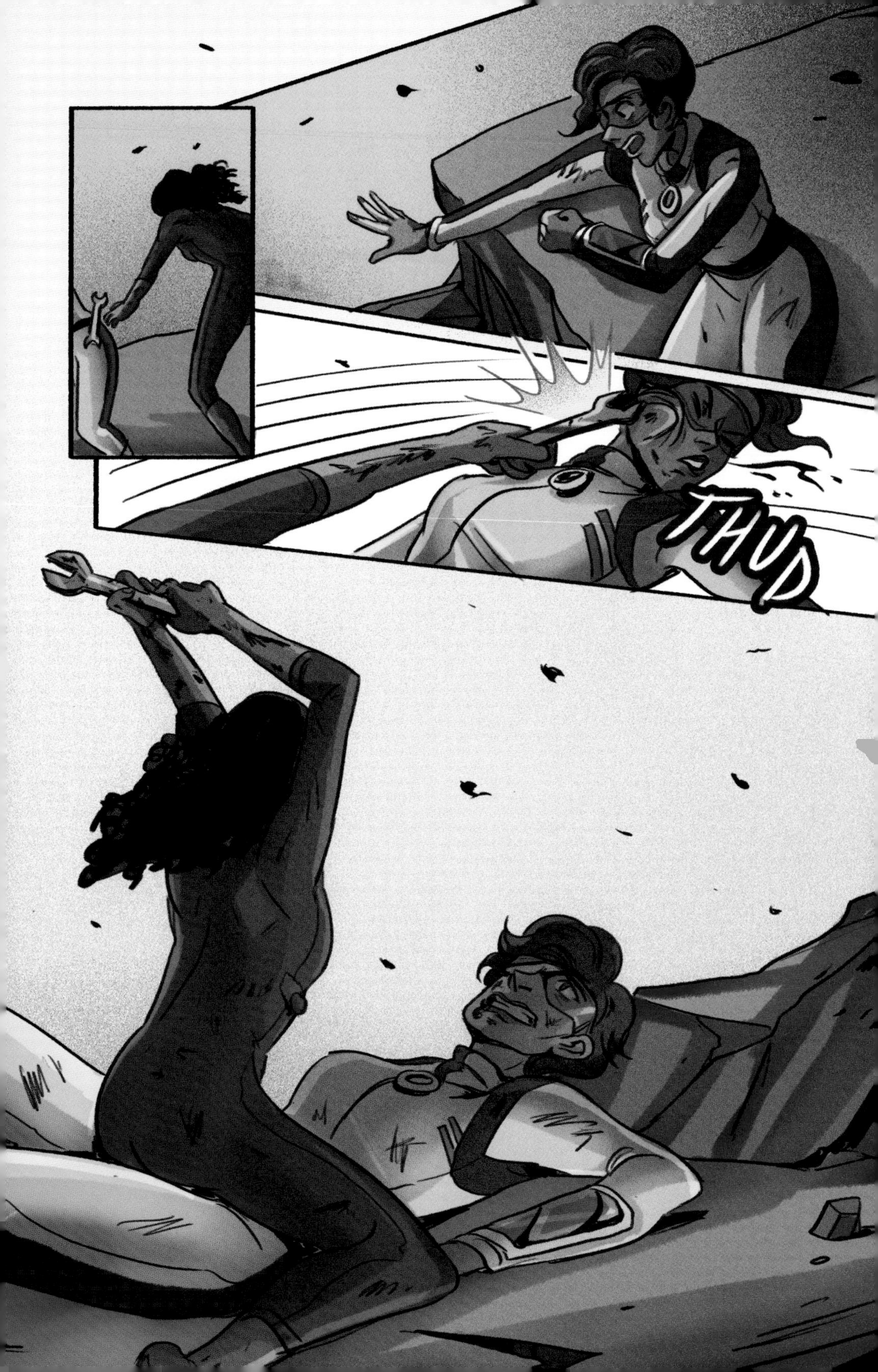
THUD

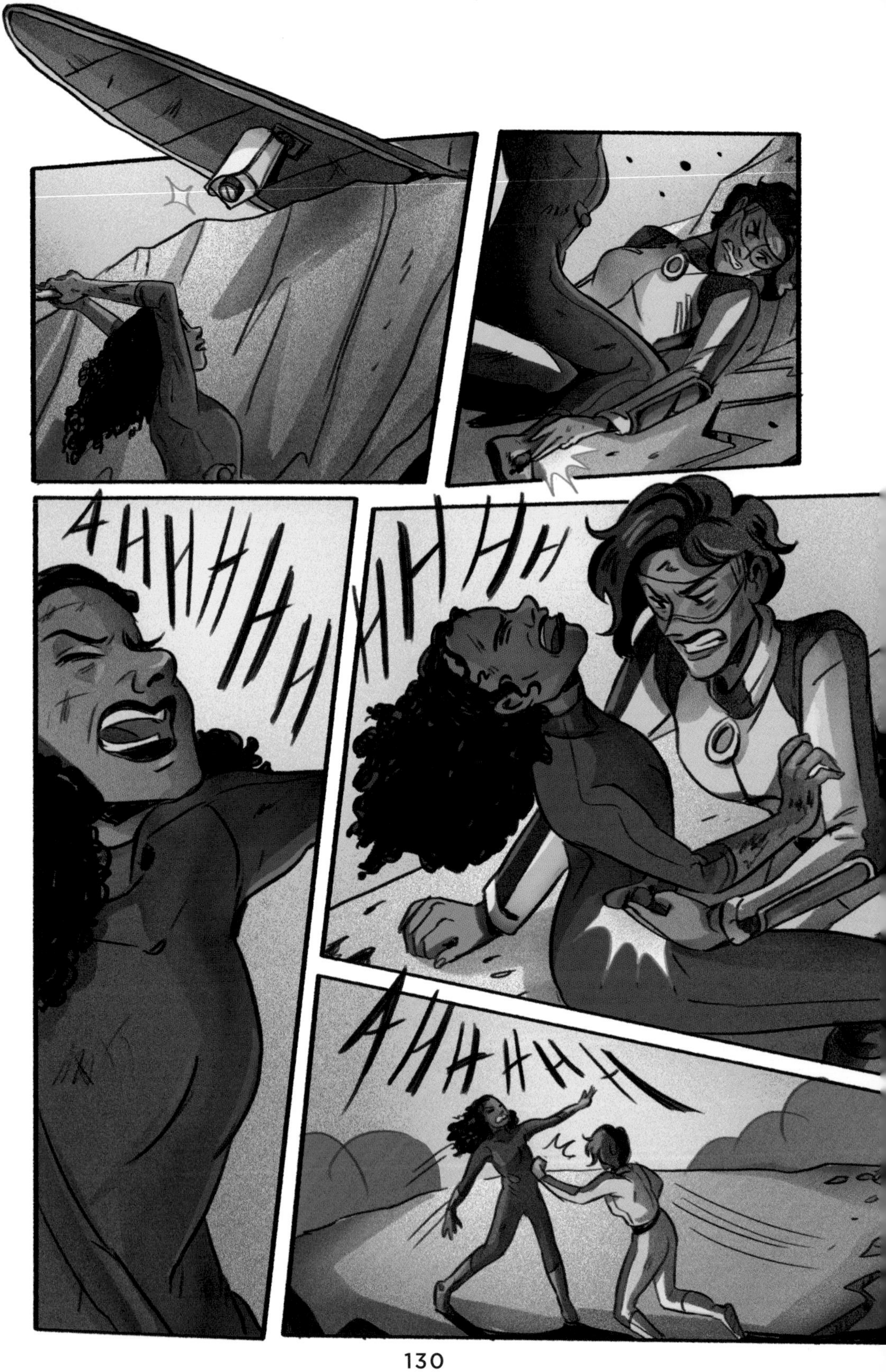
AHHHHHHH
HHHHHHHHH
AHHHHHH

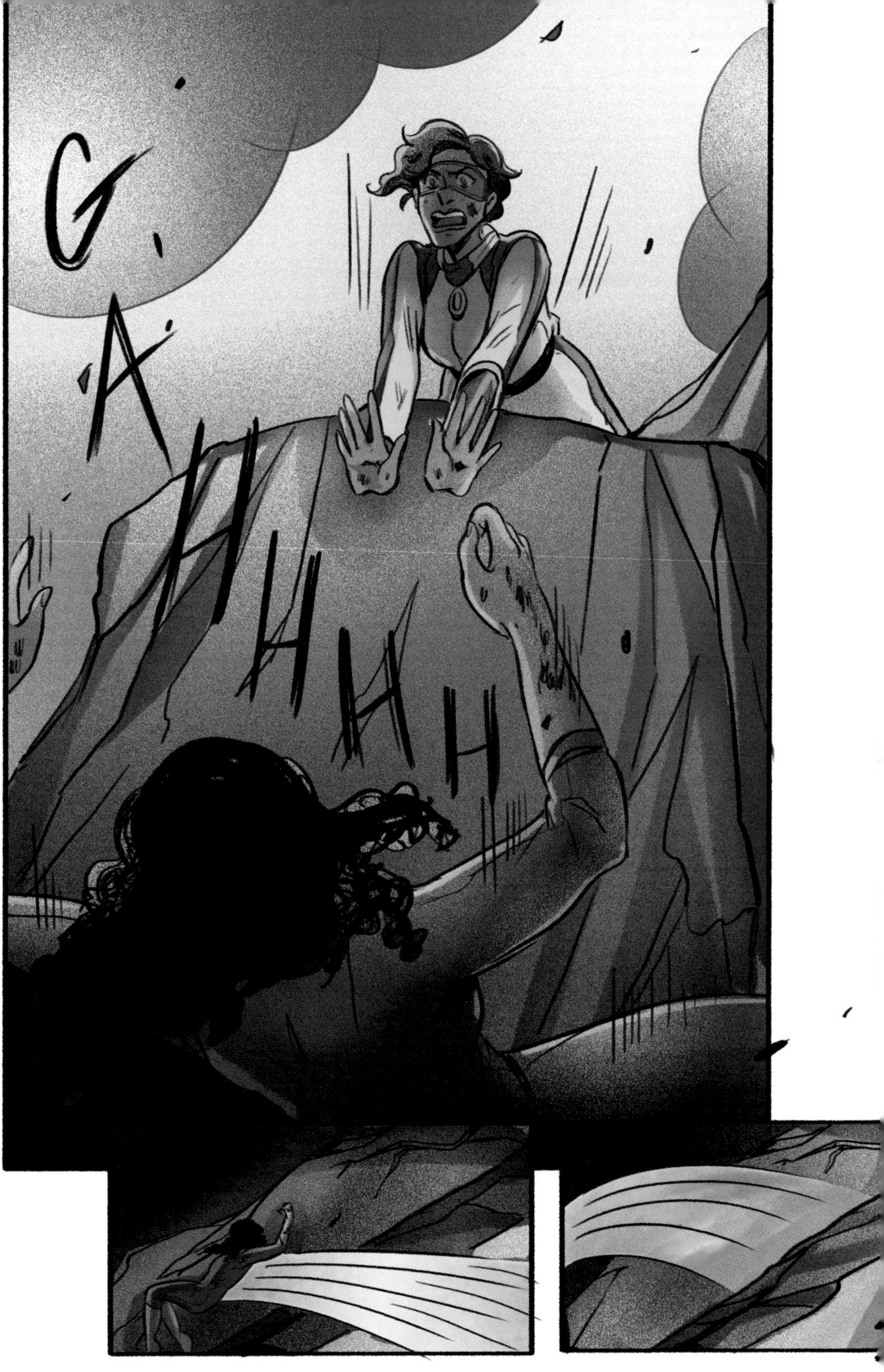
GAHHHHH

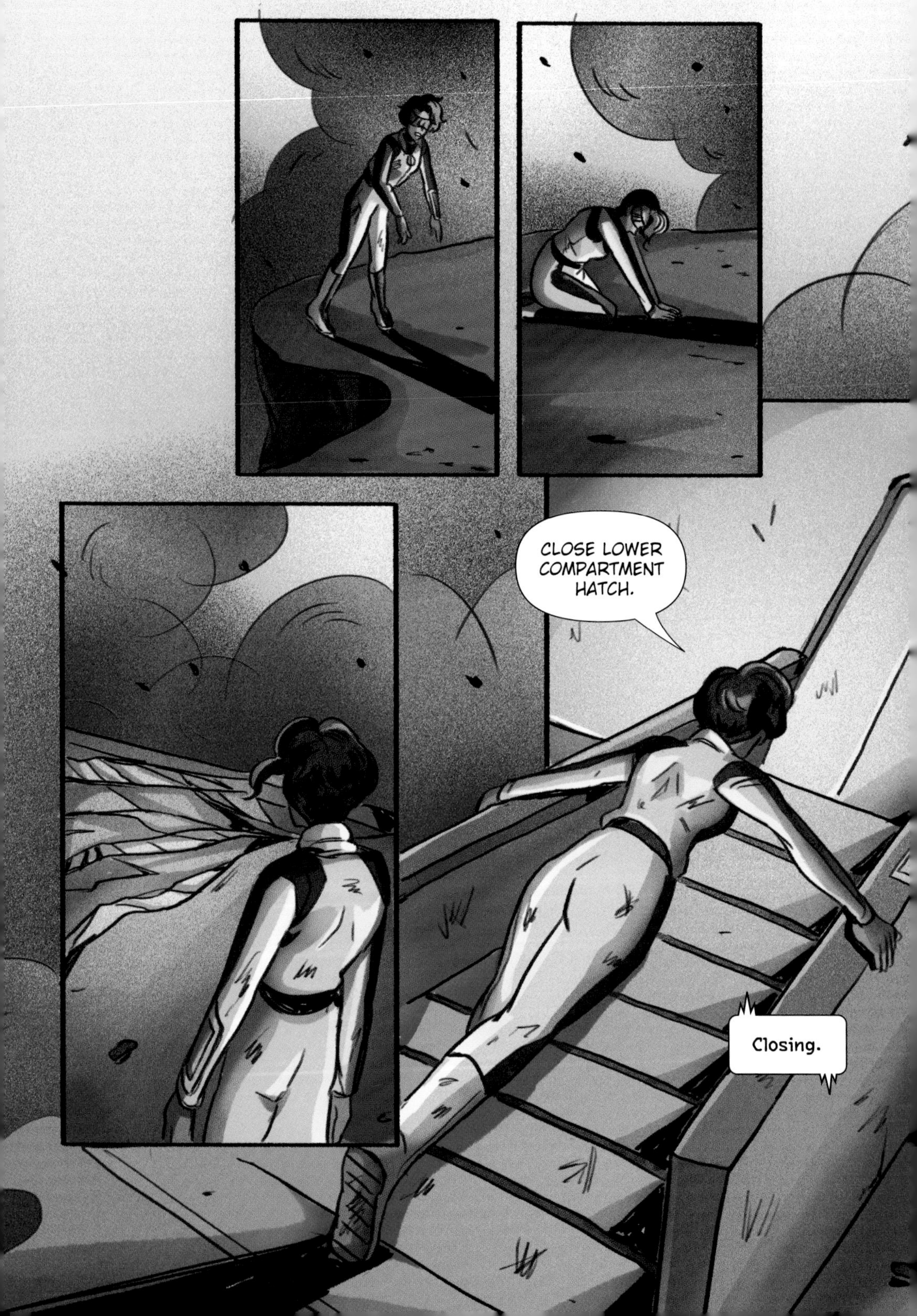
CLOSE LOWER COMPARTMENT HATCH.
Closing.

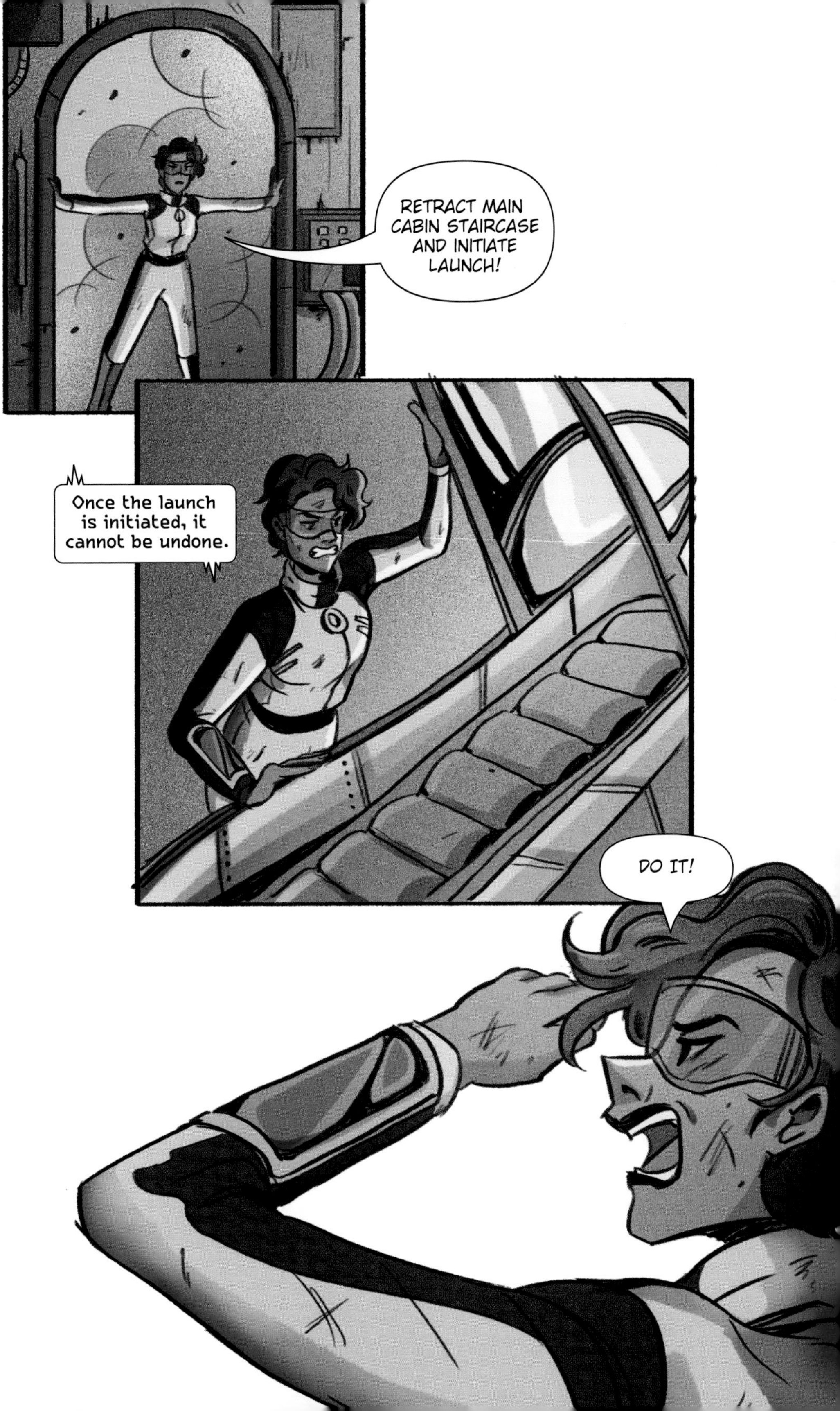
RETRACT MAIN CABIN STAIRCASE AND INITIATE LAUNCH!
Once the launch is initiated, it cannot be undone.
DO IT!

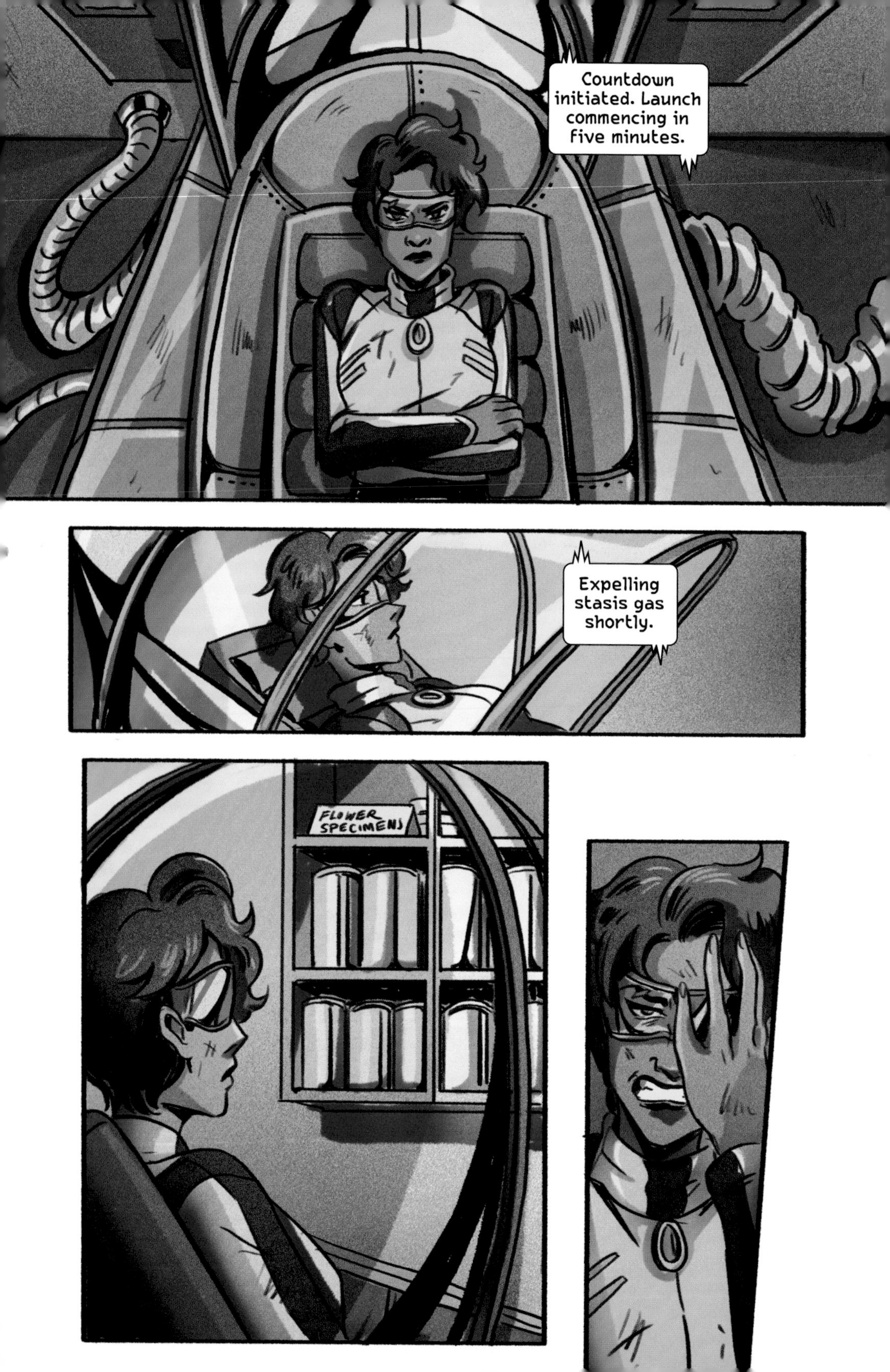
Countdown initiated. Launch commencing in five minutes.
Expelling stasis gas shortly.
FLOWER SPECIMENS

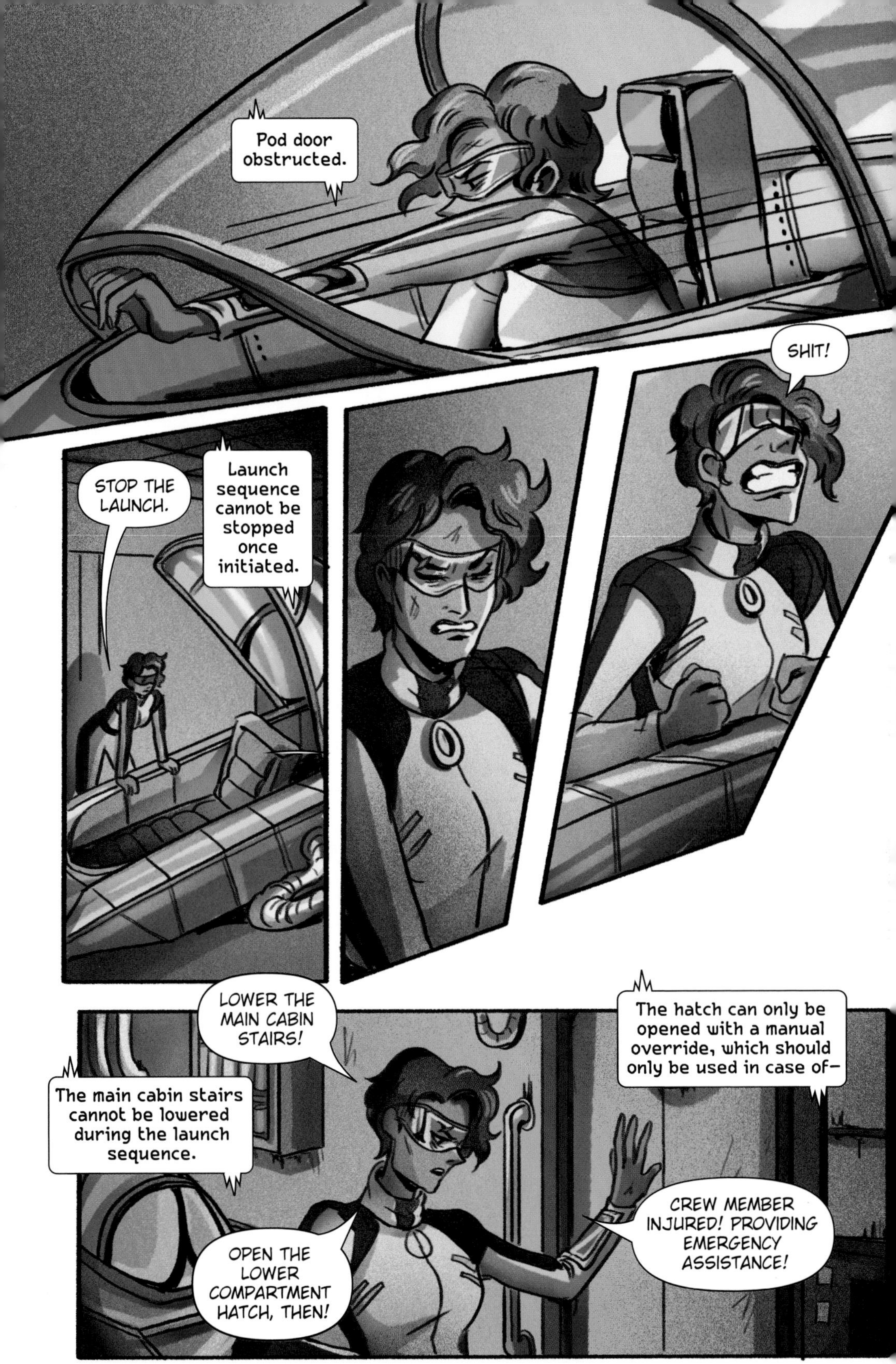

Pod door obstructed.
STOP THE LAUNCH.
Launch sequence cannot be stopped once initiated.
SHIT!
LOWER THE MAIN CABIN STAIRS!
The main cabin stairs cannot be lowered during the launch sequence.
OPEN THE LOWER COMPARTMENT HATCH, THEN!
The hatch can only be opened with a manual override, which should only be used in case of–
CREW MEMBER INJURED! PROVIDING EMERGENCY ASSISTANCE!

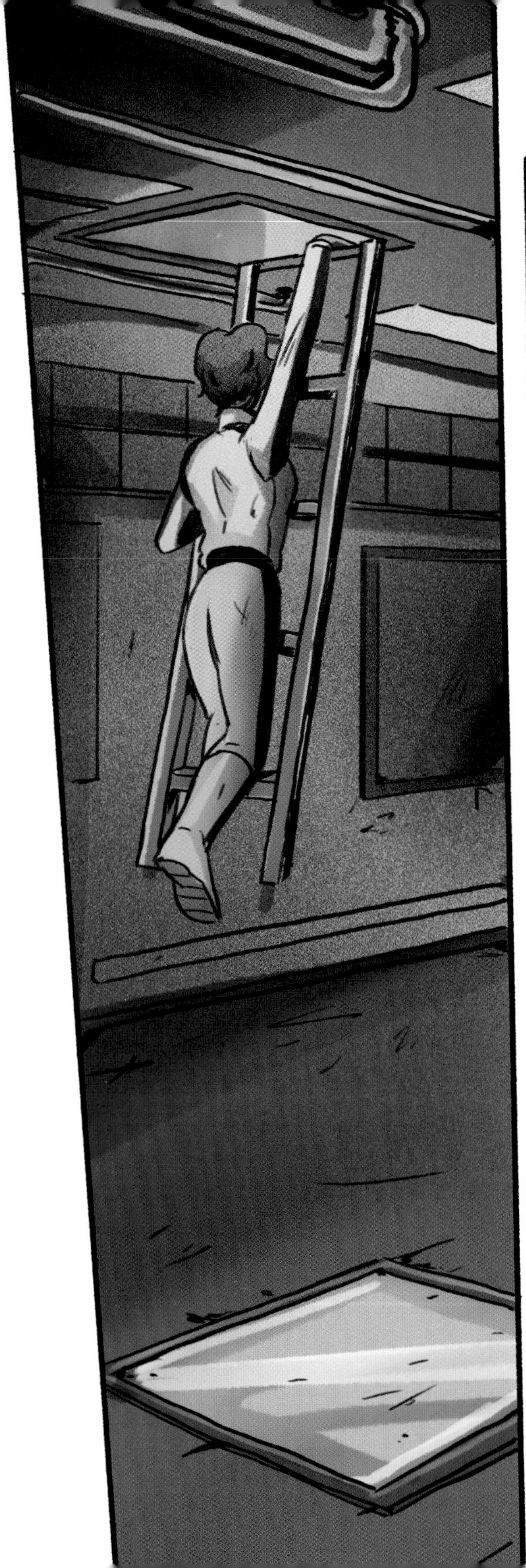
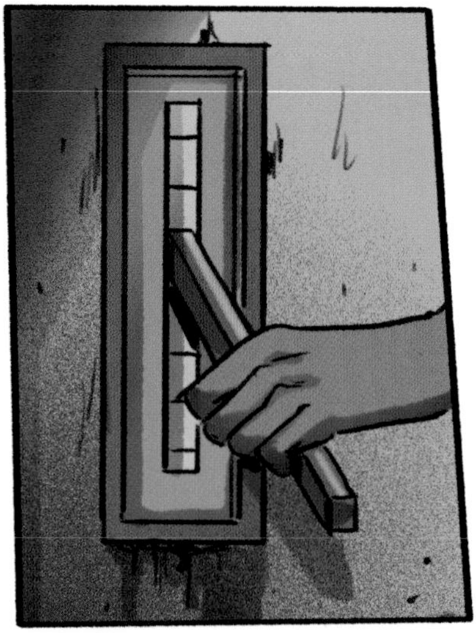
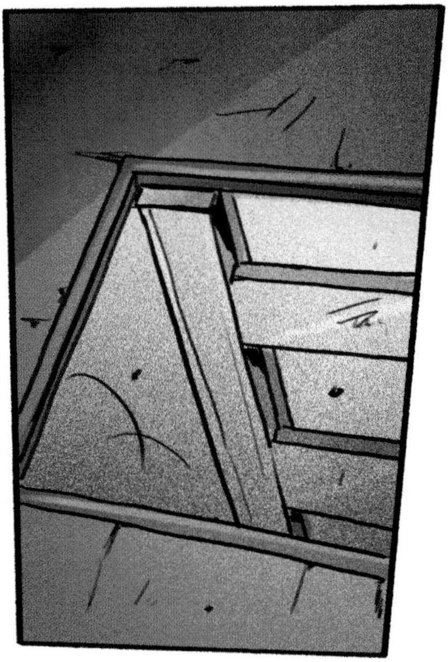

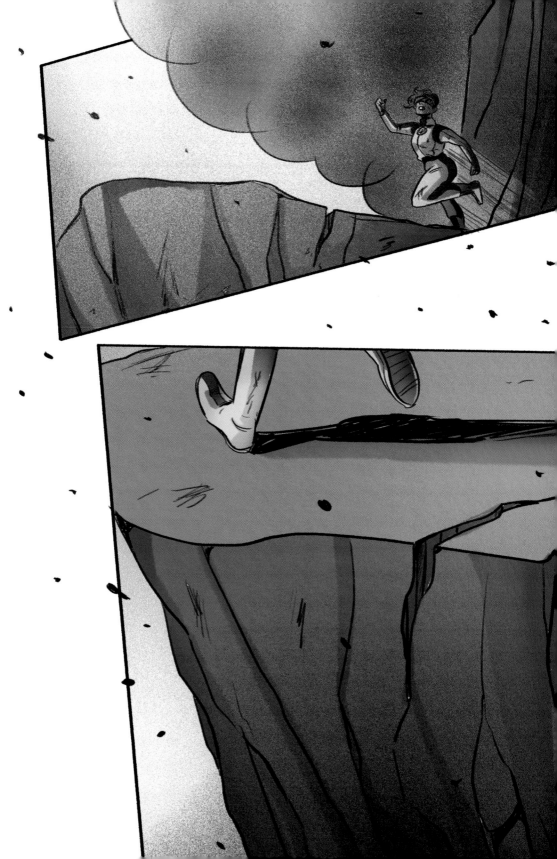

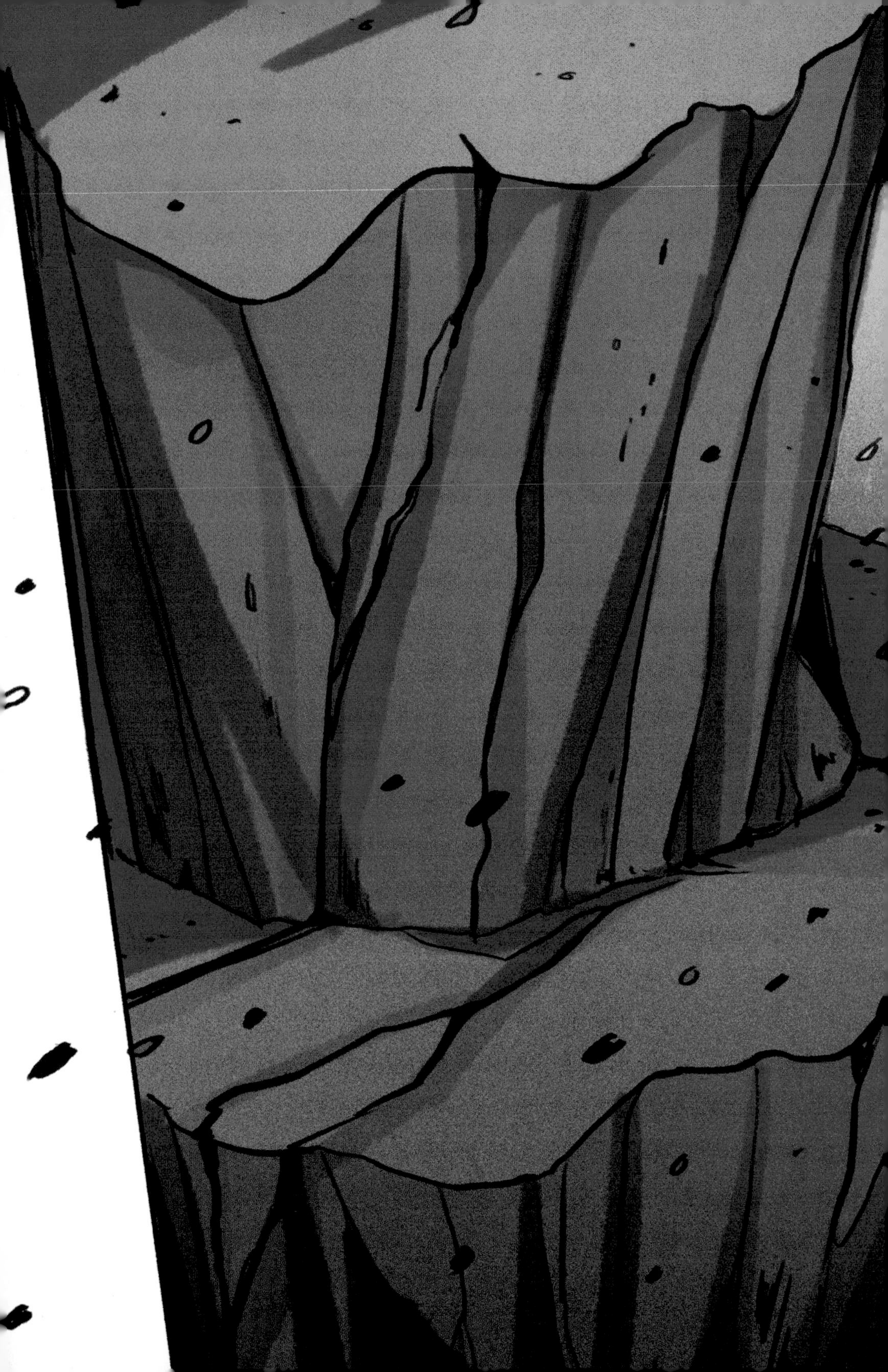

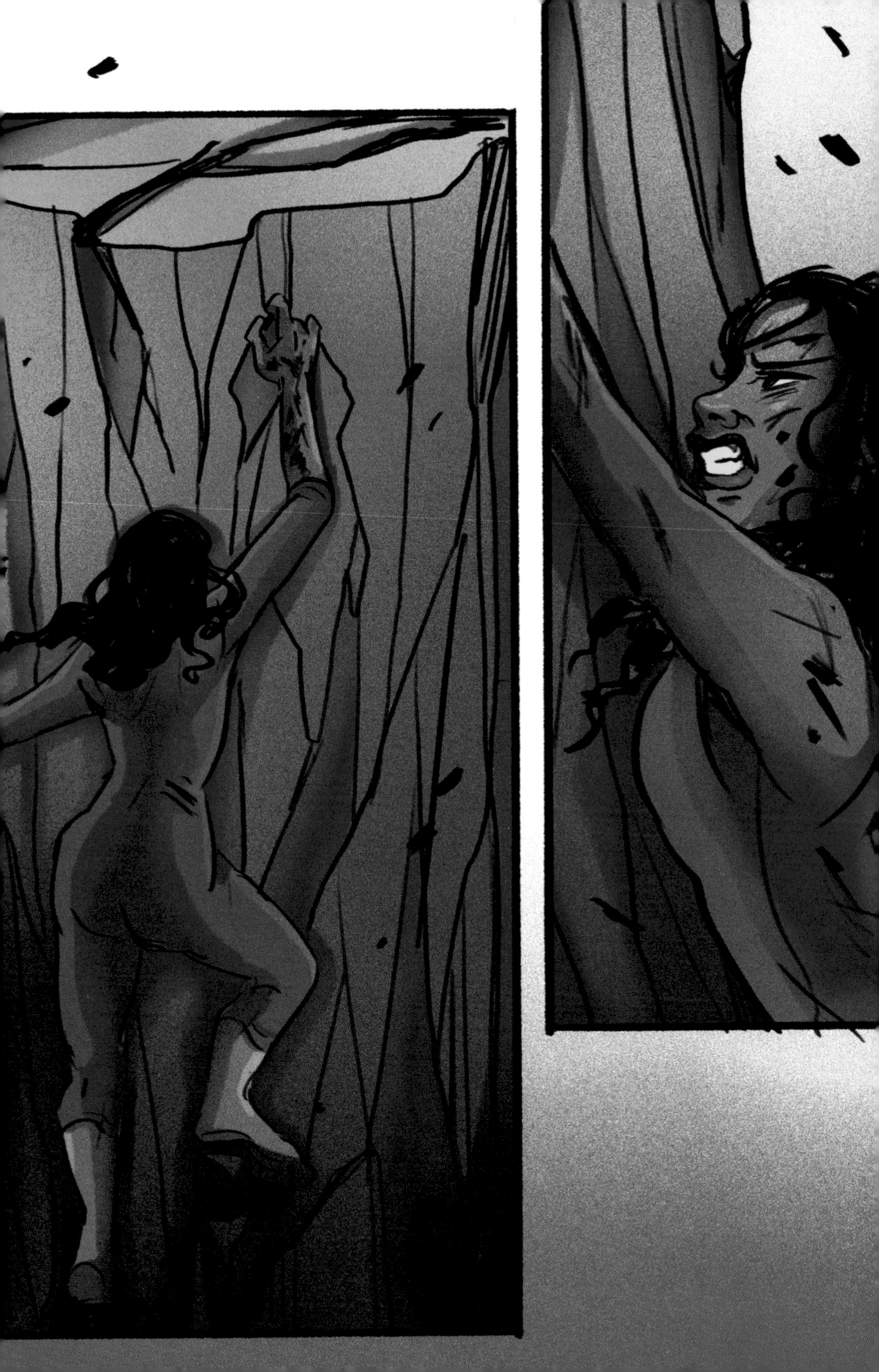

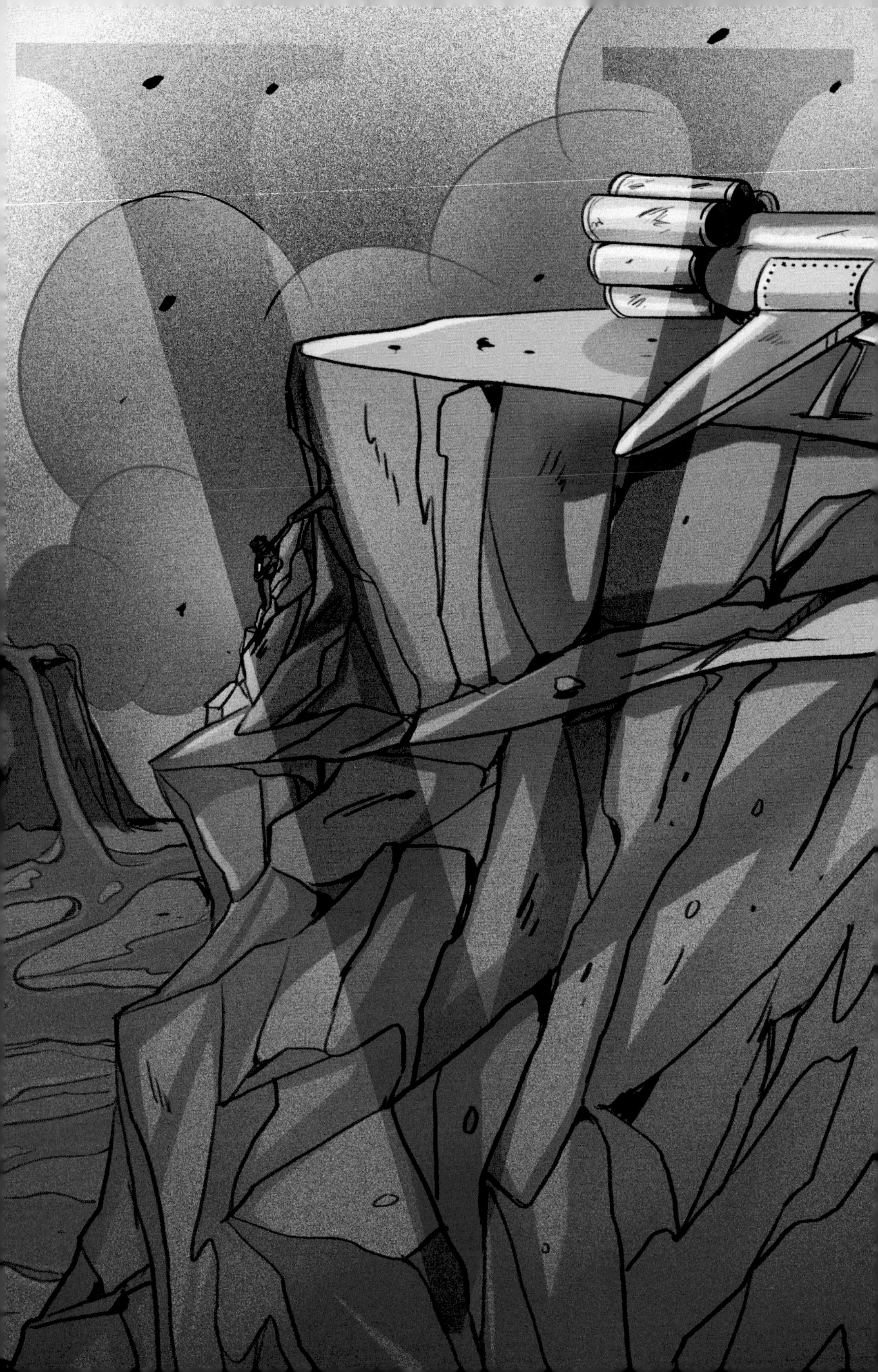

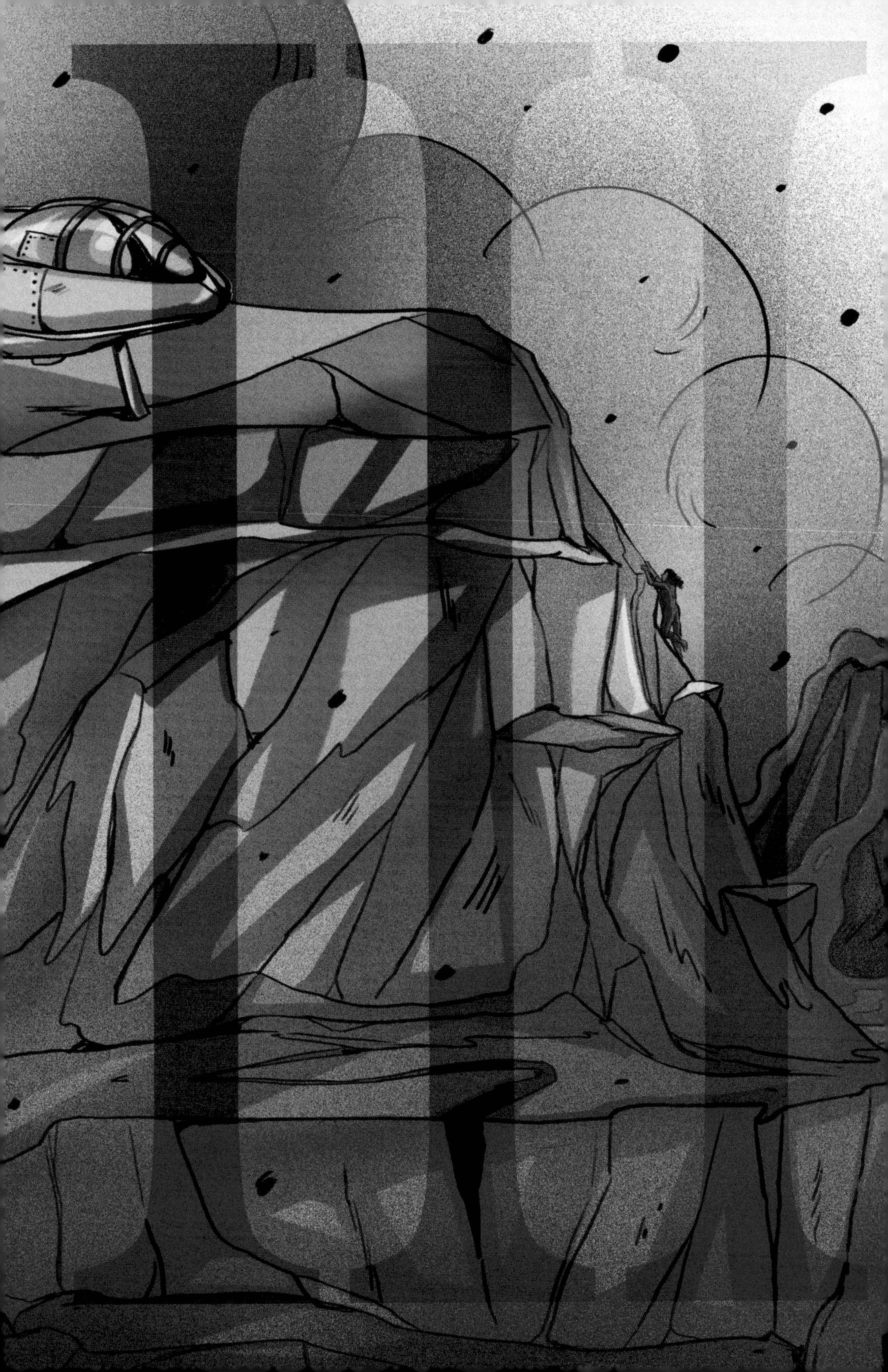

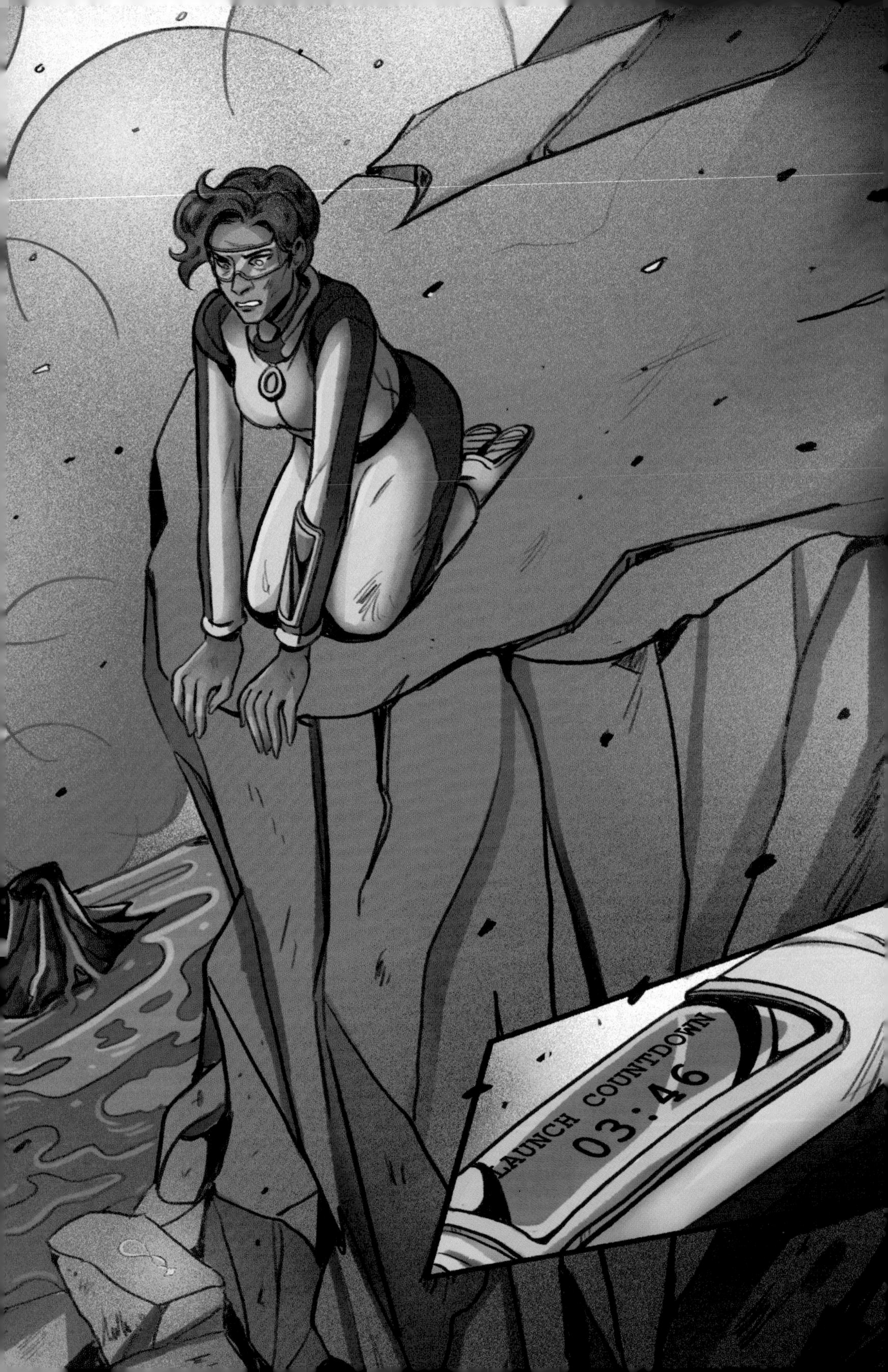
LAUNCH COUNTDOWN
03:46

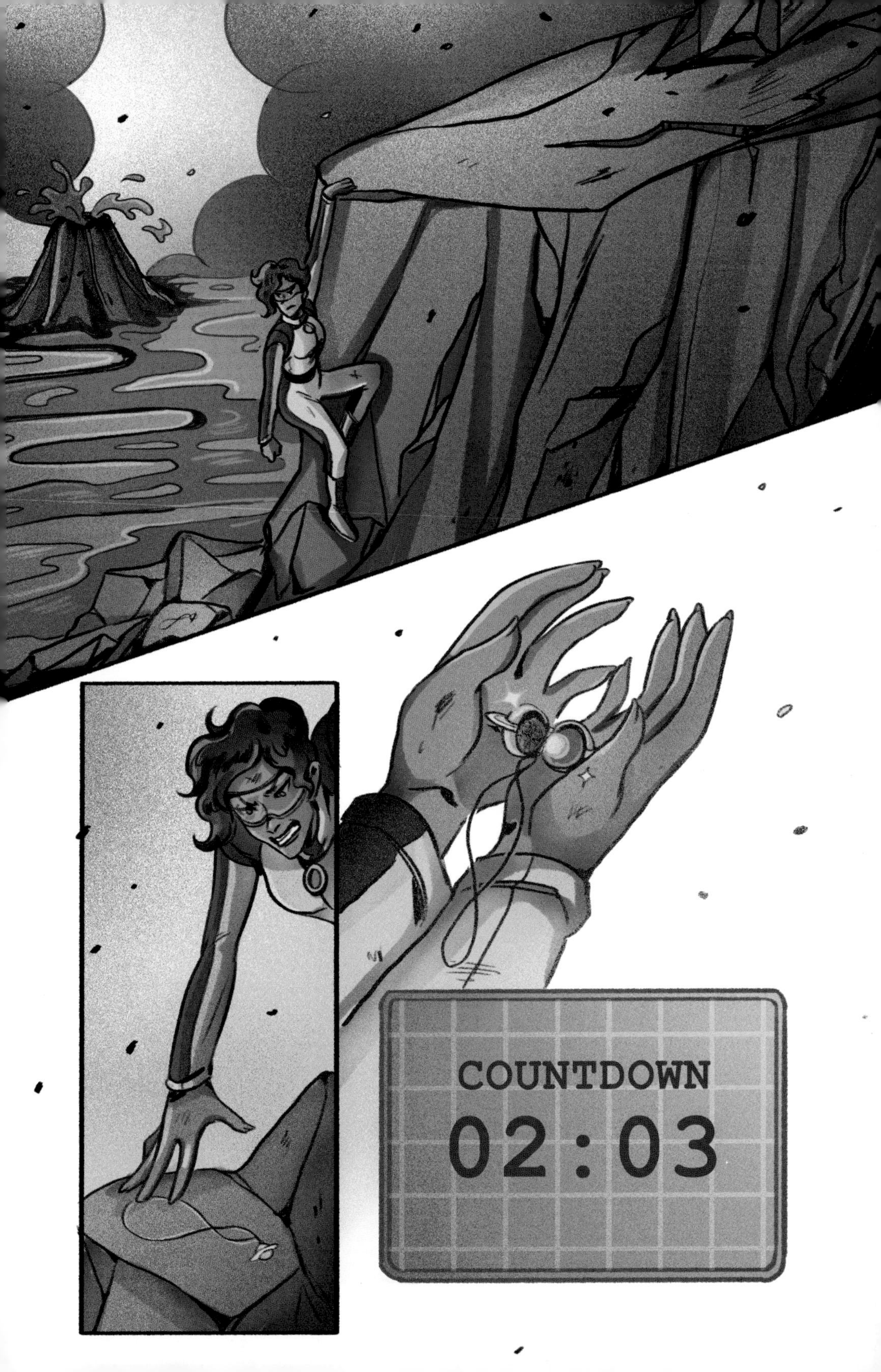
COUNTDOWN
02:03

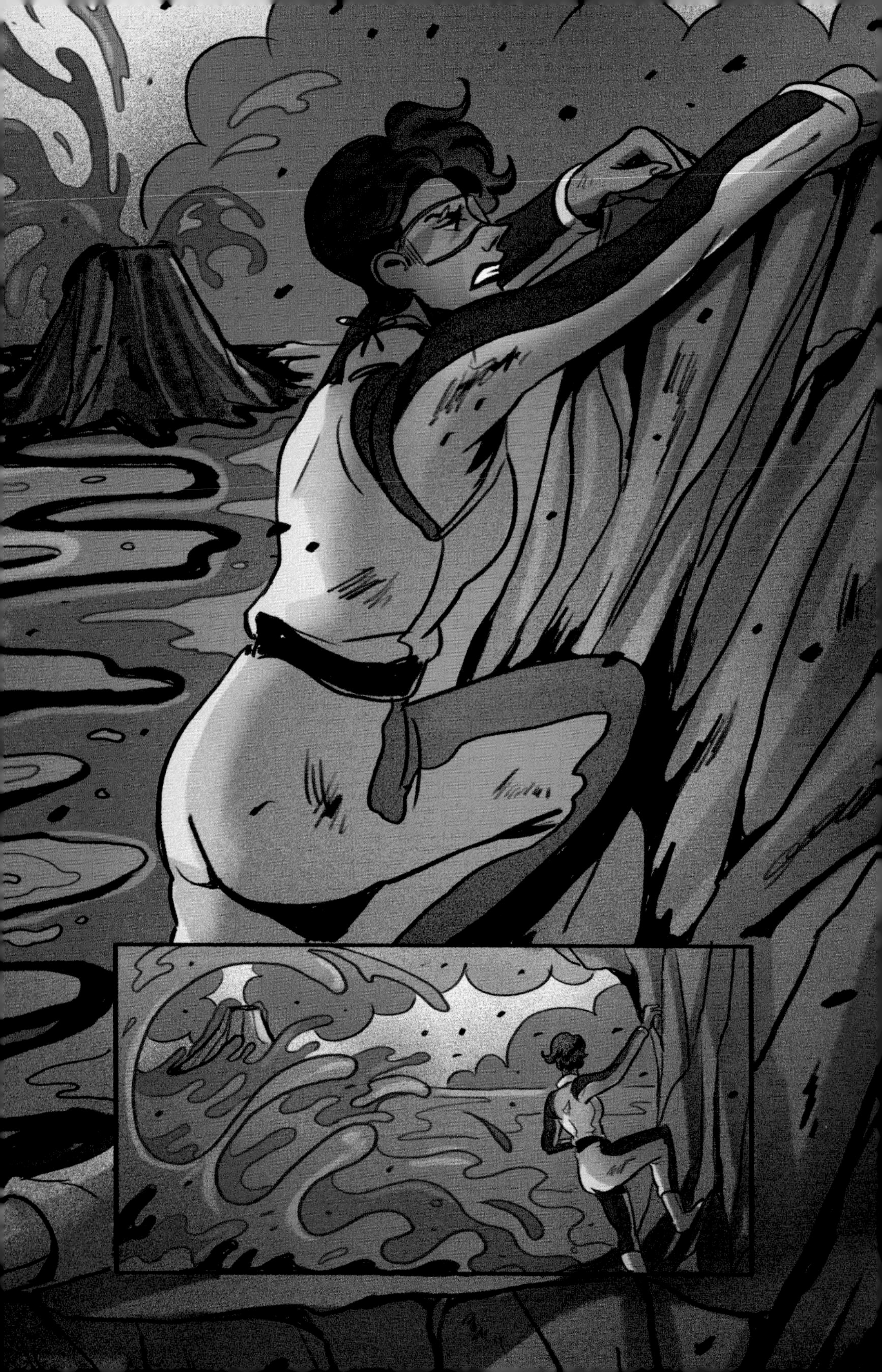

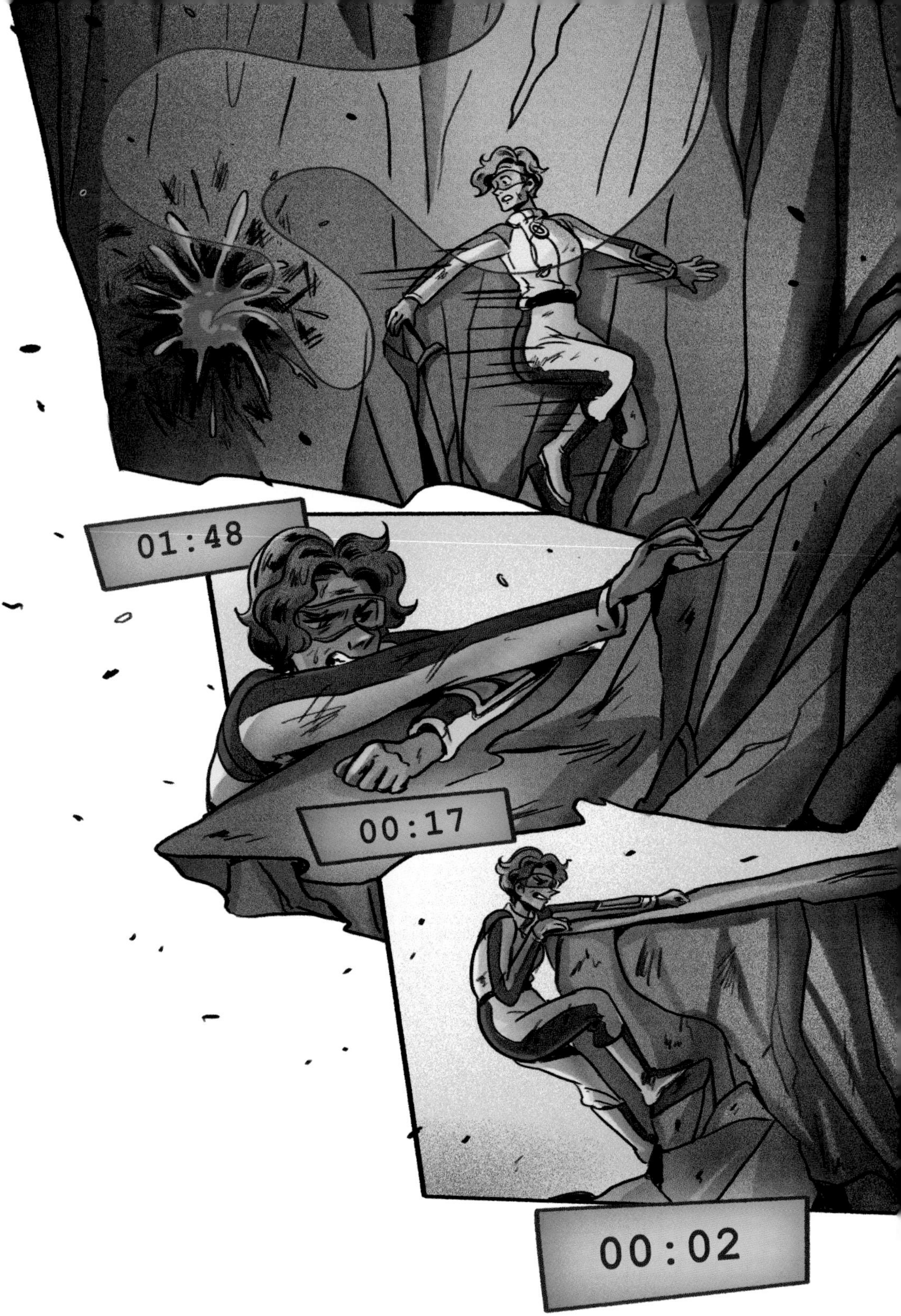
01:48
00:17
00:02

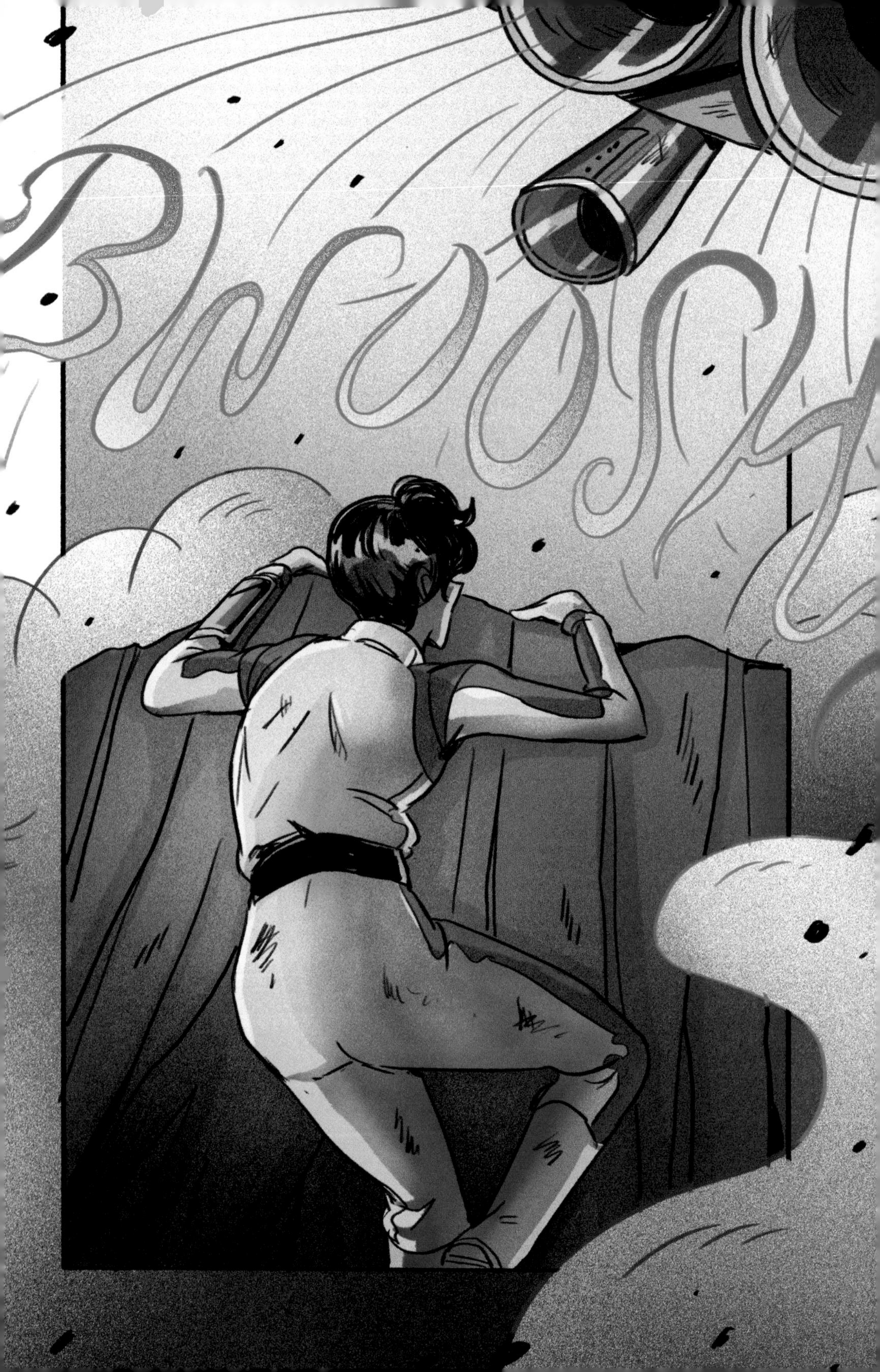
BWOOSH

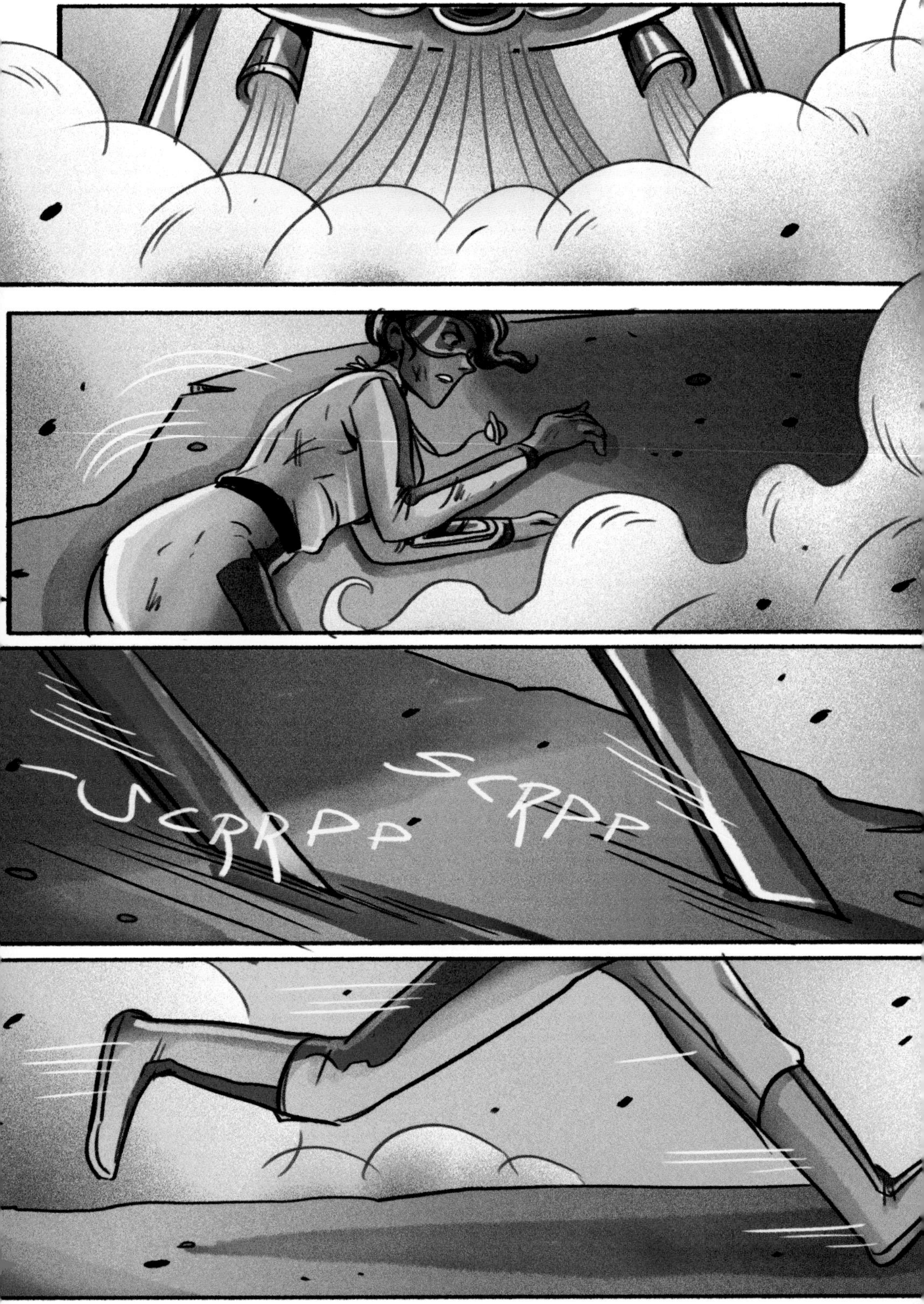
SCRPP
SCRPP

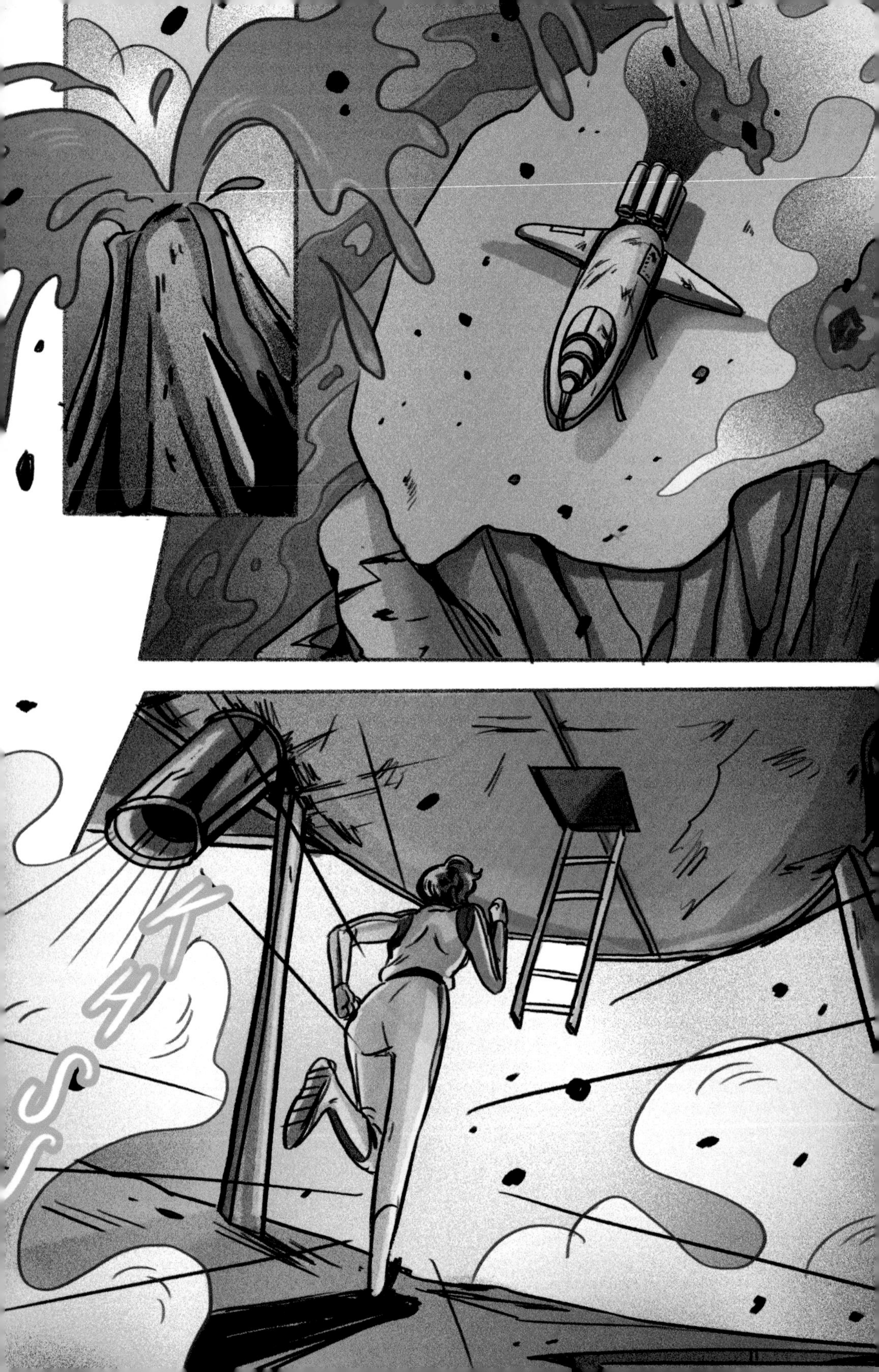

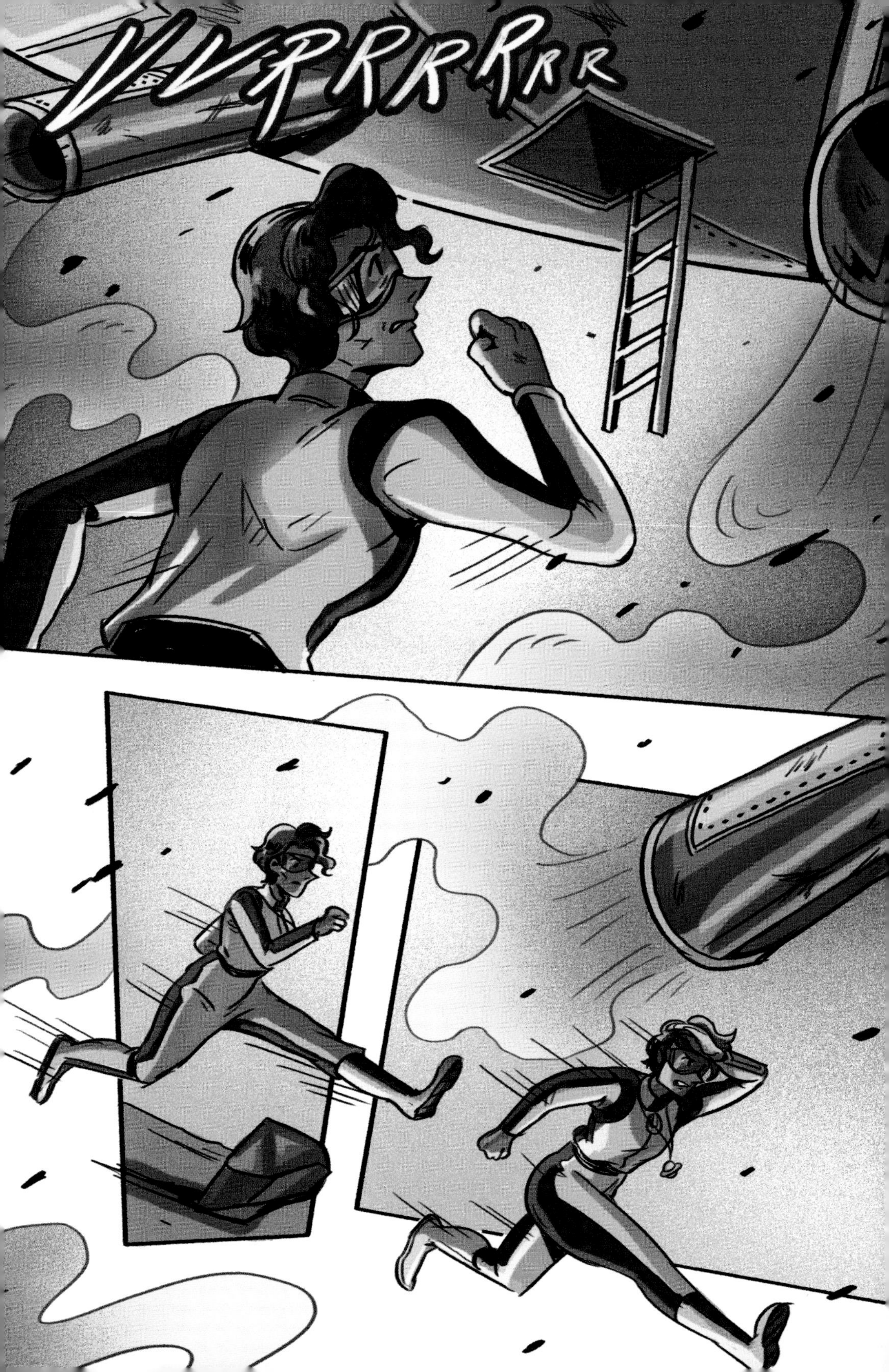
VVRRRRrr

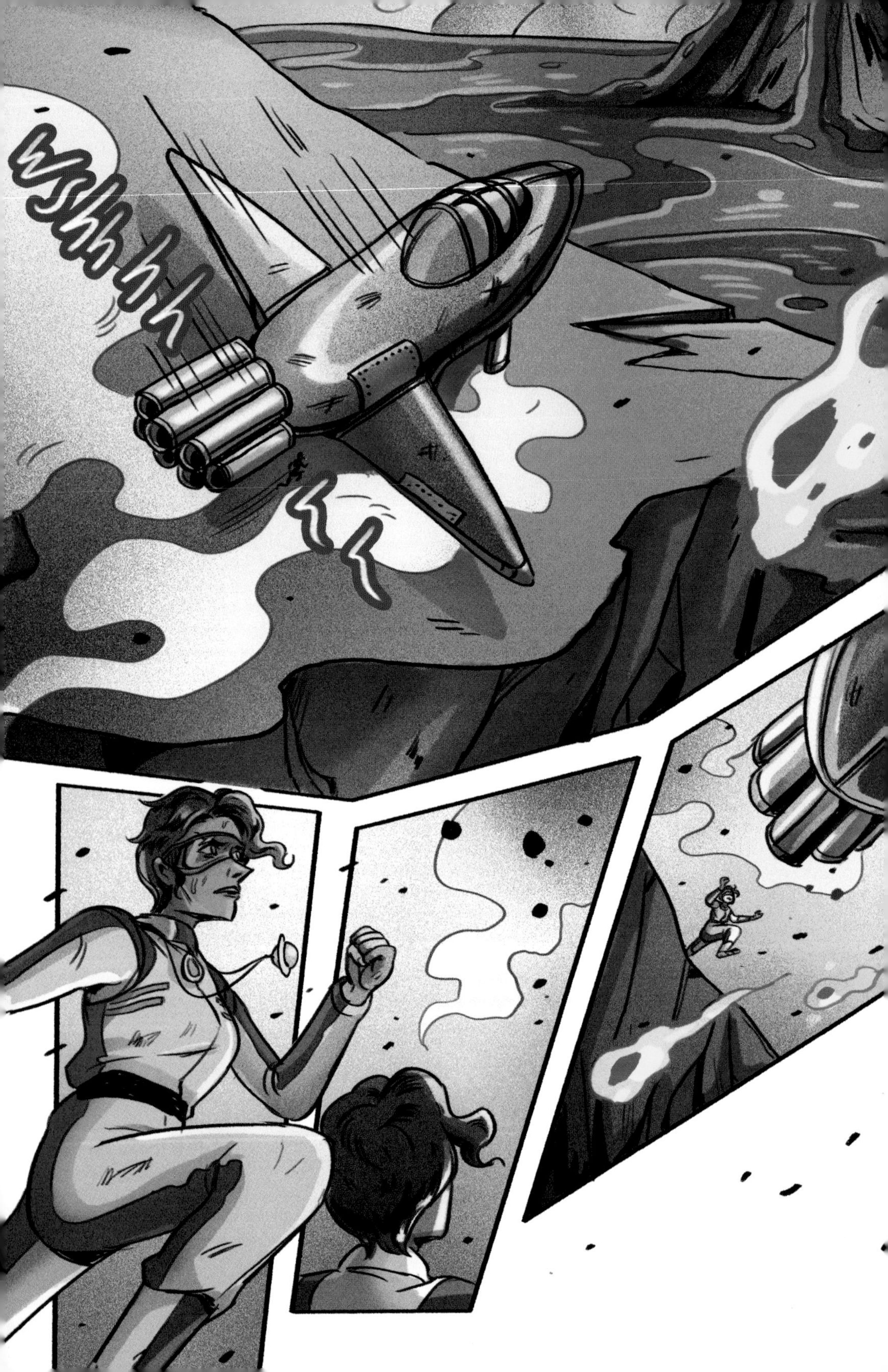

wshhhh

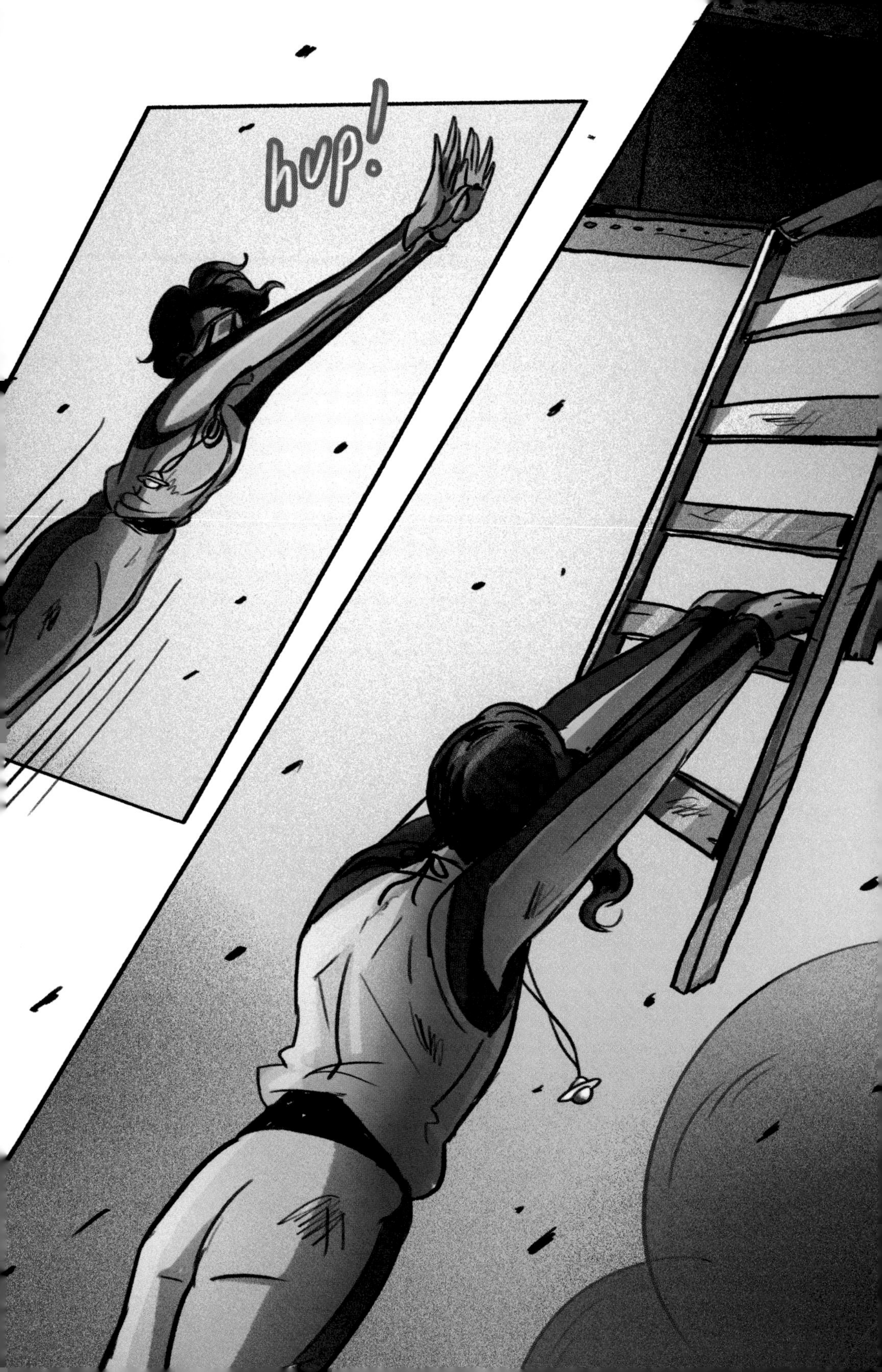
hup!

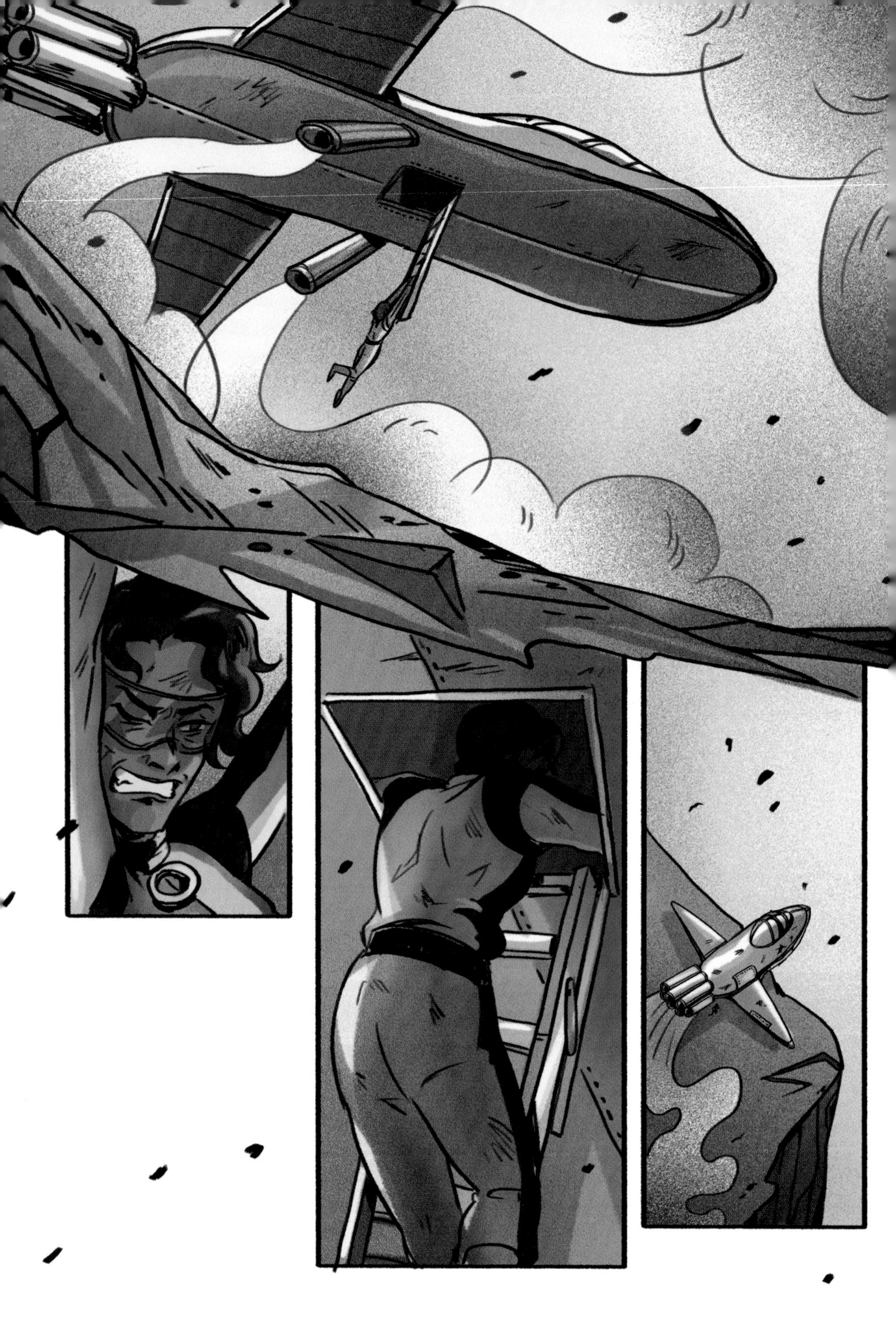

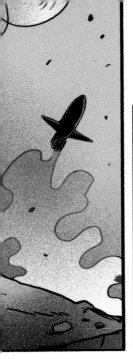

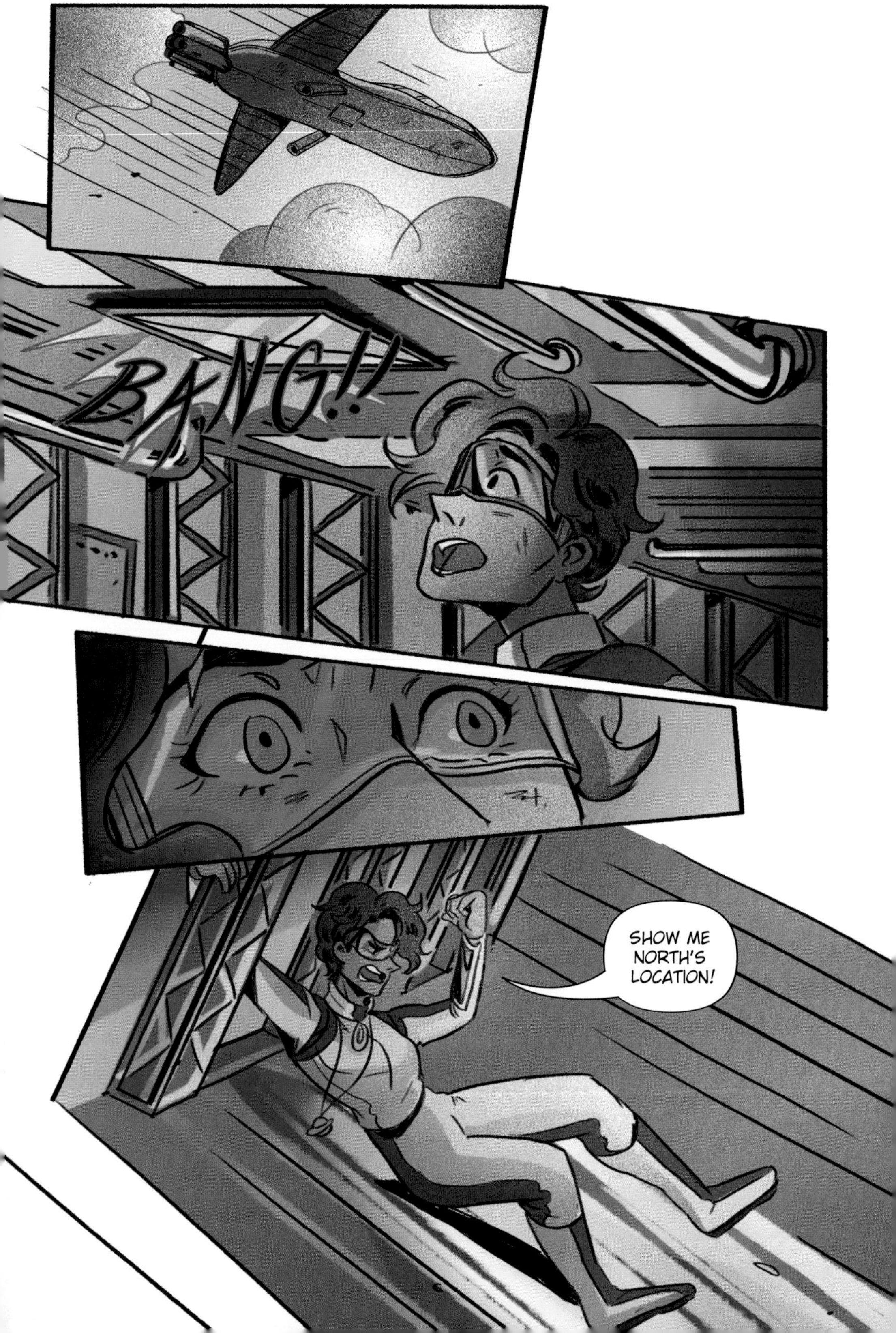
BANG!!
SHOW ME NORTH'S LOCATION!

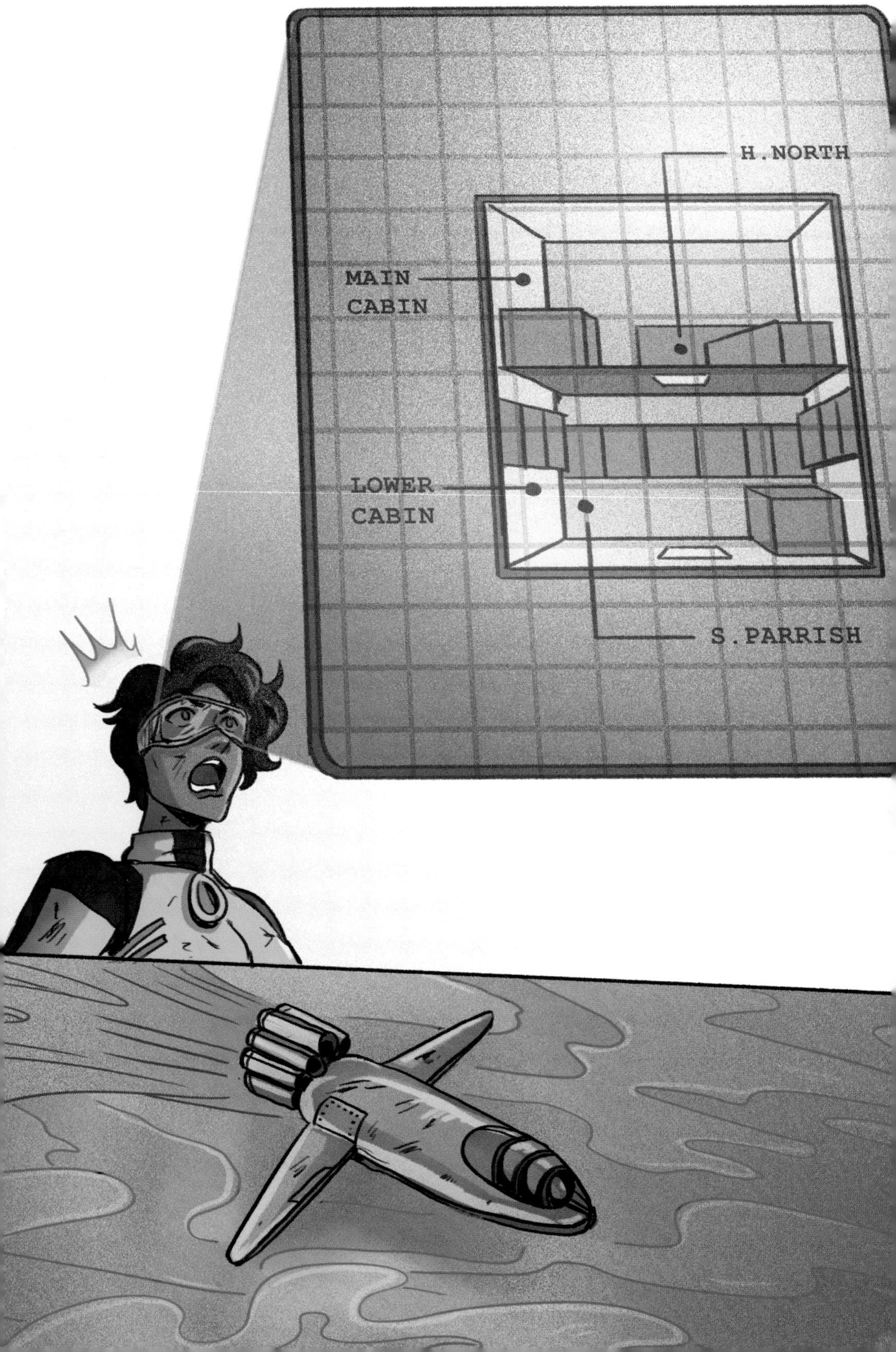
H.NORTH
MAIN CABIN
LOWER CABIN
S.PARRISH

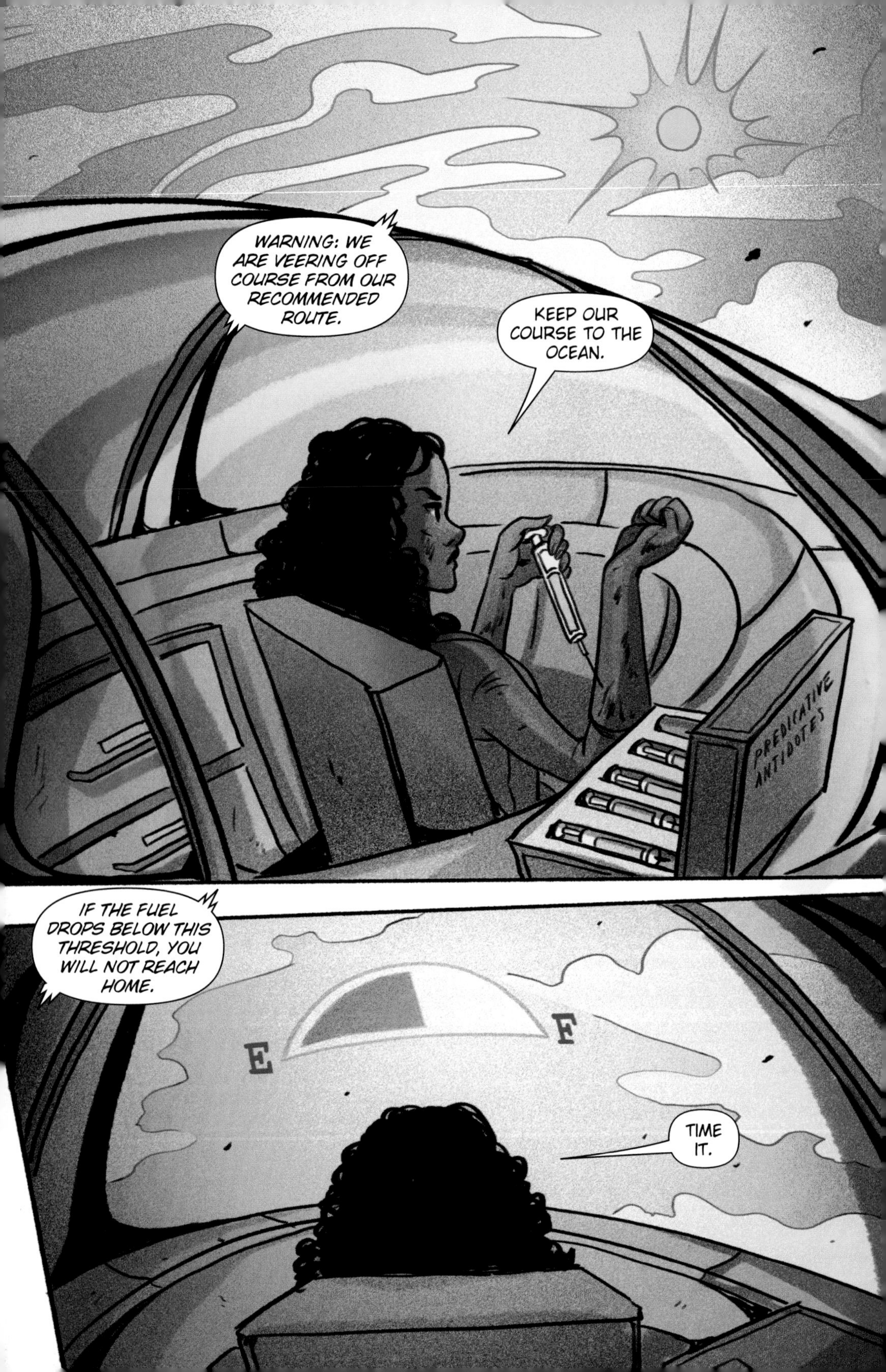
WARNING: WE ARE VEERING OFF COURSE FROM OUR RECOMMENDED ROUTE.
KEEP OUR COURSE TO THE OCEAN.
PREDICATIVE ANTIDOTES
IF THE FUEL DROPS BELOW THIS THRESHOLD, YOU WILL NOT REACH HOME.
E
F
TIME IT.

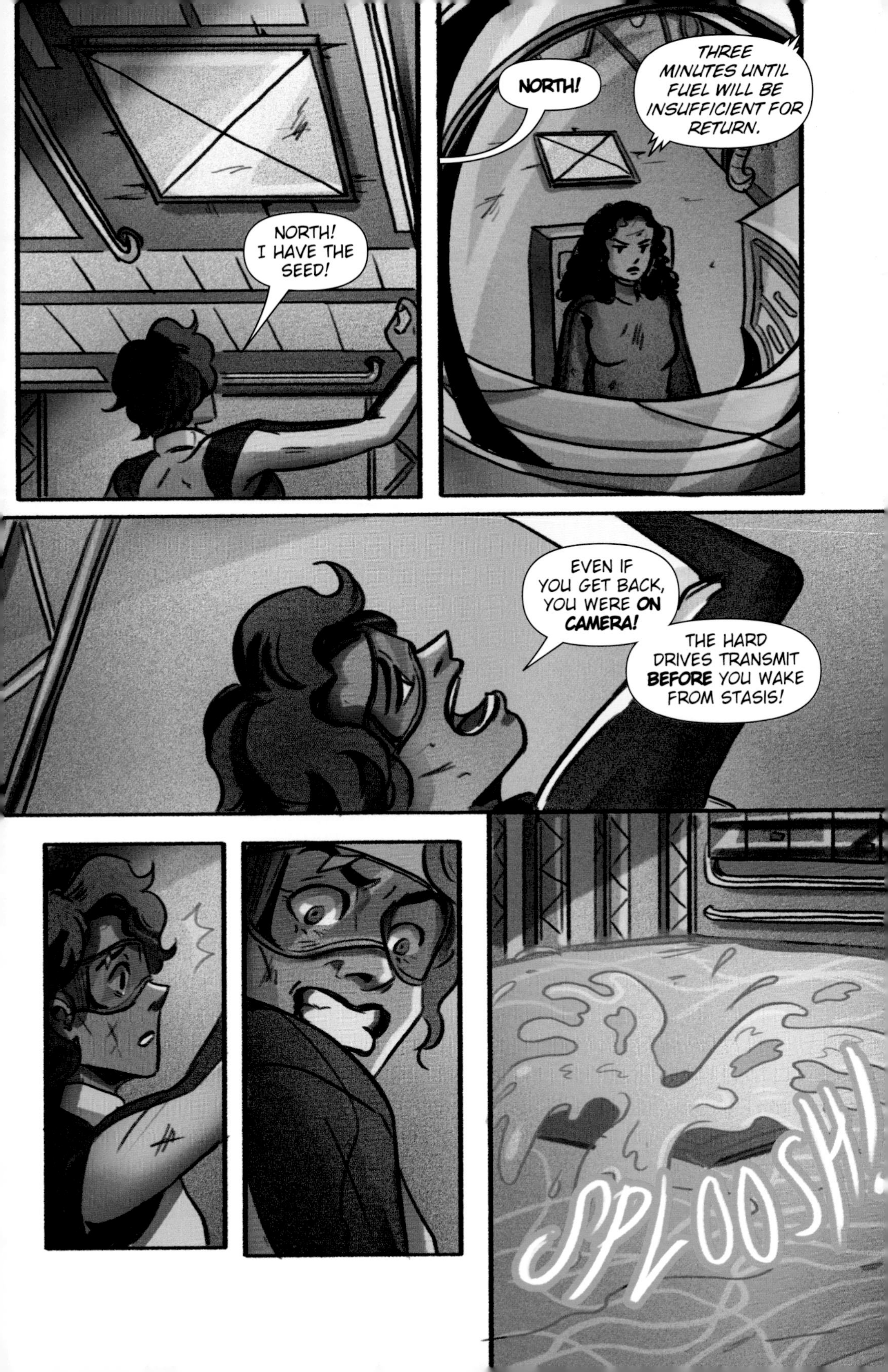
NORTH! I HAVE THE SEED!
NORTH!
THREE MINUTES UNTIL FUEL WILL BE INSUFFICIENT FOR RETURN.
EVEN IF YOU GET BACK, YOU WERE ON CAMERA!
THE HARD DRIVES TRANSMIT BEFORE YOU WAKE FROM STASIS!
SPLOOSH!

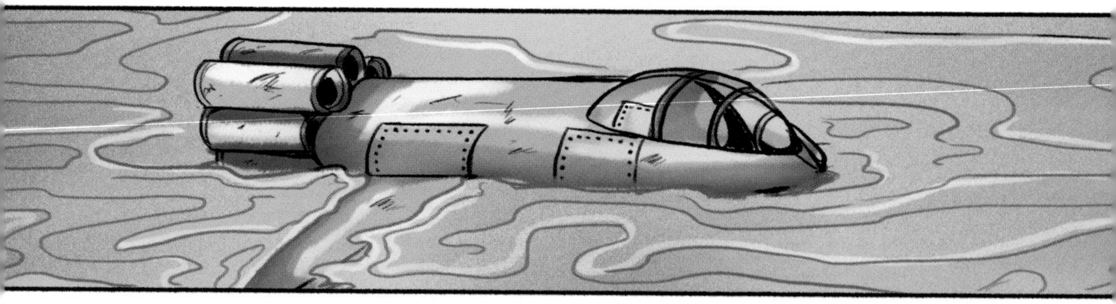

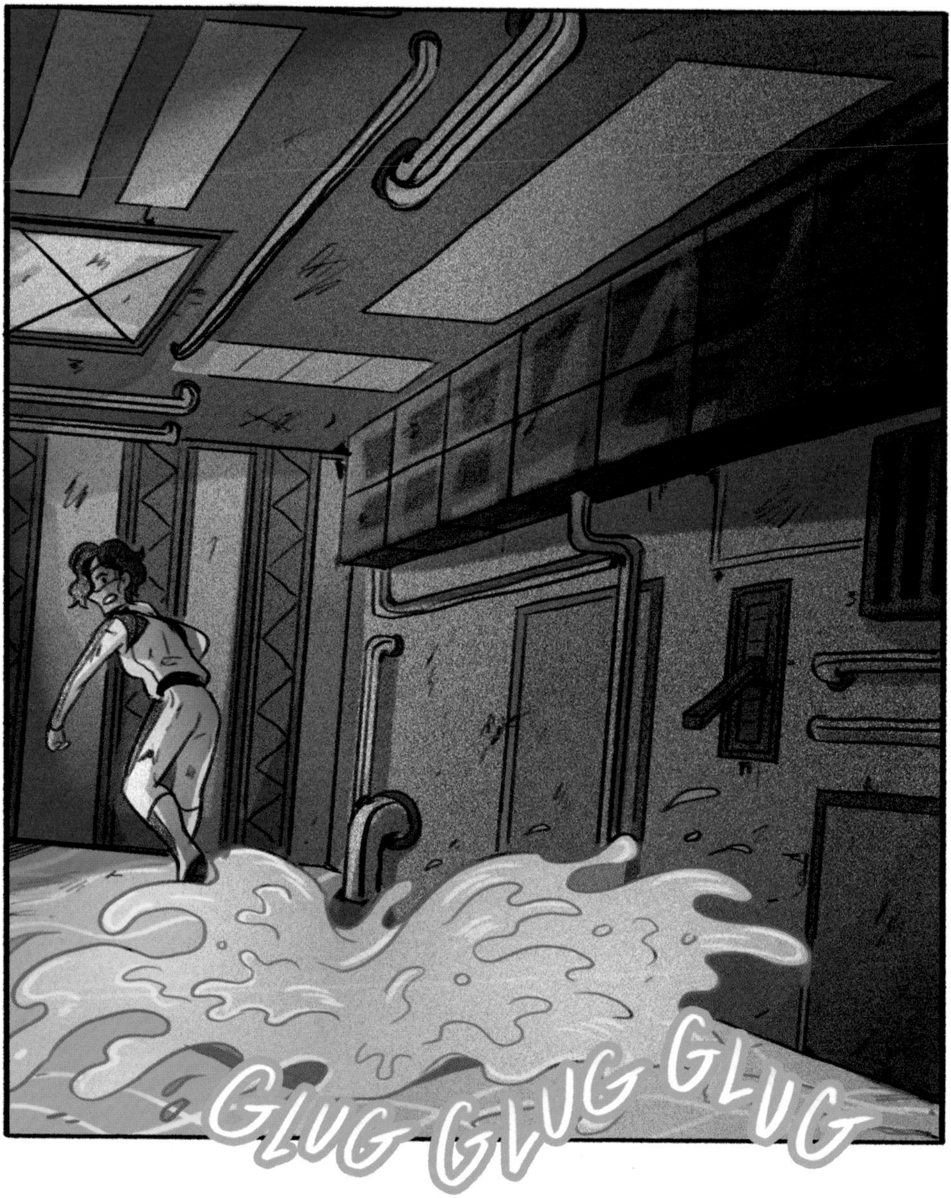
GLUG GLUG GLUG

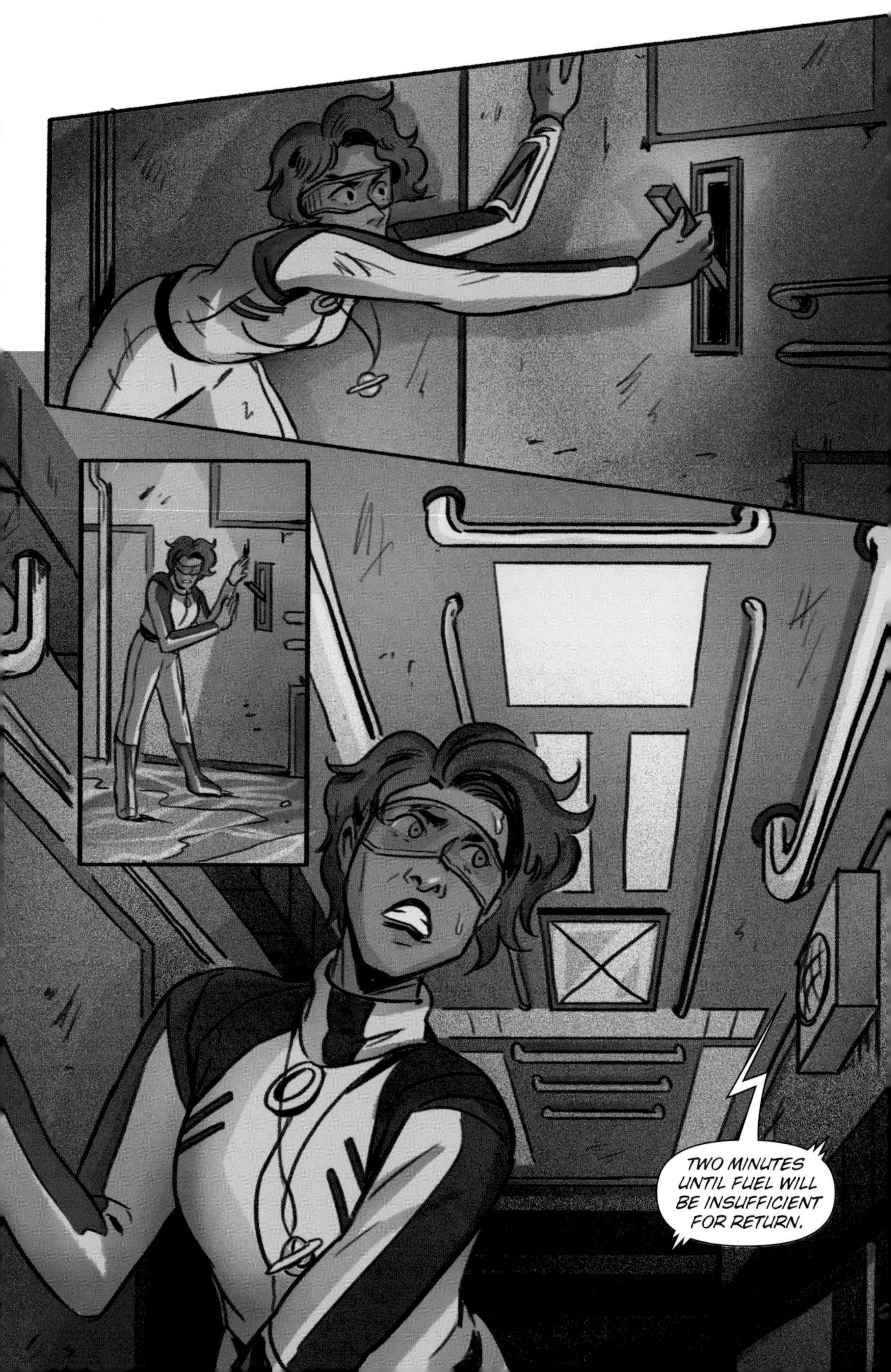
TWO MINUTES UNTIL FUEL WILL BE INSUFFICIENT FOR RETURN.

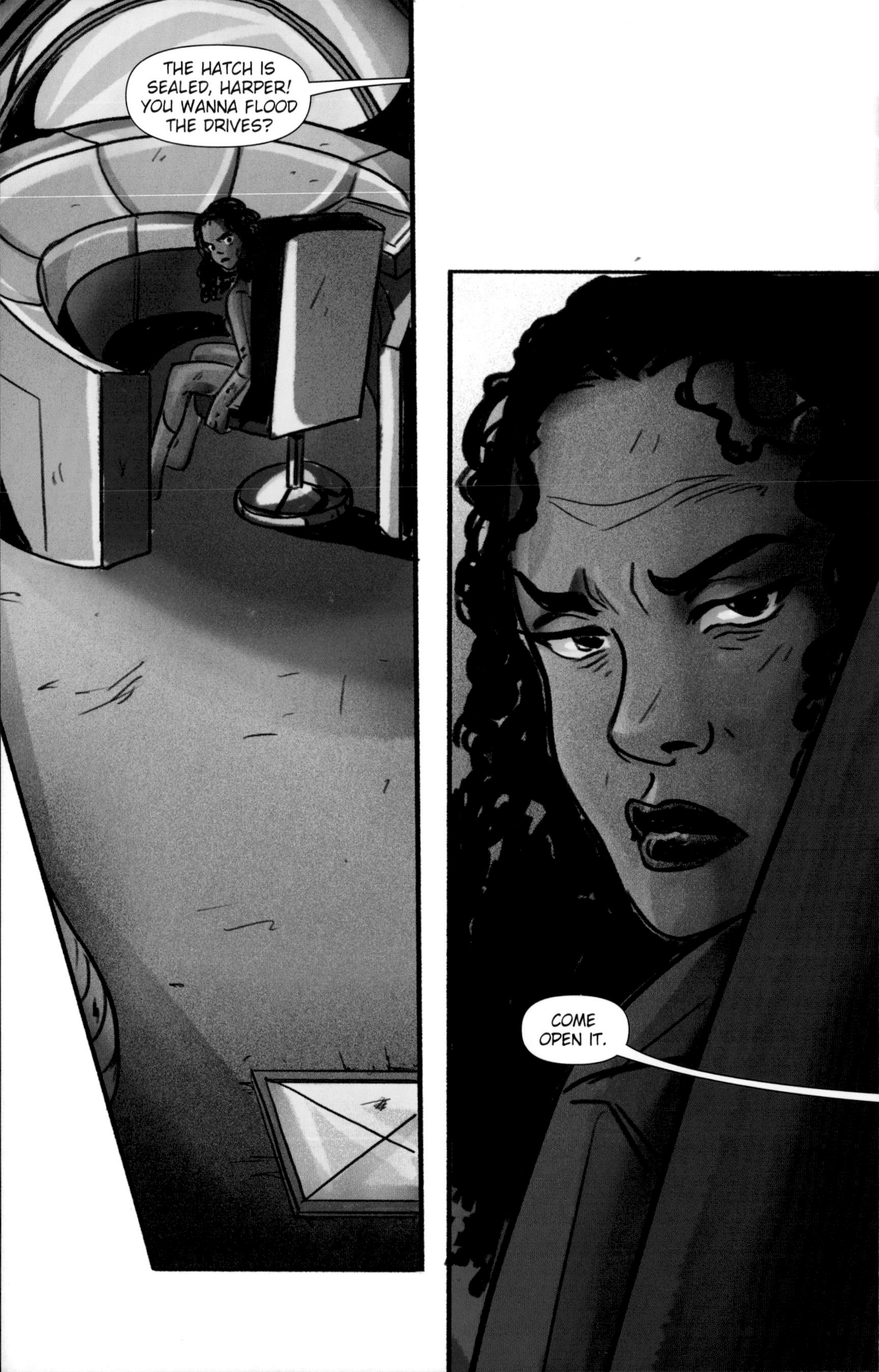
THE HATCH IS SEALED, HARPER! YOU WANNA FLOOD THE DRIVES?
COME OPEN IT.

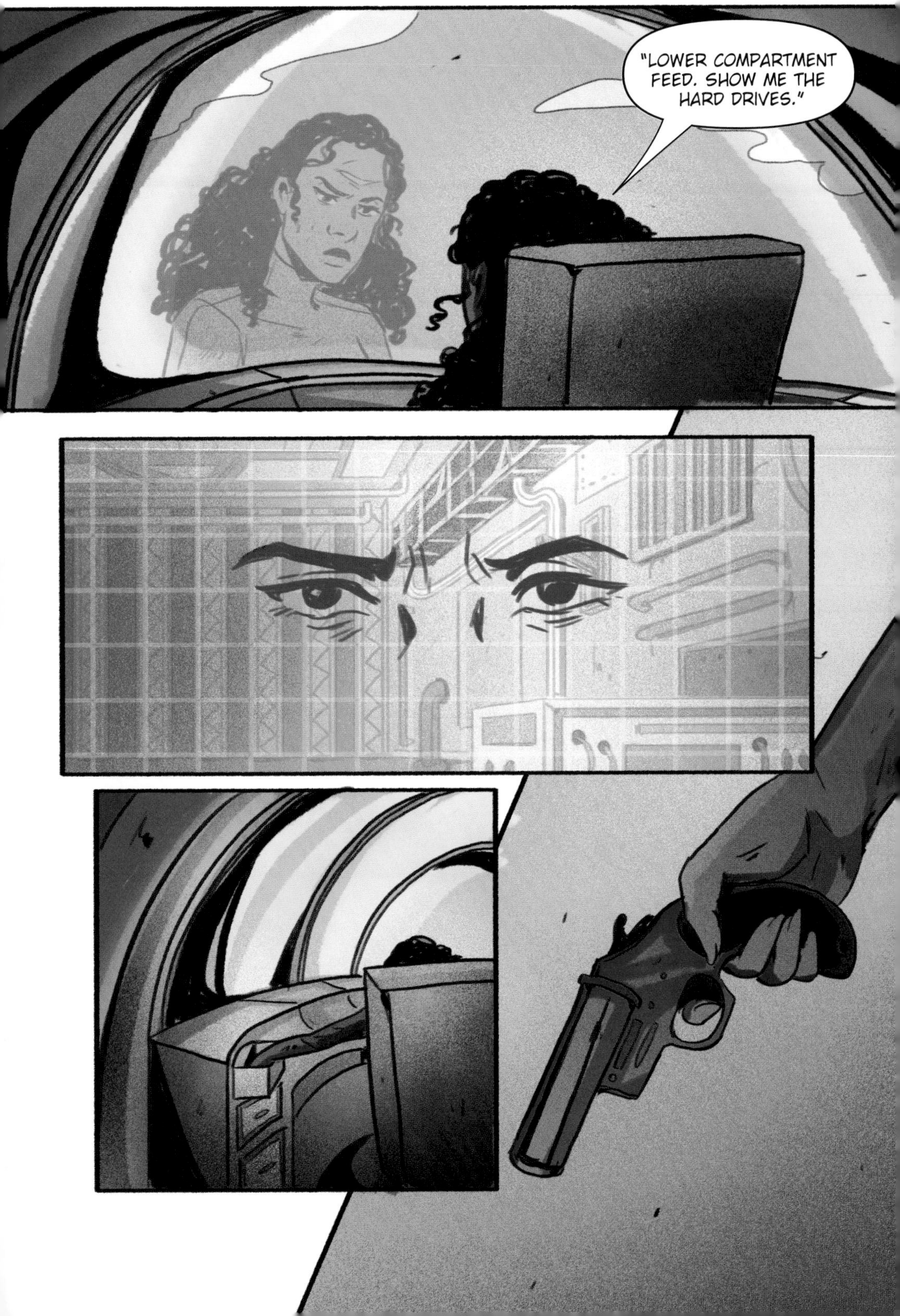
"LOWER COMPARTMENT FEED. SHOW ME THE HARD DRIVES."

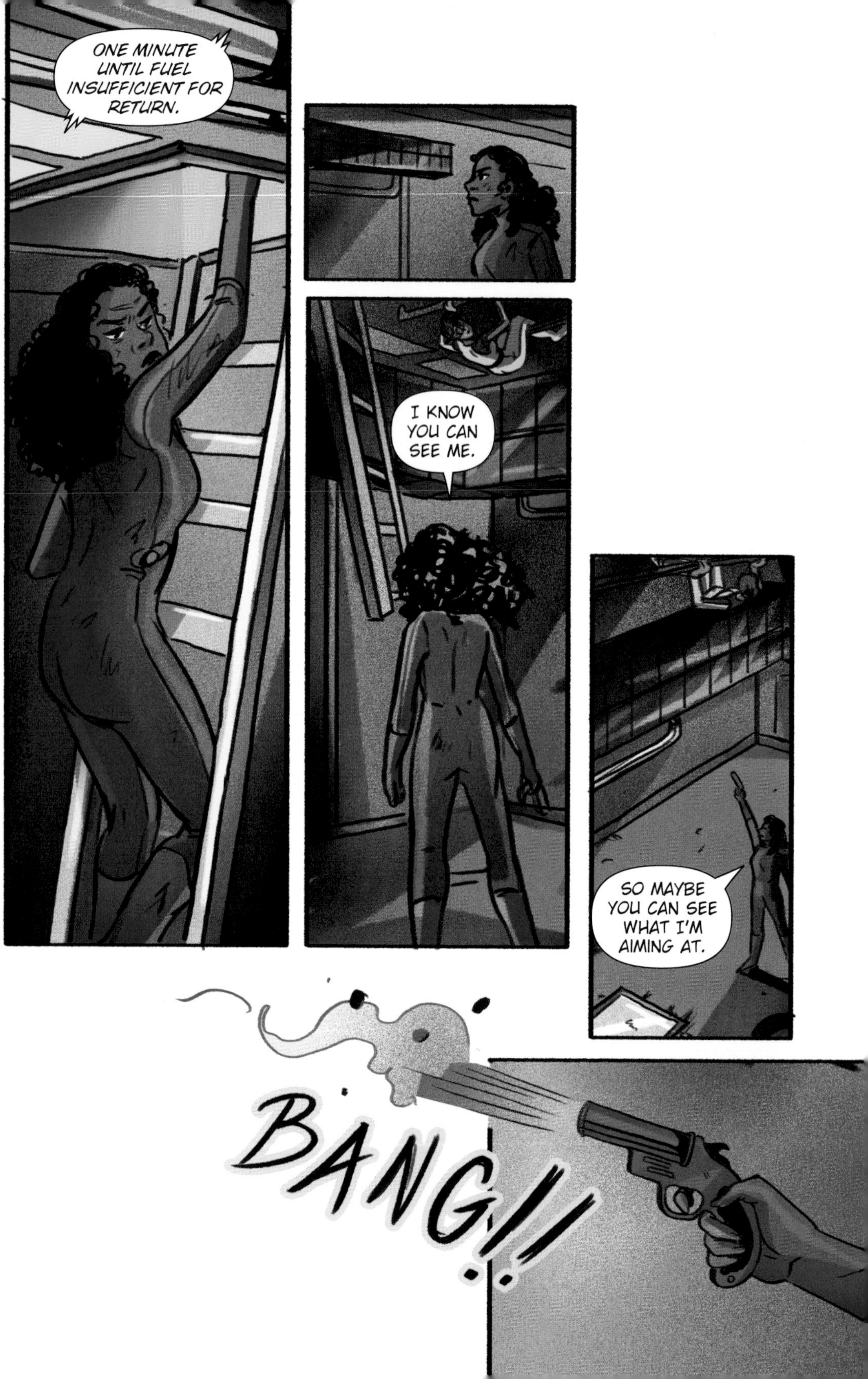
ONE MINUTE UNTIL FUEL INSUFFICIENT FOR RETURN.
I KNOW YOU CAN SEE ME.
SO MAYBE YOU CAN SEE WHAT I'M AIMING AT.
BANG!!

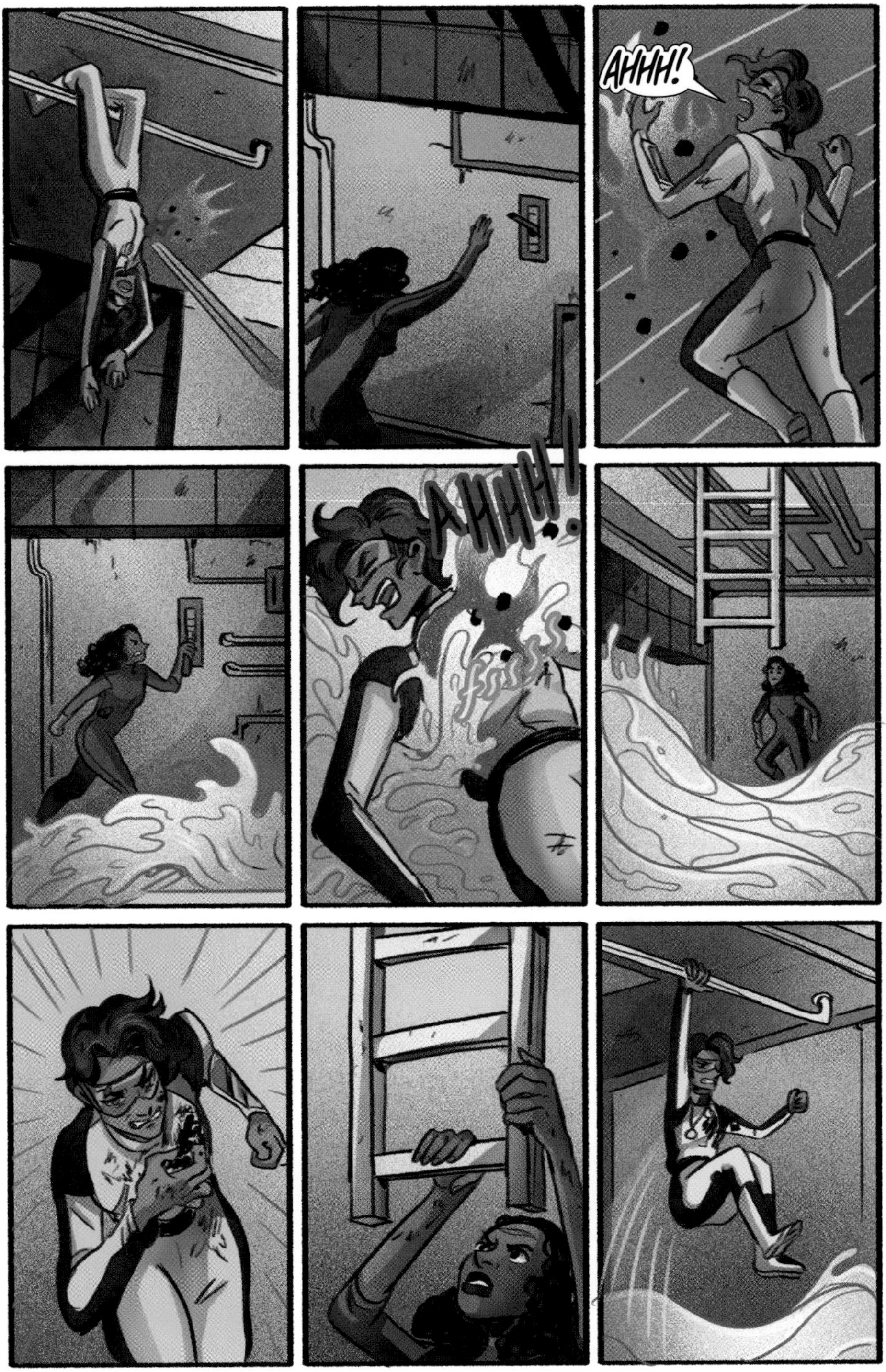
AHHH!
AHHH!

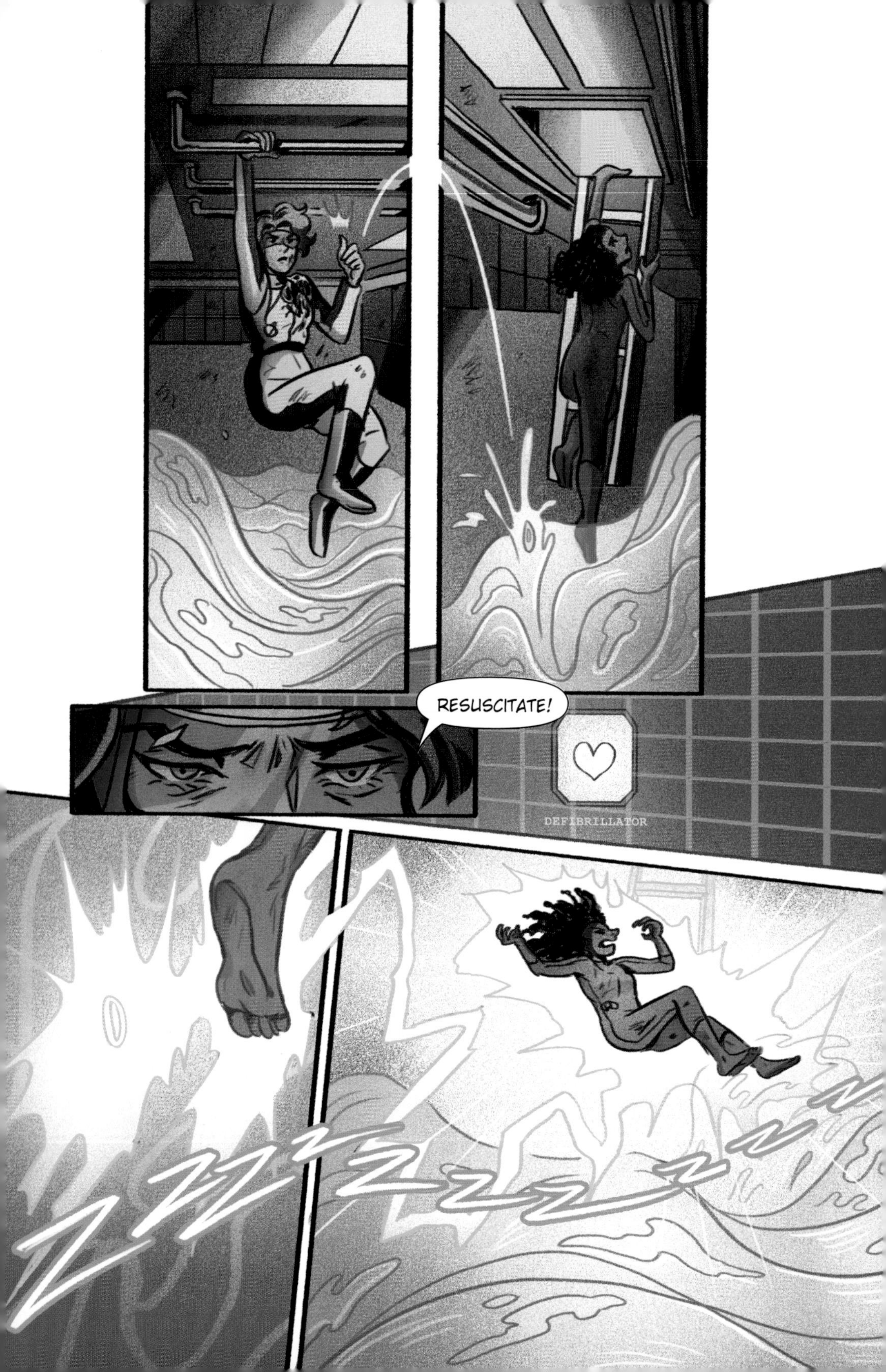
RESUSCITATE!
DEFIBRILLATOR
ZZZZZZZZZZNNNN

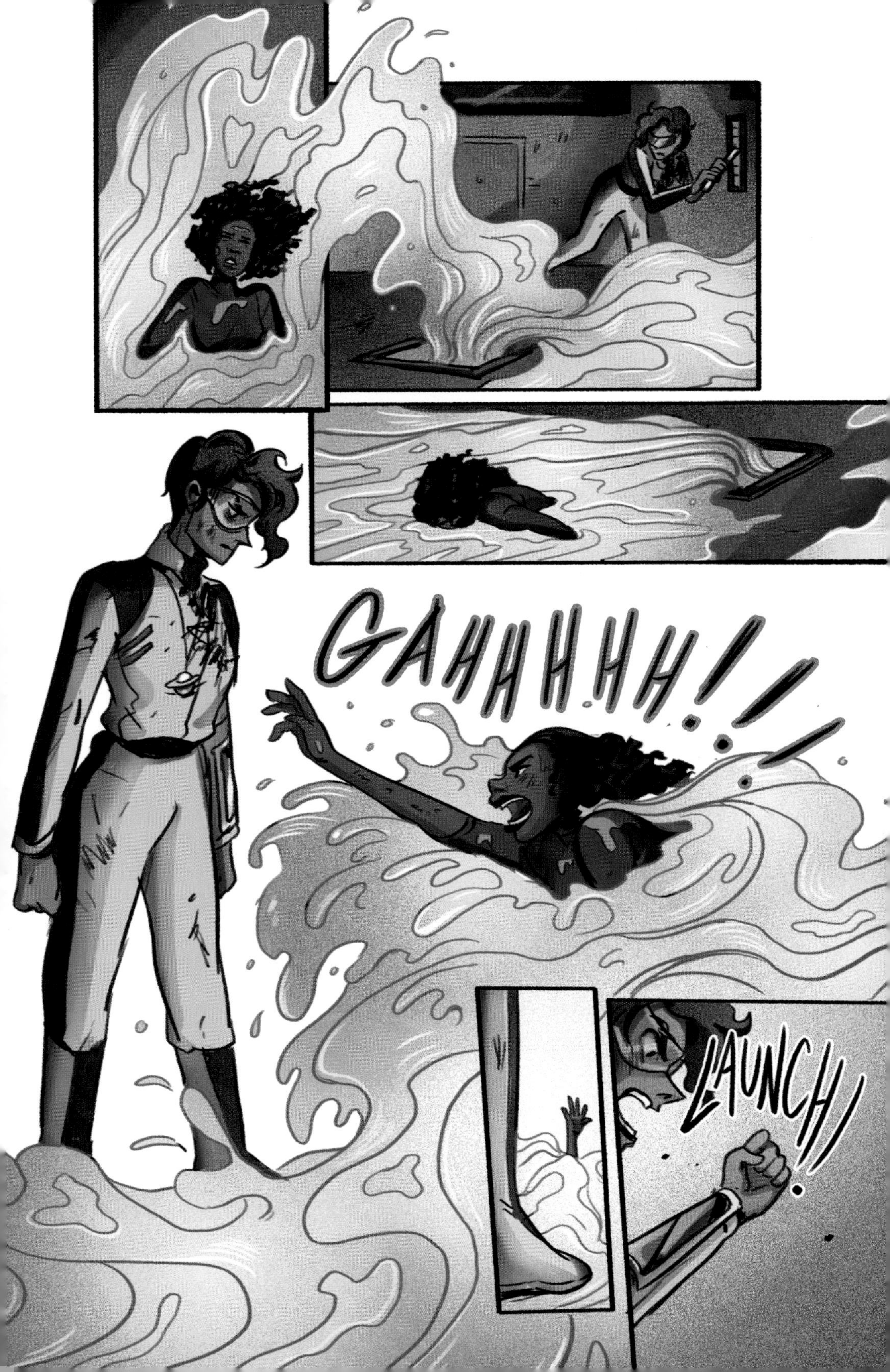
GAHHHHH!!!
LAUNCH!!

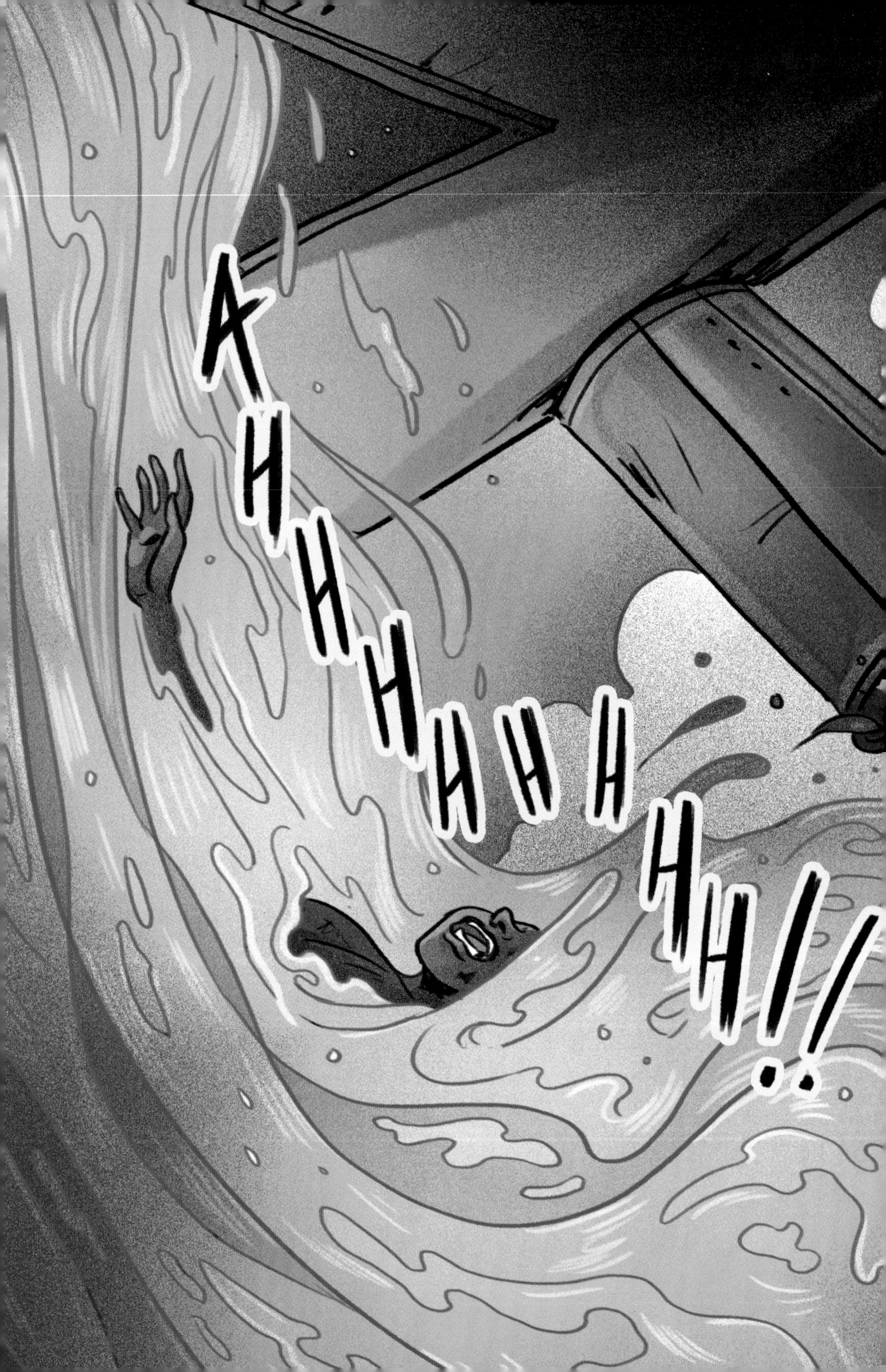
AHHHHHHHHH!!

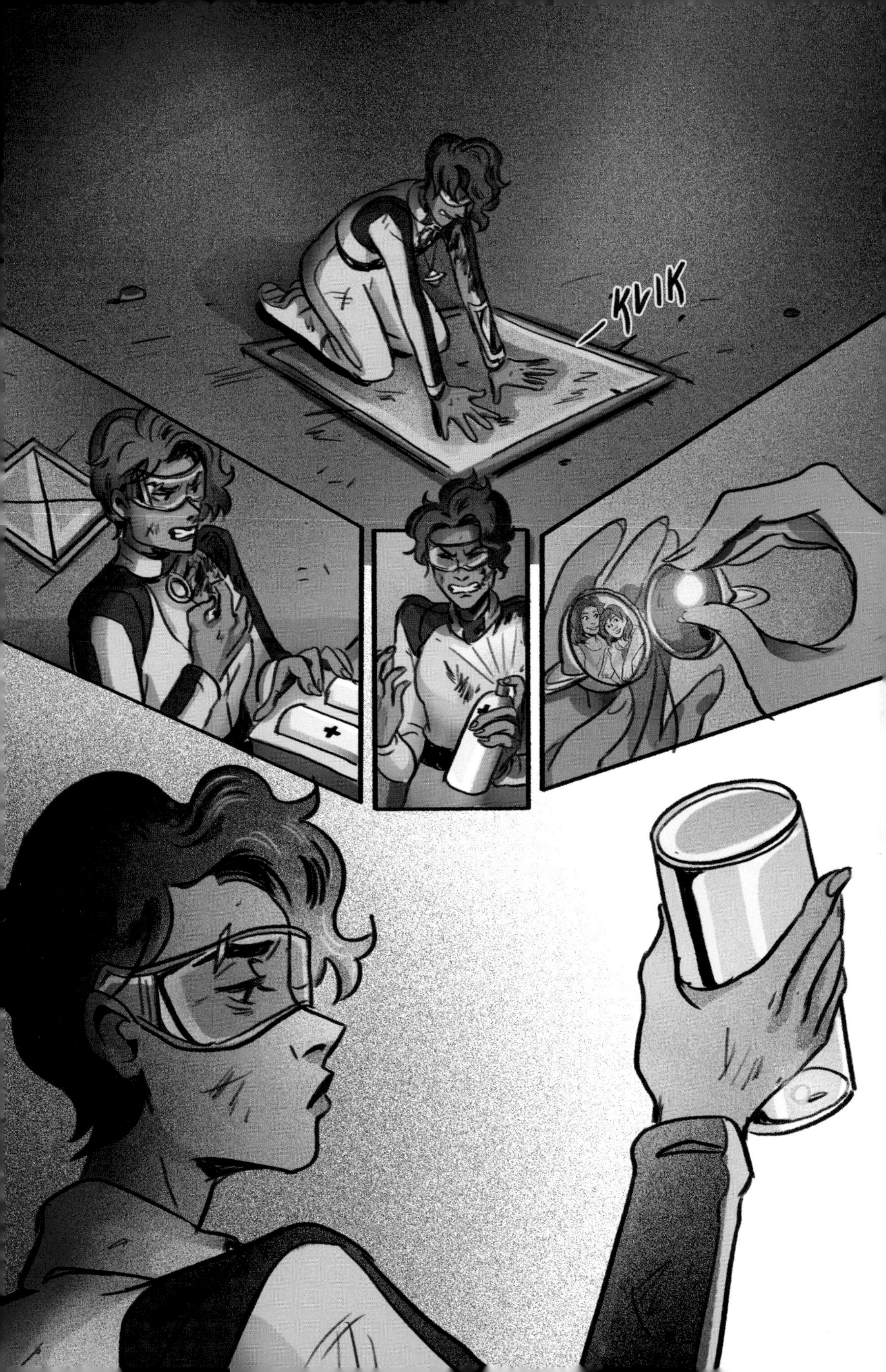
KLIK

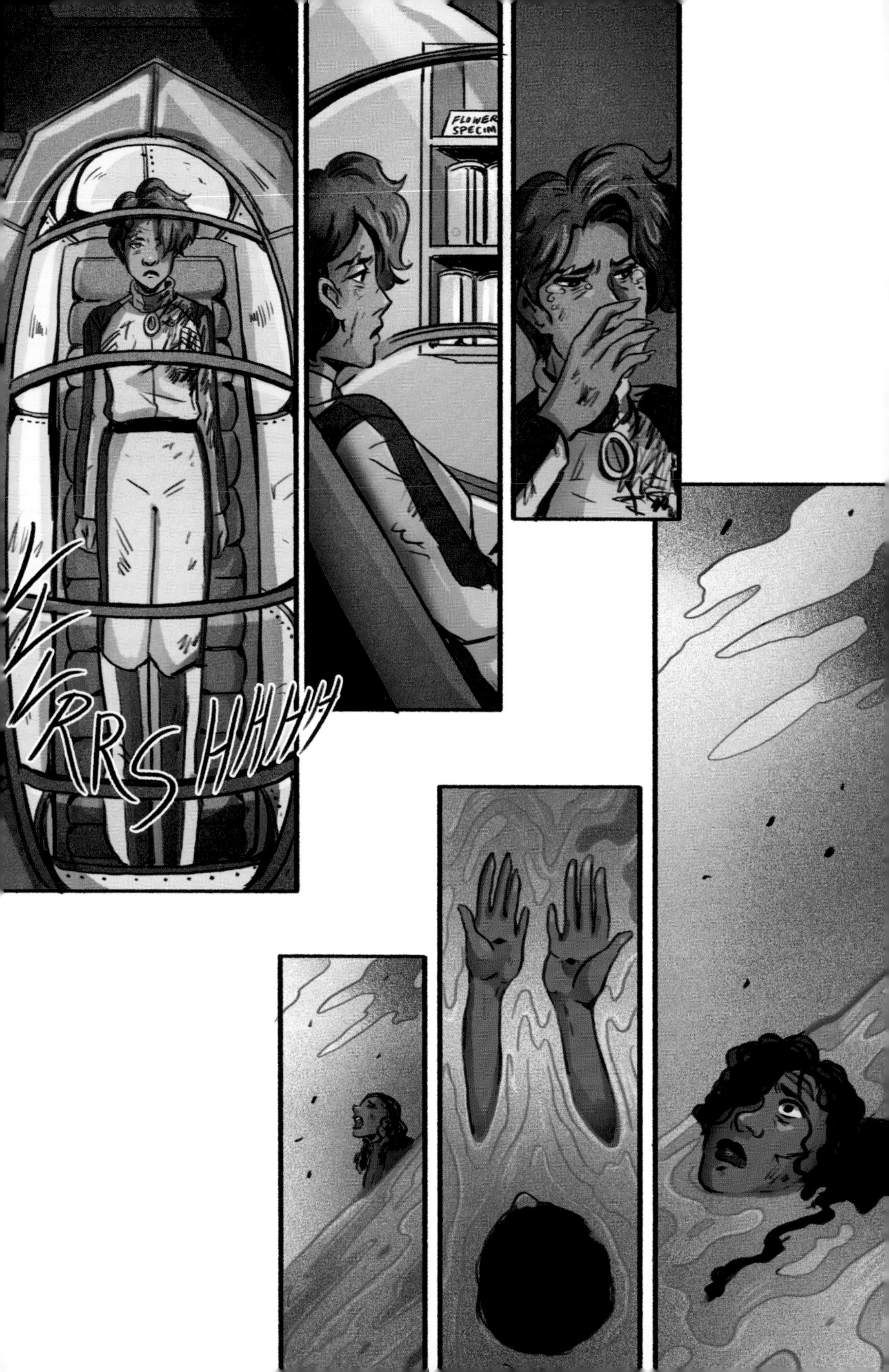
FLOWER SPECIM
VVVRRSHHHH

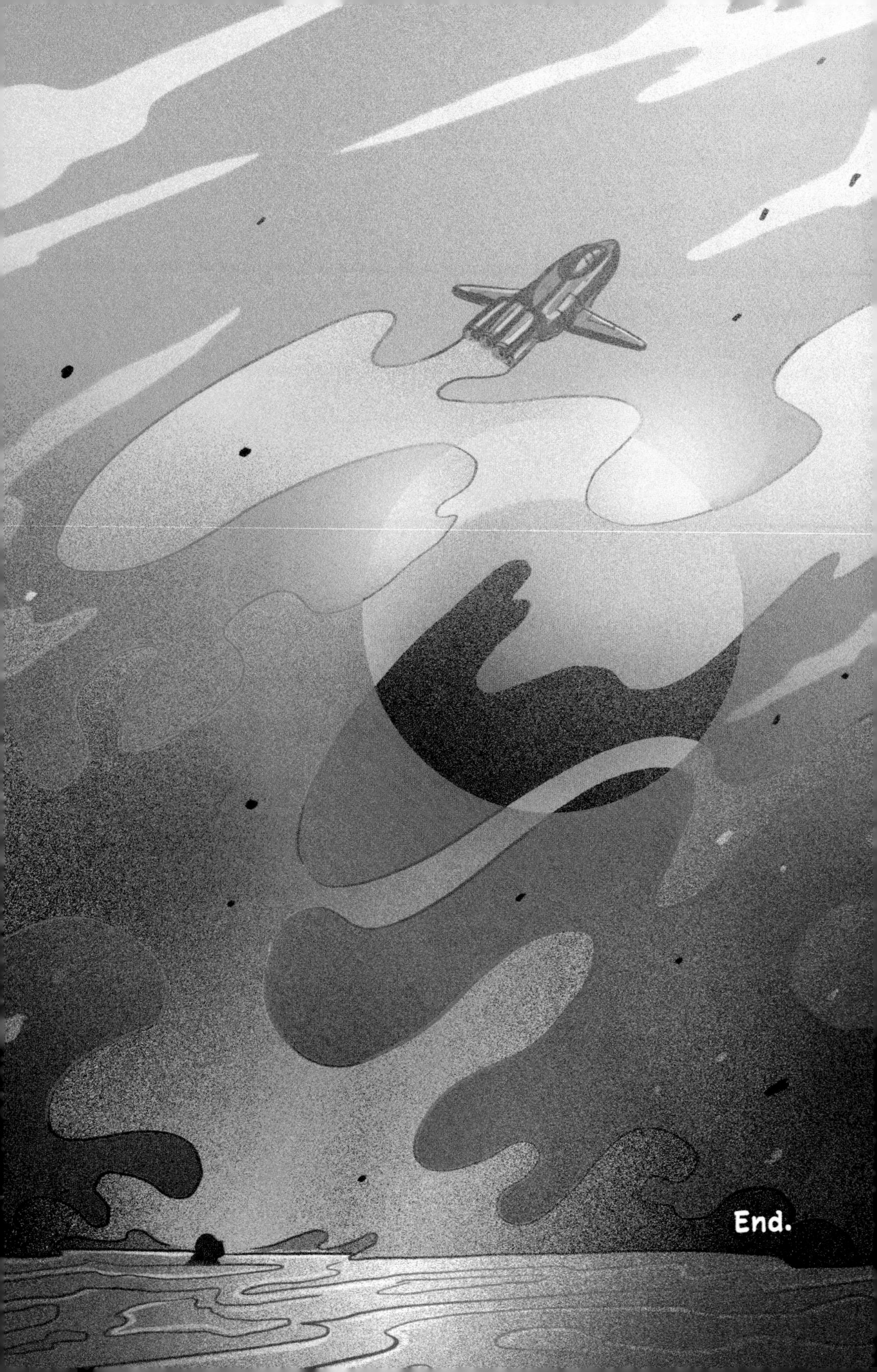
End.

MANY THANKS to my editor, Charlotte Greenbaum, who pushed the hardest of anyone to make this book a reality. I am also grateful to Maxwell Neely-Cohen, without whom this project would never have come about. Thank you to Arielle Jovellanos, whose art elevated my script in ways I couldn't have anticipated.

Additionally, I'd like to offer my eternal gratitude to Vicki Simons, who has enthusiastically supported my writing from the very beginning; Rob Rodems, for the comfort he provides between battles with my keyboard; as well as Dylan Morgan, Lukas Fauset, and Taylor Pavlik, whose early feedback on this story (and so many of my stories since) has made me a better writer.

—Eric Anthony Glover

TO MY mom and dad for everything.

To Charlotte for making sure I kept going.

To Eric who let me play in his world.

To my color assistants, Andrew, James, and Alexandra. I couldn't have done it without you.

To Ate, Jaemari, Emma, Nicole, Gail, Janet, Melva, and Tim for staying up and logging FaceTime hours with me on long work days.

Thank you, everyone!!

—Arielle Jovellanos

VISUAL DEVELOPMENT

by Arielle Jovellanos

CHARACTER DESIGNS

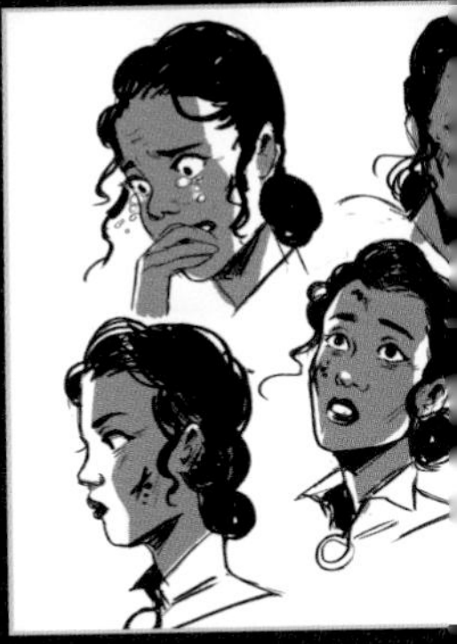

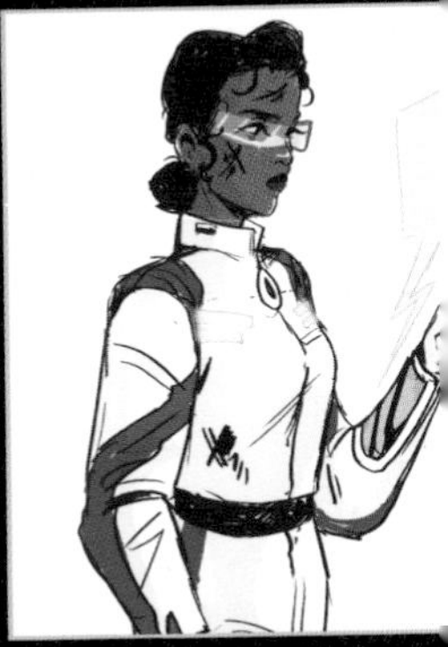

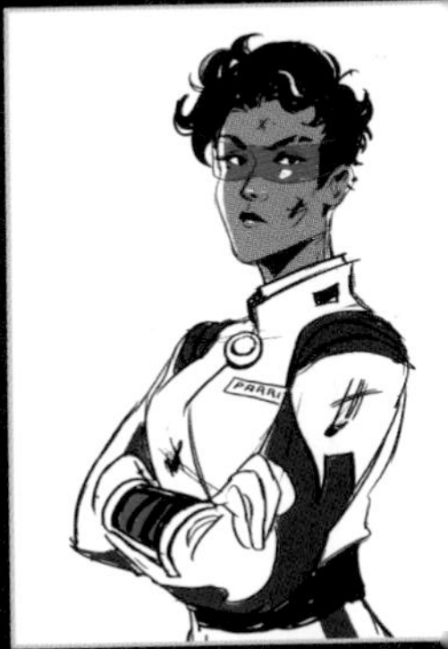

North was an interesting character to work with because I had to find ways to visually show how the planet wears her down as the story goes on. For example, putting her hair in a bun at the start allowed me to use the state of her hair as a marker dramatizing how she goes from a reclusive scientist on a mission to someone just desperately trying to survive.

When I was first designing the suit, I was mostly looking at Ripley from *Alien* and the plugsuits from *Neon Genesis Evangelion* as inspiration. In a couple pieces of concept art, I originally had the suit a darker color, but wound up going with an off-white because it would stand out more in most panel compositions and served as a better canvas for the rips and dirt stains North suffers on her journey.

The story is essentially a game of cat-and-mouse, so I clocked on using color to distinguish North and Parrish pretty early in the process. I think Parrish's red offsets North's blue in a very striking way, and the palette of the book generally contrasts between cool blues and warm reds, sometimes coalescing into purples when the two characters clash. I didn't plan for this, but the final page wound up a happy accident with the two characters' colors swapping: North is left behind in a reddish, fiery haze as Parrish flies out into a clear blue sky.

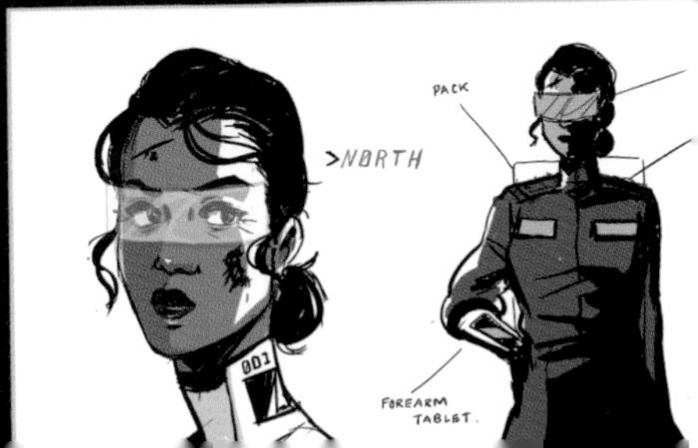
PACK
>NORTH
FOREARM TABLET.

DIGITAL INTERFACE

When I first received Eric's manuscript, I noticed that so much of the story relies on North using her tablet, and I wanted to find a way to dramatize the visual language of something as simple as typing, receiving a notification, or watching a video. Here I was playing with various ways to make the Guardian interesting—really just finding ways to make its presence loom as its own character.

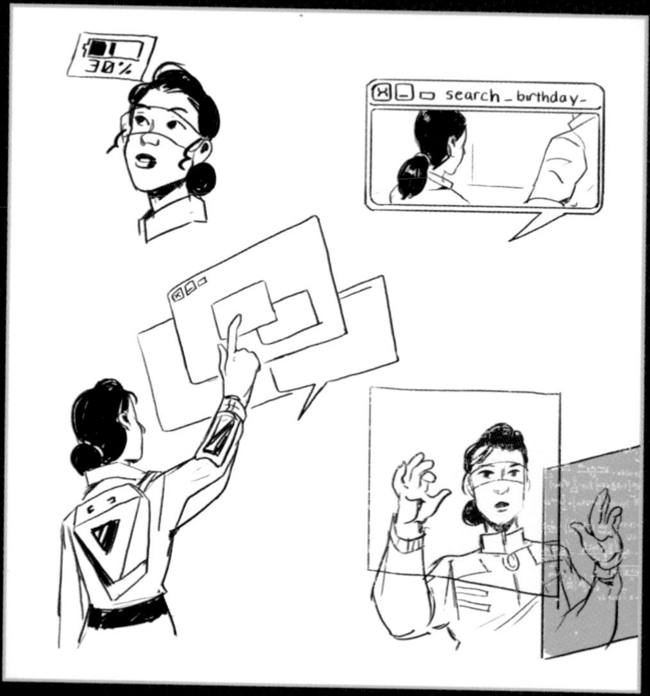
30%
search_birthday_

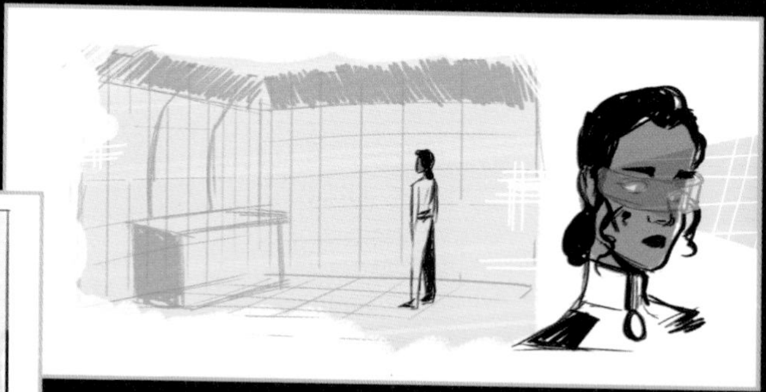

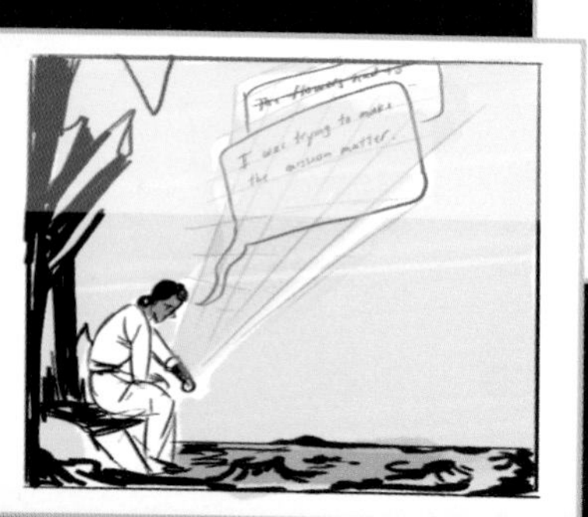
I was trying to make the mission matter.

MOUNTAIN AND WASTELAND

I looked at Chesley Bonestell's space landscapes for inspiration and did a few concept sketches for the terrain of Eleos. While this didn't wind up being used in the book, I liked playing with the idea of a mountain that had ice rings around it, similar to the composition of Saturn's rings.

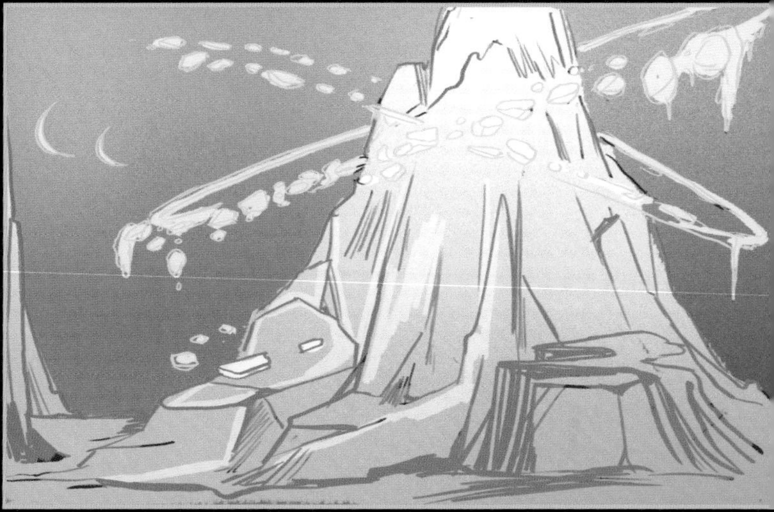

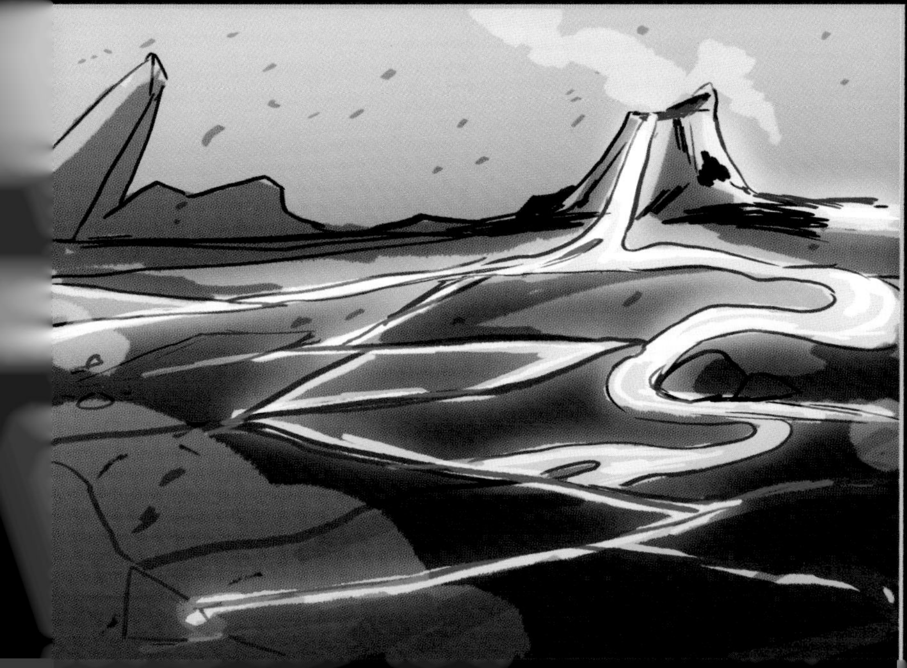

MEGASCOPE Curator: John Jennings
Editor: Charlotte Greenbaum
Designer: Kay Petronio
Managing Editor: Elizabeth Palumbo
Production Manager: Erin Vandeveer
Lettering: Dave Sharpe
Additional Colors: Andrew Dalhouse

ibrary of Congress Control Number for the
hardcover edition: 2020944148

ISBN 978-1-4197-4229-3
eISBN 978-1-68335-778-0

Printed and bound in China
10 9 8 7 6 5 4 3 2 1

Abrams ComicArts books are available at
pecial discounts when purchased in quantity
for premiums and promotions as well as
ndraising or educational use. Special editions
can also be created to specification. For
details, contact specialsales@abramsbooks.
com or the address below.

ABRAMS The Art of Books

ABRAMS COMICARTS
MEGASCOPE

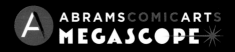

MEGASCOPE is dedicated to showcasing speculative and non-fiction works by and about people of color, with a focus on science fiction, fantasy, horror, history, and stories of magical realism. The megascope is a fictional device imagined by W. E. B. Du Bois that can peer through time and space into other realities. This magical invention represents the idea that so much of our collective past has not seen the light of day, and that there is so much history that we have yet to discover. MEGASCOPE will serve as a lens through which we can broaden our view of history, the present, and the future, and as a method by which previously unheard voices can find their way to an ever-growing diverse audience.